SPREADSHEETS	WORD PROCESSING	
Up one cell	Up one line	To prev...
To top of column	Up one sentence	To field names (above first record)
Down one cell	Down one line	To next record (1); next field (2,3)
To bottom of column	Down one sentence	To last record
Right one cell	Right one character	To next field
Right to first column in region	Select word to right	To last field of current record
Left one cell	Left one character	To previous field
Left to last column in region	Select word to left	To first field of current record
To top of current page, then up one page	To top of displayed text in frame, up one frame at a time	To record at top of Database frame (2) To previous record (2,3)
To top of column	Up one paragraph	To field names (above first record)
To bottom of current page, then down one page	To bottom of displayed text in frame, then down one frame at a time	To record at bottom of Database frame (1) To next record (2,3)
To bottom of column	Down one paragraph	To last record
To first column, current row	To beginning of current line	To first field of current record
To top left cell	To first character in frame	To first field name (above first record)
To last column of current row	To end of current line	To last field of current record
To bottom right cell	To last character in frame	To last field of last record
Into frame (to last selection)	Into frame (to last selection)	Into frame (to last selection)
Same as In	From outer frame: to lowest level (to last selection)	From outer frame: to lowest level (to last selection)
To frame border	To frame border	To frame border
Same as Out	To highest level (desktop)	To highest level (desktop)
Open menus	Open menus	Open menus
N/A	Drag frame	Drag field (2)
Resize columns	Size frame	Size field on form (2)
Recalculate spreadsheet/selection	Execute formula behind frame	Recalc (in frame or in selected field)
Select range	Select text	Extend selection over fields/records
Move range	Move selection *	Move selection
Copy range	Copy selection *	Copy selection
Zoom spreadsheet	Zoom document	Zoom database
N/A	N/A	Switch to Table, Form, or dBASE view
Accept entries, down one cell	Create new paragraph	Accept entry; move down one field (1,3) Open/close form element (2)
Accept entry; right one cell	Tab text	Right one field (in same record)
Accept entry; left one cell	N/A	Left one field (in same record)
Left one cell	Erase character to left of cursor	Left one field (in same record)
Erase cell contents	Erase character or selection	Erase field or selection contents
Toggle between frames and cabinets	Toggle between frames and cabinets	Toggle between frames and cabinets

* Also Cut (Shift-F7), Paste (Shift-F8), and Edit Cut text (Shift-F2)   1 Table View   2 Forms View   3 dBASE View

Mastering
Framework III

Mastering
Framework III™

Douglas Hergert
Jonathan Kamin

 San Francisco • Paris • Düsseldorf • Soest

Acquisitions Editor: Dianne King
Editor: Tanya Kucak
Word Processor: Bob Myren
Series Designer: Julie Bilski
Chapter Art: Suzanne Albertson
Screen Graphics: Sonja Schenk
Typesetters: Cheryl Vega and Winnie Kelly
Proofreader: Eddie Lin
Indexer: Debbie Burnham-Kidwell
Cover Designer: Thomas Ingalls + Associates
Cover Photographer: Casey Cartwright

Framework, Framework II, Framework III, FRED, dBASE, dBASE II, dBASE III, dBASE III PLUS, dBASE IV, and MultiMate are trademarks of Ashton-Tate.

Apple and Apple IIe are trademarks of Apple Computer Corporation.

CompuServe is a servicemark of CompuServe, a subsidiary of H & R Block, Inc.

Dow Jones News/Retrieval Service is a registered servicemark of Dow Jones & Co., Inc.

Easycom/Easygo is a trademark of Transend.

IBM, Personal Computer AT, and DisplayWrite are trademarks of International Business Machines Corporation.

1-2-3, DIF, and VisiCalc are trademarks of Lotus Development Corporation.

MS, MS-DOS, and Multiplan are trademarks of Microsoft Corporation.

The Source is a servicemark of Source Telecomputing Corporation, a subsidiary of Reader's Digest Association, Inc.

Telenet and Telemail are servicemarks of GTE, Inc.

MCI Mail is a servicemark of MCI Telecommunications, Inc.

WordStar is a trademark of MicroPro International Corporation.

SideKick and SuperKey are trademarks of Borland International.

Lexis and Nexis are trademarks of Mead Corporation.

The Knowledge Index is a trademark of Dialog Information Services.

Hayes Smartmodem, Hayes Smartmodem 1200B, and Hayes Smartmodem 2400B are trademarks of Hayes Microcomputer Products, Inc.

PC Paintbrush is a trademark of IMSI.

Calendar Creator is a trademark of Channelmark Corporation.

WordPerfect is a trademark of WordPerfect Corporation.

SYBEX is a registered trademark of SYBEX, Inc.

SYBEX is not affiliated with any manufacturer.

Library of Congress Card Number: 89-60278
ISBN 0-89588-513-1
Manufactured in the United States of America
10 9 8 7 6 5 4 3

ACKNOWLEDGMENTS

THIS BOOK REFLECTS THE WORK OF MANY PEOPLE. We wish to thank them all for their contributions. We owe a great debt to Barbara Gordon, who edited the first version of this book, *Mastering Framework*; Tanya Kucak, who edited the second and present versions; David Kolodney, who managed the project; and Rusel De Maria, for his help with revising the current version.

Many people at the Forefront Corporation, developers of Framework III for Ashton-Tate, have contributed in ways too numerous to mention. For their help with previous versions, we would like to thank Steve Aubrey, David Greene, Chris Kirkpatrick, Marilyn McMahon, Hal Schectman, Rich Strauss, and Dave Welch, who gave unstintingly of their time and expertise. Thanks also to Kent Irwin of Ashton-Tate, Rosemary Morrissey of IBM, and Joe Campbell, who gave us the benefit of his considerable knowledge of telecommunications. For their help with the current version, we are grateful to Dave McLaughlin and David Altounian of Ashton-Tate.

CONTENTS AT A GLANCE

TABLE OF CONTENTS

INTRODUCTION

Framework III is an integrated software package that offers all of the most important personal computer applications in one coherent program.

With Framework III, you can use your computer to perform all of the following tasks:

- Building spreadsheets of numbers
- Creating word processed documents
- Assembling and working with databases
- Producing graphs
- Communicating directly with other computers via modem and telephone lines
- Sharing data with other software packages

To tie these diverse elements together, Framework III supplies you with a tool called *outlining*. An outline can serve either of two essential functions in your work: you can use outlining to combine several different applications that you have already developed, creating a single integrated document from them; or you can use outlining as a way of planning and organizing a task that you have not yet begun.

On your computer's display screen, Framework III provides you with a visual "desktop" on which all of your work will take place. You will create "frames" on the desktop to contain each different task that you undertake. Just as on a real desktop, you might find yourself working with many different documents at once in Framework III—spreadsheets, word processed texts, databases, and graphs.

To create and work with these documents, Framework III gives you several essential tools, all of which are easy to find and easy to use. Framework III is primarily a menu-driven program, which means that its main operations are displayed on the screen for you to examine and select. Choosing a menu option seldom requires more than two or three keystrokes.

But in addition to the menus, Framework III also supplies a set of ten frequently used operations that you access through the ten function keys on your keyboard. These function keys, along with the menu operations, give you complete control over the size, shape, and contents of the document frames that you place on the desktop.

One of the great advantages of Framework III is that all these menu and function-key operations work consistently throughout the program. Learn to use them for one kind of application, and you will almost instinctively be able to apply your knowledge to all the other kinds of Framework III documents.

Finally, Framework III includes a complete programming language, called FRED—a language designed to operate exclusively within the Framework III environment. FRED includes all the features and facilities of most other PC programming languages, such as BASIC or Pascal. Yet FRED is in many ways even more powerful than these traditional languages, because it is designed to work along with all the tools included in Framework III itself. You can exploit the powers of FRED programming at many levels; new computer users and seasoned programmers alike will find themselves using aspects of FRED to increase the versatility of Framework III documents.

This book is designed to introduce you to both the mechanical details of operating Framework III and the kinds of business tasks you will be able to perform with the program.

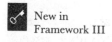 New in Framework III

Framework has evolved over several years, and there have been several versions of the product. Though all versions have shared certain characteristics, each has added its own features and operational changes. For instance, Framework III is the first version to make extensive (though optional) use of the mouse, to add footnotes and a thesaurus to the word processing, and so forth. This book is about Framework III, but we would be remiss if we ignored anyone still using Framework II. Therefore, throughout the book, you will see notes like the ones in the margin, which will alert you that a feature or procedure is different. Whenever possible, we have indicated the way to do things in earlier versions of Framework.

 Version Note

This book is written from the perspective of a user at a keyboard. However, some of you may use the mouse for many of the operations detailed here. If you use a mouse, please refer to the Mouse Techniques section of Chapter 1 for an overview of how the mouse techniques parallel the keyboard techniques. You will have no trouble translating the keyboard instructions to mouse techniques once you have reviewed this information.

In addition to the Mouse Techniques section, Chapter 1 gives you a broad look at all that Framework III can do; thereafter, each chapter of the book is devoted to one of Framework III's major functional applications: outlining, spreadsheet programming and graphing, word processing, database management, telecommunications, FRED programming, and working with other programs.

In this book, you will learn about Framework III by studying examples of the program in action. Each of the many examples in this book is designed specifically to illustrate one or more of Framework III's features. The best place to read this book, then, is in front of your own computer, with Framework III running; the examples are presented as hands-on tutorials, for you to work through, step by step, on your computer.

Each chapter in this book is divided into four main sections: an overview, describing the details and the conceptual background of a given application area; a set of practical examples, demonstrating how the application might actually be put to work in a business environment; a section called Exploring Further, which will help you expand and deepen your understanding of Framework III; and finally, a summary.

The chapters are meant to be read in sequence, as each one builds upon the material of its predecessors. Following is a brief description of what you will find in each chapter.

Chapter 1: A First Look at Framework III. This chapter supplies a general introduction to the operational elements and the functional components of Framework III. You'll learn how Framework III makes use of your computer system's hardware, including the display screen, the keyboard, the mouse, the disk drives, the printer, and the computer's internal memory, RAM. You'll also start to explore the practical significance of each of Framework III's major components: outlining, spreadsheet programming, graphing, word processing, database management, and telecommunications.

Chapter 2: Outlining. Here you will begin learning about outlining as an application and as a tool for integrating other applications. You'll find out how to create, expand, and modify an outline. You'll also discover how outlining can be used both for planning new projects or for pulling together a set of documents that you have already developed. Outlining never strays far from the center of our attention throughout this book.

Chapter 3: Spreadsheets. In this chapter, you'll learn how to create and work with tables of numbers within Spreadsheet frames. You'll find out how a spreadsheet is organized and how you can control its appearance and format. You'll learn how to write formulas to produce calculated values for spreadsheets, and then you'll learn how to *copy* formulas across rows and down columns of a spreadsheet. You'll also begin using FRED functions in this chapter; FRED will take on increasing importance from this point forward in the book. Finally, you'll discover how a spreadsheet can be used as a tool for exploring "what-if" scenarios.

Chapter 4: Word Processing. Framework III's word processing capabilities are elegantly simple to use, yet as powerful as many stand-alone word processing programs. This chapter will show you how to create, format, style, edit, save, and print a word processed document. In particular, you'll learn how to exploit the options of the Words menu, how to check your spelling, search for synonyms, create footnotes, and print your documents in just the format you require. You'll also continue working with Framework III's outlining facility to combine Word frames with other kinds of frames, producing integrated documents.

Chapter 5: Databases. Database management is a carefully designed component of Framework III, not just an extra feature tacked onto a spreadsheet program. In this chapter, you'll learn what a database is and how you can design and create your own databases in Framework III. You'll work through the essential database management operations: sorting, searching, replacing, appending records and fields, writing formulas to calculate field values, and filtering the database to display a selected subset of your data. You'll also discover Framework III's Forms view and dBASE view for databases, and you'll learn how you can use these alternative views of the database. Finally, you'll continue to expand your understanding of *integration;* here, you'll learn how to link a database with a spreadsheet, to increase the power of both, and how to link a database with a word processed document to create a form letter, or mail merge.

Chapter 6: Telecommunications. This chapter introduces Framework III's telecommunications component. It begins by explaining some of the terms and requirements of telecommunications. You'll learn how to use telecommunications to interact with a remote computer through a terminal, to send files from your disks or the desktop, to receive files directly on your disks, and to send and receive files using routines that test for accuracy in transmission. You'll also learn how to use the conveniences of Framework III's Telecommunications menu, to write files that store the information you need to link up with a particular remote computer, and to send files directly to another computer without the use of a modem.

Chapter 7: An Introduction to FRED Programming. This chapter describes the features of the FRED programming language, and offers some significant programming examples for you to examine and study. Even if you have never written a computer program before, this chapter will be worth your attention. You will learn about the features of Framework III's desktop Library, which allows you to write several kinds of programs that appeal even to beginners: macro programs, abbreviations, and assumptions. You'll also glimpse the expanded power that is available to you should you choose to become a FRED programmer. If you have already learned to program in some other language, this chapter will help you to translate your programming skills into practice with FRED. In particular, you'll want to focus on the complex programming examples at the end of the chapter.

Chapter 8: Working with Other Programs. This chapter explains the various ways to run other programs while using Framework III. You'll learn how to write a program to call another software package and how to install your program on Framework III's menu. You'll also learn about the other file formats that Framework III can read and write, and how to use them.

This book ends with several appendices. **Appendix A, Installing and Customizing Framework III**, will show you how to make Framework III run smoothly and efficiently on your particular computer system, and point you toward the many ways you can customize Framework III for your particular style of working. **Appendix B, FRED Functions**, provides a listing and brief explanation of all the FRED programming functions, with their syntax forms. **Appendix C, Tables of ASCII Characters**, lists the MS-DOS displayable characters and their ASCII codes, as well as the standard ASCII control codes.

If you are just getting started in Framework III, you may want to take a look at Appendix A, on configuring the program for your own computer system. However, you will have a chance to tell Framework what kind of system you are using when you run the SETUPFW program as part of the installation process. Appendix A will guide you.

When you start Framework III on a hard disk system, you will see the screen shown in Figure I.1. Press the Return key, and you will soon find yourself looking at the Framework III desktop. Although this book assumes a hard disk system, you can easily run Framework III on a computer with two floppy disk drives. Two of the ten disks supplied in the Framework III package are required to get Framework III running on your computer. To start Framework III on a system with two floppy drives (after running the Setup program), follow these steps:

1. If necessary, turn on your computer with your DOS disk in drive A, and set the correct date and time. Remove the DOS disk.

2. Place System Disk 1 in drive A, and a disk for your data files in drive B.

3. At the DOS prompt A>, enter the command

   fw

4. After the program is loaded into your computer from System Disk 1, the screen shown in Figure I.1 will appear, with the additional message

Please insert SYSTEM DISK 2 in DRIVE A:

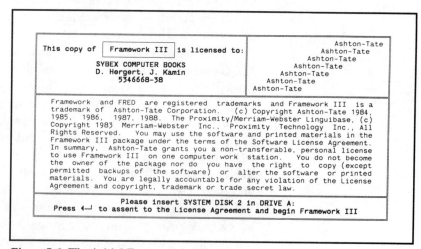

```
┌──────────────────────────────────────────────────────────────────────────┐
│                                                                            │
│  ┌───────────────────────────────────────────────┬───────────────────┐   │
│  │                                                 │      Ashton-Tate  │   │
│  │ This copy of │ Framework III │ is licensed to: │    Ashton-Tate    │   │
│  │                                                 │  Ashton-Tate      │   │
│  │         SYBEX COMPUTER BOOKS                    │Ashton-Tate        │   │
│  │         D. Hergert, J. Kamin                    │  Ashton-Tate      │   │
│  │              5346668-38                         │    Ashton-Tate    │   │
│  │                                                 │      Ashton-Tate  │   │
│  ├─────────────────────────────────────────────────────────────────────┤   │
│  │ Framework  and  FRED  are  registered  trademarks  and Framework III is a │
│  │ trademark of  Ashton-Tate  Corporation.   (c) Copyright Ashton-Tate 1984, │
│  │ 1985,  1986,  1987, 1988. The Proximity/Merriam-Webster Linguibase, (c)   │
│  │ Copyright 1983  Merriam-Webster  Inc.,  Proximity  Technology  Inc., All  │
│  │ Rights Reserved.   You may use the software and printed materials in the  │
│  │ Framework III package under the terms of the Software License Agreement.  │
│  │ In summary,  Ashton-Tate grants you a non-transferable, personal license  │
│  │ to use Framework III  on one computer work  station.   You do not become  │
│  │ the  owner  of  the package nor do  you have  the right  to copy (except  │
│  │ permitted  backups of  the software)  or  alter the software  or printed  │
│  │ materials.  You are legally accountable for any violation of the License  │
│  │ Agreement and copyright, trademark or trade secret law.                   │
│  ├─────────────────────────────────────────────────────────────────────┤   │
│  │              Please insert SYSTEM DISK 2 in DRIVE A:                     │
│  │  Press ←┘ to assent to the License Agreement and begin Framework III    │
│  └─────────────────────────────────────────────────────────────────────┘   │
│                                                                            │
└──────────────────────────────────────────────────────────────────────────┘
```

Figure I.1: The initial Framework III screen

Remove System Disk 1 and place System Disk 2 in drive A.

5. Press the Return key, and the Framework III desktop will appear on your screen.

You are now ready to begin reading Chapter 1.

CHAPTER

A First Look
at Framework III

OVERVIEW

INTRODUCTION

FRAMEWORK III IS A MULTIFUNCTIONED, MULTI-layered personal computer program for business use. Within a single software environment, the program offers you tools for performing and organizing your work under some of the most important general categories of personal computer activity:

- Working with numbers
- Working with words
- Working with records of information
- Working with graphs
- Communicating with other computers

We refer to these activities as *spreadsheet programming, word processing, database management, business graphing,* and *telecommunications,* respectively.

Framework III is rich and complex enough to handle elaborate business tasks in all of these categories. At the same time, Framework III's design is simple, consistent, and intuitive. As a result, when you use Framework III, you will be able to concentrate on the business tasks at hand rather than on the intricacies of operating your computer.

This first chapter will introduce you to Framework III. Later chapters will present a sequenced, hands-on approach to learning the details of Framework III. In this first chapter, you should not try to memorize anything, but rather acquire a general sense of Framework III's characteristics. You'll learn what the program can do for you and how you can best approach accomplishing jobs with it.

You'll also begin to see how Framework III operates on your computer. You'll examine the important features of the keyboard and the display screen, the mouse (if you use one), the functions of the disk drives and your printer, and the requirements Framework III imposes on your computer's internal memory (RAM).

Finally, you'll get a preview of the skills you'll develop and the capabilities you'll add to your computer repertoire as you master

Framework III. We'll be looking at examples of each of the program's major capabilities. Here, briefly, are the activities we'll be studying:

1. *Working with numbers: spreadsheet programming.* A spreadsheet is a table of numbers and headings, organized in rows and columns. Framework III will help you create spreadsheets and work easily and flexibly with the numeric information that spreadsheets contain. You can perform simple arithmetic on that information, calculating totals and averages from the rows and columns of numbers. Or you can perform more complex tasks, choosing among the large set of statistical and financial functions that Framework III offers. If you change a number somewhere in the middle of a spreadsheet, Framework III automatically redoes all your arithmetic for you.

2. *Working with words: word processing.* You can utilize Framework III to prepare and store any kind of written documents, from short memos and letters to book-length projects. The word processing features in Framework III give you flexible ways to create, edit, and revise your document, and then print it out on paper in just the format you choose.

3. *Working with records of information: database management.* Framework III will help you organize your personal or business record-keeping jobs. A list of addresses, a collection of information about your business clients, a personnel file, an inventory of parts or supplies—all of these are candidates for Framework III's data-handling facilities. You'll be able to create such records and then place them in any order. You can also revise records, delete records, add new records, and locate any record or group of records instantly.

4. *Working with graphs: business graphing.* Given a set of numbers that you have been working with—either in a spreadsheet or a database—Framework III can quickly create elaborate business graphs from those numbers. You can look at these graphs on your display screen, or you can print them on paper.

5. *Communicating with other computers: telecommunications.* Framework III includes a powerful, easy-to-use telecommunications function. If you have the necessary peripheral equipment, you can use it to send information from your computer to other computer users via telephone lines, receive information in a similar manner, gain access to information services and computerized bulletin boards, and communicate directly with mainframe computers.

   (In addition, Framework III includes facilities to convert files from the formats used by several popular programs—Lotus 1-2-3, WordStar, MultiMate, Multiplan, Display-Write, Framework II, WordPerfect, and the dBASE programs—as well as from other widely used formats, and to convert its own files to any of these formats. Therefore, even if you work in an environment where your co-workers use other programs, you can be assured that you can share your files with many of them. (See Chapter 8 for details.)

Framework III is called an *integrated software package* because it gives you tools for all of these activities, along with consistent ways of using and managing the program itself. Framework III also helps you to *combine* and *organize* these different elements of your computer work.

This is one of the advantages of an integrated package over stand-alone, single-function programs. Real-life jobs are seldom as clear-cut and distinct as words versus numbers or data versus graphs. More often we are required to combine different elements of our work, producing creatively integrated results.

For example, consider these typical business tasks:

- Inserting a spreadsheet table of sales statistics into a word processed memo you are writing to your regional sales managers.

- Finding the total current value from your inventory database, and moving that value to a financial spreadsheet you are preparing.

- Writing a word processed form letter and creating a personalized copy for each of the people listed in your database of business clients.

- Preparing a presentation-quality bar graph to summarize the financial data contained in a spreadsheet, and then incorporating both the spreadsheet and the graph into a word processed document you are preparing.

- Using an online information service to look up the recent performance of a stock on the New York Stock Exchange and graphing the statistics in a form that shows high, low, and closing prices.

Each of these jobs involves sharing information and mixing functions in ways that could be complex, time-consuming, or just plain messy without the benefit of a good integrated software package. With Framework III, you'll learn to manage all these jobs efficiently, letting your computer work out the mechanical details while you concentrate on the more creative and interesting parts of your work.

Finally, along with its major productivity components—spreadsheet programming, word processing, database management, business graphing, and telecommunications—Framework III also gives you a special tool to organize all of the work that you accomplish under its auspices. This tool takes the form of another of Framework III's working components: *outlining.* We'll explore outlining in detail in Chapter 2, but, in fact, the outlining facility is so essential to the character of Framework III that we'll see examples of its use throughout this book. As we set out to look specifically at the elements of Framework III, we should begin by discussing the significance of outlining.

DIVIDING YOUR WORK INTO PARTS . . . AND PUTTING IT BACK TOGETHER

A simple but essential piece of practical philosophy lies behind the design of the Framework III program:

People work most effectively when they can divide large jobs into smaller, interrelated tasks, which they can then accomplish one at a time.

Whether you are working with words, numbers, data, graphs, or some combination of these elements, Framework III encourages you to work in small, manageable components. After all the components are complete, you can go back and organize them into a coherent whole.

Two essential elements of the Framework III program—frames and outlines—will lead you naturally toward this approach:

1. *Frames.* For every job you perform in Framework III—whether it involves spreadsheet programming, word processing, database management, telecommunications, or business graphing—you will always begin by creating a *frame* for the job. A frame is simply an area on your display screen that represents, and contains, a specific kind of work. You may find yourself with many frames on the screen at once, but generally you will work with just one frame at a time.

2. *Outlines.* Whenever you need to establish a relationship among several frames you have created, you can put those frames in an outline. An outline imposes a hierarchy on the diverse elements of a large job, and it also gives you a practical way of handling many frames at once.

Let's consider a short example that illustrates this approach. At the end of a given tax year, you decide that you need to gather data about your financial activities over the year, so that you can estimate your tax liability. On the surface, you think the job should be simple: Determine your total income for the year, subtract business expenses and deductions, and look up the tax you owe on the remainder. But upon closer examination, you see that the picture is more complex. Several kinds of income, expenses, and deductions come into play, each of which will have to be tallied up on its own.

You begin creating spreadsheets for several different calculations. These spreadsheets include the following elements:

Business income

Interest income

Business expenses

Depreciation expenses

Interest deductions

Charitable contributions

Deductible professional fees

Deductions for state and local taxes

Each of these spreadsheets covers a single aspect of your financial picture for the year; you work on each of them individually, producing a ''bottom-line'' total in each category. Finally, you need some way to bring all this information together to come up with a figure for your actual taxable income.

In Framework III, each of these small spreadsheets would be contained within its own individual frame. To bring the frames together, you could create an outline like the following:

Taxes—1988

    Income

        Business

        Interest

    Expenses

        Business

        Depreciation

    Itemized Deductions

        Interest

        Charitable Contributions

        Professional Fees

    Taxable Income

The lowest-level headings in this outline all represent the spreadsheets that contain your financial information. The final spreadsheet, Taxable Income, will take bottom-line information from all the other spreadsheets to show you your taxable income.

Framework III actually allows you to use outlining in two different ways:

- You can begin by creating an assortment of spreadsheets, word processed texts, databases, and graphs, each contained within its own frame. When you are ready to organize these diverse elements of your work, you can create an Outline frame and move the work frames into the outline.

- Or you can begin by creating an outline of your work, and then filling in the details in individual frames beneath your outline headings.

In the tax example we chose the first approach, beginning with a series of spreadsheets and then using an outline to impose an order on them. Let's look at an example of the other approach.

As the sales executive of a national retail firm, it is your job to keep in touch with the regional sales managers. At the end of the current quarter, you are planning to write a memo to the regional managers to let them know how the company is doing and how each region is doing. Your memo will be a combination of text, spreadsheets, and graphs. Before you begin writing the memo, you decide to create an outline of all the information it will contain:

Memo to Regional Managers

    The Big Picture

        The Company's Sales This Quarter (text)

        Quarterly Sales (spreadsheet)

        Illustration of Quarterly Sales (graph)

    The Regional Picture

        From the Best to the Worst (text)

        Comparative Quarterly Sales (spreadsheet)

        Illustrated by Region (graph)

    The Salespeople

        The Best (text)

        Bonus Calculations (spreadsheet)

        Illustrated by Salesperson (graph)

When you create an outline like this one in Framework III, each low-level heading in the outline (that is, each heading that does not contain subheadings of its own) represents a frame for you to work in. And, as we have seen, each working frame can contain any one of the following:

- Word processed text
- A spreadsheet
- A database
- A graph
- An outline

In summary, outlining is a special element that helps you organize all the work you do in Framework III. An outline consists of headings and subheadings, each of which can, in turn, represent a frame for part of the work you are actually performing—work in any one of the functional categories that Framework III offers you. Now let's begin looking at Framework III on your computer.

THE ELEMENTS OF FRAMEWORK III

Like all computer programs, Framework III has its own distinctive appearance on your display screen. The program also makes use of your keyboard for its own special purposes; its keyboard functions are different from those of any other program you may be familiar with. Fortunately, though, the display screen and keyboard are designed to work consistently throughout all the Framework III components. Once you have become familiar with the way the program presents itself to you on the screen—and with the way you control the program's functions from the keyboard—you will learn to rely on the program's logical consistency as you move from one kind of work to another.

This consistency is another one of the advantages of working with an integrated software package like Framework III. You can do all your work in one unified software environment, without having to deal with the different syntax and command structure of differently designed programs.

In this section, we'll study how Framework III uses your IBM Personal Computer and most compatibles. (If you use one of the IBM PC compatibles, you may find some minor differences between the details we discuss here and the actual workings of your computer.)

Starting with the display screen, the keyboard, and the mouse, and then moving on to the other components of your computer, we'll examine the way Framework III makes use of the resources of your computer hardware.

THE DISPLAY SCREEN

Figure 1.1 shows how Framework III appears when you first begin running the program on your computer. The screen consists of several distinct areas. Framework III uses these areas for displaying your current work or for displaying certain messages to you during your work. Each of these areas has a name that describes its function in Framework III:

- The desktop
- The menu line
- The clock
- The status panel
- The message area

You don't need to remember the names of these areas, but after a little experience in running Framework III, you'll get used to looking in certain areas of the screen for the particular information you need.

Figure 1.1: The opening Framework III screen

THE DESKTOP   The *desktop* takes up the bulk of the display screen, and it is where most of your work in Framework III will take place. Whenever you create a frame or retrieve a frame from disk, it will appear on the desktop, where you can examine its contents and work with it. You will learn that this metaphoric desktop gives you the same kind of flexibility that your real-life desktop does for arranging your work in just the way that suits you:

- You can increase or decrease the number of frames that are on the desktop at a given time.

- You can put frames aside in "trays" on the desktop, where they'll still be available to you but out of the way of your other work.

- You can "drag" frames around to different areas of the desktop, so that you can look at more than one frame at once.

- You can increase or decrease the size of a frame, so that you can see more or less of the frame's contents.

- You can move your work frames into an Outline frame so that you can establish a relationship between different elements of your work.

We'll be looking at the keyboard and mouse functions that allow you to perform all of these desktop feats. Meanwhile, for a preview of what a working desktop might look like, Figure 1.2 shows you three different frames—a Word frame, a Spreadsheet frame, and a Graph frame—all arranged on the desktop for viewing at once. You can see that these frames overlap and have been set at different sizes. Figure 1.3 shows the same three frames placed in their respective "trays" at the lower right corner of the desktop. We say that a frame is *closed* when it is put away in its tray, and *open* when it is displayed on the desktop. Shifting a frame between the desktop and its tray requires only a single keystroke from you.

WORKING WITH DRIVES AND DIRECTORIES   Near the upper right corner of the desktop reside the trays of some special frames, which you will be using constantly. These frames, called *file cabinets*, have two types. Each cabinet of the first type is devoted to a single

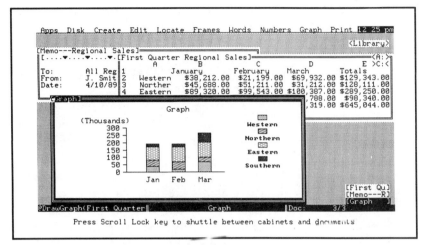

Figure 1.2: Three frames on the desktop

Figure 1.3: Three closed frames in their trays

disk drive, so you have as many cabinets of this type as you have drives. The second type is actually a unique cabinet called the *Library cabinet.* The disk drive cabinets display the names of the disk drives. In Figure 1.3, they display the names

    <A:>

and

>C:<

but the names will vary depending on the number and kind of drives your computer has.

Although you can use Framework III on a computer with two floppy disk drives, its large size—it uses several disks for the program and for special files—makes it cumbersome to use without a hard disk. If you do use two floppy disk drives, the one on the left (or the top) is named A and the one on the right (or the bottom) is B. (Disk drive names are usually followed by a colon, as shown in the illustration.) In a system with two floppy disk drives, you'll usually keep one of the Framework III program disks in drive A, and you'll use drive B to save the information you create.

If you use a hard disk, it is probably named C. To keep track of your Framework III program files, you should create a special *subdirectory* for the program. You may also want to create subdirectories for those files you originate using Framework III, as well as for any other programs you use. If you use a hard disk and you are not familiar with subdirectories, consult your DOS manual.

Any other disk drives you may use—external hard drives, hard disk cards, or RAM disks—will also have their own file cabinets. The system represented in Figure 1.3 has a single floppy disk drive called A and a hard disk drive called C. If your system has a RAM disk, it may be labeled D, and in network configurations, you may have drives such as I, J, and K for network servers and remote drives.

When you save a frame on the desktop to a disk, it becomes a *file*. You can save a frame onto disk or read a file from the disk at any time.

When you first begin a Framework III session, one drive (usually the one you started Framework from) will be the *default drive*. You can change the default drive in the Setup program.

New in
Framework III

In Framework III, you can recognize the default drive because it is bracketed by a greater-than and less-than sign:

>C:<

Ordinary drives are bracketed by a less-than and greater-than sign:

<A:>

When you open one of the disk drive cabinets, the frame will show a directory of the disk. If you use subdirectories, the directory displayed will be the current subdirectory. You can see a sample disk directory of drive C in Figure 1.4. We'll discuss disks, drives, and directories more later in this chapter.

The Library cabinet is a place to store various types of files that you always want to have available for immediate use. It is designed to make using Framework III speedy and effortless. We'll look into the Library cabinet later in this chapter as well.

THE MENU LINE   Just above the desktop, on the top line of your display screen, appear a series of ten words:

> **Apps   Disk   Create   Edit   Locate   Frames   Words
> Numbers   Graph   Print**

These words represent Framework III's main *menu.* Just like a menu in a restaurant, a program menu gives you a series of options. Framework III's menu has ten main options, represented by the ten words in the menu line. These options allow you to control, modify, and work with the frames you create.

We'll postpone looking at these options until we know a little more about Framework III; but if you think you can guess what most of the

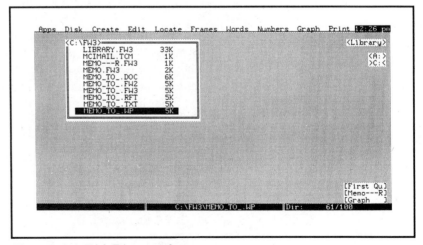

Figure 1.4: A Disk Directory frame

options do, you're probably right. Framework III's intuitive design often allows you to accomplish tasks with a minimum of previous knowledge about how the program works.

THE CLOCK   Just to the right of the menu is Framework III's clock. The display on this clock changes every minute, and the colon between the numbers blinks every second. Framework III takes the time from the computer's system clock and displays it on the screen for you. From time to time the clock may stop—for example, when you are performing disk operations (saving frames on disk or reading files from disk). But when the operation is complete, the clock will start up again at the correct time.

Of course, the time displayed on the Framework III clock depends on your setting the time correctly when you set up your computer, or, if you have no battery-operated internal clock, when you first turn on your computer. If you fail to set the time, or if you set it incorrectly, Framework III's clock will not display the right time. If your system does not have a clock that sets the time for you automatically, you should get in the habit of setting the correct time each time you turn on your computer to use Framework III.

THE STATUS PANEL   Directing your attention down the display screen, you can see that there are two areas of information located below the desktop. The single reverse-video line directly below the desktop is called the *status panel*. This line is divided into three parts, and it always displays certain information about the frame you have selected for your current work. You can see in Figure 1.1 that the disk drive cabinet, C, is the current frame selection. The name of the frame is displayed in the center section of the status panel. The section on the right tells you that C is the third of three cabinets:

Cabinet: 3/3

When we look in more detail at the structure of a frame, we'll find out more about this status panel.

THE MESSAGE AREA Below the status panel is the message
area. This area of your display screen has two lines: the *edit line* and
the *message line*.

When you enter a value into a frame or choose to edit a value that
is already in a frame, the value will first appear on the edit line. As
you enter keystrokes to change the value itself, the changes will often
also occur on the edit line, and will also be reflected in the original
location.

Below the edit line, on the bottom line of your display screen, is
Framework III's message line. Framework III reserves this area to
display special information. The information in the message line is
always relevant to your current activity in Framework III. The message may concern something you are about to do, something you
have just done, or some action that is available to you at a given turn
in the program.

For example, as you prepare to select activities from Framework
III's menu, the message line will explain briefly what action a given
menu choice will perform. Or, if you hit one or more keystrokes that
Framework III doesn't know what to do with at a given point, the
message line will display some sort of *error message*. Often Framework
III will also beep when an error occurs, so you will know to check the
message line to see what has happened.

Your understanding of Framework III's display screen organization will increase as you begin using the program. There is little
about the display screen that you need to memorize; most of the
time, you will simply get into the habit of looking in a certain area of
the screen for the information you want.

We have already seen some frames displayed on the desktop;
before we begin mastering the Framework III keyboard, we should
pause to examine the structure of a frame.

WORK FRAMES

You know by now that Framework III lets you create frames for
any of six types of activities:

1. Spreadsheet frames, for working with numbers

2. Word frames, for word processing

3. Database frames, for database management

4. Graph frames, for displaying graphs

5. Telecommunications frames, for sharing data with other computers

6. Outline frames, for organizing your work and grouping other frames together

Even though frames for different activities look quite different on the screen, all of the frames you create in Framework III have certain elements in common. Every frame has four distinct parts:

- A border

- A label (or name)

- A contents area

- A programming area behind the frame

Figure 1.5 shows a Spreadsheet frame that has just been created. The spreadsheet is empty: it doesn't yet have any values entered into its rows and columns. We'll use this figure to discuss the four structural parts of a frame.

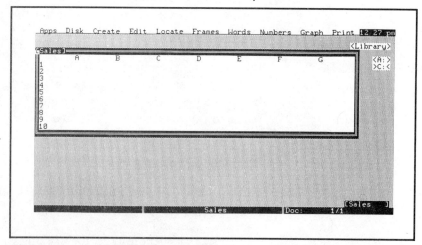

Figure 1.5: A Spreadsheet frame—The elements of a frame

THE BORDER   The border of a frame is represented by the thin double lines that surround the rectangular frame area. When you *select* a frame for your current work, the border is filled in with a thick reverse-video rectangle. This is called the *highlight*. You can see that the frame in Figure 1.5 has been selected for some activity.

Another visual indicator that Framework III gives you to let you know where you are currently working on the screen is the *cursor*. The cursor is a small rectangle that takes up the space of one character on the screen. In Figure 1.5, you can see the cursor at the upper left corner of the Spreadsheet frame's border.

What you can't see on a printed page—but will notice right away on the screen—is that the cursor constantly flashes on and off. This makes it easy for you to find your current location on a crowded desktop. When the cursor and the highlight are located on the border of a frame that you have selected, you can perform any Framework III action that affects the frame as a whole. For example, you can drag the frame to a new location on the desktop, move the frame into an outline, change the display size of the frame, or save the frame as a disk file.

If you use a mouse, an additional cursor—the mouse cursor—will help you locate the current position of the mouse.

THE LABEL   At the upper left corner of every frame's border is a space, enclosed in square brackets, that is reserved for a frame label. A label is simply a name that you supply for a frame you have created. In Figure 1.5, you can see that the name *Sales* has been given to this Spreadsheet frame. Notice that the same name also appears in the frame's tray at the lower right corner of the desktop. (The central portion of the status panel also displays the label of the currently selected frame.)

Frame labels are important for several reasons. First, they allow you to identify, with names that you yourself assign, each frame that you create and work with. Second, when you save a frame onto disk, the disk file in which you save your work will take the name that you have assigned to the desktop frame. For this reason, you cannot save a frame until you have given it a name.

Finally, as you advance in your knowledge of Framework III, you'll discover all sorts of activities that link different frames or establish relationships between frames. These activities often depend on the ability to refer to a frame by name.

THE CONTENTS AREA   The visible area *inside* a frame is, of course, reserved for the frame's contents—that is, the main work for which you have created the frame. The contents of frames will be at the center of our attention throughout this book. Each type of frame—Spreadsheet, Word, Database, Graph, Telecommunications, and Outline—has a distinctive inner organization, designed specifically to meet the requirements of a specific kind of work. You can see, for example, that the contents of the three frames in Figure 1.2 are organized in quite different ways. You'll quickly learn to recognize the different frame types by their appearance.

THE PROGRAMMING AREA   Every frame has yet another area that is normally out of view. This area, which we say is located *behind* the frame, is reserved for special programming activities. In accomplishing most tasks in Framework III, your use of this area is completely optional; still, you should be aware that the area exists. Behind every frame is an area reserved for you to write a formula or a program.

For advanced users, Framework III includes a complete programming language that can control and expand the capabilities of the Framework III program. If you have ever worked in BASIC on your computer, you know that a programming language consists of a large set of commands that your computer can perform. You can write and store a series of such commands—called a *program*—that will perform a planned sequence of actions on the computer.

Framework III's programming language is called FRED (an acronym for Frames Editor). We'll be dealing with FRED from time to time, on a rather casual basis, throughout this book. When these occasions arise, you'll be reminded about the programming area behind frames. Chapter 7 will also give you a quick introduction to the rules and capabilities of FRED, and Appendix B summarizes the FRED functions. For now, simply remember that a FRED program can reside behind any frame.

In summary, the visible and most active elements of a frame are its border, its label, and its contents. In order to work with frames, you have to learn to use the keys on your keyboard that control the movement of Framework III's cursor and highlight from one point to another. (Remember, the cursor and the highlight indicate the location of your current work on the desktop.) You can move the cursor and the highlight in several different ways, to select frames and to select a working location inside a frame. In the next section, we'll discuss the keys that allow you to move from one place to another on the desktop. In the section after that, we'll introduce the mouse. Throughout the remainder of this chapter, we'll use the terms *cursor* and *highlight* more or less synonymously. Just remember that both of these visual markers show you where you are working on the display screen. Starting with Chapter 2, we'll begin to distinguish more carefully between their respective functions.

THE FRAMEWORK III KEYBOARD

If you've used other programs on your PC, you know that your keyboard is divided into roughly three areas. The largest area, in the center, works pretty much like the keyboard of a typewriter. The letters, the digits, and an assortment of punctuation marks are all located where you would expect to find them on a typewriter.

At the right side of the keyboard is a number pad, which also serves as the *cursor-control area.* On some keyboards, separate cursor-control keys are located between the main keyboard and the number pad. You can use these keys interchangeably with those of the number pad for cursor control. At the left side of some keyboards are two columns of *function keys,* labeled F1 to F10. On other keyboards, the function keys are arranged along the top and may be labeled F1 to F12. Only the first ten function keys are of interest to us here, however. (As you move from one program to another on your PC, these function keys tend to be the most elusive of all, because they are usually designed to offer completely different functions in each program you use.)

The cursor-control keys and the ten function keys, along with several other important keys located on either side of the alphabetic keys, are all essential to the design of Framework III. They give you a rich array of functions you cannot do without. They also make Framework III easier to use than many other programs of equal complexity. If you compare Framework III to other integrated packages, you will find that Framework III's menu—represented by the ten words above the desktop—is remarkably concise and simple. One of the reasons for this is that Framework III has moved so many control functions directly to the keyboard.

THE CURSOR-MOVEMENT KEYS The number pad at the right side of the keyboard works in two different ways. It can give you an alternative way of entering numbers into your computer, or it can give you ways of controlling the movement of the cursor on the display screen. The key that shifts the number pad between these two modes of operation is labeled Num Lock.

We call Num Lock a *toggle key* because it toggles a part of the keyboard back and forth between two different modes. When you press Num Lock in Framework III, you will see a small message appear at the far right side of the status panel:

NUM

This means that the right side of the keyboard has been shifted into its number-pad mode. You can use it for ten-key numeric data entry. Press the Num Lock key again, and the NUM message disappears from the screen. Now the right side of the keyboard is available for cursor-movement functions.

Usually, you will use the right side of the keyboard for cursor movement in Framework III. Whenever Framework III does not respond to the keyboard in the way you were expecting, always check to see if you have inadvertently pressed the Num Lock key, toggling the keyboard into the wrong mode.

Table 1.1 summarizes the basic cursor-movement keys. (To use them, make sure the NUM message is *not* showing on your screen.) Framework III gives its own special names to these keys. To help you remember the names and functions of these keys, the Framework III package includes two plastic templates that you can place on your keyboard. One of the templates fits over the function keys (at the left side of the keyboard), reminding you what the F1 to F10 keys do in Framework III. The other template can be glued onto the flat area at the top of your keyboard, just above the number pad. This second template describes the cursor- and highlight-movement keys.

As you study Table 1.1, notice the different kinds of cursor and highlight movement that are possible:

- Between a frame's border and its contents (the Out [−] and In [+] keys; you can also use the F11 key for Out and the F12 key for In)

Table 1.1: The Cursor- and Highlight-Movement Keys

KEYBOARD NAME	FRAMEWORK III NAME	DESCRIPTION
–	Out	Moves the cursor and the highlight from the contents area of a frame to the border of the same frame.
+	In	Moves the cursor and the highlight from the border of a selected frame to the contents area of the frame.
←	Return	Opens a frame that is in its tray, or puts an open frame back into its tray.
Scroll Lock	Shuttle	Moves the cursor between the desktop frames and the disk drive cabinets.
Ins	Instruct	Selects the Framework III menu, allowing you to select one of the menu's activities.
Del	Delete	Deletes frames from the desktop; deletes files from the disk directory; or deletes words, numbers, or data from the contents of a frame.
Num Lock	Num Lock	Toggles the keyboard between number-pad mode and cursor-movement mode.
↑, ↓, ←, →	Arrow keys (↑, ↓, ←, →)	On the desktop, these keys move your selection from one frame to another.

- Between desktop work frames and the disk drive cabinets (the Shuttle [Scroll Lock] key)

- Between one frame and another on the desktop (the arrow keys)

- From the desktop to the menu (the Instruct [Ins] key)

In addition, the Ctrl key, when used in conjunction with the cursor-movement keys, can amplify the cursor movements. We'll talk about these extended effects as they become relevant in different types of frames.

THE FUNCTION KEYS The function keys, F1 to F10, help you work with frames in some important ways. We'll be studying their use as we need them. If you want a preview of what they do, Table 1.2 provides a summary.

Table 1.2: The Framework III Function Keys

KEYBOARD NAME	FRAMEWORK III NAME	DESCRIPTION
F1	Help	Supplies you with a help screen that describes your current Framework III activity.
F2	Edit	Allows you to create or edit a formula or program that resides behind a frame.
Shift-F2*	Edit Cut Text	Allows you to edit text that has been copied from the desktop to the electronic clipboard (using Shift-F7).
F3	Drag	Lets you move a frame from one place to another on the desktop.
F4	Size	Lets you increase or decrease the visible portion of a frame on the desktop.
F5	Recalc	Recalculates a frame or the formula behind a frame.
F6	Extend Select	Allows you to select a group of frames or data as the object of a subsequent action.
F7	Move	Allows you to move frames or data from one place to another.

Table 1.2: The Framework III Function Keys (continued)

KEYBOARD NAME	FRAMEWORK III NAME	DESCRIPTION
Shift-F7*	Cut	Allows you to place a copy of the selected text in the electronic clipboard.
F8	Copy	Allows you to copy frames or data from one place to another.
Shift-F8*	Paste	Allows you to insert a copy of the electronic clipboard's contents at the cursor.
F9	Zoom	Enlarges your view of a selected frame to take up the entire display screen.
F10	View	Toggles between Outline view and Frames view.

* New in Framework III

One function key that you should learn about right away is the Help key, F1. You can press the Help key at any point during your work, and Framework III will quickly put you into its online help facility. This facility consists of an extensive series of help screens that describe in detail the entire Framework III program. When you press the Help key, Framework III first determines the nature of your current work. Then it places you at exactly the help screen that applies to the activity you are involved in. (In the words of the Framework III documentation, help is *context-sensitive*. This means that Framework III determines what kind of help you need from the context of your current activity.) If you are in the menu and you press the Help key (F1), Framework III will show you a help screen that describes the menu option you were about to select.

The Escape key (labeled Esc, at the upper left corner of your keyboard) gets you out of the help facility and back to your work on the desktop. You should get into the habit of pressing the Help key (F1) whenever you have a question about Framework III.

Now let's look at an alternate way to move around the screen and issue commands in Framework III—the mouse.

MOUSE TECHNIQUES

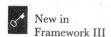
New in
Framework III

You can use a two- or three-button mouse to perform many Framework III operations. Many of the keyboard operations that require several steps are performed quickly and intuitively using a mouse.

First, we'll look at mouse basics. The following terms refer to mouse actions:

- *Click*: Press a button quickly and let go.
- *Press*: Press a button and hold it down.
- *Double-click*: Click twice in rapid succession.
- *Drag*: Press and hold the button down, then move the mouse.

In the following paragraphs, we'll explain the basic mouse techniques. At the end of this section, we'll show you how these techniques compare to keyboard actions.

To select any frame, outline level, spreadsheet cell, database field, or character position in word processing and telecommunications, simply place the mouse cursor over the desired element and click the left button.

To select any menu item, simply position the mouse cursor on the desired menu, click the left button once (equivalent to pressing Instruct [Ins], or pressing Ctrl and the first letter of the menu item), drag the mouse to the desired option (the highlight will move as you move the mouse), and click again.

To leave the current menu, move the mouse cursor outside the menu and click the left button (equivalent to pressing Out (−).

To leave all menus, press the left and right mouse buttons together (equivalent to pressing Escape).

There are three special places to use a mouse within a frame:

1. The upper left corner of the frame: If you press the left mouse button in that corner, then drag the mouse, you can move a frame anywhere on the desktop.

2. The lower right corner of the frame: If you press the left mouse button in that corner and drag the mouse, you can resize a frame, as shown in Figure 1.6.

3. The edge of the frame: If you press the right mouse button on the edge of the frame, you can scroll the contents of the frame. If you hold the button down, the contents of the frame will scroll slowly. If you click the button, the contents will move a screen at a time. The position of the mouse cursor will determine the direction of the scrolling. If the mouse cursor is toward the top of the frame, the contents will scroll toward the beginning; if it is toward the bottom, the contents will scroll toward the end. You can change the direction of the scrolling by moving the mouse.

You'll notice that these special mouse techniques take the place of some of the function and cursor keys. For instance, using the mouse in the upper right corner to move the frame is like using Drag (F3),

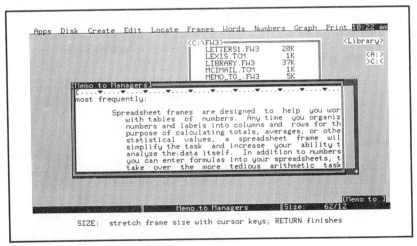

Figure 1.6: Special places to use the mouse

and using the mouse in the lower right corner to size the frame is like using Size (F4). Scrolling with the mouse is like using the PgUp and PgDn keys.

The mouse can also take the place of several other keys:

KEY	*MOUSE EQUIVALENT*
Return	Double-click the left mouse button to open and close frames, load them from disk, and change directories.
Extend Select (F6)	Press the left mouse button and drag to select an area of text, numbers, or multiple frames. To select multiple frames on the desktop, select the first or last frame from the trays (not the frames themselves), then drag the mouse over the other trays you want to select. Note that you cannot select noncontiguous frames or data.
Zoom (F9)	Double-click the left mouse button anywhere in a frame to zoom it. In a zoomed frame, the same action will unzoom.
Formula Edit (F2)	To begin a formula edit in a spreadsheet, click the mouse in the formula area of the cell (located in the first third of the status panel), then begin entering the formula, as shown in Figure 1.7.

Let's look at how you would translate keyboard instructions into mouse movements. Suppose you had the following instructions:

Ctrl-C	(to open the Create menu)
E	(to create an Empty frame)
Size (F4) and arrow keys	(to change the size of the frame)
Drag (F3) and arrow keys	(to finish sizing and start moving the frames to a new location)

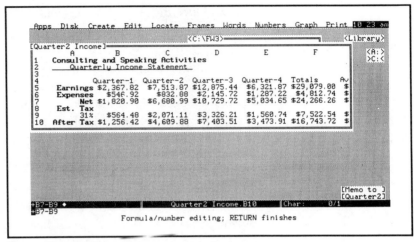

Figure 1.7: Beginning a formula with the mouse

Return	(to finish dragging)
In (+)	(to enter the first frame)
Zoom (F9)	(to zoom the frame)

To perform the same steps with the mouse, you would:

1. Click on the Create menu.
2. Move to Empty and click on it.
3. Place the mouse cursor on the lower right corner of the frame. Press and hold the button. (You'll notice that the lower right message line changes to read *Size:*, and shows the current size of the frame.)
4. Move the mouse until the outline of the frame is the size you want it to be, then release the button. (Notice that the message line changes as you drag the mouse around.)
5. Place the mouse cursor on the upper left corner of the frame, and press and hold the left mouse button. (Notice that the lower right message line now reads *Drag:*, and displays the current position of the frame's upper left corner.)
6. Move the mouse until the outline of the frame is in the proper position, then release the button. (Notice how the position indicator in the message line changes as you move the mouse.)

7. Click the left button anywhere inside the frame.

8. Double-click the left button to zoom the frame.

Extending selections is just as easy. Anywhere you see instructions involving Extend Select (F6), you can simply position the mouse cursor at the beginning of the selection, press the left button, and drag the mouse until the desired selection is made.

If you practice all the techniques outlined here, you will quickly be able to use the mouse without having to think about it. You will still have to use the keyboard, however, to perform many Framework tasks. If you don't see a mouse equivalent for a specific activity here, then it must be done on the keyboard. A good example is pointing during formula entry in a spreadsheet, which you'll learn about in Chapter 3. It might seem logical to use the mouse to point to spreadsheet cells, but you must use the keyboard's cursor keys for that.

Like the function keys, the full power of Framework III's menu comes into focus only after you have begun creating frames in each working category. We'll investigate the menu in a preliminary way now, filling in many of the details in subsequent chapters.

FRAMEWORK III'S MENU

As we have already seen, the menu is displayed as a group of ten words at the top of your screen. Each of these words represents a set of options you can select for working with frames or the contents of frames. When you select one of the ten words, you are presented with a *submenu* of still more selections. Through this hierarchy of menu selections, Framework III presents you with an elaborate yet simple-to-use set of options for accessing the program's control functions.

Table 1.3 summarizes, in general terms, some of the most elementary menu operations. This summary is by no means a complete description of the menu; each submenu option has several operations that you'll probably find yourself using all the time, and others that you'll use only rarely.

As we have seen, the key that puts you into the menu is the Instruct key, labeled Ins on your keyboard. (You press this key to "instruct" Framework III what to do next. Most programs call Ins the *Insert* key.) When you press the Ins key, Framework III immediately displays the submenu for one of the ten menu options at the top

Table 1.3: A Summary of the Framework III Menu

MENU OPTION	DESCRIPTION
Apps	Controls telecommunications, network mail, spelling check, and thesaurus. Also allows you to run other programs directly from the desktop, toggle the Safety feature, and change colors.
Disk	Reads files from disk and stores frames onto disk. Gives you access to submenus through which you can read files created by other programs into Framework III, or convert Framework III files into formats that other programs can read. Also provides a way to quit Framework III and return to DOS.
Create	Creates new Outline, Word, Spreadsheet, or Database frames. Allows you to specify the dimensions of a Spreadsheet or Database frame before you create it. Also allows you to add new rows or columns to a current Spreadsheet frame, or new records or fields to a current Database frame. In addition, permits you to record a series of keystrokes as a *keyboard macro,* which you assign to a specific key to be pressed in combination with the Alt key, to be played back at any time, or to which you give an abbreviation, which Framework III will replace with your keystrokes.
Edit	Potentially undoes the most recent Framework III action (for example, an inadvertent deletion). Deletes columns or rows from a Spreadsheet frame; deletes records or fields from a Database frame. Allows you to protect selected frames or contents from editing. Includes word count and typeover toggles as well as submenus for hyphenation and footnote options.
Locate	Provides three important functions for all types of frames: sorting (arranging data in alphabetical or numeric order), searching (looking for a certain sequence of data within a frame), and search and replace (replacing instances of a certain value with a new value, either selectively or throughout a frame).

Table 1.3: A Summary of the Framework III Menu (continued)

MENU OPTION	DESCRIPTION
Frames	Works on the appearance and characteristics of frames on the desktop; particularly valuable for setting the format of an Outline frame.
Words	Controls the style and format of text in Word frames and other frames. Boldface and italics are examples of styles. Right justification and centering are examples of formatting.
Numbers	Offers you a range of number styles for Spreadsheet and Database frames—for example, currency, percent, scientific. Also includes options for recalculating formulas in the spreadsheet and for setting entry formats for cells and database fields.
Graph	Allows you to create a graph from a selected set of numbers in a Spreadsheet or Database frame. Offers an assortment of bar, pie, line, and point graphs, plus options for determining how they will be created.
Print	Sends a selected frame to the printer to produce a hard copy. Determines the layout of the printed page, and includes four submenus of additional controls.

of the screen. For example, Figure 1.8 shows the submenu for the Create option.

Once you have pressed the Instruct key to select the menu, you can use the ← and → keys to move from one menu option to the next. Each time you press an arrow key, a new submenu will be displayed on the screen, below the corresponding menu option.

When you have reached the menu option that you wish to work from, you can use the ↑ and ↓ keys to move within the submenu. The cursor and highlight will show you the current selection in the submenu. To choose an option in a submenu, you position the cursor appropriately and press the Return key. This tells Framework III to act on your selection.

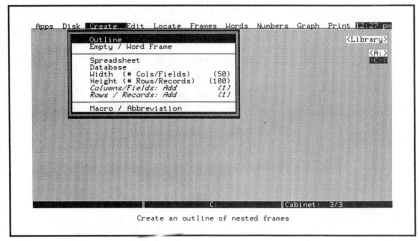

Figure 1.8: The Create submenu

Let's look at an example of using the menu, keystroke by keystroke. Say you want to create a new Spreadsheet frame, like the one shown in Figure 1.5. Here is the sequence of keystrokes you will follow:

Instruct	(to get into the menu)
→	(to move to the Create option)
↓	(to position the cursor over the Spreadsheet option)
Return	(to select the Spreadsheet option)

In response to this sequence, Framework III will create a new Spreadsheet frame for you and place it on the desktop.

You may have to press each of the arrow keys more than once to move the highlight to the correct options. When you enter the menu for the very first time during a given session with Framework III, the Instruct key places you in the second submenu, the Disk option. But subsequently, each time you press the Instruct key to go to the menu, Framework III will return you to the menu option that you chose during your *previous* menu activity. You can always use the → and ← keys to move to a new menu option, and the ↑ and ↓ keys to move to a specific submenu option.

Once you get used to the menu and learn about the most commonly used options inside each submenu, you'll be able to use a faster technique for making menu selections, one that bypasses both the menus and the cursor-movement keys. The technique is to use the Ctrl key (called the *Control* key) along with the first letter of the option you wish to select. The Ctrl key works just like the shift keys on a typewriter. You have to hold it down along with a second key for it to have any special effect.

To indicate that you have to press the Ctrl key and another key concurrently, we often use a special hyphenated notation in print. For example, the following notation means, "Hold down the Ctrl key and press the C key":

Ctrl-C

Let's say that you want to create a new Spreadsheet frame, this time using the faster keyboard technique. Here are the keystrokes necessary for the operation:

Ctrl-C   (to open the Create submenu)

S   (to select the Spreadsheet option)

That's all. The Spreadsheet frame will be created for you, just as before. You don't even need to pause to look at the Create submenu when it comes onto the screen. The operation will be accomplished as soon as you press the S key.

You may not want to use this faster technique at the beginning. Sometimes, it can be more reassuring to examine the menu carefully before you select an option. But as you become more adept with Framework III, keep in mind that this technique is available.

Before reading further, you should look through the entire Framework III menu on your own screen and compare the menu options with the summarized descriptions in Table 1.3. You can see that some of the options will interest us primarily in the context of one specific type of frame, while other options have a more general applicability.

Conveniently, Framework III has a way of telling you at any point in your work precisely which menu options can be used. The options in a given submenu that are applicable to your current work will always appear in a high-intensity text on the display screen, and the options that do not apply—and that you cannot choose—will appear in normal intensity. (On a graphics display, the options that are applicable to your current work appear in normal type, and the options that do not apply are italicized. You can configure for color text or Hercules monographics.)

Now that we have discussed the features of Framework III's desktop, the elements consistent to each working frame, the cursor-movement and function keys, mouse techniques, and the Framework III menu, we need to take a brief look at Framework III's use of your computer's hardware.

HARDWARE CONSIDERATIONS

There are many ways in which you can put together a complete computer system around the PC. Here are just a few of the variables:

- The amount of internal memory (RAM) in your computer
- The kind of display device attached
- The kind of printer you have
- The kind and number of disk drives you have

In general, Framework III does a good job of adjusting itself to whatever hardware configuration it finds itself in. But if you are preparing to do extensive work with Framework III, or if you are planning to buy a computer system specifically for running Framework III, there are a few considerations you should keep in mind.

MEMORY   One of the most important hardware resources for running Framework III is memory. As PCs with large amounts of memory have become commonplace, a new generation of software products, including Framework III, have appeared that require such memory. The minimum recommended memory for Framework III is 512K; however, it operates more efficiently with 640K. Moreover, if you have a Personal Computer AT with extended memory (more than 640K), or an expanded memory board that meets the Lotus-Intel-Microsoft standard, Framework III can be customized so that it uses this type of memory as well.

We have discussed ways in which you might establish relationships between frames in Framework III. This includes exchanging data between frames, creating graphs from Spreadsheet and Database frames, and grouping several frames together under one outline. In order to perform any of these feats, all of the frames involved have to be present on the desktop, not just stored on disk. Because each frame on the desktop takes up some of your computer's RAM, you can see that the more elaborate a system of frames you plan to create, the more memory you will need.

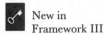
New in
Framework III

DISPLAY SCREEN   For your display screen, you can choose either a monochrome or a color monitor and either a graphics or text configuration, and with either choice you can be assured of enjoying the full range of the program's capabilities. Framework III can create business graphs on either kind of configuration, using any of the major IBM or non-IBM display adapter cards. (Some other major integrated packages can display graphs only in a high-resolution graphics environment. Graphs in these programs are not available on a monochrome monitor that is controlled by an IBM monochrome display card.)

On a color monitor, Framework III will give you high-resolution color graphs, just as you would expect. On an ordinary monochrome monitor, Framework III creates graphs out of the special graphics characters that are available in the high range of the IBM PC character set. Each of these graphics characters takes up the space of one normal character on the screen, but they can be used in groups to build interesting graphics effects. This works just fine for bar graphs and point graphs. A pie chart is a bit more of a problem, but even so, Framework III makes a valiant attempt. See Table A.1 in Appendix A for a comparison of text and graphics modes.

PRINTER   When you get ready to send text, numbers, and graphs to your printer, Framework III is once again ready to adjust as necessary to the hardware you own. Graphics will be printed to the extent of the resolution possible on your printer. (On a daisy-wheel printer, Framework III selects convenient characters to build graphs with. For example, the H character may be used to build bar graphs.)

Most printers use special sets of control codes to switch into particular printing modes (condensed print, for example). When you give Framework III the information that it needs about your printer, the program lets you select most of these printing modes from a menu. In addition, there is a function that will allow you to send any printing codes that do not appear on the menu, so that you can make full use of your printer. We will discuss printing in Chapter 4.

In summary, Framework III's flexibility extends not only to your work on the desktop, but also to the hardware devices you have attached to your computer.

So far, we have concentrated on the appearance and the characteristics of Framework III rather than on the actual kinds of work you can accomplish with the program. Let's now explore in a more concrete way the meaning of the major Framework III components: outlining, spreadsheet programming, graphing, word processing, database management, and telecommunications.

FRAMEWORK III COMPONENTS

In this section, we'll see what the different types of frames look like, and we'll explore some of the specific features that Framework III offers in each of its functional categories.

OUTLINING

As we have already discussed, outlining can serve two quite different purposes in your work with frames:

- You can create a complete outline of a project before you actually begin doing any of the work.

- You can create a series of frames, work on their contents, and then establish a logical relationship among the frames by placing them all in an outline.

To accommodate these two different approaches to outlining, Framework III's menu gives you two ways to establish an Outline frame.

The first way is to choose the Outline option in the Create submenu. In response, Framework III creates a frame that looks like the one in Figure 1.9. This frame contains a kind of template for an outline. The template has room for three major outline headings, numbered 1 to 3. Each heading in turn has three subheadings, numbered 1.1, 1.2, 1.3, and so on.

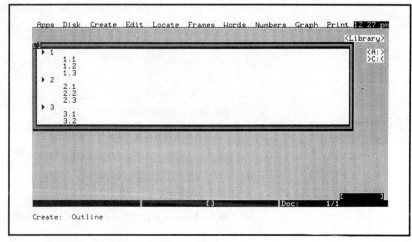

Figure 1.9: An Outline frame

> 1
>> 1.1
>> 1.2
>> 1.3

These are all Empty frames. An Empty frame is available to you for word processing. This means that each of these three subheadings contains three Word frames that you can work with.

How can you use this Outline template? Let's say you are planning to write a long memorandum to your salespeople describing a new product that your company is getting ready to put onto the market. You want first to focus on the product itself, then describe the marketing approach for the product, and finally discuss your competition.

You can use Framework III's Outline template to plan your memo. Your first step will be to enter headings and subheadings into the outline itself. Let's look at a possible outline for the Product Memo.

> 1 The Product
>> 1.1 general description
>> 1.2 technical aspects
>> 1.3 pricing
> 2 The Market
>> 2.1 who will buy
>> 2.2 distribution
>> 2.3 advertising

3   The Competition
   3.1   other products
   3.2   other marketing strategies
   3.3   where we stand

Once you have created your outline, you can use each of the Empty frames for word processing. In other words, you will write your memo into the outline itself.

Of course, you have to open up the Empty frames before you can work in them. To open frames that reside in an outline, Framework III gives you two function keys, which work in quite different ways:

- The Zoom key (F9) opens an individual frame (or a group of frames) in the outline and devotes the entire screen to its contents. You will use the Zoom key whenever you want to focus your attention on one or more frames. Figure 1.10 shows the effect of Zoom on the first subheading of the Product Memo outline. Notice that the name of the subheading appears in the status panel, below the desktop. Pressing the Zoom key a second time will return you to the original format of the outline.

- The View key (F10) shifts your outline between *Outline view* and *Frames view*. Figure 1.11 shows part of the Product Memo

Figure 1.10: The effect of the Zoom key

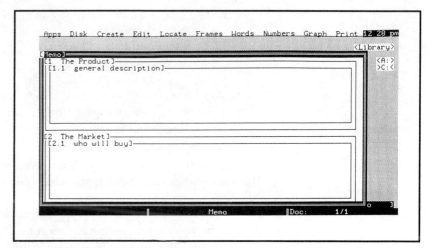

Figure 1.11: Frames view of an outline

outline in Frames view. You can see that each of the sub-headings consists of an Empty frame. Pressing the View key again will return you to the original Outline view.

You have a great deal of flexibility in working with Outline frames. Outlines would not be very useful if you were always required to work within three sets of three subheadings. Framework III allows you to change the size, organization, and contents of your outline in any way that meets your requirements:

- You can add new major headings and give them new sub-headings of their own.

- You can create new logical levels, producing an outline that contains frames that are many levels deep.

- You can delete headings or subheadings.

- You can move headings or subheadings to a new location in the outline. Framework III will automatically renumber the outline to reflect the new sequence of headings.

- You can number your outline sections in either traditional or technical style.

- Finally, you can insert Spreadsheet, Database, and Graph frames into the outline, so that your outline will not be restricted to Word (or Empty) frames only.

The second way you can create an outline is to begin with an Empty frame. Notice the second option in the Create submenu in Figure 1.8:

Empty / Word Frame

Choose this option, and Framework III will create an Empty frame for you, as shown in Figure 1.12. You can always use an Empty frame for word processing. You can also use an Empty frame to contain other frames in an outline form. If you have already created some other work frames that you want to place in an outline, you can simply move them into an Empty frame.

At the beginning of this chapter, we discussed an outlining example involving tax forms. To organize these forms, you would first create an Empty frame. Then you would move the various tax spreadsheets into the frame to create your outline. Framework III's Move key, F7, is your tool for moving frames from the desktop into an outline.

In summary, outlining in Framework III is a way for you to plan ahead, to organize your thoughts before you begin working. Outlining is also a way to bring together pieces of work that you have

Figure 1.12: An Empty frame

already completed. In Chapter 2, you'll learn exactly how all this can be done.

SPREADSHEET PROGRAMMING

Tables of numbers are an inescapable part of our lives. Tax tables, mortgage tables, test scores, sales figures, population statistics, discount rates, insurance payments—these are the kinds of numeric data that pass daily across our desks and demand attention.

Such tables typically have a row of headings at the top, to explain the significance of the columns, and a column of labels at the left, to describe the rows. Figure 1.13 shows a small example: sales statistics for three products—X, Y, and Z—over a six-month period. Notice that the last column on the right shows the total sales for each month, and the last row (at the bottom of the spreadsheet) shows the total sales for each product.

Producing tables like this one by hand is no fun, as anyone who has worn out the erasers on a collection of stubby pencils can attest. Just as you finish totaling up all the columns and rows, and you finally come up with a grand total at the lower right corner of your spreadsheet, you look at your original data and discover an incorrectly entered figure. Typically, the way these things go, the error will be

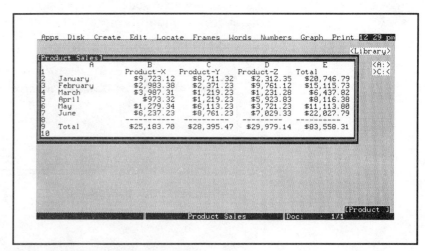

Figure 1.13: A spreadsheet example

located right in the middle of the table, such as the figure for Product Y sales in the month of March. Correcting your mistake means redoing a lot of arithmetic—retotaling rows and columns, and finding a new grand total.

Electronic spreadsheets like Framework III's were made for situations like this one. Spreadsheet programming simply means setting up a table of numbers and letting the computer do all the associated arithmetic for you. In Framework III, the painful task described above would be reduced to the following simple steps:

1. Create a Spreadsheet frame big enough to hold your table.

2. Enter the column and row headings into the first row and first column.

3. Enter all the numbers.

4. Write *formulas* for the row and column totals, and *copy* those formulas across and down the spreadsheet.

5. To correct an error—for example, the figure for Product Y in March—simply type a new number in the correct location. Framework III will automatically recalculate all your totals for you.

Look for a moment at the way a Framework III spreadsheet is organized. The columns are all identified by letters, and the rows by numbers. At each intersection of a row and column, you can enter (by typing at the keyboard) a number or a label. These intersections are called *cells,* and you can refer to each cell in a spreadsheet by its *address.* An address is made up of a column letter and a row number. For example, the sales figure for Product Y in March is at cell address C4, as you can see in Figure 1.13.

Because each cell has a name, you can write arithmetic formulas that refer to cells, or rather to the *contents* of cells. Adding the contents of three cells and putting the total into a fourth cell is as simple as entering a formula like this one:

+B2 + C2 + D2

This is the formula that yields the total sales for January. Once you've written a formula like this, you can copy it to apply it to other rows in your spreadsheet.

In Chapter 3, you will learn how to do all this and much more. For now, simply remember that an electronic spreadsheet is a table of numbers that is designed to respond to change. You might hear people talking about ''what-if's'' when they discuss the power of a spreadsheet. What if you decide to change the estimated tax rate? What if you revise your bonus plan? What if the price of Product X increases again? Or what if you simply make a mistake in data entry? A Spreadsheet frame can respond instantly to numeric changes like these—it gives you newly calculated results before you can get up to sharpen your pencil.

GRAPHING

We have long been taught that a picture is worth a thousand words. In the business environment, one picture is worth a thousand numbers. Busy people would often rather spot trends off a graph than pore over the numeric data that lies behind the graph.

Framework III's graph-drawing ability is related directly to its components that deal with numbers: spreadsheets and databases. Anytime you create a table of numbers, you can also make a graph from those numbers. Amazingly, creating a graph in Framework III seldom requires more than a half-dozen keystrokes from you.

Figures 1.14, 1.15, and 1.16 show three different graphs that Framework III created from the Product Sales spreadsheet we've been looking at. Examine these graphs, and notice the details that Framework III automatically works out in each case:

- The scale of the graphs

- The labels on the horizontal axes

- The numbers on the vertical axes

- The keys that explain the different elements of the graphs

- The choice of visual textures to distinguish among the elements represented on the graphs

Framework III offers seven different graph types in all: bar, stacked bar, pie, line, marked points, high-low-close (for analyzing stock quotations), and x-y. We'll look at examples of these graphs and explore the

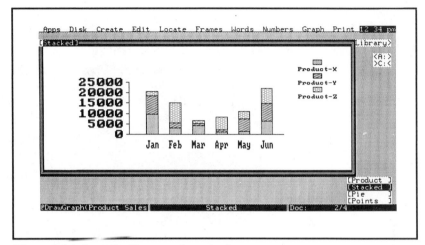

Figure 1.14: A stacked bar graph example

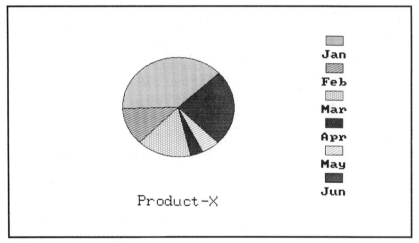

Figure 1.15: A pie chart example

use of Framework III's Graph submenu in Chapter 3. One important point to keep in mind is this: when you create a graph from a Spreadsheet frame, the graph, like the spreadsheet itself, can respond to changes in your numeric data. Change a number on the spreadsheet, and Framework III can quickly redraw the graph to reflect your new data.

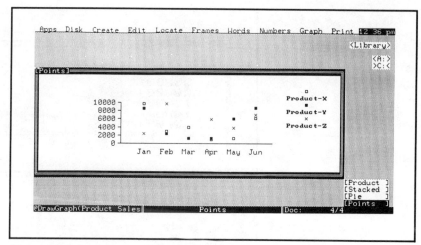

Figure 1.16: A marked points graph

WORD PROCESSING

People who love to write and people who hate to write often have one characteristic in common: a remarkable fondness for editing, revising, and rewriting. Whatever the genre—from business documents to personal correspondence to the Great American Novel— writers love to experiment with variations in their own writing: trying out new words, inserting sentences, changing the order of paragraphs, deleting the unnecessary adjective, until every word sounds and looks just right.

Clearly, this kind of attention to literate and literary detail is good. But no one enjoys typing someone else's words—or even one's own words—several times in a row. What secretary has not at some point pondered the life-threatening effects of a typewriter speeding through the air, upon hearing the familiar request, ''Could you just make these few corrections, and switch those two paragraphs around—and have it ready before lunch?''

Small wonder that computerized word processing has produced a stir in the business world. Now all the variations of text editing, including inserting, deleting, changing, correcting, and, yes, switching things around, can be done electronically, within your computer's memory, before a single word ever appears on paper. You can even check spelling, look up words in the online thesaurus, and incorporate footnotes into your documents.

In Framework III Word frames, you can create documents and accomplish all kinds of editing tasks with a minimum of effort. Seldom has word processing been so easy to learn. Chapter 4 will get you started; we'll also examine special effects such as boldface, underlining, italics, right justification, headers, footers, and so on. The special effects—underlining, boldface, and italic type—will show up not only in your printed documents, but right on the screen. (If you install Framework III in one of the full-color graphics modes, special effects will appear in different colors.) Some of these effects are illustrated in the Word frame shown in Figure 1.17; note that italic type appears as underlined text in graphics mode.

DATABASE MANAGEMENT

A database is simply a collection of related information. A personal or business address book is a database. So are the records you keep for periodic activities such as banking and paying bills. The card catalog at your local library is a rather large database, arranged in several different ways for the convenience of locating books. The telephone book is yet another database that we all use daily.

The main practical differences between a paper database and an electronic database are ease of handling and ease of use. When you

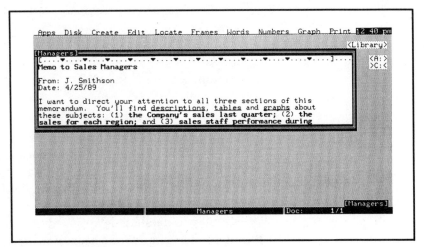

Figure 1.17: A sample Word frame

create a database in Framework III, you can expect all of the following activities to be easy to perform:

- Sorting (arranging the information in some order)
- Searching (locating just the information you want)
- Adding new records
- Deleting old records
- Performing arithmetic calculations on the database
- Creating printed reports from the database

Database terminology uses the words *record* and *field* to describe categories of information. A record is one complete unit of information in a database. Consider a list of names, addresses, and phone numbers. A single record in such a list consists of all the information about one person. For example, a record might include the following information:

First name

Last name

Address

City

State

Zip code

Home phone

Work phone

We can expect that each record in the database will contain all of these items of information about someone. These items are called fields. In the case of this address book, a record consists of eight fields of information. Every record in a single database will contain the same number and type of fields.

Typically, a database is arranged in columns and rows, in a way that is similar to a spreadsheet. But the structure of a database is more consistent than a spreadsheet needs to be. Each row of a database is guaranteed to contain one record. Each of the fields of the database resides in a separate column. The column headings are therefore called *field names* in a database.

Figure 1.18 shows a Database frame. It contains the sales records of a group of ten salespeople. These are the field names of this database:

Last (name)

First (name)

Region

Sales

Bonus

This database illustrates several of the most important features Framework III offers for managing data:

- The data can be *sorted* in any of the fields. We could select any order we wished—for example, placing the people in order by region or last name, or in ascending or descending order of total sales.

- The bonus amount for each salesperson was calculated by Framework III from a formula that was entered in the bonus

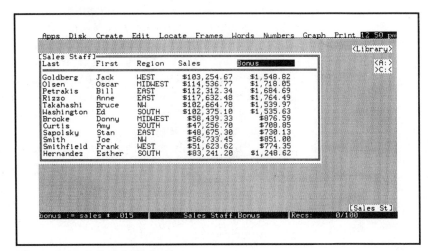

Figure 1.18: A Database frame

column. (Each person receives a bonus of 1.5 percent of total sales.) This bonus amount can be changed simply by changing the formula.

- We can *filter* this database, instructing Framework III to select and display only certain records that match *criteria* that we establish. In such a small database, this would just be a learning exercise, but you can imagine the importance of filtering if your database had hundreds of records. You might want to look at all the salespeople who work in the Midwestern region, or all the people who had total sales greater than $50,000.

Chapter 5 will show you how to create and manage a database in Framework III.

TELECOMMUNICATIONS

The Framework III package includes one final part: a telecommunications component that will help you hook up your own computer, via telephone lines, with other computers. To use it, you must install a device called a *modem* in your computer. A modem *mo*dulates outgoing computer data into audio signals that can be sent over telephone lines, and it *dem*odulates incoming audio signals into data that your computer system can work with.

For both business and recreational uses, the field of telecommunications continues to increase in importance. Some working people use modems to hook up with office computers from their home computers. Many banks offer home computer banking services, which allow you to use your PC to pay bills and transfer money from one account to another.

But probably the most widespread use of personal computer telecommunications involves *information services,* such as The Source, CompuServe, and Dow Jones News/Retrieval. These are all special-interest information sources, updated daily, that you can access only with your computer. They offer business news, current events, computer recreation, and so on.

To use any of these services—or to use any of the free bulletin boards, or simply to send data directly to another computer—you need software to handle the technical details involved in making the connection. Framework III's telecommunications component is designed for the purpose. With the telecommunications component, you can send a file that you have already prepared directly from your disk (which is called *uploading*). You can also *download* files, which means receiving them via your modem and storing them immediately on disk. You'll learn about the telecommunications component in Chapter 6.

As you begin creating frames for your own work, you'll want to learn about saving frames on disk and printing them on paper. These are the subjects of the next two sections.

SAVING FRAMES

The file cabinets for your disk drives are always available to you on the desktop. They are there for two purposes: to allow you to examine, at any time, the contents of your disks; and to provide you with a convenient means of reading files from the disks and saving files to the disks.

We have seen that Framework III's Shuttle key (marked Scroll Lock on your keyboard) moves the highlight from your work frames to the disk cabinets. Here is the complete sequence of keystrokes you will use to read a file from your data disk:

Shuttle (Scroll Lock)	(to move the highlight to the disk frames)
Arrow keys	(to select the correct disk)
Return	(to open the frame)
In (+)	(to move the highlight into the frame)
↑ or ↓	(to select a file)
Return	(to move the file to the desktop)

The extension name .FW3 identifies Framework III files on your disk; these files become frames when you move them onto the desktop. The file name you see on the disk directory may be only part of the frame's complete label. This is because DOS file names are limited to eight characters, plus an extension name that can be up to three characters long. Framework III frame labels can be practically any length (up to 32,000 characters).

When Framework III saves a frame on disk, it takes the first eight characters of the frame's label as the file name. For this reason, you have to write labels carefully: the first eight characters of each frame label must be distinct from other frames that you intend to save on a given disk.

DOS imposes certain restrictions on file names. Some characters, such as commas, periods, and the space character, are not allowed. Framework III labels, however, can contain any character except the square brackets, [and]. Frame labels that contain illegal DOS file name characters will be transformed automatically when you save a frame on disk. Illegal DOS characters will be changed to an underscore character (_). So, for example, a frame called Sales Memo will be saved on disk under the file name

SALES_ME.FW3

We have seen how to get a file by shuttling into the disk drive cabinet. A second way you can move a file to the desktop from a disk is via the Disk submenu's Get File by Name option:

Ctrl-D   (to select the Disk submenu)

G   (to invoke the Get option)

Framework III will ask you for the name of the file you wish to bring to the desktop. You must specify the entire file name, although you need not include the extension if the file is a Framework III file. (You'll learn in Chapter 8 how to bring other types of files to the desktop.) You can also indicate a disk drive—for example:

A:TAXES.FW3

If you do not specify a disk drive, Framework III always assumes that you want to read from or write to the *default* drive. The default drive is B in a system that has two floppy disk drives, or C in a system that has a hard disk. (You can change the default disk drive by selecting another disk drive cabinet and pressing Ctrl-Return. This new cabinet will be your default drive until you exit from Framework III or change the default again.)

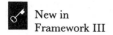
New in
Framework III

You can also work with DOS files and directories directly from
Framework III. You can:

- Rename any file by pressing the spacebar when the file is
  highlighed, then entering the new name.
- Open any directory by selecting it and pressing Return.
- Move to up the directory tree by pressing Out (–) from the
  drive frame's border.
- Create a new subdirectory by entering the drive frame and
  selecting Empty from the Create menu. You will have an
  opportunity to name the new directory.
- Delete entire directories and their contents by selecting the
  directory and pressing Delete.
- Copy and move files between directories and drives using
  Move (F7) and Copy (F8). (To copy files into an empty subdirectory, use Move or Copy normally, but don't attempt to
  enter the directory. Instead, highlight it and press Ctrl-In
  [+]. This is true only if the target directory is empty.)

Framework III gives you several ways to save a file on disk. One
important procedure is called Save and Continue. You use this procedure whenever you want to save a frame that you are in the process
of completing. Save and Continue saves a copy of the frame in its
current condition, and then it leaves the frame on the desktop so you
can continue working with it.

You can perform a Save and Continue operation in one of two
ways. First, if there is more than one frame on the desktop, you have
to make sure that you have selected the frame you want to save. The
highlight can be either on the border of the frame or inside in the contents of the frame. Then you can select the Disk submenu's Save and
Continue option:

Ctrl-D   (to select the Disk submenu)

S   (to invoke the Save and Continue option)

If the frame you are saving is an outline, all of the frames contained in
the outline will be saved in the one file you are writing to disk.

An even more convenient way to perform a Save and Continue operation is with the following keystrokes:

Ctrl-Return   (Save and Continue)

Pressing these two keys will automatically save to disk any frame that you are currently working on.

The Save and Continue operation is a good way for you to secure the safety of your current work. People who use personal computers have to learn, sometimes through painful experience, the importance of regularly creating *backups* of computer-generated documents and information. You never know when some minor mishap will result in a loss of data—someone accidentally unplugging your computer, a power failure in your neighborhood, or an inadvertent sequence of keystrokes. If you have recently saved your work, you will be confident that you can lose only what you have done since the last save operation.

Yet another way to save a frame is to use the Disk submenu's Put Away option:

Ctrl-D   (to select the Disk submenu)

P   (to invoke the Put Away option) .

This operation saves the currently selected frame on disk and then deletes the frame from the desktop.

By the way, if you get a file from disk, change the frame in some way on the desktop, and then save the frame back to disk, Framework III will remember the directory the frame originally came from, and send it back to the same place.

You can always delete a frame from the desktop *without* first saving it to disk if you really want to. Simply select the frame and press the Delete key (labeled Del on your keyboard).

If you have the Safety feature set to on, Framework III will prompt you before deleting a frame.

New in Framework III

Happily, Framework III can bring back a deletion if you have second thoughts. The Edit submenu has an Undo option that will undo the last operation you performed. To invoke this handy operation, press these keys:

Ctrl-E   (to select the Edit submenu)

U   (to invoke the Undo option)

If you delete a file from a disk cabinet, however, you cannot bring the file back. For this reason, Framework III asks you to confirm that you truly want to delete a file from your disk. To delete a file, select the correct file name in the disk cabinet and press the Delete key.

You can get a fuller view of a disk directory—complete with dates and times—by pressing the View key (F10) while the disk's cabinet is selected.

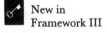
New in
Framework III

Framework III remembers which view of a cabinet you last used, even after you've exited from the program.

PRINTING FRAMES

We'll be discussing Framework III's printing options several times, in the context of each different type of frame. There will be variations to learn for printing in each Framework III component. However, the essential Print submenu is easy to use. You select the frame or frames you want to print, make sure your printer is turned on, and press

Ctrl-P   (to select the Print submenu)

B   (to begin printing)

When you print an Outline frame, you have to decide between printing just the outline or the contents of each frame in the outline. The View key (F10) controls this option: Outline view prints only the outline itself; Frames view prints the contents. (Look back at Figures 1.9 and 1.11 to review the difference between Outline view and Frames view.)

EXAMPLES

In each chapter of this book, after looking at selected elements of Framework III in detail, we'll complete our study with realistic examples. We'll be looking in on The Sophisticated Palate, Inc., a fictitious company that uses Framework III for a variety of computer applications, and we'll nose around a bit in the company's books and documents, to see how Framework III's resources might be used in a business situation.

The Sophisticated Palate is, as you might expect, a fancy food company. It produces a variety of gourmet pastries, international breads, salads, pâtés, fresh pastas, and other delicatessen and international food items, which it distributes to retail outlets and uses in its catering service. In addition, it distributes fancy imported foods such as cheeses, cookies and crackers, and jams and jellies.

The company was started as a partnership eight years ago by Eileen Wilcox and George Farley strictly as a catering service. However, demand for their products was so great that they have since incorporated and branched out into the wholesale arena. Although Eileen and George started out by preparing all the foods themselves, they now have a staff of nine cooks, five order clerks, four drivers, eighteen part-time waiters and waitresses (for the catering service), a bookkeeper, and an administrative assistant. They bought a PC with a hard disk drive two years ago, and started out using the original version of Framework for their clerical and record-keeping chores. They have since expanded the machine's memory to 640K and upgraded to Framework III, which they use almost exclusively for all their computer work. Before the PC, these tasks used to take a great deal of pleasure out of running the company.

Since this chapter's overview has taken us casually through the whole range of Framework III's capabilities, we'll try to find a few documents from The Sophisticated Palate's business office that illustrate what we've studied. We'll look at a database, a rather imaginative spreadsheet, and an outline-based integrated document.

AN EMPLOYEE DATABASE

George handles the company's personnel matters. Since the work is low-keyed and pleasant, the business is successful, and there is a great deal of camaraderie among the workers, there has been little employee turnover: most of the current group of workers have been with the company over three years.

George meets with each employee individually for an informal evaluation every six months or so. He listens to complaints, makes suggestions, handles any scheduling problems that Ariana Katz, the administrative assistant, cannot resolve, and usually offers small salary increases during these meetings.

Figure 1.19 shows a printout of a database that George has developed in Framework III to keep track of his employees' work histories and evaluation dates. He has discovered that Framework III databases can work effectively with dates. Framework has functions that allow you to enter dates into a table and then perform certain kinds of date arithmetic operations, such as finding the number of days between two dates. George's database contains the following fields of information about each employee:

       Last name

       First name

Last	First	Hired	Job	M/w.Co	LastEval	Elapsed	StSal	CurSal
Munter	Cookie	Feb 13, 1988	Cook	13	Aug 20, 1988	7	$7.50	$7.85
Dexter	Gordon	Sep 18, 1987	Clerk	18	Oct 2, 1988	6	$7.00	$7.00
Greene	Jane	Aug 31, 1986	Waitr/s	31	Oct 2, 1988	6	$2.70	$3.75
Estevez	Ray	Oct 19, 1987	Waitr/s	42	Oct 2, 1988	6	$2.20	$3.75
Lopez	Rick	Oct 3, 1987	Waitr/s	18	Oct 3, 1988	6	$3.75	$3.75
Poulos	Costas	Sep 11, 1986	Cook	31	Oct 13, 1988	5	$5.90	$7.85
Mayer	Oscar	Sep 3, 1986	Waitr/s	31	Oct 13, 1988	5	$2.70	$3.75
Costanza	Dom	Mar 15, 1986	Waitr/s	37	Oct 13, 1988	5	$2.70	$3.75
Hardy	Felicia	Apr 1, 1988	Waitr/s	12	Oct 28, 1988	5	$3.75	$3.75
Castilo	Dolores	Oct 26, 1987	Cook	17	Oct 28, 1988	5	$7.25	$7.85
Shapiro	Ernie	Mar 29, 1987	Driver	24	Nov 8, 1988	4	$6.00	$6.75
Birnbaum	Sue	Nov 6, 1986	Waitr/s	29	Nov 8, 1988	4	$2.70	$3.75
Leung	Sharon	May 12, 1985	Clerk	47	Nov 8, 1988	4	$5.50	$7.00
Whitfield	Julian	Nov 8, 1983	Clerk	65	Nov 8, 1988	4	$4.50	$7.25
Kyle	Selina	Oct 31, 1985	Waitr/s	41	Nov 17, 1988	4	$2.20	$3.75
Gillespie	Joan	Nov 17, 1988	Cook	4	Nov 23, 1988	4	$7.85	$7.85
Osawa	Frank	Nov 14, 1986	Bookkpr	29	Nov 23, 1988	4	$10.75	$12.10
Satdeva	Krishna	Nov 8, 1986	Cook	29	Nov 23, 1988	4	$5.90	$7.85
Jaron	Howard	Nov 20, 1981	Cook	89	Nov 23, 1988	4	$5.50	$8.25
Tate	Howard	Jun 4, 1984	Driver	58	Nov 17, 1988	4	$5.00	$7.00
Freund	Bobbie	May 22, 1987	Driver	22	Dec 1, 1988	4	$6.00	$6.25
Khoury	Jamil	May 15, 1987	Waitr/s	23	Dec 1, 1988	4	$2.80	$3.75
Goldstein	Bert	Dec 4, 1986	Waitr/s	28	Dec 1, 1988	4	$2.80	$3.75
Yee	Tony	Dec 2, 1986	Waitr/s	28	Dec 1, 1988	4	$2.80	$3.75
Jones	Kate	Dec 1, 1986	Clerk	28	Dec 1, 1988	4	$6.25	$7.50
Ortega	Maya	Jun 27, 1988	Waitr/s	9	Jan 8, 1989	3	$3.75	$3.75
Parker	Charlene	Jul 8, 1988	Waitr/s	9	Jan 8, 1989	2	$3.75	$3.75
Stavros	Sandra	Jan 23, 1989	Waitr/s	2	Jan 23, 1989	2	$3.75	$3.75
Powell	Earl	Jun 22, 1985	Waitr/s	46	Jan 23, 1989	2	$2.20	$3.75
Carroll	Nancy	Jun 20, 1985	Cook	46	Jan 23, 1989	2	$5.80	$8.25
Jordan	Alex	Jul 13, 1986	Driver	33	Feb 14, 1989	1	$5.50	$6.75
Katz	Ariana	Feb 2, 1986	Adm.Ast	38	Feb 14, 1989	0	$11.25	$13.50
Rollins	Ted	Feb 14, 1989	Waitr/s	1	Feb 14, 1989	0	$3.75	$3.75
Shimozu	Lana	Aug 15, 1987	Cook	19	Feb 23, 1989	0	$7.50	$7.85
Bromberg	Dan	Jul 12, 1987	Clerk	21	Feb 23, 1989	0	$7.00	$7.00
Nasir	Abdul	Jul 7, 1987	Waitr/s	21	Feb 23, 1989	0	$3.75	$3.75
Charles	Otis	Feb 25, 1986	Waitr/s	37	Mar 4, 1989	0	$2.70	$3.75
Silvestri	Maria	Feb 6, 1986	Cook	38	Mar 4, 1989	0	$5.90	$7.85

Figure 1.19: The Sophisticated Palate—An employee database

Date hired

Position

Months with the company

Last evaluation date

Months elapsed since last evaluation

Starting hourly wage

Current hourly wage

The field names of the database are of course abbreviated, so that all the information can appear on the screen at once. Given the date an employee was hired, a Framework III formula that George has written calculates the number of months that the employee has worked for The Sophisticated Palate. A similar formula calculates the number of months since the last evaluation. George keeps the database sorted by this months-elapsed figure, in descending order. He can glance at the list and immediately find the employees who are coming due for an evaluation, their salary history, and their length of employment with the company.

A COSTING SPREADSHEET

Eileen has been developing a line of special-order party trays, which are available both as retail items and through the catering service. She has used a Spreadsheet frame to help her keep track of costs and pricing. She generally offers a combination of five delicatessen items in each tray. The trays are available in sizes for 10, 20, 50, or 80 people. To calculate the company's costs for these trays, she must include the cost of supplies and labor for each item on the tray.

She has come up with spreadsheet formulas for determining costs and retail prices for three different party trays. A printout of the spreadsheet she used for costing one of the trays is shown in Figure 1.20. The cost of supplies is directly proportional to the number of people the tray will serve. Labor costs also increase for the larger trays, but not as quickly. After determining the cost of a tray, she calculates a 40 percent markup to obtain the retail price.

```
*****  BUFFET TRAY  *****
# People        10              20              50              80
          Supplies Labor  Supplies Labor  Supplies Labor  Supplies Labor
Beaucaire   $8.75   $6.25   $17.50  $12.50   $21.88  $31.25   $70.00  $50.00
Mousse     $10.80   $4.10   $21.60   $5.13   $27.00   $6.87   $86.40   $8.20
Shrimp/Av  $12.00   $6.00   $24.00   $6.20   $30.00   $6.50   $96.00   $6.80
Turkey      $9.20   $8.00   $18.40   $8.00   $23.00   $8.00   $73.60   $8.00
Primavera   $7.00   $3.20   $14.00   $3.70   $17.50   $4.45   $56.00   $7.70

Total      $47.75  $27.55   $95.50  $35.53  $119.38  $57.07  $382.00  $80.70
Supp+Labor         $75.30          $131.03          $176.44          $462.70
Markup (40%)      $105.42          $183.44          $247.02          $647.78
Rounded Price     $105.00          $183.00          $247.00          $648.00
```

Figure 1.20: The Sophisticated Palate—A costing spreadsheet

A PROMOTIONAL FLIER

The costing spreadsheets are, of course, for her own use only. But Eileen has found that an easy way to promote the party tray line is to announce, early in the month, what will be available for that month. Moreover, taking orders early in the week makes it easier for her to be prepared for the weekend. For this reason, she has developed a one-page promotional flier describing the month's trays. She word processes the flier, which she then duplicates for distribution to customers.

Figure 1.21 shows the printed flier. Eileen writes a short description of each tray, followed by a spreadsheet table of prices. To produce the flier, she combines these diverse elements—Word frames and a Spreadsheet frame—in an Outline frame, which she then prints.

These are three of the smallest tasks that Eileen and George perform with Framework III. We'll see the solutions they find for more significant business record-keeping problems in subsequent chapters.

EXPLORING FURTHER

Before ending this chapter, let's examine some of the advanced features available to you in Framework III. We'll look at a way for you to access DOS programs without quitting the Framework III program, and we'll discuss the Library.

```
Party Trays for This Weekend

Cocktail Tray I

Two cocktail sandwiches are featured on this tray: Nova Scotia
smoked salmon on a dill rye and the English Classic, cucumber
sandwiches.  In addition, the tray features California figs
wrapped in prosciutto, Belgian endive leaves onto which a Greek-
style red caviar spread is piped in attractive rosettes, and
miniature artichoke-heart quiches.

Prices

# of People        10          20          50          80
Price              $35         $65         $150        $220


Cocktail Tray II

Marinating in a special mixture of lemon grass, cilantro, and
other exotic spices and using a mesquite grill results in an
exotic barbecued chicken that's ours alone.  Jumbo shrimp are
served with a spicy Louisiana Creole dip.  The tray also includes
new potatoes filled with sour cream and caviar; a selection of
fresh raw vegetables and dips; and cream-cheese, black-olive, and
pimento canapés.

Prices

# of People        10          20          50          80
Price              $50         $85         $185        $240

Buffet Tray

Start with the buffet tray, add one of our fresh-baked desserts,
and you have a complete dinner for your guests. Salade Beaucaire,
served on the luxury liner The France, combines Belgian endive,
celery root, ham, apples, and potatoes in a seasoned mayonnaise
dressing made with crème fraîche. The Vitello Tomato Mousse is
the classic Italian dish transformed into a light mousse of veal
subtly flavored with lemon, tuna, and capers. Shrimp and Avocado
Spread is blended from the freshest ingredients, in a cream
cheese base, and lightly seasoned with a blend of old-world
spices, topped with a fine layer of chopped egg and Hungarian
paprika. A boned turkey, filled with a mixture of veal and pork,
layered with truffles and pistachios, is rolled into a sausage
shape for our Galantine of Turkey. It is sliced and served cold
with a sherry-scented aspic. Spring's first harvest is the basis
of Salad Primavera. Asparagus, red peppers, new peas, and sweet
corn are tossed with pasta in a light citrus dressing.

Prices

# of People        10          20          50          80
Price              $105        $183        $247        $648
```

Figure 1.21: The Sophisticated Palate—A promotional flier

A DOS FRAME

From time to time, it is convenient to be able to leave an applications program temporarily to perform an operation in the disk operating system. When you finish in DOS, you would like to return to your uninterrupted work in the applications program. Framework III allows you to do this by creating a frame that is temporarily devoted to DOS. These are the keys you press to use this feature:

Ctrl-D   (to select the Disk submenu)

D   (to invoke the DOS Access option)

To access DOS, Framework III must go by way of a frame. If your currently selected frame is empty, it will use that frame. If the current frame is a Word frame, it will open the frame, and display the following message:

Delete all contents (y/n)?

If you press N, or if your current selection on the desktop is not a Word frame or an Empty frame, Framework III will create a new frame for DOS access, and label it

Dos Access Frame

If a Word frame is selected, and you respond to the prompt by pressing Y, the contents will be deleted, and that frame will be used for DOS access, although it will retain its label. Figure 1.22 shows a typical DOS Access frame.

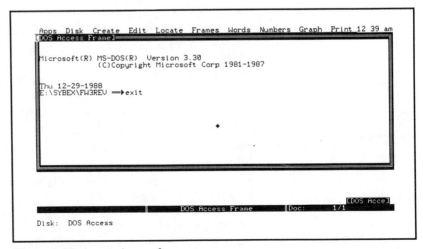

Figure 1.22: A DOS Access frame

Ordinarily when you exit from a DOS Access frame, it retains whatever characters appeared on the screen while you were using DOS. However, if you have the ANSI.SYS device driver installed, or use certain "background" programs such as SuperKey, DOS access works somewhat differently. In a short time, the desktop will disappear, and you will have a blank screen with a DOS prompt. If your Framework III subdirectory is called FRAMEWK, the screen will display

    C:\FRAMEWK>

While you are in the DOS frame, you can perform any of the DOS internal or external commands, or any program that runs on DOS. To return to Framework III from DOS or any other program, you simply enter the DOS command

    EXIT

This command will put you back in the Framework III desktop, with any frames that you were working on still intact.

Using the DOS Access frame can be convenient in a variety of situations; for example:

- You can use it to perform some advanced disk operation that is not available while you are in Framework III.

- You can run a BASIC program that you have written yourself.

- You can temporarily work in some other applications package, without disturbing your desktop work in Framework III.

After any of these activities, you can return to Framework III and continue whatever you were doing before you entered the DOS frame. You'll learn more about DOS Access frames in Chapter 8.

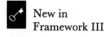 New in Framework III

In Framework III, if you have set the DOS roll-out feature to on (see Appendix A for more information), DOS access will behave differently. In particular, no characters will be captured to the DOS frame. On the other hand, you will have more memory to work with in DOS.

THE LIBRARY

The Library is a unique part of the desktop. It is always loaded automatically. Therefore, it is a good place to store any pieces of information that you need frequently.

The Library is a file cabinet, not a frame (although it behaves like a frame in many ways). Therefore, if the highlight is on a frame, you must press the Shuttle key (Scroll Lock) to look at it. To view the contents of the Library, press the following keys:

Shuttle (Scroll Lock)	(to move to the file cabinets)
↑ or ↓	(to select the Library cabinet)
Recalc (F5)	(to get a full-screen view of the Library cabinet's contents)

The Library is in outline form, containing these major headings:

Macros

Abbreviations

Printing templates

User-defined functions

Phone book

One important feature of Framework III is that when it searches for a frame, it always looks in the Library, as well as on the desktop. Moreover, it will search the entire Library, so it will find anything in the Library no matter how deeply it is nested within a subheading of an outline. This feature makes the Library a powerful tool for customizing the way Framework III behaves. You can add any number of special frames that you use frequently, and Framework III will always find them.

FEATURES OF THE LIBRARY

Let's take a brief look at the types of items that are supplied with the Library. These are only some of the sorts of things that you might want to include in your own library.

PREDEFINED MACROS AND ABBREVIATIONS The Library includes ten predefined macros and several abbreviations. A *macro* is a series of keystrokes (which can include both text and Framework III commands) that can be played back when you press an Alt-key combination. An *abbreviation* is a series of keystrokes that, when properly treated, will be replaced by a longer series of keystrokes. Abbreviations are more appropriate than macros when you want to insert a large body of text. Both macros and abbreviations are created by way of the Create submenu. The macros are all combinations of the Alt key and a function key. Although they are intended as samples for you to study, you will find most of them quite useful. The abbreviations are self-explanatory. We'll learn how to create macros and abbreviations in Chapter 7, and we'll use some of the predefined macros in Chapter 6.

PRINTING TEMPLATES Whenever you print a document, you are given the option of specifying a printing template to use. Printing templates contain all the printer settings for a specific type of document—the ones in the library are just samples for you to look at. We'll explore printing templates in Chapter 4.

USER-DEFINED FUNCTIONS You can use the FRED language to create new functions to perform various tasks for you automatically. If you store them in the library, you can call them by name just as if they were a native part of the FRED language. We'll create a user-defined function in Chapter 7.

PHONE BOOK If you have a modem, Framework III can dial phone numbers for you. If you include your phone directory in the Library, a single keystroke-combination will display it for you. Then all you need to do is use the search function to find the name of the party you want to call, and use another keystroke-combination to dial the phone automatically. We'll explore these capabilities further in Chapter 6.

SUMMARY

Framework III is an integrated package that you can use for spreadsheet programming, word processing, database management, business graphing, and telecommunications. Outlining is a sixth essential component of the package that allows you to tie together your work in the other components. In addition, Framework III provides an easy way of sharing files with other application programs, and of running other application programs from within Framework III.

You create a separate frame for each component of your work in Framework III. Each frame has a border, a label, a contents area, and a background programming area.

Framework III encourages you to divide your work into small, easily handled modules. The elements of Framework III that help you work with the frames you create are the menu, the mouse, the function keys at the left side of the keyboard, and an important set of cursor-movement keys at the right side of the keyboard.

All your work in Framework III takes place on the desktop. In addition to work frames, in which you create business documents, the file cabinets for the disk drives and the Library are always available on the desktop. Files that you read from disk become frames on the desktop; likewise, a frame that you save from the desktop becomes a disk file, with the DOS extension name .FW3. The Library is a place to store any frames that you use frequently. Framework III's Print submenu supplies you with an easy way to send any frame to the printer.

With Chapter 2, we'll begin our detailed study of the Framework III components, starting with outlining.

Outlining

OVERVIEW

INTRODUCTION

IN CHAPTER 1, WE DISCUSSED THE TWO REASONS for outlining in Framework III. On the one hand, you can think of outlining as a productivity component in its own right. No matter what kind of project you are planning, you can use the outlining feature to organize your thoughts, to anticipate the order and logic of the work ahead of you, and to establish a successful approach for accomplishing your goals. All this can occur before you begin concentrating on the *content* of your work.

On the other hand, you can also think of outlining simply as a useful tool that improves your productivity with Word, Spreadsheet, Database, Graph, and Telecommunications frames. With outlining, you can group documents together in meaningful ways and establish links among the various elements of your work.

In this chapter, we'll practice using Framework III's outlining functions. The first step will be to learn the mechanical details: using the keyboard and the Framework III menus to create, modify, and expand outlines. You'll recall that you can begin outlining with either an Outline frame or an Empty frame. We'll examine both of these approaches.

We'll begin working with several of the Framework III function keys that manipulate frames and outlines: the Move (F7) and Copy (F8) keys, which move frames from one place to another inside an outline or from the desktop to the inside of an outline; the Zoom (F9) and View (F10) keys, which look at outlines and frames in different kinds of detail; and the important Extend Select key (F6), which makes it possible to work with several frames or elements at once.

We'll also master several of the menu options that work with frames and outlines; the Frames menu offers several interesting options for creative use of outlines. In addition, we'll be looking at the Create, Disk, and Print menus.

This is a lot of detail to learn all at once. Fortunately, the function keys and the menus work in similar ways in other Framework III contexts. Once you learn to use these function keys and menus for outlining, you will find that you can almost automatically apply the same tools

CH. 2

to all your other work, whether in spreadsheet programming, word processing, database management, or telecommunications.

Let's begin, then, with Outline frames.

CREATING AN OUTLINE

As you can see in Figure 2.1, Outline is the first of the options in the Create menu. Let's review the two approaches you can use to create an outline:

- Use the Instruct (Ins) key to open the menu, then use the ← or → key (if necessary) to choose the Create option.

- Or press Ctrl-C, for a shortcut into the Create submenu.

With the Create menu displayed on the screen, you have three ways of choosing the Outline option:

- Use the ↑ or ↓ key, if necessary, to position the highlight over the word Outline, and press Return.

- Press the Home key (to get to the top of the menu), and press Return.

- Or simply press the O key.

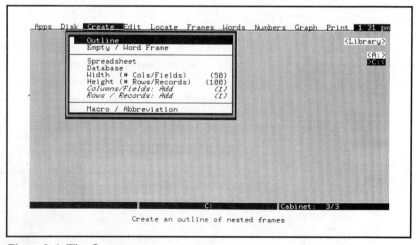

Figure 2.1: The Create menu

In summary, here are two sequences of keystrokes you can use to create an outline:

Instruct	(to open the menu)
→ or ←	(to select Create)
↑ or ↓ or Home	(to select Outline)
Return	(to invoke the option)

or

Ctrl-C	(to select the Create submenu)
O	(to invoke the Outline option)

Figure 2.2 shows the Outline frame that is placed on the desktop as a result of any of these keystroke sequences. You'll recall that this outline begins with room for three major headings, with each major heading allowing room for three subheadings. Your next step is to enter a frame label. Then you can begin entering outline headings.

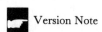 Version Note

Framework versions I and II used the edit line for entering frame labels. Therefore, where this section refers to editing in the frame label, earlier versions were actually editing in the edit line below the status panel.

ENTERING FRAME LABELS   The first thing you'll normally want to do when you create any frame is to assign the frame a label. You should write labels that will serve to identify the contents of

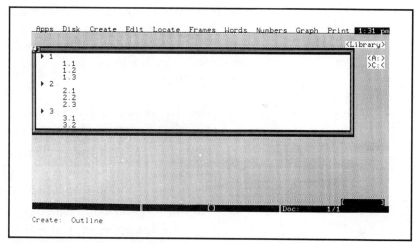

Figure 2.2: An Outline frame

the frames you create. Imagine that you have created a couple dozen frames with Framework III, and you've stored them all as files on a hard or floppy disk. You're going to want to be able to examine the disk directory and recall more or less what each of your files contains. Hence, you should be guided by two criteria in writing good frame labels:

1. The whole label should function as a descriptive title for a frame on your desktop.

2. The first eight characters of the label must serve as a unique identifier for the file that will ultimately store your frame on disk.

You enter a frame label when the highlight is located on the frame's border, as shown in Figure 2.2.

Let's imagine a situation in which you are likely to create an outline to help you plan ahead. You have been assigned the responsibility of preparing a 30-minute talk to present at an upcoming business meeting. Your proposed topic is the effective use of personal computers in the business environment. You decide that the best way to organize your thoughts on the subject is to start with an outline. Let's call your Outline frame *Computer Talk*; we'll use this exercise to illustrate the whole range of outlining techniques in Framework III.

Begin entering the frame label simply by typing the characters themselves. As soon as you press the uppercase C, the first letter of your label, some interesting action will take place on the display screen. Several things will happen below the desktop—where the cursor is, in the frame's tray on the desktop, in the status panel, and on the message line:

1. The characters you type will appear in the label area. As you type, the edit cursor will lead one space ahead of each character.

2. The first eight characters you type for the frame's label are echoed in the tray at the lower right corner of the desktop, and also in the central section of the status panel.

3. The third section of the status panel, in the lower right corner of your display screen, will give you information about the length of the frame label you are creating.

4. The message line will tell you exactly what activity you are involved in, and what you should do to complete the activity:

Label editing; RETURN finishes (ESC cancels changes)

Figure 2.3 shows the appearance of the screen after you have typed the first ten characters of the label. Notice the status panel's message:

Char: 11/1

This message tells you that the cursor is currently located at the eleventh character position of the first line of your label. (We will discover later that labels can consist of more than one line of text.)

Also note that the label you are entering is actually appearing at three different locations on the screen. Each of these locations ultimately serves a different function in Framework III's screen presentation:

1. The frame label—this is where you are actually entering (and changing, if necessary) the label.

2. The central section of the status panel—this section always tells you the name of the currently selected frame on the desktop.

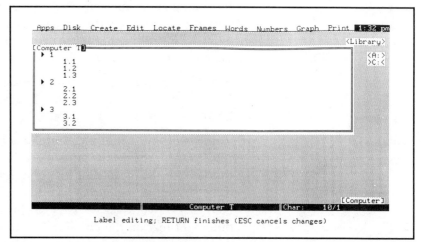

Figure 2.3: Entering a label for a frame

3. The tray, at the lower right corner of the desktop—with room for only eight characters, the tray tells you what the name of this frame will be when you save it as a file on disk.

USING CURSOR-MOVEMENT KEYS   While you are entering information in Framework III, you can use several cursor-movement keys to help you complete your data entry correctly. You will use these cursor-movement keys for many kinds of data entry in Framework III, not just for entering frame labels. Here are the special keys you can use:

- *The Backspace key.* This key, located on the top row of the keyboard, just to the left of the NumLock key, *erases* the last character you entered on the line you are editing; it also moves the edit cursor one space backward.

- *The ← and → keys.* These keys move the cursor backward and forward on the line you are editing without erasing the characters you have already typed. You might want to use these keys to reposition the cursor so that you can insert some new characters inside the line you have already begun to enter.

- *The Home and End keys.* The Home key moves the cursor to the beginning of the line you are editing, and the End key moves it to the space beyond the last character you've entered on the line you are editing. You can use these keys to move quickly back and forth within the data you are entering.

- *The Delete key.* This key deletes the character at the current cursor location and moves the characters located after the cursor to the left, to take up the empty space.

- *The Return key.* This key completes your data entry and returns the cursor to its original location on the desktop—in this case, the frame label area. (The edit cursor does not have to be located at the end of the current line before you press Return.) As you will see later in this book, you will sometimes edit text on the edit line. Pressing Return on the edit line would complete the entry and place the highlight where you started the edit.

You can see that Framework III gives you complete control over the process of entering a frame label—or entering any other information into some element of the desktop. You can move the cursor, delete characters, and insert characters before you press the Return key to complete the entry.

THE CURSOR AND THE HIGHLIGHT   In Chapter 1, we saw that the *cursor* and the *highlight* are two visual markers that Framework III uses to show you where you are currently working on the display screen. In much of your work, the cursor and the highlight will be located together. For example, when you select a frame, the cursor is located on the border of the frame, and the highlight simply extends and emphasizes the visual effect of the cursor.

However, when you are entering or editing information, the cursor shows your position on the line, character by character. From now on, we'll think of the *highlight* as the marker for the currently selected frame or element, and the *cursor* as the marker for character-by-character text entry on the line you are editing.

The edit cursor does not look exactly the same as the cursor you saw on the frame's border. On a frame's border, the cursor is a small, flashing rectangle, taking up one character space. While editing, the cursor is a reverse-video space or a contrasting color that displays the current letter or digit. Beneath the letter or digit is a flashing underscore character.

In summary, the *general* role of the cursor and the highlight together is to show you where you are currently working on the display screen. The highlight (along with the cursor) marks a frame or several frames that you have selected for some specific activity. The cursor alone marks your place in a line of text that you are entering or editing.

EDITING A LABEL   We have seen that you can make changes in your data entry before you press the Return key. But what if you still make a mistake in the entry of a label? For example, let's imagine you accidentally left out a letter of the name you intended to give to the frame. After you press the Return key, you see that your frame label is

Comuter Talk

There are two ways you can correct your work. The simplest way is to reenter the edit mode. The key that does this for you is the space-bar. Press the spacebar once, while the frame's border is highlighted, and you will find the cursor back in the frame label, located at the beginning of the text. To correct your mistake, then, you would press the following keys:

Spacebar (to begin editing)

→, three times (to position the edit cursor)

p (to insert the missing character)

Return (to complete the correction)

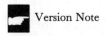 Version Note

Safety is a new feature of Framework beginning with version III.

The other way you can correct an error is simply to retype the whole label; however, your ability to do so is controlled by the Safety feature, which you can set on or off from the Frames menu. If Safety is on, then you cannot simply begin typing to reenter a label. This will prevent you from accidentally typing over an existing label. If Safety is off, you can simply begin typing. As soon as you enter the first character (C), the original version of the frame label will disappear, and the cursor will be positioned in the frame label, ready for you to enter a new sequence of characters.

To turn Safety on or off, press:

Ctrl-F (to select Frames)

S (to toggle the Safety option)

As usual, if Safety is off, two dashes will appear to the left of the menu option. If it is already on, the word *on* appears to the left.

ENTERING OUTLINE HEADINGS

Once you have given your Outline frame an appropriate name, you'll be ready to go inside the frame and begin typing the headings of the outline itself. The data-entry technique is identical, and you can use the same cursor-movement keys to modify your work as you go along.

The first step, however, is to position the cursor inside the Outline frame. To do this, you'll recall, you use the In key, located at the lower right corner of the keyboard. (This key is labeled with a plus sign on the keyboard.) When you press this key, the highlight will be positioned over the first line of your outline, as shown in Figure 2.4.

Now that you are ready to work with the outline itself, you should examine the symbols and characters that Framework III uses to designate the structure of the outline. In Chapter 1, we discussed the numbering system of an outline. The main headings are numbered sequentially: 1, 2, 3. The numbers of subheadings have two parts: the first part identifies the subheading's location in the entire outline, and the second part indicates the sequential order inside a given section of the outline.

For example, consider the subheading number 2.3. The number tells you that this is the third subheading beneath the second major heading. However complex your outlines ultimately become, you will always be able to identify a subheading's location and logical order simply by examining its number.

As we talk about headings and subheadings, keep in mind that the outline actually represents a hierarchy of frames. Each major heading is a *containing frame*; each subheading, a subframe. Framework III supplies symbols within the outline that tell you what type of frame each heading represents. Notice that each major heading in the outline is preceded by a pointer—a small triangle that points toward the

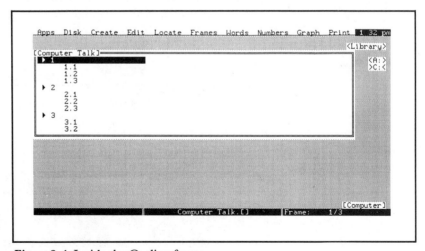

Figure 2.4: Inside the Outline frame

heading number. Framework III uses the pointer to tell you that this heading represents a containing frame—that is, a frame that contains other frames.

An Empty frame can serve your outlining requirements in one of two ways. You can perform word processing tasks inside the frame, in which case the frame becomes a Word frame. Or you can put other frames inside the frame, creating a new level in the hierarchy of your outline. In this case, the subframe itself becomes a containing frame.

You'll recall that each of the subheadings in an outline represents an Empty frame. Let's try a little experiment. Press the following keys:

Ctrl-F   (to select Frames)

R   (to invoke the Reveal Type option)

You'll notice, in Figure 2.5, that each subheading now has

(E)

following its numerical designation. This stands for Empty. When you choose the Reveal Type option, each type of frame is labeled with a letter—E for Empty frames, W for Word frames (which is what Empty frames become once you have entered text in them) and Telecommunications frames (which will also contain text once they have been used), S for Spreadsheet frames, and D for Database

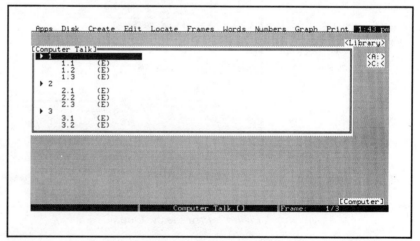

Figure 2.5: An outline with the frame type shown

frames. Outline frames—or any frames that contain other frames—never have an identifier of this type.

Although Framework III doesn't normally display the indicator that tells you what types of frames are contained in an outline, we will continue with the Reveal Type option selected for the rest of this exercise, so that you can see what happens when you make changes to your outline.

But for the moment, let's not worry about the *contents* of the frames in our outline. In fact, let's go back to thinking of the outline as a set of headings and subheadings that you are using to organize your upcoming computer talk. We were about to begin entering labels into the outline to describe the sequence of this talk.

With the highlight positioned at the first major heading of the outline, as shown in Figure 2.4, notice the messages supplied in the status panel below the desktop. The central section of the panel gives you the *full name* of the current selection:

Computer Talk.[ ]

A full name is a sequence of labels, separated by periods, indicating the hierarchy of the outline. The first label shows the name of the outline frame itself: Computer Talk. This name is followed by a period; then the empty brackets show that you have not yet entered a label for this first outline heading.

The right-hand section of the status panel shows the following message:

Frame: 1/3

This tells you that you are located at the first of the three major headings in your outline. You can see that Framework III has many overlapping ways of telling you exactly where you are working in an outline. The messages and symbols that supply this information are often deliberately redundant: you are free to make use of the display screen's resources in whatever way makes sense to you.

Let's see what happens as you begin entering a label at this first heading position in the outline. The first part of your upcoming talk is going to be a general introduction to business computing. So you want to enter the word *Introduction* at heading 1. Begin typing the letters and watch the display screen. Figure 2.6 shows the screen as

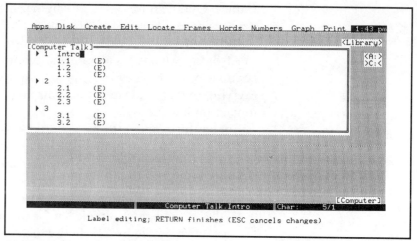

Figure 2.6: Entering an outline heading

you're entering the word. The status panel shows the new full name of the outline heading and the character-by-character progress of the edit cursor. When you finish typing the label, press the Return key. Heading 1 will be highlighted, indicating that you are no longer in the edit mode.

So we see that the process of entering labels into the outline is the same as the process of entering a frame label. Let's enter the other labels into the major heading positions of the outline. You decide that the second part of your talk is going to be about word processing, and the third will cover spreadsheet programming. So you want to reposition the highlight and enter the following headings:

2   Word Processing
3   Spreadsheets

From the position of major heading 1, you can use the ↓ key to move the highlight down the outline. There are two ways to proceed. You can move one step at a time, subheading by subheading, until you reach your destination. Or, for a quicker way to move from one *major* heading to the next, you can press two keys at once:

Ctrl-↓   (to move to the next major heading)

Likewise, the ↑ key moves you back up the outline, and Ctrl-↑ moves you up to the previous major heading. Mouse users can use standard point and click techniques.

After you have entered labels for the three major headings of your outline, you are going to enter subheadings. Figure 2.7 shows the entire outline, including subheadings for the three sections of your talk. Before you read on, practice entering labels by creating this outline on your desktop.

Now that we have the beginnings of an outline, let's see what techniques are available for working with it.

CHANGING THE OUTLINE

First, you may have noticed that Figure 2.7 devotes the entire screen to the outline rather than just the space inside the frame on the desktop. The Outline frame itself, as shown in Figure 2.6, was not big enough for you to see the entire outline at once. When you move

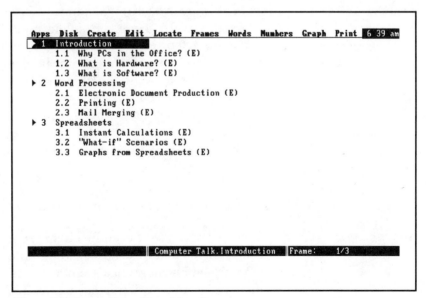

Figure 2.7: An outline with subheadings

the highlight down to the subheading numbered 3.3, the outline *scrolls* one line up the screen. In other words, to make room to display the bottom line of the outline, Framework III has to push the top line temporarily out of view.

Scrolling is a common phenomenon in all kinds of computer work, because your display screen has only enough room for showing a certain number of contiguous lines at once. You can scroll either up or down with the cursor keys. Lines that are out of view are still part of the document; they are just temporarily off the screen. You can reach them again by scrolling back to their location.

ENLARGING YOUR VIEW OF THE OUTLINE

Framework III gives you a couple of ways to devote more than the normal frame area to a given document. One way is to use the Zoom key (the function key labeled F9). To zoom in on a frame, place the cursor on the frame's border and press the Zoom key.

To reach the border of the Outline frame from inside the outline, you use the Out key (the key labeled with a minus sign, on the far right of your keyboard). Each time you press Out (–), the highlight moves one level higher in the outline, until it reaches the border of the frame itself. For example, from subheading level 3.3, you would have to press Out twice to reach the border: first to reach the heading level 3, then to move to the border of the frame.

Alternatively, you can press two keys at once, Ctrl-Out, to reach an Outline frame's border from any location inside the outline. So to zoom in on the entire outline, producing a display like the one in Figure 2.7, here are the keys you will press:

Ctrl-Out(–)   (to move the highlight to the border)

Zoom (F9)   (to zoom in on the frame)

Now you can see the entire outline at once, without scrolling. Of course, if you add new sections to the outline, as we are going to do next, the outline may once again be too large to fit on the screen. In this case, scrolling will still take place when you move from one part of the outline to another.

FOCUSING ON PARTICULAR SECTIONS

There is another simple technique for changing the amount of information shown on the screen. Occasionally you may want to concentrate on one particular section of your outline. You may find it convenient to have a temporary way of hiding the details of other sections. With one keystroke, Framework III allows you to *close* an entire section of your outline, so that you see only the main heading of that section. Closing a section of an outline is equivalent to closing a frame by putting it in its tray. The frame—or the outline section—is still available to you when you need it. You have simply put it out of view for the moment.

For example, let's say you have temporarily finished working on the Introduction section of your talk, and you want to concentrate on the other two sections. You can close this section by moving the highlight to the first major heading and pressing the Return key. The result is shown in Figure 2.8—the subheadings of the Introduction section are no longer visible.

To reopen the Introduction section, press Return again while the highlight is positioned over the same heading. When you do so,

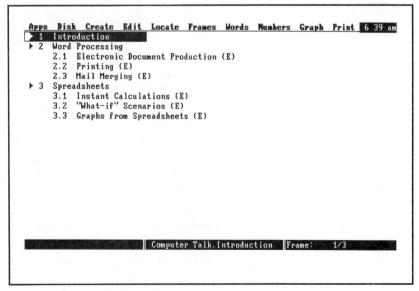

Figure 2.8: Closing an outline section

the subheadings will reappear on the screen. You can use this technique to open or close any section of your outline.

In the following paragraphs, we'll explore several ways in which you can change the size and organization of your outline, including the following:

- Adding new headings
- Deleting headings
- Adding new levels to the structure of the outline
- Moving and copying sections of the outline
- Moving frames from the desktop to the outline
- Changing your view of the outline

To illustrate all these functions, we'll continue making plans for your upcoming computer talk.

ADDING NEW HEADINGS

There are several techniques for adding or inserting new headings to your outline. The technique you choose will depend on the type of frame you want to insert. It will also depend on whether you want to insert a new Empty frame, or one that you have already developed somewhere else on the desktop. In this section, we'll look at two ways to add frames to your outline.

Let's say you have decided to add a new subheading to the section of your talk that deals with spreadsheets. Between sections 3.1 and 3.2, you want to place an actual example of a spreadsheet. Recall that headings 3.1 and 3.2 are both Empty frames, potentially available for word processing. The new frame that you place between them will be a Spreadsheet frame, the contents of which you will develop after you have completed your outline.

You will need to use the Create option of Framework III's menu to add this new frame—or, rather, to add this new *outline subheading*, since we are still thinking of our work as an outline rather than a group of frames. To add a subheading at a specific point in your outline, you must be careful to position the highlight properly. Here is the rule for doing so:

> Place the highlight at the heading immediately *above* but *at the same outline level* as the position where you want the new heading to appear.

In other words, if you want a new subheading to appear between 3.1 and 3.2, you will move the selection highlight to heading position 3.1 in the outline.

Once you have put the highlight in the correct place, you simply invoke the appropriate option of the Create menu to create the new heading. In this case, to create a Spreadsheet frame, you will press the following keys:

Ctrl-C   (to open the Create menu)

S   (to create a Spreadsheet frame)

Figure 2.9 shows what the outline will look like after you press these keys. Several interesting things have happened. First of all, the new subheading has been given the number 3.2. Furthermore, the subheadings located farther down in this section have been automatically incremented. The former headings 3.2 and 3.3 have become 3.3 and 3.4, respectively.

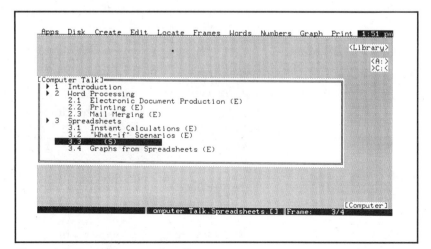

Figure 2.9: Inserting a new heading

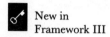
New in
Framework III

In Framework III, a new built-in macro command will add a new first frame heading on the current outline level. To use this macro, position the cursor anywhere within a particular outline level and press Alt-F2. A new outline heading is created at the beginning of the current level.

Because we have selected the Reveal Type option, the new subheading's frame type has also appeared on the screen:

3.2   (S)

We can see that the frame represented by this position in the outline will be available to us for spreadsheet programming. The next step you should take is to give this new subheading a name. Call it *Example*:

3.2   Example (S)

At this point, you decide that your talk should have a fourth major section, covering database management. Like the other major sections, this one will have several subheadings of its own. You need to find a convenient way to add a new group of headings to your outline.

Again, you have several techniques to choose from to expand your outline. Perhaps the simplest way in this case is to use the Outline option of the Create submenu. Just as when we created the original outline, this option will add three major headings, each with three subheadings. Since we want only one new major heading, we'll then have to delete the other two.

You must carefully determine the correct position for the highlight before adding the new headings. Since you are adding major headings to your outline, you need to position the highlight at the major heading you want the new headings to follow. In short, place the highlight at heading 3, the one labeled *Spreadsheets*. Then press the following keys to create the new headings:

Ctrl-C   (to open the Create menu)

O   (to create new headings)

You can see the new sections in Figure 2.10.

```
    Apps  Disk  Create  Edit  Locate  Frames  Words  Numbers  Graph  Print 12 17 am
  ▶ 2    Word Processing
         2.1   Electronic Document Production (E)
         2.2   Printing (E)
         2.3   Mail Merging (E)
  ▶ 3    Spreadsheets
         3.1   Instant Calculcations (E)
         3.2   Example (S)
         3.3   "What-if" Scenarios (E)
         3.4   Graphs from Spreadsheets (E)
  ▶ 4
         4.1    (E)
         4.2    (E)
         4.3    (E)
  ▶ 5
         5.1    (E)
         5.2    (E)
         5.3    (E)
  ▶ 6
         6.1    (E)
         6.2    (E)
         6.3    (E)
                            Computer Talk.[]        Frame:    4/6
```

Figure 2.10: Adding new sections

DELETING OUTLINE HEADINGS

Since you need only one additional section in your outline, instead of the three that you now have, you have to find some way to get rid of the rest. The Delete key will do the trick. You can delete either entire sections or just subheadings. Simply position the highlight over the part of the outline you want to delete, and press the Delete key.

In this case, you want to delete sections 5 and 6. But just to experiment, place the highlight over heading 4 instead. Press Delete once. You'll see that when you delete 4, the old sections 5 and 6 are renumbered as 4 and 5. Press Delete again. Now the old section 5 has become section 4, leaving you with precisely the outline length you want.

Deletions in Framework III are just easy enough to be dangerous. One of the major reasons for loss of valuable data on a computer is simple human error, leading to inadvertent deletions.

Fortunately, Framework III has a helpful way of bringing back accidental deletions. You may recall from Chapter 1 that the Edit menu has an Undo option. The keys you press to invoke this option are

Ctrl-E   (to open the Edit menu)

U   (to undo the last operation)

You may want to practice using this option now, so you'll know how to take advantage of it when you need it. You may find this option especially useful with frame labels. Recall that you can correct an error in a label simply by retyping the label, unless you have Safety on. This means that you can also erase a label by pressing a key while a label is highlighted. To get back the old label, press Escape. If you have already pressed the Return key to accept the accidental edit, press Ctrl-E U to recover your original label.

After practicing the Undo option, make sure your outline has exactly four sections. Section 4 is to have only two subheadings, as follows:

    4   Database Management
        4.1   Definitions (E)
        4.2   Practical Applications (E)

Enter these headings into your outline. Then delete the third sub-heading from section 4. Use the same process: place the highlight over the unwanted subheading and press the Delete key.

ADDING NEW LEVELS TO THE OUTLINE

Up to now, all but one of the subheadings in your outline have rep-resented Empty frames, potentially available to you for word process-ing. The outline has only two *levels*: the major headings, 1, 2, 3, and 4; and the subheadings 1.1, 1.2, and so on.

In many outlines, two levels are not adequate to express the logical organization of a given task. So the next thing to learn is how to add more levels to your outline.

The discussion of database management in your talk is currently divided into two sections: Definitions and Practical Applications. You decide that the Definitions section needs more detail—that is, more subdividing. You want to specify the database definitions that you will be presenting. In the context of databases, you are planning to discuss three terms that you think your audience will want to learn about: files, records, and fields. You would like your outline to look like this:

> **Database Management**
>   **Definitions**
>   **Files**
>   **Records**
>   **Fields**
>   **Practical Applications**

Follow these steps to create a new level in your outline:

1. Place the highlight at the heading below which you want to create a new level

2. Press two keys simultaneously: Ctrl and In (+).

Let's try it. First move the highlight to subheading 4.1, with the label *Definitions*. Then press

> Ctrl-In (+)   (to create a new level of outlining)

Here is what you will see in your outline:

> **4   Database Management**
>   **4.1   Definitions**
>   **4.1.1   (E)**

Notice that subheading 4.1 is no longer an Empty frame. It has lost its (E) designation, and on the screen you can see that it has a pointer, to show you that it is a containing frame. The new subheading (or sub-subheading, if you like), numbered 4.1.1, is an Empty frame.

Now you need to add two more subheadings at this new, third level of your outline. Place the highlight at subheading 4.1.1 and press

> Ctrl-C   (to open the Create menu)
>
> E   (to create heading 4.1.2)
>
> Ctrl-C   (to open the Create menu again)
>
> E   (to create heading 4.1.3)

Make sure you understand the difference between adding a new heading at an already established outline level and adding a new, deeper level. The former action uses the Create menu; the latter, the Ctrl-In (+) keystrokes.

Now type headings for the three new sublevels, 4.1.1, 4.1.2, and 4.1.3. Recall that the headings will be *Files*, *Records*, and *Fields*. Figure 2.11 shows the current organization of your outline.

As you examine your work up to now and consider the material you'll be presenting to your audience, you suddenly realize that you've made a mistake in organizing your talk. Your audience will be a group of managers, and their primary interest will be in spreadsheet programming. For this reason, you decide that you might risk losing their attention if you discuss word processing near the beginning of your presentation. A better approach would be to begin with spreadsheets.

This kind of change is, of course, a common occurrence in the thought process represented by an outline. When you look at the whole outline, you will often decide that you would like to rearrange some of the sections. Let's see how this can be done in a Framework III outline.

MOVING PORTIONS OF THE OUTLINE

The Move key (function key F7) and its companion the Copy key (F8) have important applications in every Framework III component. They are both involved in transferring desktop information

Figure 2.11: Adding a new level

from one place to another. The keys' names clearly indicate the difference between their respective functions:

- The Move key (F7) actually displaces information. After a move, the information will no longer be found in its original location; instead, it will be at the target location.

- The Copy key (F8) leaves the information intact at its source *and* produces a new, identical copy of the information at the target location. (Perhaps the most important use of Copy is in spreadsheet programming, where the word *identical* does not always apply to the copy or copies that are produced. We'll see why in Chapter 3.)

At this point in our outlining work, we require the services of the Move key. Before the end of this chapter, we'll also see examples of the Copy operation in an outline.

Your goal at this point is to rearrange the Computer Talk outline in this new order:

1   Introduction
2   Spreadsheets
3   Word Processing
4   Database Management

Here are the steps you will take to accomplish this change:

1. Place the highlight on the third major heading, labeled *Spreadsheets*.

2. Press the Move key (F7).

3. Move the highlight up to the first major heading, *Introduction* (the easiest way to do this is with the Home key).

4. Press the Return key.

To generalize the steps of a Move operation: you begin at the *source* location (that is, the location of the information you want to move), press the Move key, move the highlight to the *destination* location, and press the Return key to complete the operation.

In an outline, you indicate the destination of a move by placing the highlight on the heading immediately *above* the target location.

Figure 2.12 shows what your outline will look like after the move. The Spreadsheets section of the outline has become the second major heading. All of its subheadings have been renumbered correctly. The Word Processing section has become the third major heading; its subheadings have also been renumbered.

We've seen how easy it is to rearrange the order of your outline using the Move key. Now we'll use the same key to move frames from the desktop to the outline.

INCORPORATING OTHER FRAMES INTO THE OUTLINE

Once again, you decide to make some changes in the way your outline is organized. As you examine the section on Spreadsheets, you realize that you need to have at least two examples to show your audience: a Spreadsheet frame and a Graph frame. You decide to eliminate the current Spreadsheet frame, 2.2, and to create a fourth subheading, numbered 2.4, to contain the two examples you want to show.

You move the highlight to subheading 2.2 and press the Delete key. Then you move down to 2.3 and create a new subheading below it by pressing the sequence

Ctrl-C   (to open the Create menu)

E   (to create an Empty frame)

You label this new subheading *Examples*. Here is the new order of the Spreadsheets section:

```
2   Spreadsheets
    2.1   Instant Calculations (E)
    2.2   "What-if" Scenarios (E)
    2.3   Graphs from Spreadsheets (E)
    2.4   Examples (E)
```

For a moment, let's assume that you have been working with Framework III for a couple of months. Looking through the Framework III files that you have stored on disk, you find a Spreadsheet file and a Graph file that you have already developed. These will serve as

```
 Apps  Disk  Create  Edit  Locate  Frames  Words  Numbers  Graph  Print 12 21 am
▶ 1   Introduction
▶ 2   Spreadsheets
    2.1   Instant Calculations (E)
    2.2   Example (S)
    2.3   "What-if" Scenarios (E)
    2.4   Graphs from Spreadsheets (E)
▶ 3   Word Processing
    3.1   Electronic Document Production (E)
    3.2   Printing (E)
    3.3   Mail Merging (E)
▶ 4   Database Management
  ▶ 4.1   Definitions
      4.1.1  Files (E)
      4.1.2  Records (E)
      4.1.3  Fields (E)
    4.2   Practical Applications (E)



              | Computer Talk.Spreadsheets | Frame:    2/4 |
```

Figure 2.12: Rearranging the outline

good examples for your presentation, and they will save you the trouble of creating new ones. You bring the two files onto the desktop and rename them Spreadsheet and Graph, respectively.

Your task now is to move these two frames from their trays at the side of the desktop to the outline, a level below subheading 2.4. This is how you want the outline to look after the move:

> 2.4   Examples
>   2.4.1   Spreadsheet (S)
>   2.4.2   Graph (G)

Completing this operation is a little tricky. The problem is that you must create the new outline level, beneath heading 2.4, before you can move the two examples into it. There is no way to move frames into an outline level that doesn't exist yet. So you'll have to perform this operation in three steps: first create an Empty frame at the new level; then move the two example frames to locations below the Empty frame; and finally delete the unused Empty frame.

The first step, then, is to move the highlight to subheading 2.4 and press Ctrl-In (+) to create the Empty frame at the new level. Here is what you'll see:

> 2.4   Examples
>   2.4.1   (E)

The second step involves learning how to use a new function key—the Extend Select key (F6). You are planning to move *two* frames from the desktop into the outline. It would be a waste of time to have to move them one at a time. Fortunately, whenever you want to perform an identical operation with more than one frame (and the frames you want to select are adjacent), Framework III gives you a special way to *extend* the frame highlight over all the frames you want to work with. Let's see how this is done.

Figure 2.13 shows your current desktop. In the open Outline frame, you can see the new Examples subheading, with its own subheading, numbered 2.4.1. In the tray area of the desktop, you can see the Spreadsheet and Graph frames that you want to move into the outline. Here are the keys you press to get out of the open Outline frame and to move the highlight to the closed tray frames:

Ctrl-Out (–) (to move to the border of the Outline frame)

↓ (to move to the first of the trays)

Now you need to select *both* frames, so that they can both be moved together into the outline. To do so, you press the Extend Select key (F6). Extend Select is certainly one of the most powerful of the ten Framework III function keys. We'll be using it in many different ways as we examine spreadsheets, word processing, and database

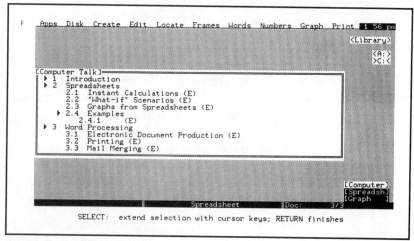

Figure 2.13: Using Extend Select

management. When you press this key, Framework III displays the following instructions on the message line:

SELECT: extend selection with cursor keys; RETURN finishes

In this case, you want to select both the Spreadsheet and the Graph trays. The highlight is already positioned on the Spreadsheet tray. After pressing Extend Select, you simply press the ↓ key to extend the highlight over the second of the two trays.

You can begin to see the significance of Framework III's highlight feature. Up to now, we have used the highlight to select individual frames or headings in the outline. Now you can see that the highlight can be enlarged, or extended, to select many frames or headings at once.

To complete the Extend Select operation, you press the Return key (following the instructions displayed on the message line). This leaves the two trays selected for the next step of our move procedure.

Next, press the Move key (F7). Again you'll see instructions on the message line:

MOVE: cursor to the move destination; RETURN finishes

To complete the move operation, you must now move the highlight back into the Outline frame and position it at the correct destination for the two frames you have selected. The following sequence of key-strokes will accomplish the move:

↑	(to move to the Outline frame)
In (+)	(to move into the frame)
↓, several times	(to highlight subheading 2.4.1)
Return	(to complete the move)

As soon as you press the Return key, the two trays on the desktop are instantly moved into the outline. All during the move operation, Framework III remembers which two frames you selected for the move. (Note that the original trays will *not* remain on the desktop; we are moving, not copying.) Something odd has happened, though; the two new outline subheadings do not look like the rest of the outline.

They don't have numbers or type indicators:

> 2.4 Examples
>   2.4.1   (E)
> – – Spreadsheet
> – – Graph

NUMBERING AND INCLUDING THE TYPE INDICATORS

This situation is typical of a move from the desktop to an outline. Frames that you move into the outline do not start out with outline numbers or type indicators. If you want to add this information to the outline, you must invoke two options from the Frames menu.

Figure 2.14 shows the Frames menu. The two options that we want to use at this point are

> – – Number Labels
> – – Reveal Type

You can switch any of these options on by selecting the option. A Framework III menu option is in effect when you see the word *on* in the menu; for example:

> on Number Labels

The option is off when you see two hyphens before the option.

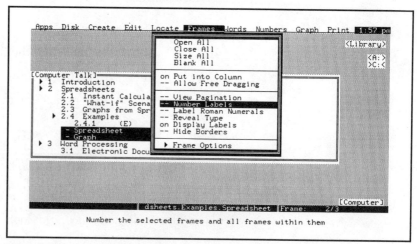

Figure 2.14: The Frames menu

These options work on whatever parts of the outline are currently selected for activity. At this point, both the Spreadsheet and Graph headings are still highlighted; the Extend Select operation is still in effect. Thus, as we invoke these two Frames options, they will work on both of the headings. Here are the keystrokes:

Ctrl-F   (to open the Frames menu)

N   (to number the selected frames)

Ctrl-F   (to open the Frames menu)

R   (to reveal the types of the frames)

Finally, Figure 2.15 shows your outline after all these operations are complete. Only one detail remains: you must still delete the Empty frame numbered 2.4.1.

At this point, you are satisfied with your outline, and you are ready to begin using it as a template for preparing the contents of your presentation. Up to now, we have been completely preoccupied with organizing the outline itself, and we have never once concerned ourselves with the contents of the frames in the outline. In the next section, we'll discuss two ways that you can use to move inside the Empty frames.

```
Apps  Disk  Create  Edit  Locate  Frames  Words  Numbers  Graph  Print  12 25 am
▶ 1   Introduction
▶ 2   Spreadsheets
      2.1  Instant Calculcations (E)
      2.2  "What-if" Scenarios (E)
      2.3  Graphs from Spreadsheets (E)
    ▶ 2.4  Examples
        2.4.1   (E)
        2.4.2  Spreadsheet (S)
        2.4.3  Graph (G)
▶ 3   Word Processing
      3.1  Electronic Document Production (E)
      3.2  Printing (E)
      3.3  Mail Merging (E)
▶ 4   Database Management
    ▶ 4.1  Definitions
        4.1.1  Files (E)
        4.1.2  Records (E)
        4.1.3  Fields (E)
      4.2  Practical Applications (E)


                    Computer Talk.Introduction  Frame:    1/4
```

Figure 2.15: Moving frames from the desktop to the outline

ENTERING THE OUTLINE FRAMES

We have already seen how the Zoom key (F9) can be used to devote the entire screen to the contents of the Outline frame. When you get ready to enter information into any of the Empty frames in the outline, you can also use the Zoom key.

For example, let's say you want to start writing some notes for the very first topic of your presentation: the first subheading in the Introduction section. If you open the Introduction section again (by placing the highlight over the first major heading and pressing Return), you can review this part of the outline:

```
1   Introduction
    1.1   Why PCs in the Office? (E)
    1.2   What is Hardware? (E)
    1.3   What is Software? (E)
```

Now you want to open the Empty frame represented by subheading 1.1, so you can begin typing some notes. Move the highlight to 1.1 and press the Zoom key (F9). As a result, the entire screen will be given over to this one Empty frame, as shown in Figure 2.16. You

Figure 2.16: Zooming into an Empty frame

can begin writing whatever information you want directly into this frame.

As soon as you start typing, this Empty frame will become a Word frame, for word processing. When you finish your work on this first section and you want to return to the outline, simply press Zoom (F9) again. The Zoom key is actually a toggle; it switches you into and out of full-screen mode for a given frame.

When you return to the outline, you shouldn't be too surprised to find that the type indicator of the first subheading has changed:

1.1 Why PCs in the Office? (W)

The W, for Word, shows that this frame is no longer empty. We'll be discussing the details of word processing in Chapter 4; but meanwhile, you shouldn't hesitate to experiment with entering words and sentences into the Empty frames of your outline.

The View key (F10) is also a toggle; it switches an outline between *Outline view* and *Frames view*. We've been working in Outline view throughout this chapter. Frames view transforms the display of each heading in the outline into an individual frame on the display screen. When you are working in Frames view in a large outline like the one we have developed, you will have to scroll from one frame to the next; generally, only two or three frames can be seen on the screen at a time in this mode.

Figure 2.17 shows a Frames view of the Introduction section of the outline. To produce this screen, place the highlight on the first major heading and press the View key (F10). Then, to devote the entire screen to the Frames view, press the Zoom key. (You can also produce this screen by simply pressing the Zoom key with the highlight on the first major heading.) Notice that you can see all three subframes of the Introduction section at once. To move inside any one of the frames, select the frame's border and press the In key (+). To return to the Outline view, press the View key again.

Note that if you want to return all the way to a frame's outer border, you can do so by pressing Ctrl-Out (–) from any point in an outline, even if you have used the Zoom key to get a full-screen view of a small portion of your outline.

We've seen all the ways that you can use an Outline frame to organize your thoughts for a given task. To summarize, Framework III

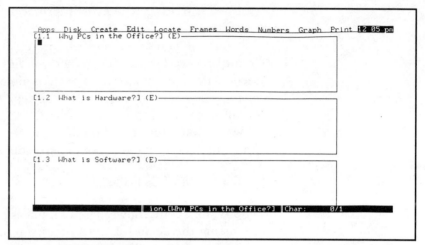

Figure 2.17: Frames view

gives you simple techniques for adding headings and levels to the outline, for deleting headings or entire levels, for rearranging the order of selected sections in the outline, for bringing in frames from the desktop, and for viewing the outline as a group of frames that you can enter information into.

BUILDING AN OUTLINE FROM AN EMPTY FRAME

You can also use an Empty frame as the starting point for an outline. You might decide to do so if the major purpose of your outline is to organize a set of work frames that you have already created. Building such an outline involves the same techniques that we discussed above. You can take advantage of several Framework III tools.

- The Move key (F7), to begin moving desktop frames into your outline

- The Create menu, to incorporate new frames (of any type) into the outline

- The Ctrl-In (+) keystroke combination, to create new levels in your outline

- The Frames menu, to control the appearance of the outline, including the appearance of numbering and type designators
- The Move (F7) and Copy (F8) keys, to rearrange the order of frames in the outline
- The Zoom (F9) and View (F10) keys, to examine and work in the contents areas of the frames

CREATING A TABLE OF CONTENTS

The Frames submenu has other interesting options that can be used on Outline frames or on outlines that you have built in Empty frames. Among these options is one that transforms an outline into a table of contents that includes page numbers. This option is called

– – View Pagination

Let's say you complete the preparation for your talk on business uses of personal computers, and the day comes for you to present the talk to your audience. Everyone is favorably impressed with the clarity of your ideas and the organization of your talk. Several people ask if you can produce a written version of your presentation, turning your notes and examples into a report that can be distributed to the managers who didn't make it to the meeting.

You agree to print what you have written. The report turns out to be a number of pages long, so you decide to include the original outline as a table of contents. The pages of the report are numbered, and you would like to find an easy way to incorporate these page numbers into the table of contents. Here's how to do it:

Ctrl-Out (–)	(to select the frame's border)
Ctrl-F	(to select the Frame menu)
V	(to view page numbers)

Figure 2.18 shows what you get; you can see that the entire report covers eight pages of documents. Your table of contents will help readers zero in on just the information they need. Note that when Reveal Type is on, /p appears after the frame type if a frame has ever been printed, as shown in the figure.

```
 Apps  Disk  Create  Edit  Locate  Frames  Words  Numbers  Graph  Print  2:57 am
▶ 1  Introduction /p . .  . . . . . . . . . . . . . . . . . .      1
     1.1  Why PCs in the Office? (W) . . . . . . . . . . .      1
     1.2  What is Hardware? (W)  . . . . . . . . . . . . .      1
     1.3  What is Software? (W) . . . . . . . . . . . . .      2
▶ 2  Spreadsheets  . . . . . . . . . . . . . . . . . . .      2
     2.1  Instant Calculations (W) . . . . . . . . . . .      2
     2.2  "What-if" Scenarios (W) . . . . . . . . . . . .      3
     2.3  Graphs from Spreadsheets (W) . . . . . . . . .      3
   ↗▶ 2.4  Examples  . . . . . . . . . . . . . . . . . .      3
         2.4.1  Spreadsheet (S) . . . . . . . . . . . . .      3
         2.4.2  Graph (G) . . . . . . . . . . . . . . . .      4
▶ 3  Word Processing  . . . . . . . . . . . . . . . . . .      4
     3.1  Electronic Document Production (W) . . . . . .      4
     3.2  Printing (W) . . . . . . . . . . . . . . . . .      5
     3.3  Mail Merging (W) . . . . . . . . . . . . . . .      5
▶ 4  Database Management  . . . . . . . . . . . . . . . .      6
   ▶ 4.1  Definitions  . . . . . . . . . . . . . . . . .      6
         4.1.1  Files (W) . . . . . . . . . . . . . . . .      6
         4.1.2  Records (W) . . . . . . . . . . . . . . .      6
         4.1.3  Fields (W)  . . . . . . . . . . . . . . .      7
     4.2  Practical Applications (W) . . . . . . . . . .      7
                        ║ Computer Talk.Introduction ║Frame:    1/4
```

Figure 2.18: Creating a table of contents

SAVING OUTLINES—
USING THE DISK MENU

The Disk menu, shown in Figure 2.19, saves entire Outline files on disk. Here is a brief description of the two relevant options of the menu.

The *Save and Continue* option saves a copy of your current outlining work and then lets you continue where you left off on the desktop. You can invoke this option from any position inside an outline; the highlight does not need to be located on the outside border of the outline. Recall that there are two ways to perform a Save and Continue operation. If you go through the Disk menu, you press these keys:

Ctrl-D　(to open the Disk menu)

S　　　(to Save and Continue)

You can also use a shorter alternative that does not go through the menu; all you press is

Ctrl-Return　(Save and Continue)

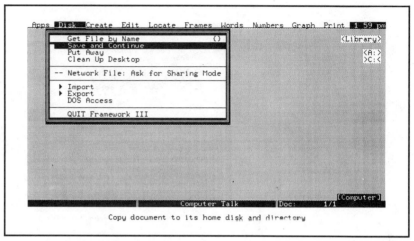

Figure 2.19: The Disk menu

The *Put Away* option saves the current Outline frame on disk and then removes it from the desktop. Once again, you can perform this operation either from inside the outline or from the border of the Outline frame.

Both of these operations save your entire Outline frame on disk, with all of the frames it contains. The Outline frame will be stored as a single file, under the name determined by the Outline frame's label.

Sometimes you may want to save as individual files one or more of the frames located *inside* an Outline frame. For example, look at the Computer Talk outline in Figure 2.20. Let's say you've decided to save the three Word frames located in the Database Management section of your outline under the Definitions subheading. You want these three Word frames each to become individual files on the disk, so you can work with each of them separately later on. Unfortunately, neither the Save and Continue nor the Put Away option of the Disk menu will help you with this operation. These Disk menu options work only with your entire Outline frame.

To save the three Word frames individually, you'll use either the Move key or the Copy key. Here are the steps you'll follow:

1. Use the Extend Select key (F6) to highlight the three Word frames (you can see in Figure 2.20 that this has already been done). Position the highlight over heading 4.1.1 and press

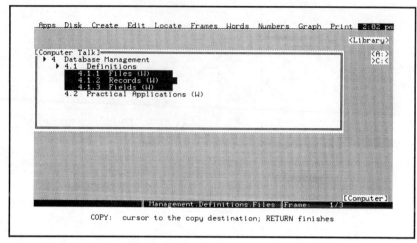

Figure 2.20: Saving subframes to disk

the following keys:

Extend Select (F6)	(to extend the highlight)
↓	(to include 4.1.2)
↓	(to include 4.1.3)
Return	(to complete the selection)

2. Press the Move key (F7) or the Copy key (F8); we'll discuss in a moment the difference between these two operations in this case.

3. Move the highlight to the inside of the disk drive cabinet B, and complete the Move or Copy operation. Here is how to do it:

Shuttle (Scroll Lock)	(to select the disk drive cabinet)
In (+)	(to move into the drive cabinet)
Return	(to complete the move)

(Recall that the Shuttle key always moves you to the disk drive cabinets.)

When you press Return, the three Word frames will be saved one at a time on your disk, as three different files. You'll be able to see them the next time you look at the disk directory.

There is an important difference between using the Copy key and the Move key for this operation. If you use the Move key (F7), the headings will disappear from your outline. They will literally be displaced—moved into the disk directory. If you use the Copy key (F8), however, the headings will be *copied* to the disk cabinet, and the originals will remain in your outline.

Near the end of this chapter, we'll come back to our discussion of the disk drive cabinets to see how Framework III handles your disk if you have divided it into DOS subdirectories.

PRINTING OUTLINES— USING THE PRINT MENU

When you set out to print an Outline frame on paper, you have to decide which part of the frame to send to the printer:

- Outline headings only
- Contents of the subframes only
- Both the headings and the contents

The View key (F10) will help you carry out your decision. Recall that View toggles an Outline frame between Frames view (where you see the contents of the frames in the outline) and Outline view (where you see only the headings of the outline). The Print operation will conform to the current View setting.

If you want to print an outline or a table of contents, print the Outline frame while it is displayed in Outline view.

If you want to print the contents of the Word, Spreadsheet, Database, or Graph frames that are contained inside your Outline frame, print the frame while it is displayed in Frames view.

The Print menu appears in Figure 2.21. To print a frame, place the highlight on the frame's border, select the view of your choice, and then press

Ctrl-P (to open the Print menu)

B   (to begin printing)

Don't be surprised if you see your disk drive lights go on before the printer begins to print. If you have set Allow Print Spooling on from the Print menu, Framework III goes through an efficient process called *spooling* while it is getting ready to print your frame. It first stores an image of the printed frame as a file on your disk, and then it transfers that file to the printer. While this is happening, Framework III displays

PREPARING TO PRINT

in the message area at the bottom of the screen. The advantage of this process is that you can work on the desktop while Framework III is printing your document. (When the printing process is complete, Framework III erases the print file from the disk.)

If the Allow Print Spooling option is off, Framework III will print your document from memory while you wait.

You can see in Figure 2.21 that the Print menu has several submenus of its own. One of them turns print spooling on or off. The one you see in the center of the desktop is the submenu for Output Options. You can look at this submenu on your own screen by pressing

Ctrl-P   (to open the Print menu)

O   (to select Output Options)

The Output Options submenu gives you three important options for controlling the way an outline is printed. You can switch any of these options on simply by selecting it on the submenu.

The Skip Closed Frames option tells Framework III not to print any sections of your outline that are closed. (Remember how we closed the Introduction section of the Computer Talk outline by pressing the Return key with the highlight over the first outline heading.) If you want to print parts of your outline selectively, this is the option to work with.

The Print Frame Labels option, which is on by default but can be toggled off and on, tells Framework III to print the outline headings (that is, the frame labels, if you think of your outline as a collection of frames) along with the contents of the outline.

 Version Note

The Allow Print Spooling option is new to Framework III. Previous versions always used print spooling.

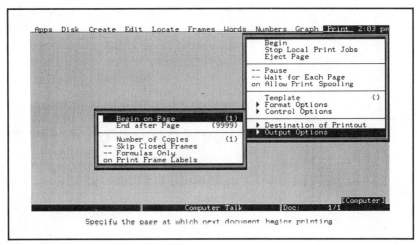

Apps Disk Create Edit Locate Frames Words Numbers Graph Print 2:03 pm

```
                                            Begin
                                            Stop Local Print Jobs
                                            Eject Page

                                         -- Pause
                                         -- Wait for Each Page
                                         on Allow Print Spooling

                                            Template               ()
                                         ▶  Format Options
                                         ▶  Control Options
      Begin on Page        (1)
      End after Page       (9999)         ▶  Destination of Printout
                                         ▶  Output Options
      Number of Copies     (1)
   -- Skip Closed Frames
   -- Formulas Only
   on Print Frame Labels
```

```
                                                            [Computer]

                      Computer Talk            Doc:      1/1
```
Specify the page at which next document begins printing

Figure 2.21: The Print menu

Finally, an advanced feature: the Formulas Only option. We have seen that each frame on the desktop can hold a formula or a program; formulas reside *behind* frames. It turns out that an Outline frame is often a convenient structure for building a FRED program—a collection of formulas stored behind a hierarchy of frames. If you write such a program and you want to print it out on paper, the Formulas Only option tells Framework III to print the program behind the outline rather than the outline itself. We'll talk more about this in Chapter 7, which discusses FRED programming.

We've discussed in detail the techniques you can use for creating Outline frames and changing them to match your own thought processes. We've also seen how to save and print outlines. Now it's time to check back with Eileen Wilcox and George Farley at The Sophisticated Palate.

EXAMPLES

In Chapter 1, we examined an outline that Eileen developed to create an advertising flier for her party trays. Let's look at exactly how she created this flier.

You'll remember that her flier contains three party tray descriptions, with a small spreadsheet below each description. The spreadsheets display a range of prices for each tray, depending on the number of people the tray is to serve.

OUTLINING
THE PROMOTIONAL FLIER

To develop this document, Eileen began with an Outline frame. She deleted the subheadings in each of the original three outline sections and entered labels for the three remaining headings:

    1   Cocktail Tray I
    2   Cocktail Tray II
    3   Buffet Tray

Her next step was to develop a template for the small spreadsheet that follows each major heading. She used the Create menu to insert a Spreadsheet frame between the first and second headings of her outline:

    1   Cocktail Tray I
    2
    3   Cocktail Tray II
    4   Buffet Tray

Then she pressed the View key (F10) so she could work on the contents of her frames. She developed the necessary two-line spreadsheet, with column headings for the number of people and a row for the prices of each tray. She left the prices out for the moment. You can see her work up to this point in Figure 2.22.

Returning the frame to Outline view, she gave her Spreadsheet frame a name—Prices—and copied it twice, placing copies beneath each of the other two tray descriptions. Placing the highlight over the Spreadsheet label, she performed the following keystrokes to produce the copies:

Copy (F8)   (to begin the copy operation)

  ↓   (to move the highlight to heading 3)

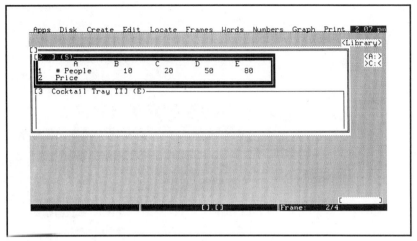

Figure 2.22: Developing the party tray flier

Return	(to produce the copy)
Copy	(to copy again)
↓	(to position the highlight)
Return	(to produce the third copy)

Here is the resulting outline:

1 Cocktail Tray I
2 Prices
3 Cocktail Tray II
4 Prices
5 Buffet Tray
6 Prices

At this point, before entering any specific data into the frames of the outline, Eileen decided to save a copy of this outline onto disk. She realized that she would be able to use this empty outline to produce quick advertising fliers for other party trays she offers in future weeks. She called the copy TRAYTEMP, for *tray template*.

Finally, she typed the text describing this week's trays into each of the Empty frames (which then became Word frames), and she entered the appropriate prices for each tray into the three spreadsheets. She moved the highlight to the border of the Outline frame and pressed the View key (F10) to put the outline in Frames view. Just before printing out the flier, she used an option in the Frames menu to get rid of the outline numbers. Then she used the Print menu to begin printing. You can look back at her work in Figure 1.21.

ORGANIZING EXPENSE SPREADSHEETS INTO AN OUTLINE

George has also begun to use outlining, as a way to keep track of the company's monthly expenses. He has asked Frank Osawa, the bookkeeper, to maintain a series of expense spreadsheets for each month, to record the cost of running the company. Here are the names of Frank's spreadsheets:

- Advertising Expenses
- Cost of Goods Sold
- Equipment Loan Payments
- Equipment Maintenance
- Insurance
- Rent
- Utilities
- Wages

We'll examine some of these spreadsheets in Chapter 3. For now, simply imagine the rows and columns of numbers that might be involved in each kind of expense. The bottom line on each spreadsheet will represent the total expense, in a given category, for the month.

Over time, George finds himself asking for more and more new spreadsheets for specific expense categories. As the number of spreadsheets increases, George realizes that he needs some way to organize all these documents and pull them together for a given month's expense accounting. An Outline frame seems to be what he needs.

He creates an Outline frame and calls it Monthly Expenses. The frame begins with just two headings:

1   Fixed Expenses
2   Variable Expenses

To fill in the outline, he brings all of the various expense spreadsheet files from disk to the desktop. Figure 2.23 shows his desktop with the spreadsheet files in trays. He realizes that he will ultimately use the Move key (F7) to move the desktop frames into the outline. But before he can do this, he has to create new sublevels beneath each of the current headings. Consulting with Eileen, he learns that the correct keystroke combination is

Ctrl-In (+)   (to create a new outline level)

He presses these keys twice, with the highlight positioned over each of the major headings. Here is what he gets:

1   Fixed Expono00
 1.1
2   Variable Expenses
 2.1

Now he can move each of the Spreadsheet frames from the desktop into the appropriate outline sections. He begins by moving the Cost of Goods Sold spreadsheet, his only variable expense. He returns to the frame border and uses the Frames menu to add numbers and a

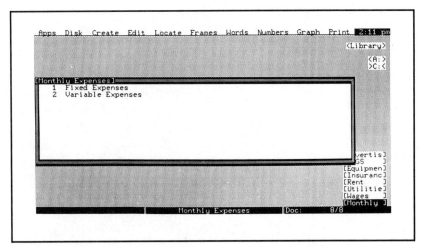

Figure 2.23: Developing an outline of expense spreadsheets

type indicator to his new outline:

```
1  Fixed Expenses
   1.1     (E)
2  Variable Expenses
   2.1     (E)
2.2 COGS (S)
```

Finally, he uses the Extend Select key (F6) to extend the highlight over all of the other spreadsheets on the desktop, so he can move them all at once into the Fixed Expenses category. He quickly deletes the two extraneous Empty frames, and smiles at a job well done:

```
1  Fixed Expenses
   1.1  Advertising (S)
   1.2  Equipment Loans (S)
   1.3  Equipment Maintenance (S)
   1.4  Insurance (S)
   1.5  Rent (S)
   1.6  Utilities (S)
   1.7  Wages (S)
2  Variable Expenses
   2.1  COGS (S)
```

SHARING DATA AMONG THE SPREADSHEETS

Eileen looks over George's shoulder on the way to the kitchen and asks him what he's doing. He's delighted to have the chance to show her how he's been able to use Framework III's outlining capabilities.

But Eileen points out that he's forgotten the most important part. Outlining is, of course, a great way to bring together groups of related documents—to organize them, to save them on disk together, and to print them in a single printing operation. But in spreadsheet work, the most useful function of all is Framework III's ability to link different spreadsheets for exchanging data—and, in this case, to produce a complete summary of all the various expense categories.

Eileen leans over George's shoulder to add one final frame to the outline:

```
3 Summary of Expenses (S)
```

She tells him that this summary spreadsheet can be organized to take bottom-line data from each of the other spreadsheets in the outline and produce a total expense figure for the month. If he then made changes in the detail spreadsheets, the summary would automatically be updated.

We'll have to wait until Chapter 3 to pursue Eileen's idea about spreadsheets. In the meantime, let's take a quick look at a few more features of Framework III.

EXPLORING FURTHER

RESET NUMBERS

Framework III creates new outlines starting with heading 1 and automatically numbering upward. But suppose you are adding the current outline frame to another one later on, or suppose you will be adding sections in the middle of the outline, and you want to show the numbers as they will appear, but leave out any entries that haven't been completed yet.

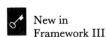 New in Framework III

You can change the numbering of any part of an outline by selecting Reset Numbering to. You will find Reset Numbering to in the Frame Options submenu. To reset outline numbers, press

Ctrl-F   (to open the Frame menu)

F   (to open the Frame Options submenu)

R   (to select Reset Numbering to)

Now you can enter the desired outline level.

There are three ways to reset the numbering—by the whole document, by a single frame (heading), or by multiple headings:

- To reset the numbering on a whole outline, press Out (–) to reach the frame border, then select Reset Numbering and type a number to set the beginning outline level.

- To reset the numbering for a single heading, simply highlight that heading and follow the procedure to reset the numbering.

- To reset the numbering for several headings, first use Extend Select (F6) to choose which headings to change, then follow the procedure to change the numbering.

If you want to change the numbering back to the way Framework III originally did it, place the cursor in the frame border and reset the numbering to 0.

OPENING SPECIFIC OUTLINE LEVELS

Sometimes you will have an outline that contains many levels, and it may become difficult to view the information when all the sublevels are displayed. You could move from one heading to another and close the lower levels, but now, with Framework III, there is an easier way to select the level of an outline to display.

To open an outline to the third level, press:

Ctrl-F	(to open the Frame menu)
F	(to open the Frame Options submenu)
O	(to select Open to Depth of)
3	(to open to level 3)
Return	(to accept the new setting and return to the desktop)

You'll notice that the current level is displayed in brackets to the right of the menu choice.

INDENTING LABELS

New in
Framework III

Although Framework III automatically indents subheadings in an outline frame, a new feature lets you choose how many spaces to indent. You can change the spacing for a single outline heading and all its subheadings, or select several main headings. The default setting is a three-space indent. Move to the frame border to change the indentations for the whole outline.

To change the indentation on an outline, heading, or selection to five spaces, press:

Ctrl-F   (to open the Frame menu)

F   (to open the Frame Options menu)

I   (to select Indent Labels)

5   (to change the indentations to five spaces)

Return   (to accept the new value and return to the workspace)

MULTIPLE-LINE FRAME LABELS

At the beginning of this chapter, we learned how to enter a label onto the border of a frame. We learned that a frame label serves to identify the frame on the desktop and to supply a file name when you store the frame on disk.

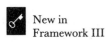 New in Framework III

Actually, frame labels may consist of many lines of information, even though only the first line is ordinarily displayed on the frame's border. In Framework III, you can not only create multiple-line labels, but you can also display them on your outlines if you set Multi-line Labels from the Frame Options submenu. From time to time, you may find it useful to enter several lines of notes into the label of a frame, simply as comments—to remind yourself of the information that the frame contains. In other cases, the multiple lines may serve to create a more complete outline with explanations of important headings.

For example, let's add a few sentences to the label of George's Monthly Expenses outline. To move the current label back to the edit line, you simply press the spacebar, as we learned earlier. Now, to expand the label into more lines, you press the Zoom key (F9). Framework III devotes the entire screen to the frame label and gives you the chance to enter any information there that you want to save along with the frame itself.

Figure 2.24 shows some notes we might want to keep in the label of the Monthly Expenses Outline frame. Once they are stored there, these notes are available for reading at any time. All you have to do is place the cursor on the frame border and press

Spacebar   (to move the label to the edit line)

Zoom (F9)   (to give the whole screen to the label)

Press the Zoom key again to return to the normal view of the desktop.

If Multi-line Labels is not currently set on, or if the frame you are viewing is the outermost one, you won't see the new lines of the label. To view the whole new label, press

Ctrl-F   (to open the Frame menu)

F   (to open the Frame Options submenu)

M   (to set Multi-line Labels on)

Of course, if you select Multi-line Labels when it is already on, you will turn it off.

If the multiple-line label does not seem to fit well in the outline, use Wrap Labels for Indentation from the Frame Options menu to create a neat appearance for any unsightly labels, as shown in Figure 2.25.

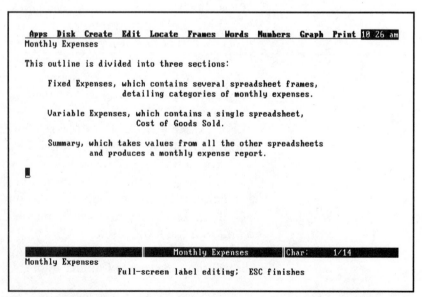

Figure 2.24: A multiple-line frame label

Figure 2.25: Wrapping multiple-line frame labels

DRAGGING AND SIZING FRAMES

Two function keys that we haven't discussed yet are Drag and Size. These keys allow you to slide a frame into a new position and change the size of a frame on the desktop. Their respective actions are both amusing and useful.

To use the Drag key, place the highlight on the border of the frame you want to move. Press the Drag key, F3. Then use the ↑, ↓, →, and ← keys to move the frame to any new location on the desktop. Press the Return key to complete the move.

The Size key has applications throughout Framework III. To use it with a frame, make sure the highlight is on the border and then press the Size key (F4). The → key increases the horizontal length of the frame's area on the desktop; the ↓ key increases the vertical height. Likewise, the ← and ↑ keys *decrease* the size of the frame.

Both sizing and dragging operations can be amplified by pressing the Ctrl key at the same time as an arrow key. When you've pressed the Size key (F4), the Ctrl key, in conjunction with an arrow key, increases or decreases the size of a frame by several screen rows or text columns. You can use the Ctrl-arrow keys to quickly make major adustments, and then use an arrow key alone to fine-tune the size of your frame. In addition, pressing the Size key (F4) twice will expand the selected frame so that it fills the entire desktop.

When you've selected Drag (F3), the Ctrl key amplifies the movements of the selected frame so that it jumps across the screen at larger intervals. If you make a mistake and want to return your frame to its original size or position, press Escape instead of Return, and your desktop will be restored as though you had never performed the operation.

Create several experimental frames, and play with the Size and Drag keys. You'll be amused with the results. You can switch from one of these functions to the other without pressing Return first. Pressing the Escape key returns the frame to its original size and positions.

These keys can also be used with frames contained in an Outline frame. Normally, frames in an outline are arranged in a column, but you can use an option in the Frames menu to allow you to move frames horizontally in an outline. The option is

    – – **Allow Free Dragging**

You can turn this option on for a given frame by pressing

    Ctrl-F   (to open the Frames menu)

    A   (to allow free dragging)

Dragging and sizing frames in an outline can be useful when you want to arrange—and print—information in parallel columns. Figure 2.26 shows an example of this—an alternative way of presenting Eileen's party tray flier. This display was produced by reducing the size of the Word frame, on the left, and dragging the Spreadsheet frame up to the side of the Word frame. Of course, you must do this sort of work in Frames view rather than in Outline view.

Just as on the desktop, Framework III allows you to correct your mistakes easily if dragging frames inside a containing frame produces unintended results. (For example, if your free-drag frames overlap on the screen, their contents will also overlap when you print the frames.) An additional option on the Frames menu, labeled

    – – – –Put into Column

will restore your frames to their original arrangement, lined up in a column against the left side of the containing frame.

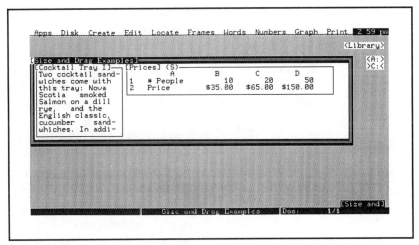

Figure 2.26: Dragging and sizing frames in an outline

The flexibility that the Drag and Size keys give you will also be useful when you want to display several independent frames (frames that are not within an outline) on the desktop at once.

SNAKING COLUMNS

New in
Framework III

In Framework III, you can use newspaper-style snaking columns in outlines. Now you can have text flow from one column to another. A built-in macro (Alt-F7) will automatically set up the necessary frames for you, or you can do so manually.

Snaked columns work by allowing text to flow from one frame to another, but the frames must be at the same level—within the same containing frame. Therefore, you must have at least three frame levels for snaked columns—the document, the containing ("page") frame, and the column frames.

To set up snaked columns manually, you must follow these steps:

1. Create a document frame and then, within it, a separate frame for the first page of the outline document that will have the flowing columns.

2. Within the page frame, create column frames the exact size of the printed columns you want. To do so, change to Frame

view by pressing View (F10), if necessary, then use Size (F4) and Drag (F3).

3. Next, select one of the column frames and turn on Snaked Columns by selecting it from the Frames menu's Frame Options submenu. This will automatically turn on Allow Free Dragging and turn off Display Labels.

Figure 2.27 shows an example of snaked columns.

You can instruct Framework III to create new pages automatically when you fill the last column in an existing page frame. To do so, select Automatic Page Creation from the Frame Options submenu. When you have reached the end of the last column in a page, another identical page is automatically created, and the text flows into it.

When you work with text in snaked columns, you can treat it as if it were all in the same frame. If you insert text, it pushes other text ahead of it through all the linked columns and pages. If you delete text, the following text will move back. You can also move through the text using standard cursor-movement commands such as PgUp and PgDn.

You can use snaked columns with other frames to create sophisticated layouts. For instance, you could create a layout that mixed free-floating snaked column frames with graphic frames, as shown in Figure 2.28. In this way, you could cause the text to flow around the graphic frame.

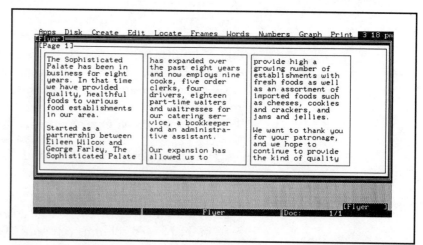

Figure 2.27: Setting up page and column frames for snaked columns

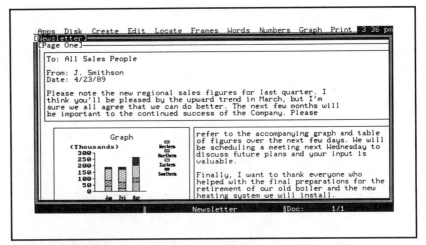

Figure 2.28: Creating a layout with text flowing around a graph

OTHER WAYS OF LABELING OUTLINE COMPONENTS

In addition to the number labels discussed earlier in this chapter, Framework III gives you the option of labeling your outline headings and subheadings in the traditional—rather than the technical—style, which you probably learned in elementary school. To select this option, choose

– – – –Label Roman Numerals

from the Frames menu. Figure 2.29 shows an outline with several levels of nesting, with traditional-style heading numbers.

Moreover, you can mix traditional, technical, and unnumbered sections in the same outline if it suits your purposes to do so. Remember that Framework III's menu commands operate only on what is selected. Thus, you can use different numbering systems for different parts of your outline by selecting the major heading of the section you want to change and toggling the *Label Roman Numerals* and *Number Labels* options on and off. Try experimenting with these options before you use them in a frame you intend to keep, because the results can be confusing if you're not careful.

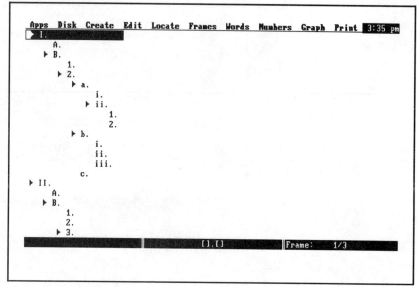

Figure 2.29: Outline with traditional numbering

DISPLAYING DISK SUBDIRECTORIES IN AN OUTLINE FORM

Finally, Framework III has incorporated its outlining capability into its display of disk subdirectories. Recent versions of the PC disk operating system, PC-DOS (or MS-DOS on compatibles), have allowed the creation of subdivisions of storage areas on a disk. This feature is designed primarily for organizing the relatively large area on a hard disk, but it can also be used with floppy disks.

PC-DOS gives you ways to create subdirectories and to store files in them as though these subdirectories were separate disks. When you have more files than can fit on a single screen directory listing, you may find it helpful to organize the files under several subdirectories. Framework III, in turn, supports the use of subdirectories. If you use a data disk in Framework III that contains subdirectories, the disk frame will display those directories in an outline form when you open them. Subdirectories have a triangle to the left of the name in the listing.

Figure 2.30 shows an example of a subdirectory outline. Only one of the subdirectories in this outline is open, revealing the names of the

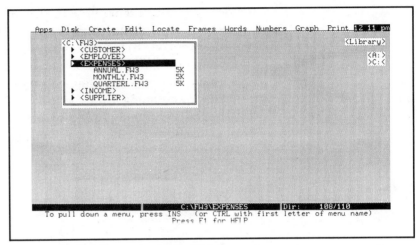

Figure 2.30: Subdirectories in the Disk frame

files it contains. Many of the keystrokes that we learned for controlling outlines also apply to the use of subdirectories in Framework III. For example, you can *open* a subdirectory by placing the highlight over its name in the disk drive cabinet and pressing the Return key. (For more information about Framework III's DOS file and directory functions, see the section in Chapter 1 on saving frames.)

Once a subdirectory is open, you can load frames onto the desktop in the normal way. Place the highlight over the file or files you want to read, and press Return.

You can designate a given subdirectory as the *current* directory, for default disk operations, in the following way: Place the highlight over the directory and press

Ctrl-Return   (to designate a default directory)

SUMMARY

Framework III gives you complete control over the creation of outlines, whether you are using the outlining process to record your extemporaneous thought processes or to organize a group of important business documents. You can start an outline with either an Outline or an Empty frame. You can add new headings, delete headings, create new sublevels, rearrange portions of the outline, zoom in on details of the outline, view the frames of an outline, change the sizes of frames, drag the frames horizontally and vertically, and even flow text from one frame to another—an impressive array of powers.

Outlining is a general, almost abstract kind of task that can apply in specific ways to everything you do in Framework III. We'll be returning to outlining as we move on to Framework III's productivity components: spreadsheet programming, word processing, database management, and telecommunications.

Spreadsheets

OVERVIEW

INTRODUCTION

SPREADSHEET PROGRAMMING MEANS DESIGNING tables of numbers that allow Framework III to do all the necessary arithmetic to summarize, evaluate, and explore the meaning of those numbers. A skillfully designed spreadsheet table will always respond arithmetically to your requirements, even when those requirements change over time. In Chapter 1, we discussed some of the advantages you will enjoy in using Framework III spreadsheets:

- You can minimize the tedium of performing repetitive arithmetic operations on groups of numbers.

- You can easily explore "what-if" scenarios; that is, you can find out how specific calculated values will change in response to changes in the raw data those calculations are based upon.

- You can instantly produce a variety of presentation-quality graphs from any table of numbers.

In this chapter, we will study examples of all these activities. The screen in Figure 3.1 shows an empty Spreadsheet frame. Let's briefly review how Framework III organizes the rows and columns of a spreadsheet.

Notice first that Framework III identifies each column with a letter of the alphabet, starting with A, and each row with a number, starting with 1. The intersection of a row and a column is called a *cell;* in each cell, you can store a single data item. The *address* of a cell is the name by which you can refer to the value the cell contains. An address consists of a cell's column letter and row number. For example, the cell at the intersection of column C and row 4 is called C4.

In each cell of a spreadsheet, you can enter data in one of three forms:

1. *Labels,* which you might create to explain the significance of the rows and columns of numbers (labels can consist of combinations of letters, symbols, and numbers)

Figure 3.1: An empty Spreadsheet frame

2. *Numbers,* upon which you can ultimately expect to perform various arithmetic operations

3. *Formulas,* which perform the arithmetic calculations of your spreadsheet

One of the most important things you will learn in this chapter is how to write formulas to perform arithmetic on the numbers in your spreadsheets. Most formulas you'll write for a given cell will contain *references* to the values in other cells. For example, the following formula contains references to the values stored in three different cells, and it results in a single number that is calculated from these cells:

+A2 + B2 − C2

This formula instructs Framework III as follows: ''Start with the value stored in cell A2, add the value stored in cell B2, and then subtract the value stored in cell C2.'' The numeric *result* of this formula will be stored in whichever cell you enter the formula itself.

We'll be studying exactly how to enter a formula into a cell, how to edit that formula if necessary, and—most importantly—how to *copy* the formula into other cells, to produce new calculated values in your spreadsheet.

To make formula writing even more powerful and versatile, Framework III supplies you with a large set of special-purpose tools that you can work with; these tools are called *functions*. We'll be introducing several categories of functions in this chapter, including the following:

- *Statistical functions,* which are used to find a variety of statistical values—sums and averages, the largest and smallest values in a group of numbers, and even complex statistics such as the variance and standard deviation of a group of numbers

- *Numeric functions,* which are used to round off values, take square roots, and work in higher mathematical realms such as trigonometry and exponentials

- *Financial functions,* which can be used to compute a surprising range of simple and difficult financial values: for example, mortgage payments, the present value of an investment, or the internal rate of return of a business project

- *Date functions,* which allow you to incorporate dates into your spreadsheets and perform *date arithmetic*—such as finding the number of days between two dates

Framework III also gives you many important ways to control the appearance and organization of your spreadsheet; for example:

- You can change the width of columns, to accommodate more or fewer characters per cell.

- You can move values or blocks of values from one place to another in your spreadsheet.

- You can insert or delete entire rows or columns.

- You can determine the *style* in which numbers will be presented on your spreadsheet—dollars and cents, percentages, scientific notation, and so on.

Exercising this control involves learning to use Framework III's menus and function keys. As promised, the use of these menus and keys will already seem familiar to you after your work with Outline frames.

Finally, as you work on spreadsheets, you should keep in mind the essential philosophy behind the design of Framework III: the best way to approach a large, complex project is to divide it into small, relatively simple tasks.

Other spreadsheet programs give you just one large spreadsheet area to work in. If you want to divide your current work into sections, you must set aside different blocks of cells inside that single spreadsheet to perform the various tasks; however, this can lead to confusion.

In Framework III, you can have many Spreadsheet frames on the desktop at once, with each one just the right size for the task it performs. Since you can give each frame a name, you can always locate the specific spreadsheet you want to examine or work with. Furthermore, a given spreadsheet on the desktop can contain references to one or more values contained in another spreadsheet; thus, you can *link* spreadsheets by sharing values among them.

We'll explore all of these features in this chapter. Let's begin by finding out how to create a Spreadsheet frame and enter data into it.

CREATING A SPREADSHEET

Like any other type of frame, a new Spreadsheet frame is placed on the desktop through the Create menu. Three different options on the Create menu are involved in the process of making a spreadsheet; you can study these options in Figure 3.2.

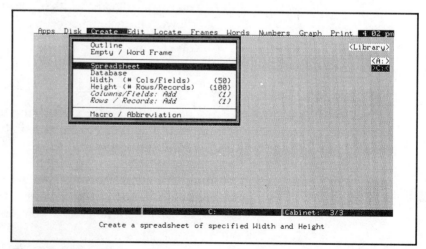

Figure 3.2: The Create menu

The central section of the Create menu begins with the Spreadsheet option. Selecting this option results in the appearance of a new Spreadsheet frame on the desktop. The sequence of keystrokes that creates a spreadsheet is

Ctrl-C   (to open the Create menu)

S   (to create a Spreadsheet frame)

But before you begin any new spreadsheet job, you will want to think about the dimensions of the spreadsheet you'll be working in.

HOW MANY ROWS? HOW MANY COLUMNS?

How many rows and columns will be required in your new spreadsheet? Exactly how big is the table of numbers you are planning to work with? Different numeric tasks call for differently organized spreadsheets; it is up to you to plan specifically for a given table of numbers before you begin your work. Framework III allows you to plan Spreadsheet frames that will exactly fit the job for which they were created.

Consider a few examples. Figures 3.3 to 3.5 show three tables of numbers, dealing with three different subjects. All three include combinations of numeric input data and arithmetically calculated values, so they would all be good candidates for Spreadsheet frames. One of the tables is oriented vertically, one horizontally, and the

```
Names                        Scores
Alcott, Susan                 92.3
Bobs, John                    59.3
Carlson, Daniel               72.0
Duncan, Rober                 78.9
Everet, Elinore               82.4
Fineman, Jack                 80.2
Himes, Liz                    95.0
Jackson, Don                  66.4
Katz, May                     62.9
Mann, April                   55.0
Nesbit, Jerry                 93.0
Ralston, Pat                  71.0
Smithson, Billy               70.2
Stern, Mary                   80.1
Wu, Tim                       85.0
Average Score-----------------76.2
Best Score--------------------95.0
Worst Score-------------------55.0
```

Figure 3.3: A table of test scores

third has more of a two-dimensional appearance. Let's think about how we would go about planning to create these tables in Spreadsheet frames.

The table in Figure 3.3 is a list of students' test scores; it records the scores and then analyzes them in a brief set of statistics at the bottom of the table. The table contains only two columns—one for the students' names, and a second for the scores themselves. There are 15 students, but the table contains 19 rows in all—with the extra 4 rows containing the headings for the columns and the statistics at the bottom of the table.

In contrast, Figure 3.4 shows a horizontally oriented table, containing 2 rows and 14 columns. The table contains conversions between degrees centigrade and degrees Fahrenheit, over a range from freezing to boiling. The first column has labels identifying the two rows of figures. Each subsequent column juxtaposes a Fahrenheit temperature with its equivalent in centigrade.

Finally, Figure 3.5 contains a table of numbers representing quarterly income calculations for a small business. This table has five columns and seven rows. Notice that the first row is devoted to column headings—identifying the four quarterly periods—and the first column describes the various elements of each quarter's activity.

Each of these three tables has different dimensions. So before you create a Spreadsheet frame for any of these tables, you would want to

F	32	47	62	77	92	107	122	137	152	167	182	197	212
C	0	8	17	25	33	42	50	58	67	75	83	92	100

Figure 3.4: A temperature conversion table

```
               Consulting and Speaking Activities
                    Quarterly Income Statement

             Quarter-1   Quarter-2    Quarter-3   Quarter-4

 Earnings  $2,367.82   $7,513.87  $12,875.44   $6,321.87
 Expenses    $546.92     $832.88   $2,145.72   $1,287.22
      Net  $1,820.90   $6,680.99  $10,729.72   $5,034.65
 Est.Tax
      31%    $564.48   $2,071.11   $3,326.21   $1,560.74
After Tax  $1,256.42   $4,609.88   $7,403.51   $3,473.91
```

Figure 3.5: Quarterly income statement

specify the precise size of the spreadsheet required. As you can see in Figure 3.2, the Create menu has two options that allow you to do this:

Width (# Cols/Fields)   {50}
Height (# Rows/Records)   {100}

The numbers in braces after each of these options show you the *default* values Framework III uses for the dimensions of a spreadsheet. Unless you specify otherwise, Framework III will create a spreadsheet that is 50 columns wide by 100 rows high. Depending on the task you have in mind, these dimensions may be too large or too small.

If you want to change these specifications, you must do so *before* you invoke the Spreadsheet option of the Create menu. To change the dimensions, choose the Width and Height options in turn; for example:

Ctrl-C   (to open the Create menu)

W   (to invoke the Width option)

At this point, the *current width value* will appear on the edit line, below the desktop, along with a message informing you that you are about to edit a value on the menu itself:

Width (# Cols/Fields) > > 50
Menu editing; RETURN finishes

To change the spreadsheet width setting, you simply enter the number of columns you want your new spreadsheet to contain and press the Return key. The new value will then be displayed on the Create menu. For example, if you change the width setting to five columns, the Width option will appear as

Width (# Cols/Fields)   {5}

Likewise, to change the height setting, you invoke the Height option on the Create menu and enter (on the edit line) the number of rows you want your spreadsheet to contain.

Here is an example of the entire process. Let's create a frame for the income table shown in Figure 3.5. The keys you should press are as follows:

Ctrl-C	(to open the Create menu)
W	(to invoke the Width option)
5	(to specify the number of columns)
Return	(to record the new width setting)
H	(to invoke the Height option)
7	(to specify the number of rows)
Return	(to record the new height setting)
S	(to create the spreadsheet)

Notice that the final step is to create the actual spreadsheet, by invoking the Spreadsheet option. This step results in your Spreadsheet frame appearing on the desktop.

The next time you open the Create menu (during the same session with Framework III), you will see the new settings you have just entered: 5 columns, 7 rows. To change these settings again for another new Spreadsheet frame, you go through the same process.

What happens if you discover, halfway through your work with a Spreadsheet frame, that you have not given it the correct dimensions? If your frame has too few—or too many—rows or columns, Framework III allows you to insert new elements or delete parts of the spreadsheet at any time. The Create menu has options for adding rows and columns:

```
Columns/Fields: Add      {1}
Rows/Records: Add        {1}
```

And the Edit menu has options for deleting rows and columns:

```
Columns/Fields: Remove
Rows/Records: Remove
```

We'll see how to use these options as we begin working with spreadsheets.

In Framework III, you can turn the column and row labels on or off in a Spreadsheet frame. To do so, select Display Labels from the

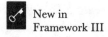
New in
Framework III

Frames menu. Display Labels is a toggle, so if labels are currently on and you select that option, they will be turned off. Normally, column and row labels will be on when you first start Framework III.

In summary, Framework III encourages you to create Spreadsheet frames whose dimensions are tailored to the tasks they are to perform. But as you work with spreadsheets, you can always increase or decrease the number of rows or columns if you find that your plans have changed.

Once your spreadsheet is on the desktop, you are ready to give the frame a label and then move inside to begin your work. To illustrate the material in the coming sections of this chapter, we are going to develop and work with the quarterly income statement shown in Figure 3.5. Imagine yourself in the following situation, explaining the need for this spreadsheet. You are a consultant and sometime lecturer, specializing in the use of personal computers in the office environment. You run this small business out of your home, where you have set up an office for yourself in the den. Your expenses are simple—they include supplies, transportation, and telephone costs. Because your office is in your home, you can also count a portion of your rent and utilities as a business expense.

It is now the end of your business year, and you wish to summarize the year's activities—partly to estimate your tax liability and partly to investigate the year's progress. Following the instructions outlined above, you have created an empty Spreadsheet frame, containing five columns, from A to E, and seven rows, 1 to 7.

With the highlight positioned on the frame's border, you enter the following label for the frame:

Quarterly Income

Now let's move inside the frame and begin working with spreadsheets.

MOVING AROUND THE SPREADSHEET

Several important keyboard functions work the same way with spreadsheets as with other frames. The In key (labeled +) moves the Framework III highlight into the spreadsheet itself. Likewise, the Out key (labeled –) moves you back up to the frame's border. Try moving back and forth a few times, and notice the changes that occur on the display screen as you move into the spreadsheet.

The highlight (which, you'll remember, always marks your current working place on the desktop) initially lands in cell A1, and it fills the entire cell with a reverse-video rectangle. Additional information about your location is supplied in the status panel. The central section of the panel tells you the current cell's full name:

Quarterly Income.A1

You can see that the full name consists of two elements separated by a period: the name of the Spreadsheet frame and the address of the cell you are in. While we are working inside the Spreadsheet frame, we can safely abbreviate this name to the cell address, A1.

The right side of the status panel supplies the current cell's location in a different form:

SS: 1/1

The letters SS stand for spreadsheet, and the numbers inform you that the highlight is located at the first column of the first row in the spreadsheet. As you move the highlight to new locations in the spreadsheet, you will see the messages in the status panel change in response.

As we have already noted, different areas of the desktop often give you the same information in different forms. This duplication is not superfluous: depending on the situation, you may find one kind of message more helpful than another.

Inside the spreadsheet, the most essential keys for moving the highlight from one cell to another are the four arrow keys: ←, →, ↑, and ↓. Recall that these keys act as direction keys only if the Num Lock key is toggled correctly. If you see the NUM message at the lower right corner of the screen, you are in the wrong mode. Press Num Lock to shift the direction keys into their cursor-movement mode.

Pressing one of the four arrow keys moves the highlight one cell in the direction indicated. These keys *autorepeat,* like the rest of the IBM PC keyboard: holding a key down for a few seconds is equivalent to pressing the key several times. If you hold an arrow key down, the highlight will be moved a number of columns or rows in the expected direction. (If you find the highlight—or the cursor—getting away from you, press Ctrl-Break to make it stop.)

But there are other, more controllable, ways to move the highlight several cells at a time. The Home and End keys, the PgUp and PgDn keys, and the Ctrl key, used in association with any one of the cursor-movement keys, are all special tools for moving the highlight more efficiently around the spreadsheet. Table 3.1 describes all these keys

Table 3.1: Keys for Moving the Spreadsheet Highlight

KEYS	ACTION
←, →, ↑, ↓	Moves the highlight one cell in the direction indicated.
Home	Moves the highlight to the first cell in the current row of cells.
End	Moves the highlight to the last cell in the current row of cells.
PgUp	Moves to top of current frame, then scrolls one entire frame up; or, in a spreadsheet that occupies less space than the frame, moves the highlight to the top row.
PgDn	Moves to bottom of current frame, then scrolls one entire frame down; or, in a spreadsheet that occupies less space than the frame, moves the highlight to the bottom row.
Ctrl-←, Ctrl-→, Ctrl-↑, Ctrl-↓	Moves the highlight to the beginning of the next block of data or the end of the current block of data.
Ctrl-Home	Moves the highlight to cell A1.
Ctrl-End	Moves the highlight to the cell at the lower right corner of the spreadsheet.
Ctrl-PgUp	Moves the highlight to the top row in the current column of cells.
Ctrl-PgDn	Moves the highlight to the bottom row in the current column of cells.
Return	Enters data, or moves the highlight one cell down.
Tab	Enters data and/or moves the highlight one cell to the right.
Shift-Tab	Enters data and/or moves the highlight one cell to the left.

and key combinations. You should spend some time practicing them before you read on. Some of the keys will make more sense once you have begun entering data into the spreadsheet; we will continue discussing them as we create our Quarterly Income spreadsheet.

There is one final characteristic to notice about moving the highlight. If the highlight is already located at one of the spreadsheet's boundaries—that is, at the first or last row or the first or last column—and you try to move the highlight outside the frame, the computer will beep gently at you, to let you know that you cannot move outside the defined dimensions of the spreadsheet.

The Zoom key (F9) also works with Spreadsheet frames. Our current spreadsheet is so small that we can see all of it within the frame on the desktop. But later, when we work with larger spreadsheets, it will be convenient to be able to devote the entire display screen to the rows and columns of data. Press the Zoom key once, and the usual elements of the desktop will disappear, giving way to a full-screen spreadsheet. Press Zoom again to redisplay the frame on the desktop.

Finally, a large spreadsheet will be *scrolled,* horizontally or vertically, as you move the highlight from place to place. Or, to mix metaphors a bit, the screen will become a *window* onto the spreadsheet, showing you a portion of the spreadsheet at a time. This will happen whenever you create a spreadsheet that has too many rows and columns to be displayed at once. When you move the highlight beyond the borders of the current display (not the actual borders of the spreadsheet), the window will move to show you new columns and rows. This is another effect we will explore later.

ENTERING DATA INTO THE SPREADSHEET

As we begin entering data into the spreadsheet, you'll discover that the data-entry techniques will vary, depending on whether you are entering labels, numbers, or formulas. Let's first enter the labels at the left of our Quarterly Income spreadsheet.

LABELS   Look again at Figure 3.5, and examine the five labels in the first column. They read as follows:

Earnings

Expenses

Net

Est.Tax

After Tax

(Notice that 31%, although it also appears in this column, is not a label but a number.) Since these labels begin in the second row of the table, the first one, *Earnings,* will go into cell A2. If your spreadsheet highlight is positioned at A1, press the ↓ key once to move to A2. (If you have moved to some other location in the spreadsheet, Ctrl-Home will move the highlight to cell A1.)

Enter the uppercase E of the first label. As soon as you do so, Framework III recognizes that you are entering a label—not a number or a formula—into this cell of the spreadsheet. The characters you enter into the label will appear on the edit line, above the following message:

Text editing; RETURN finishes

This message is important and is always worth noting when you begin entering a data item. It tells you what *type* of data Framework III is accepting from your input; in this case, the word *text* in the message confirms that this is a label. If you have to edit your work, you can use the arrow keys to move the edit cursor backward or forward, and the Backspace and Delete keys to delete characters, as we discussed in Chapter 2.

The Return key completes the data entry. After you press Return, the label you've entered will appear in the spreadsheet, at cell location A2. Now you are ready to move to cell A3 to enter the next label.

You have two choices for moving the highlight down the spreadsheet. The more obvious choice is the ↓ key. But if you are entering a long column of labels or numbers quickly, there is a more convenient key for moving down the column: the Return key. You have just hit the Return key once to complete the data entry; now simply hit it again to move down to the next cell. Touch typists will particularly appreciate this Framework III keyboard feature; you don't have to search around for the ↓ key between entering one columnar data item and the next.

Practice entering data into a column by typing the rest of the labels into column A:

Expenses	(the label)
Return	(to complete the data entry)
Return	(to move down one cell)
Net	(the label)
Return	(to complete the data entry)
Return	(to move down one cell)

and so on. For the moment, leave row 6, between *Est. Tax* and *After Tax,* blank.

We'll enter one more label before we begin placing numeric data in the spreadsheet: the column heading *Quarter-1*. From the highlight's current location, A7, there are several ways to move up to cell B1. One fast way is to press

Tab	(to move one cell to the right)
Ctrl-PgUp	(to move to the top of the spreadsheet)

The Tab key is an alternative to the → and ← keys. Pressing Tab by itself moves the highlight one cell to the right. Shift-Tab moves the highlight to the left.

You can also use Tab for data entry when you are entering adjacent values into a single row. Normally, you would have to press two keys between one entry and the next:

Return	(to complete the data entry)
→	(to move to the next cell to the right)

The Tab key takes the place of both of these keystrokes, entering the previous value and moving the highlight one cell over.

Once the Tab key has moved the highlight into cell B7, Ctrl-↑ will move it to the top of the spreadsheet. In Table 3.1, you can read about the use of the Ctrl key with the cursor-movement keys. These key combinations can be used for moving the highlight to the beginning of the next block of data, or to the end of the current block of data in your spreadsheet. At this point in our Quarterly Income spreadsheet, column B does not yet have any data in it. So Ctrl-↑ simply moves you up to row 1.

With the highlight at B1, enter the label

Quarter-1

Then press Return twice, once to complete the data entry and once to move down one cell. Now we're in a position to begin entering the numbers.

NUMERIC VALUES   Your consulting business showed earnings of $2,367.82 during the first quarter of the year. For the moment, enter this value as

2367.82

As soon as you press the key representing the first digit of this number, your data entry will appear on the edit line, below the desktop. You will also see the following message:

Formula/number editing; RETURN finishes

Because you began your data entry with a digit, Framework III immediately recognizes that you are entering a numeric value. As we proceed in this chapter, we'll discover other initial characters that will indicate to Framework III that you are entering a number—or a formula that will result in a number—into a cell.

Once again, you can edit the data before you press the Return key. When you complete the data entry, the number will appear in cell B2 as expected.

Press the Return key again to move the highlight down to cell B3. The expenses for the same quarter were $546.92, so enter that value (without the dollar sign) and press Return. When you do, the first four rows of your spreadsheet will appear as follows:

Quarter-1
Earnings   2367.82
Expenses   546.92
Net

Studying this data carefully, you can learn a good deal about the way Framework III normally displays data on the screen. Unless you specify otherwise, here are the rules Framework III follows:

- Labels are left-justified within the space of their respective cells; this means that the first character of the label appears in the very first, or leftmost, space of the cell.

- Numbers are right-justified within the space of their respective cells; however, Framework III always leaves one blank space after a number in a cell.

These are the *default* rules for data display; later in this chapter, we'll learn how you can change the way Framework III displays data to suit your own requirements.

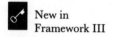 New in Framework III

With Framework III's new Entry Format for Data command (found in the Numbers menu), you can also preset cells or ranges for numeric input. Although this might not seem to be necessary, since it is so easy to enter numbers in the Spreadsheet frame, this preset format adds some features. For one, you can more easily enter labels that begin with numbers (for example, *1st Quarter* instead of *Quarter-1*). You don't have to press the spacebar first.

When you use Entry Formats to define a cell for numeric data, it means that the cell will read the first number as the cell value *regardless of whatever else you enter*.

For instance, cell entries of

4 bushels

and

more than 4 bushels

are read as the number 4. This format is more versatile, because you can add any text identifiers without changing the numeric content of the cell. If used in a formula, both of the cells mentioned above would function as the number 4. See later in this chapter for more information about Entry Format for Data.

With the first-quarter earnings and expenses stored in the spreadsheet, the next step is to find the net income for the company during the quarter—obviously, a simple matter of subtracting expenses from earnings. We'll use this simple calculation to examine the different techniques Framework III allows for entering formulas into the spreadsheet.

FORMULAS   Up to now, we have alternately used the words *name* or *address* to describe a cell indicator such as B2. Both of these terms, though perhaps informal, are correct: B2 is at once the name by which we can identify a certain cell and the column-row address at which we can find that cell. Now, however, it is time to introduce yet another, almost synonymous term: a cell *reference*.

A cell address that appears as part of a formula is called a reference. The distinction is simple but important: a cell reference stands for the *value that is contained in a certain cell,* whereas a cell address represents a location in the spreadsheet. In an arithmetic formula, a cell reference represents some actual numeric value that is currently stored somewhere in the spreadsheet. Now let's begin entering formulas.

Move the highlight down to cell B4, where the net income should appear. Knowing that a formula consists of arithmetic operations and cell references, your first inclination might be to enter the formula into B4 as follows:

B2 – B3

After all, B2 contains the earnings and B3 the expenses; what more can be required than to subtract one from the other? But if you were to enter the first character, B, of this formula as shown above, you would receive a surprising message at the bottom of the screen:

Text editing; RETURN finishes

Clearly, something is wrong; you do not mean this to be a text—or label—entry at all. How do you make Framework III understand that this is a formula—that B2 is a cell reference, representing a numeric value?

We have learned already that Framework III determines the *type* of any data entry from the first character of that entry. If the first character is a letter of the alphabet, Framework III assumes you are entering a *label* into the spreadsheet. If the first character is a digit,

Framework III assumes numeric data entry. So we have to find an initial character that will flag this data entry as an arithmetic formula rather than as text.

One solution is this: we can use the plus sign (+) as the initial character of a formula. Framework III reads this sign as the beginning of numeric or formula entry. (Notice that the plus sign is located on the same key as the equal sign on your keyboard, above and to the right of the P. Be careful to distinguish between this key and the In key, which is also labeled with a plus sign but is shaded gray.)

New in
Framework III

In Framework III, you can predefine a format for any cell or range of cells using Entry Format for Data in the Numbers menu. From the Entry Format for Data submenu, you can select one of seven preset formats:

- Unspecified (the default setting)
- Character (to enter labels, even if they begin with a number or other symbol)
- Numeric
- Date
- Time
- Logical (yes/no, true/false)
- Formula

Entry Formats are used primarily in databases (see Chapter 5), but they can also be used on a cell or range of cells in a Spreadsheet frame. We already saw how they can be used with numeric entries. Thus, if you know that a cell or range of cells will contain only formulas, you can predefine that cell or range using Entry Format for Data.

What do you do if you somehow get started in the wrong type of data entry (and you're not using predefined entry formats)? For example, what if you mistakenly begin your formula with a B rather than a + ? Two keys, Escape and Delete, will get you out of the error:

Escape   (to move out of the edit line)

Delete   (to delete the contents of the current cell)

After pressing these two keys, you can start your formula entry over again in an empty cell.

Looking back at the Quarterly Income spreadsheet, the highlight should still be positioned at cell B4. Begin the formula entry with the plus sign, and continue as follows:

+ B2 – B3

As soon as you enter the plus sign, Framework III displays the message you are looking for:

Formula/number editing; RETURN finishes

Framework III users could set the Entry Format for cell B4 to Formula, then enter:

B2 – B3

without the plus sign. Since the entry format is already set to Formula, you'll notice that the *Formula/number editing* message displays as soon as you enter the first letter of the formula. However, if you plan to use pointing (explained below) at the beginning of the formula, you may prefer to begin a formula entry with the + sign, even if you are using the Formula entry format.

When you complete the formula and hit the Return key, the *result* of the formula is instantly displayed in cell B4:

1820.90

In summary, to write effective formulas you have to keep three things in mind:

1. You must use the Formula entry format, or choose an appropriate initial character for the data entry, so that Framework III will know that you are typing a formula, not a label. (Besides +, you can use –, *, /, @, or a number.)

2. You must create an arithmetic expression that, when evaluated, will result in the correct calculation.

3. You must find the correct cell references to put into the formula.

When you enter such a formula into a cell, Framework III displays the numeric result of the formula in the cell. If you want to reexamine the formula itself, you will find it displayed in the first section of the status panel.

Typing cell references into a formula is only one of the ways you can enter a formula into a spreadsheet. Another (often simpler) way is to use *pointing*. Framework III allows you to indicate the cells that go into a formula by moving the spreadsheet highlight to those cells.

Let's reenter the formula for the net income, this time using the pointing technique. Delete the current contents of cell B4 by pressing the Delete key while the highlight is positioned over the cell.

As before, you should first type a plus sign, to begin the formula entry. The plus sign will appear on the edit line, followed by the edit cursor. The highlight temporarily disappears from the spreadsheet. From the edit line, the ↑ (or ↓) key initiates pointing in Framework III. As soon as you press ↑, several changes occur on the screen:

1. The highlight returns to the spreadsheet, to cell B4.

2. You will see the following message appear below the desktop:

    CURSOR POINTING; RETURN finishes

3. The formula on the edit line will suddenly expand to

    +B4

When you point to a cell in the spreadsheet, that cell automatically becomes a reference in the formula you are building. Pointing thus provides you with a visual way of telling Framework III exactly which references you want included in a formula.

But B4 is not the reference you want in this formula, so now you must use the arrow keys to move the spreadsheet highlight to the cell you do want to appear in the formula. In this case the cell is B2, representing first-quarter earnings. When you move the highlight up to this cell, your formula on the edit line will change to

    +B2

The next element of the formula is a minus sign, to subtract the expenses from the earnings. Press the minus key, and the cursor returns again to the edit line; your formula has become

+ B2 –

Now you can use pointing again to produce the second reference in your formula. Press the ↑ key. The highlight returns to the cell that you pointed to previously, and your formula on the edit line becomes

+ B2 – B2

To point at the correct cell on the spreadsheet, press the ↓ key to move the highlight down one cell and then press Return to complete the pointing. You will finally see the correct formula on the edit line:

+ B2 – B3

Press Return once more to complete the formula entry. The result is the same as before; the net income for the quarter appears in cell B4 as

1820.90

The formula for the cell appears in the first section of the status panel.

To summarize, here is the correct sequence of keystrokes for entering the net income formula in cell B4, using the pointing technique:

+	(to begin formula entry)
↑	(to initiate pointing)
↑, twice	(to move the highlight to the earnings cell)
–	(to continue the formula)
↑	(to initiate pointing again)
↓	(to move to the expenses cell)
Return	(to complete the pointing)
Return	(to enter the formula)

Two more calculations remain to complete the first quarter of the Quarterly Income spreadsheet—the estimated taxes and the after-tax income. These two values go into cells B6 and B7, respectively. But before we can perform these calculations, we have to enter a value for the estimated tax rate into cell A6.

Move the highlight to A6. Let's say that, based on last year's taxes, you are estimating a tax rate of 31 percent. Into cell A6, enter the value

.31

Now, you know that the estimated taxes will be calculated as

net income × estimated tax rate

and the after-tax income will be

net income − estimated taxes

Let's use the pointing technique to translate these two calculations into spreadsheet formulas with appropriate cell references.

Position the highlight at cell B6 to enter the formula that will calculate your estimated tax. Here are the keystrokes you will use to enter the formula by pointing:

+	(to begin the formula)
↑	(to initiate pointing)
←	(to point at cell A6)
*	(to multiply)
↑	(to initiate pointing again)
→	(to move into column B)
↑, twice	(to point at cell B4)
Return	(to complete the pointing)
Return	(to complete the formula)

These keystrokes result in the formula

+A6*B4

Notice that the asterisk character represents *multiplication* on your computer. (You can type this symbol either by pressing Shift-8 or by pressing the asterisk key on or near the numeric keypad.) The result of this formula, your estimated tax liability for the quarter, is displayed in cell B6 as

564.48

You will be able to complete the final formula on your own, using pointing. Just remember these things:

- Begin your formula with a + character, so Framework III will know that this is a formula, not a label (or use the Entry Format for Data option on the Numbers menu).

- Use the ↑ key to move the cursor from the edit line to the spreadsheet, initiating the pointing process.

- Use the arrow keys to point to the correct cells.

- Press Return twice—once to complete the pointing, and a second time to complete the formula entry.

The formula that goes into cell B7 is

+ B4 − B6

and the value that results is

1256.42

Figure 3.6 shows how your spreadsheet should look at this point. You can review the three formulas you have written into the spreadsheet by moving the highlight over cells B4, B6, and B7; whereas the spreadsheet cell shows you the *result* of the formula, the first section of the status panel shows you the formula itself. As you examine the three formulas, remember the two techniques you used to create them:

1. Typing them character by character onto the edit line.

2. Using the *pointing* method to indicate the references in the formulas.

There is no difference in the actual formulas you create using either of these techniques; the only difference is in the convenience of creating the formula.

With these three formulas written into the spreadsheet, you can now begin to experiment with Framework III's ability to respond to changes in the original data. For example, what if you find that you've entered the wrong number for the quarter's expenses? Or what if you want to modify your estimate for the tax rate? If you make changes like these, Framework III automatically recalculates any formulas that are dependent on the values you change.

Give it a try. Move the highlight to cell B3 and enter a new expense figure—say, 653.82. As soon as you enter the new amount, all the values below B3 in the column will be recalculated. This is because all of the spreadsheet's formulas are directly or indirectly related to the expense amount.

Now move the highlight to cell A6 and enter a new tax rate—.27, for example. Once again, the formulas that are dependent on the tax rate will be recalculated, and new values will appear in the appropriate cells.

These experiments begin to give you an idea of the real value of a spreadsheet. Change the original data, and Framework III automatically recalculates all formulas that depend on that data.

Before you continue, go back and reenter the original values for the expenses (546.92) and the tax rate (.31). In the next section, we'll

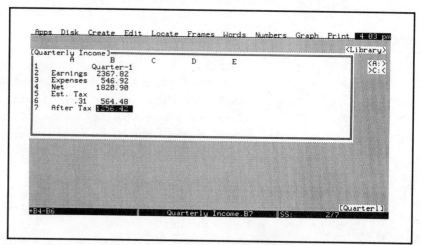

Figure 3.6: Quarterly Income spreadsheet, first quarter

discover ways of *editing* the data that is currently stored in a spreadsheet cell.

EDITING DATA IN THE SPREADSHEET

You can change the data stored in a cell whenever you want in Framework III. You have just seen one simple way to do so: simply move the highlight to the cell you want to change and enter a new value. When you begin the new data entry, the previous value disappears from the cell and the cursor moves down to the edit line, where you can type and edit the replacement.

In many instances, however, you might prefer to revise the current value of a cell rather than replace it with a new value. Framework III conveniently allows you to move the current value of a cell down to the edit line, where you can revise that value. You press one of two keys, depending on the type of data you are planning to edit:

- *The spacebar*—to edit labels
- *The Edit key (F2)*—to edit numbers or formulas

In either case, the current value of the cell appears on the edit line, where you can use the usual keys to edit it: the arrow keys, to move the edit cursor to a specific location in the value; the End key, to move the cursor to the end of the value, or the Home key, to move back to the beginning; the Delete or Backspace key, to delete characters; and the digit or character keys, to *insert* new characters into the value.

When you have made the necessary changes, press the Return key to complete the editing session. The new version of the data will return to its original cell in the spreadsheet.

Let's try editing some data in the Quarterly Income spreadsheet. Begin by moving the highlight to cell A6, where the estimated tax rate is located. Because this is a number, you will press the Edit key (F2) to change it. When you do so, you will see the number appear on the edit line, with a message below it, as follows:

.31
Formula/Number editing; RETURN finishes

The edit cursor is positioned over the first character of the value, the decimal point. Let's say you want to change the value to .33. Press the following sequence of keys:

End   (to move the cursor to the end of the value)

Backspace   (to erase the last digit)

3   (to insert a new digit)

Return   (to complete the edit)

When you press the Return key, several things will happen in the spreadsheet. First, the new value will appear in cell A6. Then, because two formulas in the spreadsheet depend on the value, the values produced by those formulas will automatically be recalculated.

You can try a similar experiment on a label on the spreadsheet. Position the highlight over a cell that contains a label, and press the spacebar. The label will appear on the edit line above this message:

Text editing; RETURN finishes

After you have tried editing the spreadsheet, restore its original values so that your version once again looks like Figure 3.6.

These particular editing experiments may seem insignificant because the values and formulas are so short. But ultimately you will be entering longer and more complex labels, values, and formulas into the cells of your spreadsheet, and the ability to edit them will become very convenient.

The Edit key (F2) and the spacebar are also useful in another situation. Sometimes when you begin a new data entry, you will want a way to specify, in advance, the type of data you are planning: label, number, or formula. The Edit key or the spacebar will move the cursor down to the edit line even when the current cell is empty.

Think of an example—imagine, for a moment, that you are creating a spreadsheet that records and totals a set of invoices. You have set aside one column for the invoice numbers and another column for the invoice amounts. Your invoice numbers each consist of three digits, a hyphen, and three letters; for example:

312-ABC

Version Note

You can use the new Framework III Numbers menu command, Entry Format for Data, to preset any cell or range to the Character format. Then, when you enter *312-ABC,* Framework will treat it automatically as a label.

Now even though *you* call this value a number, Framework III will consider it a label. Framework III has no way to deal numerically with a value that contains nonnumeric characters such as ABC. It will not accept your invoice numbers unless you enter them as text labels.

But the problem is this: as soon as you begin the data entry with a digit, Framework III puts you into the numeric data entry mode:

Formula/number editing; RETURN finishes

You need to tell Framework III that this is not a number but rather a label entry.

The solution is simply to press the spacebar before you begin the data entry. When you do so, you will see the correct entry message:

Label editing; RETURN finishes

Then you can enter the invoice number, beginning with a digit, and Framework III will accept it as a text label rather than a number.

Returning once again to our Quarterly Income spreadsheet, let's discover an alternative way of looking at cell references.

ENGLISH NAME REFERENCES

Position the highlight on cell B2 of the spreadsheet. In the central section of the status panel, you should now see the following name:

Quarterly Income.B2

This tells you that the highlight is on cell B2 of the Quarterly Income spreadsheet.

Framework III actually gives you two different ways to look at cell references in a spreadsheet. The first way, as we have seen throughout this chapter, uses a cell's column and row location, such as B2. The second way, called *English name references,* depends on the labels that you enter into the first column and first row of your spreadsheet. Because we have labels in column A and row 1, we can examine some English name references in our Quarterly Income spreadsheet.

Anytime the highlight is inside the spreadsheet, you can shift between normal address references and English name references by typing an exclamation point. Do so now, with the highlight positioned at cell B2, and you will see the following message in the central section of the status panel:

Income.[Quarter-1].Earnings

The *full* English-language name of this cell—even though there is not room in the status panel to display the whole name—is

Quarterly Income.[Quarter-1].Earnings

In this name, you can see that the column heading, Quarter-1, has taken the place of the column letter, B; and the row label, Earnings, has taken the place of the row number, 2. You will also notice some unfamiliar punctuation. The normal cell reference, B2, contains no punctuation at all. The English name reference contains a period between the two elements of the name, and the first part of the name, Quarter-1, is surrounded by square brackets.

You can see additional English name references by moving the highlight down column B. For example, the English names of cells B3 and B4 are

[Quarter-1].Expenses

and

[Quarter-1].Net

respectively. You will see these names displayed in the central section of the status panel.

What is the advantage of using English name references rather than the simpler address references? English names—which you supply yourself in the form of labels on your spreadsheet—are more descriptive and meaningful than the rather abstract address references. It's not hard to see which of the following two expressions is intuitively clearer—the English name reference formula:

[Quarter-1].Earnings + [Quarter-2].Earnings

or the address reference formula:

        + B2 + C2

On the other hand, the design of a spreadsheet may not always lend itself to the use of English name references. Sometimes it is not convenient to devote the first column and the first row of the spreadsheet to descriptive labels—which is a requirement if you want to use English name references. Or, depending largely on personal preference, address references may just seem simpler. On a small spreadsheet, such as the Quarterly Income spreadsheet, you may have no trouble at all remembering that cell B2 contains the business earnings for the first quarter of the year.

Whichever system of references you use, always remember that they represent the same thing. The two formats

        [Quarter-1].Earnings

and

        B2

both refer to the value contained in the cell itself.

You can enter formulas using English name references, too. However, formulas entered using English name references will remain in that form when you switch to address references, and formulas entered using address references will remain that way when you switch to English names.

We need one final word of explanation about the use of brackets in English name references. To avoid any ambiguity, Framework III uses square brackets whenever a label in an English name happens to contain a character that has a special arithmetic meaning. For example, the hyphen in *Quarter-1* might be mistaken for a minus sign in a formula. Putting brackets around Quarter-1 is Framework III's way of separating the reference from any other elements of a formula.

Framework III will supply these brackets as soon as you shift your spreadsheet into the English name reference mode. Therefore, you should always avoid including square brackets of your own as part of a Framework III label.

To shift back into address references, simply type another exclamation point. Once again, when you move the highlight back up to B2, you will see the familiar reference to the current cell:

Quarterly Income.B2

We will now begin exploring some ways in which you may want to change the appearance of the spreadsheet, without changing the actual values that the spreadsheet contains.

CHANGING THE SPREADSHEET'S APPEARANCE

Framework III gives you several tools that help you control the way spreadsheet data are displayed on the screen. Data items can be right- or left-justified or centered within their cells. Numbers can be displayed in a variety of styles. Special effects such as boldfacing and underlining can also be used in spreadsheets.

Another important spreadsheet characteristic that you can control is the width of the columns. When Framework III first creates a spreadsheet, each column is by default nine characters wide. Sometimes this width may be too large or too small to suit the data you want to display. Framework III allows you to change the width of one or more columns in the spreadsheet, so that each column is just right for the data it contains.

We will study all these possible changes in this section. As you start working with these tools, keep in mind the distinction between editing a value and changing its appearance. Changing the style in which a number is displayed has no effect on the numeric value itself. Formulas that depend on the numeric value will not need to be recalculated after a style change.

Looking back at the original quarterly income table in Figure 3.5, you can see several display changes that we might want to make to improve the appearance of our Framework III spreadsheet. The most obvious is the display of the currency values. They should all be shown as dollars and cents, including the dollar sign and commas where necessary.

Furthermore, the tax rate should be expressed as a percent, not a decimal. And finally, the labels in column A look better when they are right-justified; that is, aligned on the right rather than the left. They also stand out more in boldface. Let's begin working on these changes. Along the way, we'll also see how to use the Extend Select key (F6) in a spreadsheet, to perform a spreadsheet operation on several cells at once.

CHANGING NUMBER STYLES

The Numbers menu appears in Figure 3.7; the first section of this menu offers a list of styles in which you can display numbers on your spreadsheet. Table 3.2 gives you a summary and some examples of each of these styles.

When you first begin working with a spreadsheet, Framework III displays numbers in General style. Essentially, this means that numbers are displayed pretty much in the way you enter them.

In the Quarterly Income spreadsheet, we want to change the numbers in column B to Currency style. The way to change the style of a number is this:

1. Place the highlight over the value you want to change.

2. Then open the Numbers menu and choose the appropriate style option.

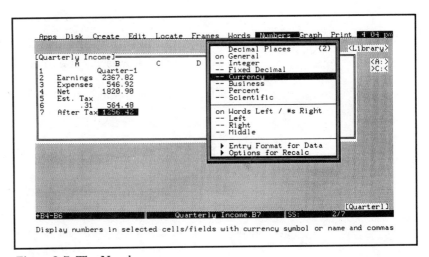

Figure 3.7: The Numbers menu

Table 3.2: Summary of the Numbers Menu: Styles

OPTION	STYLE
General	Following the style of the data entry itself: 6328.96
Integer	Rounded to the nearest integer: 6329
Fixed Decimal	Displaying a fixed number of digits after the decimal point, specified by the Decimal Places option: 6328.96
Currency	Including a dollar sign and commas: $6,328.96
Business	Including commas but no dollar sign: 6,328.96
Percent	Followed by a percent sign, with the decimal point moved two digits to the right (for display purposes only): 632896.00%
Specific	In ''exponent'' form, where the symbol E represents the exponent: 6.33E + 3 (read this as 6.33 × 103)

Note: In all styles except Integer, the number of digits displayed after the decimal point is determined by the setting of the Decimal Places option.

You can start out by trying these steps on a single value. Place the highlight over the expenses value in cell B3. Press these keys:

Ctrl-N   (to open the Numbers menu)

C   (to choose Currency style)

The expenses value will be displayed as

$546.92

Of course, it would be more convenient to be able to style a whole group of values in the spreadsheet at once. This is where the Extend

Select key (F6) becomes important. You may recall that we used the Extend Select key in Chapter 2 to select and work with several frames at a time. Likewise, we can use this function key to work with several spreadsheet cells at a time.

Place the highlight over the first number in column B, at cell B2, and press the following keys:

Extend Select (F6)   (to extend the highlight)

Ctrl-PgDn   (to move the highlight down, to the end of the column)

Return   (to complete the extend operation)

As soon as you press the Extend Select key, the following message appears below the desktop:

SELECT: extend selection with cursor keys; RETURN finishes

Notice the use of the Ctrl key with the PgDn key. Rather than extend the highlight by only one cell at a time, the Ctrl key along with the PgDn key moves the highlight to the end of the column. Ctrl along with an arrow key moves the highlight by entire blocks of data, as described in Table 3.1. Can you guess what would happen if you had used Ctrl-↓? Try it later, if you want to see the difference.

You can see the result of this operation in Figure 3.8. For the first time in our spreadsheet, the highlight covers not just a single cell but an entire *range* of cells. The significance is that you can now perform spreadsheet operations—such as changing the numeric display style—on the entire range you have selected, rather than on a single cell at a time.

Now let's make all the numbers we have selected appear in Currency style:

Ctrl-N   (to open the Numbers menu)

C   (to select the Currency option)

The results are a bit alarming and not at all what we were expecting. Somehow, we have lost several of the numbers in the column.

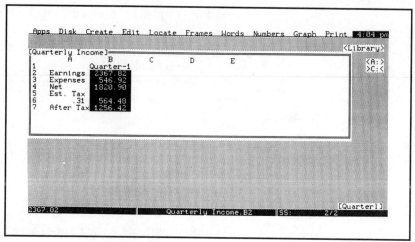

Figure 3.8: Result of Extend Select

Here's what the column looks like now:

```
* * * * * * * * *
* * * * * * * * *
   $546.92
* * * * * * * * *
   $564.48
* * * * * * * * *
```

The problem, as you may have guessed, is that the column is no longer wide enough to display the larger numbers. Recall that Framework III's default column width is nine characters. With the dollar signs and commas, the larger numbers in the column are now exactly nine characters long. But Framework III also puts an extra space after a number in a cell, as we learned at the beginning of this chapter. For this reason, the column needs to be at least ten characters wide to display these numbers.

As you can see, Framework III replaces the numbers it can't display with a string of asterisks to indicate that the column is too narrow. To correct the problem, we'll use the Size function key (F4) to increase the column width.

CHANGING COLUMN WIDTHS

In a spreadsheet, the Size key works on the column or columns that are currently selected by the highlight. Press the Size key (F4), and you'll see the following message appear below the desktop:

SIZE: stretch frame size with cursor keys; RETURN finishes

The Size key works as well with spreadsheet columns as it does with frames. Let's increase the width of column B by two spaces. Press the → key twice, and then press Return. With the column thus enlarged, the row of numbers will appear as follows:

$2,367.82
$546.92
$1,820.90
$564.48
$1,256.42

Now there is room to display all the numbers in Currency style.

We have seen, then, that Framework III will not display numbers successfully in a column that is too narrow. The width of the column must be at least one space larger than the length of the number you want to display. Interestingly enough, Framework III does not impose the same rule on labels. You can enter labels of any length into a cell. If there are empty cells to the right of the current cell, Framework III will allow the display of a label to extend across the boundaries of cells. We'll experiment with this effect a little later when we add a title to our spreadsheet. (If the cells to the right of the current cell are occupied, the label will be truncated where it crosses the cell's boundary.)

We can now use the Numbers menu again, this time to change the style of the estimated tax rate in cell A6. Move the highlight to A6. (When you first press the ↓ key, the extended highlight will once again become a single-cell highlight; then you can use the ← and ↑ keys to move to A6.) Next, go into the Numbers menu:

Ctrl-N   (to open the Numbers menu)

P   (to select the Percent option)

In response to this operation, the tax rate is now displayed as

31.00%

This is not quite what we want. In this case, there is no need to display the two digits after the decimal point. Once again, we can turn to the Numbers menu to correct the situation:

Ctrl-N   (to open the Numbers menu)

D   (to select the Decimal Places option)

The default value for the Decimal Places option is 2, as you can see on the menu. When you select this option, its current value drops down to the edit line, where you can change it. You'll also see the message

Menu editing; RETURN finishes

Enter the value 0, because we want no digits after the decimal point in this case. Press the Return key, and the tax rate will now appear as

31%

Examine the first section of the status panel to see what is actually stored in this cell. You will see the number

.31

This shows us once again that changing the display style of a number has no effect on the value of the number itself.

Next we'll work on column A, the labels that describe the information contained in the Quarterly Income spreadsheet.

CHANGING THE DISPLAY OF LABELS

We have two changes to make on the column of labels—first, we want them to be right-justified inside the width of the column, and second, we want them to appear in boldface.

In addition to numeric styles, the Numbers menu deals with the horizontal alignment of values in the spreadsheet. Looking back at Figure 3.7, you can see that the second section of the menu has four alignment options:

Words Left / #s Right
Left
Right
Middle

The first of these options is the default condition; labels are normally left-justified in a cell, and numbers are normally right-justified. You can change the alignment of any value, however, by selecting the appropriate cell and invoking the Left, Right, or Middle option. These options stand for left justification, right justification, or centering, respectively.

To right-justify the labels in column A, we should begin by selecting the range of cells that will be involved in the operation. Move the highlight to cell A2 and press the following sequence of keys:

Extend Select (F6)	(to extend the highlight)
Ctrl-↓	(to extend down through the entire block of data)
Return	(to complete the extend operation)
Ctrl-N	(to open the Numbers menu)
R	(to select the Right option)

Now, while the highlight is still extended over the entire column of labels, we can also use the Words menu to select boldfacing:

Ctrl-W	(to open the Words menu)
B	(to select the Bold option)

Now press the ↑ key to move the highlight to cell A1, and examine the column of labels. On your screen, they will appear in a high-intensity or boldfaced display. When we eventually print this spreadsheet onto paper, they will be boldfaced.

The Words menu contains several other options that deal with special display and printing effects. We'll examine this menu in more detail when we discuss word processing in Chapter 4.

To continue working with the Quarterly Income spreadsheet, the next step will be to begin entering your consulting business's income and expense values for the other three quarters of the year. Before doing so, however, we have already learned that we have to increase the width of the remaining columns, to make them wide enough to display the numbers involved. Previously, we used the Size key (F4) to extend the width of a single column. We can also use it, along with the Extend Select key (F6), to enlarge more than one column at a time. Let's see how.

Move the highlight to cell C1, and press the following keys:

Extend Select (F6)	(to extend the highlight)
Ctrl-→	(to extend to the right side of the spreadsheet)
Size (F4)	(to enlarge the columns . . .)
→, twice	(. . . by two spaces)
Return	(to complete the operation)

Now each of these columns—C, D, and E—is 11 spaces wide; there will be plenty of room to enter all the new numbers for the three final quarters.

It might also be convenient to specify a style for these columns before we begin entering the numeric values. Up to now, we have seen how to specify a style for a specific cell or block of cells within the spreadsheet. Framework III also gives you a way to assign a numeric style *globally,* to the entire spreadsheet. We'll examine this technique in the next section.

GLOBAL SPREADSHEET STYLING

In the Quarterly Income spreadsheet, most of the numbers represent dollars and cents. The only exception is the estimated tax rate. In spreadsheets like this, it is convenient to work with a global style, dealing with exceptions separately. It turns out that if you specify a style while the highlight is on the *border* of the frame, the style you have chosen will be applied globally to all numeric values inside the spreadsheet. Let's try using this technique. We'll have to begin by moving the highlight to the border:

Out (–)	(to move to the border of the frame)
Ctrl-N	(to open the Numbers menu)
C	(to choose the Currency option)
In (+)	(to move back into the spreadsheet)

Now move the highlight to cell C2, and enter the earnings for the second quarter:

7513.87

The figure will be displayed as

$7,513.87

Spend a few moments entering the remaining data for the final three quarters. You will find that each numeric value will be displayed in Currency style:

Quarter-2	Quarter-3	Quarter-4
$7,513.87	$12,875.44	$6,321.87
$832.88	$2,145.72	$1,287.22

What has happened to the estimated tax rate, now that the style has been set globally? Nothing—it still appears as a percentage:

31%

Whenever you set or reset a style *locally,* for an individual cell or block of cells inside the spreadsheet, those cells will not be affected by the global style.

Our next step, to complete this stage of the Quarterly Income spreadsheet, is to provide formulas for net income, estimated tax, and after-tax income for the three remaining quarters of the business year. We have learned how to create formulas, either by typing both the arithmetic operations and cell references onto the edit line or by typing the arithmetic operations and pointing to the cell references. One way to perform the remaining calculations would be simply to repeat this process for each quarter.

But Framework III has an easier and much more elegant way to apply these similar formulas to the entire table. We'll find out how in the next section.

USING THE SPREADSHEET

Up to now, we have concentrated on the mechanical details of entering data and controlling the appearance of the spreadsheet. Now it is time to discover some of the essential characteristics of spreadsheet programming. The first subject at hand is learning how to copy a formula, so we can complete the calculations in the Quarterly Income spreadsheet.

COPYING FORMULAS

Each calculation in row 4 of the spreadsheet will be based on the same formula:

net income = earnings − expenses

We have already developed this formula in cell B4; in spreadsheet terms, the formula was translated into

+B2−B3

In copying this formula across row 4, we will want to maintain the formula's exact format, but we will have to change the column references. For example, the correct formula for the net income of the second quarter, in column C, will be

+C2−C3

Likewise, the third and fourth quarters, in columns D and E, will require the following formulas:

+ D2 − − D3
+ E2 − E3

Framework III automatically copies this formula in a *relative* way. This means that as the formula is copied across row 4, the arithmetic operations of the formula and the *row references* will remain identical in each copy of the formula; but the *column references* will automatically be changed to represent the appropriate values in each column.

The Copy key (F8) performs the task of copying formulas in Spreadsheet frames. To produce a successful copy operation, you need to supply Framework III with two pieces of information:

1. The source location of the information that you want to copy

2. The destination of the information

You use cell pointing to specify both the source and the destination of the copy. Framework III assumes the source to be the location of the highlight at the time you press the Copy key. A message below the desktop prompts you to point to the destination.

Let's try it. Place the highlight at cell B4, which contains the net income formula that we want to copy into cells C4 to E4. Press Copy (F8); when you do, this message appears on the screen:

COPY: cursor to the copy destination; RETURN finishes

If this message does not seem specific, it is because the Copy key can be used in many different ways in Framework III, depending on the kind of frame you are working with. In a *spreadsheet* copy operation, we need to extend the highlight over the entire range of cells that we want to copy our formula to. We'll use the Extend Select key (F6) in this process. Here is the sequence of keystrokes to complete this operation:

→	(to move the highlight to C4)
Extend Select (F6)	(to stretch the highlight)
Ctrl-→	(to extend to cell E4)

Return	(to complete the extend operation)
Return	(to complete the copy operation)

When you complete these keystrokes, Framework III copies the formula instantly, and the three new calculated values appear on the screen—the net income figures for the final three quarters of the year.

Move the highlight over the cells that contain the three new values—C4, D4, and E4. As you do so, watch the formulas that are displayed in the first section of the status panel. You can see that Framework III has precisely met the requirement of producing *relative* copies of the formula. Each new formula applies itself specifically to the data in its own column.

This first example of formula copying was simple: it involved one formula, copied over only a few cells. But relative copying works just as successfully with complex formulas, copied over large ranges of data. The steps are the same:

1. Position the highlight at the location of the formula you want to copy.

2. Press the Copy key (F8).

3. Use the Extend Select key (F6) to stretch the highlight over the entire destination range of the copy.

4. Press the Return key twice, first to complete the Extend Select operation, then to complete the copy operation.

Sometimes, spreadsheets will contain values that serve as arithmetic constants. If you copy formulas that refer to such a constant, relative copying is no longer appropriate. We'll look at an example of such a situation in the next section, and we'll see Framework III's solution to the problem.

ABSOLUTE VERSUS RELATIVE COPYING   The next formula in our Quarterly Income spreadsheet calculates the estimated tax:

estimated tax = tax rate × net income

The current implementation of this formula, in cell B6, is

+A6*B4

Once again, we would like to copy this formula through all of row 6, but there is something a little different here. One of the references in this formula, the tax rate at A6, should not be copied in a relative manner. The tax rate is shown in only one location on the spreadsheet, and it must be applied uniformly to each quarter's income. In other words, its cell reference should not be revised while the copy operation is performed over the columns of the destination range. This situation calls for *absolute* copying.

To perform absolute copying, we need some way to let Framework III know that the cell that contains the tax rate, A6, should be considered a fixed reference. After the copy operation, each new formula must contain a relative reference to the net income value in its own column and an absolute reference to the tax rate in A6:

```
+A6*C4
+A6*D4
+A6*E4
```

Framework III's way of specifying an absolute cell reference is to place dollar signs in the cell reference, preceding the column letter and the row number. For example, to express A6 as an absolute reference, we would call it

```
$A$6
```

Actually, some copy operations call for *mixed* references, where only the column or the row is to be considered as absolute, and the other element is taken as a relative reference for copying purposes:

```
$A6
A$6
```

But the simplest and most common case is a full absolute reference such as $A$6.

Keep in mind that the notation for absolute references has meaning only in a copy operation. Generally, when you write a formula for a given cell in the spreadsheet, you will *anticipate* whether you are ultimately going to copy that formula into other cells. If you plan to copy the formula, you will have to decide which of the formula's references will be copied in a relative manner and which, if any, will be copied in an absolute manner.

In creating a new formula, there are two ways to introduce an absolute reference—either by typing the $ symbols directly into the reference, or by using a special extension of the pointing technique.

At the moment, we already have a formula in our Quarterly Income spreadsheet for the estimated tax. So before we try to copy this formula, we have to modify it to make the tax rate an absolute reference. Typing the $ symbols from the keyboard will be the easier technique in this case. But we will nonetheless try both techniques before we copy the formula.

Begin by positioning the highlight over the value in cell B6. Press the Edit key (F2) to edit the formula that is behind the value. The formula will appear on the edit line:

+ A6 * B4

 Version Note

In Framework III, you can copy a whole formula in the absolute mode. If you press # instead of Return when finishing the copy procedure, all cell references in the formula will be made absolute, even if they weren't originally written that way. Note, however, that this method does not allow you to create mixed references.

Here is an instance where the ability to edit a current value on the spreadsheet turns out to be convenient. To transform A6 into an absolute reference, we only need to insert $ symbols. These are the keystrokes you use to edit this formula:

→	(to move the edit cursor one space to the right)
$	(to insert the ''absolute'' symbol)
→	(to move the edit cursor again)
$	(to insert the second symbol)
Return	(to complete the edit operation)

When you press the Return key, you will see that the new formula for cell B6 is now

+ $A$6 * B4

Notice that there is no change in the calculated value shown in the cell itself. The absolute reference has no new effect on the calculation; it is there only because we anticipate making copies of the formula.

Now let's look at the second technique for producing an absolute reference, the pointing method. We'll have to start with an empty cell, so begin by deleting the current contents of cell B6 with the Delete key.

The pointing begins in the normal way:

+ (to begin the formula)

↑ (to initiate pointing)

← (to point at cell A6)

At this point, the edit line will contain the beginning of the formula:

+ A6

Now, while we are still in the pointing mode, we can simply type the $ symbol once from the keyboard, and Framework III will automatically create an absolute reference. The edit line now displays the beginning of the formula as

+ $A$6

Complete the formula just as we did originally, by supplying the multiplication symbol and pointing to the cell that contains the net income, B4:

* (to multiply)

↑ (to initiate pointing again)

→

Ctrl-↑ (to point to B4)

Return (to complete the pointing operation)

Return (to enter the formula)

The formula will appear as

+ $A$6 * B4

To summarize, the pointing technique allows you to create absolute references in three simple steps:

1. Press the ↑ key to start the pointing.

2. Use the arrow keys to point to the correct reference on the spreadsheet.

3. Type the $ symbol to make the reference absolute.

Interestingly enough, the pointing technique also allows you to create *mixed* references. To do so, you repeatedly type the $ symbol until you see the exact reference you want. Framework III steps you through all the possible combinations of references—absolute, mixed, or relative—one at a time:

```
+ $A$6
+ A$6
+ $A6
+ A6
+ $A$6
```

You'll see each version appear on the edit line, and if you keep typing $, the original version will reappear.

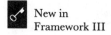
New in
Framework III

There is a useful new way to use Copy (F8) in Framework III. If you select a range, press Copy (F8), then (without moving the cursor) press #, Framework III will convert all formulas to values. As you will see in Chapter 7, we will use this feature in a macro first to calculate a formula, then convert the result to a value so it won't be calculated again when we press Recalc (F5).

You are now ready to copy the estimated tax formula into the rest of row 6. But before doing so, take another look at the Quarterly Income spreadsheet. To complete the spreadsheet at this stage, we actually still have *two* formulas left to copy—the one we've been working with, in cell B6, and the one that calculates the after-tax income, in cell B7. It would be convenient to be able to copy both formulas at once.

Framework III allows us to do that with the Extend Select key. Here are the steps:

1. First use Extend Select (F6) to stretch the highlight over the *source range*—that is, the formulas you want to copy.

2. Press the Copy key (F8) to begin the operation.

3. Use Extend Select (F6) again, to stretch the highlight over the *destination range*—the cells to which you want to copy the original formulas.

This is the process we'll follow to copy both the estimated tax and the after-tax income formulas. Beginning with the highlight positioned at cell B6, follow this sequence of keystrokes:

Extend Select (F6)	(to stretch the highlight over the source range)
↓	(to include B7 in the source range)
Copy (F8)	(to begin the copy operation)
→	(to position the highlight at the beginning of the destination range)
Extend Select (F6)	(to stretch the highlight)
Ctrl-→	(to indicate the entire destination range)
Return	(to complete the extend operation)
Return	(to complete the copy operation)

As a result of these keyboard commands, you will see two new rows of values appear instantly on the spreadsheet—the estimated taxes and the after-tax income for the second, third, and fourth quarters of the business year.

Move the highlight through this block of cells to examine the formulas that have been copied into it, and watch the display in the first section of the status panel. You will see all of the following formulas as you move from cell to cell:

	Quarter-2	Quarter-3	Quarter-4
31%	+$A$6*C4	+$A$6*D4	+$A$6*E4
After Tax	+C4 – C6	+D4 – D6	+E4 – E6

The formulas were all copied correctly; in particular, the absolute reference to $A$6 was carried forward unchanged, as a spreadsheet constant, to each cell in row 6.

This completes the initial stage of the Quarterly Income spreadsheet for your consulting and speaking business. In the following section, we'll continue adding some new elements.

ADDING ROWS AND COLUMNS

The entire five-column by seven-row spreadsheet is now completely filled with the information we planned for it. Often, at this point in your work with a spreadsheet, you'll decide to expand your original plans. You'll think of new ways in which your spreadsheet might become even more valuable if additional information were included. In the case of the Quarterly Income spreadsheet, for example, you may want to add a title, a column of totals, and a few columns of simple statistics that will help you analyze the business year.

Before you can add any information, though, you clearly have to expand the dimensions of the spreadsheet. We saw at the beginning of this chapter that the Create menu contains two options that will do this for you:

> Columns/Fields: Add
> Rows/Records: Add

To use either of these Create options, you must follow these three steps:

1. Place the highlight inside the spreadsheet, at a cell located immediately *before* the position you want the new columns or rows to appear.

2. Open the Create menu and choose either the Columns or the Rows option.

3. Specify the number of columns or rows you want to add, and press the Return key to complete the operation.

The new columns or rows will appear at the position you have specified, and the organization of the spreadsheet will be expanded appropriately. New column letters or row numbers will appear (if you have Display Labels on in the Frames menu). Even more significantly, any formulas that you have already entered into your spreadsheet will automatically be revised, if necessary, to allow for the changes in the spreadsheet.

The process of adding rows or columns presents one small problem. There is no immediate way to insert new rows at the top of the spreadsheet or new columns at the left side of the spreadsheet. You can see why if you think about the first step of the process:

- To add rows, the highlight must be placed at the row immediately above where the new rows are to appear.

- To add columns, the highlight must be placed at the column immediately to the left of where the new columns are to appear.

But there is no way for you to place the highlight above row 1 or to the left of column A.

To solve this problem in a spreadsheet that already contains data, we have to add an extra step to the process. We'll insert the rows or columns at some point below or to the right of where we actually want them. Then we'll *move* the current data into the new empty cells, creating empty rows at the top of the spreadsheet, or empty columns at the left side of the spreadsheet.

Let's look at an example. Now that you have completed your Quarterly Income spreadsheet, you decide that you would like to place a title at the top of it. The title will contain two lines and will look like this:

Consulting and Speaking Activities
Quarterly Income Statement

You would also like to see a blank line between the title and the data itself. In all, you have to add three rows to the spreadsheet.

We'll add the three rows at the bottom of the spreadsheet and then move the current block of data down by three rows. The Move key (F7) moves data to new locations in a spreadsheet. Here are the keystrokes that will add the three rows:

Ctrl-End (to move the highlight to the lower right corner of the spreadsheet)

Ctrl-C (to open the Create menu)

R (to choose the Rows option)

3 (to specify the number of rows you want to add)

Return (to add the rows)

To add rows below row 7, you can place the highlight in *any* cell in row 7. Using Ctrl-End is simply the most convenient way to move the highlight quickly to the bottom of the spreadsheet. When you complete these keystrokes, you will see three new rows inserted below row 7. Now the spreadsheet contains ten rows, numbered 1 to 10.

To move the current block of data down into the new rows, we'll use the Move key. Here are the steps that a move requires:

1. Expand the highlight over the entire block of data you want to move.

2. Press the Move key (F7).

3. Move the highlight to the destination of the move operation, and press Return to finish.

When you press the Move key, you will see the following message:

MOVE: Cursor to the move destination; Return finishes

If you are moving a two-dimensional block of cells, as in the Quarterly Income spreadsheet, you can specify the destination of the move by placing the highlight at the upper left corner of the area to which you want the block of data moved. In this case, the new upper left corner of the data will be cell A4, since we want to empty rows 1 to 3.

Here are the keystrokes to perform the move:

Ctrl-Home	(to move the highlight to the upper left corner of the spreadsheet)
Extend Select (F6) ↓	(to expand the highlight)
Ctrl-End	(to select the entire block of data)
Move (F7)	(to move the selected data)
Ctrl-Home	
↓, three times	(to move the highlight to the upper left corner of the destination)
Return	(to complete the move)

Press Ctrl-Home again to move the highlight back up to the top. Your spreadsheet should look like Figure 3.9. We now have room to place a title above the data.

We have already discussed the way Framework III handles the display of long labels: text is allowed to cross the borders between cells. Conveniently, we'll be able to enter the two lines of the title into cells B1 and B2, respectively. Move the highlight to B1 and type the first line of the title:

Consulting and Speaking Activities

As you type the text into the edit line, you'll see the characters also appear in the spreadsheet. Press Return to complete the data entry. This entire label is contained in cell B1, even though its display takes up the space of more than three cells.

Enter the second line of the title into cell B2:

Quarterly Income Statement

To center the second line below the first, you'll need to begin the text with four blank spaces. First press the spacebar once to begin the edit mode; then press it four more times for the blank spaces. Enter the text and include four trailing spaces after the word *Statement;* finally, press Return.

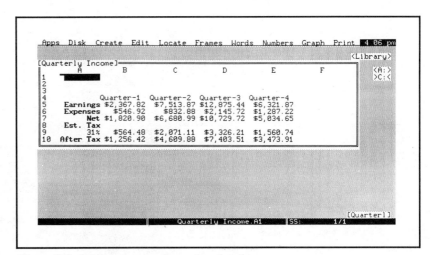

Figure 3.9: Adding rows and moving the data

Now use the Words menu to change the display of the two title lines. The first line should be in boldface, and the second should be underlined. (Use the Words menu options B and U, respectively.) The underlining extends over the blank spaces in the second title line, as you can see in Figure 3.10.

In the next section, we'll be studying ways to add totals, averages, and other statistics to your spreadsheet. We'll be placing all this new information in columns to the right of the current income table. To prepare, you should insert four new columns into the spreadsheet, beyond column E:

Ctrl-End (to move the highlight to the last column)

Ctrl-C   (to open the Create menu)

C   (to choose the Columns option)

4   (to specify the number of new columns)

Return   (to complete the operation)

These keystrokes will add columns F through I to the spreadsheet. There are now too many columns to see in Frames view, so you should press the Zoom key (F9) to expand the display of the spreadsheet over the full screen. Even on the full screen, however, you will discover that only seven complete columns can appear on the screen

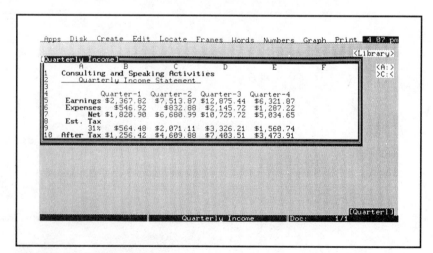

Figure 3.10: Adding a title

at once. As you move the highlight horizontally back and forth across the spreadsheet, the columns at the beginning and end will *scroll* in and out of view. Or, to put it another way, your window onto the spreadsheet will move to the right or to the left.

Take the following steps to further prepare the four new columns for the work ahead:

1. Use the Extend Select key (F6) and Ctrl-→ to select all four columns.

2. Using the Size key (F4), increase the size of the columns to 11 spaces.

3. Add the following labels into cells F4, G4, H4, and I4, respectively:

    Totals   Average   Most   Least

4. Now move the cursor into cell B2.

5. Open the Edit menu and select the Lock option:

    Lock Columns/Rows

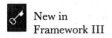
New in
Framework III

In versions of Framework earlier than Framework III, you could lock only row 1 and column A. In Framework III, you can now lock multiple rows and columns, depending on which rows and columns are displayed on the screen as well as the cursor position. Columns along the left and upper edges of the screen, and above and to the left of the cursor position, are locked when you select Lock Columns/ Rows from the Edit menu. To lock columns only, move the cursor to the top row of the column to the right of the ones you want to lock. Likewise, to lock rows only, move the cursor to the far left cell of the row below the ones you want to lock. To unlock columns and rows, select Lock Columns/Rows from the Edit menu anytime. To change locked columns and rows, first unlock them, then select new columns and rows to lock using the methods explained above.

Selecting the Lock option changes the way Framework III scrolls your spreadsheet; when you toggle the Lock option into its *on* state, any columns and rows above and to the left of the cursor will always stay in view, no matter how you scroll the spreadsheet. In this case, by positioning the cursor in cell B2, you will lock column A and row 1. This is a convenience when viewing a large spreadsheet that contains identifying labels or other data you want to keep in view.

Notice that the new columns are formatted in Currency format; the global setting also applies to columns or rows that you add later.

From the labels we added in columns F, G, H, and I, you can see that the formulas we will be writing in these columns will require different arithmetic than simple addition, subtraction, multiplication, or division. In the next section, we'll begin looking at a category of tools Framework III provides for building special spreadsheet formulas. These tools are called *functions*.

USING SPREADSHEET FUNCTIONS

Functions in Framework III can serve many different purposes. In fact, whenever you use a function or write a formula, you are actually working with the resources of FRED, the programming language that is built into Framework III. We'll have more to say about FRED in Chapter 7; for now, just keep in mind that the language consists of a large and versatile collection of functions that give you extended powers over the work you perform in Framework III. One of these extended powers is the use of functions in spreadsheet formulas.

Framework III's spreadsheet functions give you shortcuts for working with values and ranges of values. They can save you the trouble of having to write complex formulas to derive certain kinds of results.

Consider a quick example. Let's say you have entered three numbers into column A of a spreadsheet:

	A
1	476
2	529
3	764

You decide that you want to find the average of these three numbers. Of course, one way to do so would be to write a formula that adds up the numbers and divides the sum by 3:

$$(A1 + A2 + A3)/3$$

You may not object to having to write this short formula; but what if the column of numbers were 30 elements long instead of only three? To write a formula to find the average of 30 numbers would be a long and tedious task.

This is why Framework III supplies functions: to give you short, easy ways to write what might otherwise be long or complex formulas. In this particular case, you would select the function that automatically computes the average of a series of numbers. But as we will soon see, Framework III supplies functions that provide many kinds of values—not just averages—for your spreadsheets.

Framework III functions have three essential characteristics:

1. Every function has a name. To use a function in your spreadsheet, you simply refer to the function by name. Without exception, every function's name begins with a special character—the "at" symbol, @. Following this symbol, the function's name usually indicates fairly clearly what the function does. For example, the function that finds averages is called @AVG.

2. Most functions require one or more *parameters*. A parameter is simply an expression of the specific value or values that you want the function to work on. When you use a function, you enter the parameters, between parentheses, immediately after the name of the function. For example, to compute the average of the values stored in cells A1 to A3, you would write the formula as

   @AVG(A1:A3)

   We'll see that different functions require different formats for the parameter expression.

3. All functions return a value or produce some programmed result. (Just like the results of other formulas, the result of a spreadsheet function is displayed in the cell in which you enter the function. For example, if you were to enter the above @AVG formula into cell A4, the average of the three cells, A1 to A3, would be displayed in A4.)

Table 3.3 describes the four categories of functions you might find yourself using most often in spreadsheets: statistical, numeric,

Table 3.3: A Selection of Framework III Functions

Statistical Functions
Parameters for each of the following statistical functions:
n = range or list of numbers or numeric expressions
@SUM(*n*) returns the sum of all the numbers in the parameter list.
@AVG(*n*) returns the average of all the numbers in the parameter list.
@MIN(*n*) returns the smallest number in the parameter list.
@MAX(*n*) returns the largest number in the parameter list.
@STD(*n*) returns the standard deviation of the numbers in the parameter list.
Numeric Functions
Parameter for each of the following numeric functions:
n = number, a numeric expression, or a reference to a number
@SQRT(*n*) returns the square root of the number. (Parameter cannot be negative.)
@LOG(*n*) returns the logarithm, base 10. (Parameter must be positive.)
@LN(*n*) returns the logarithm, base *e*. (Parameter must be positive.)
@EXP(*n*) returns the value of *e* to the *n*, where *n* is the parameter.
@PI returns an angle in radians, requires no parameter, and yields a value of pi correct to 15 digits.
@SIN(*a*) returns the sine of the angle *a* in radians.
@COS(*a*) returns the cosine of the angle *a* in radians.
@TAN(*a*) returns the tangent of the angle *a* in radians.
@ROUND(*n*, *d*) results in the value of *n*, rounded off to *d* decimal places.
@MOD(*a*, *b*) results in the value of *a modulus b* (that is, the *remainder* from the division of *a/b*). The value of *b* cannot be zero.

Table 3.3: A Selection of Framework III Functions (continued)

Numeric Functions (continued)
@RAND yields a random number between 0 and 1, inclusive. (Requires no parameter.)

Financial Functions
@PMT(*principal, rate, periods*) computes the payment per *period* required on a *principal* loan at a specified interest *rate* per period.
@PV(*amount, rate, periods*) computes the present value of a series of equal income or payment *amounts* for a specified number of *periods*, given the discount *rate*.
@NPV(*rate, list*) computes the net present value of a *list* of periodic inflows or outflows of cash, given the discount *rate*.
@IRR(*estimate, list*) computes the internal rate of return of a *list* of period cash flows, given a first *estimate* of the rate.

Date Functions
@DATE(*yyyy, mm, dd*) displays the date in the current cell and results in a date value that can be sorted or used in the date arithmetic functions, @DIFFDATE and @SUMDATE.
@TODAY displays today's date in the current cell. (Requires no parameters.)
Both of the following date functions perform arithmetic on Framework III date values.
@DIFFDATE(*date1, date2*) finds the number of days between *date1* and *date2*.
@SUMDATE(*date, days*) adds the specified number of *days* to *date* and yields the resulting date.

financial, and date. We'll see working examples of many of these functions before the end of this chapter. (You will find a list of all the Framework III functions in Appendix B.) Remember that functions are available to you throughout your work in Framework III, not just in Spreadsheet frames.

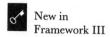 New in
Framework III

In Framework III, empty cells are considered to contain zeros (0). In earlier versions of Framework, they were null cells that returned an error

#N/A!

if referenced. However, starting in Framework III, empty cells are numeric zeros. Some statistical functions (such as @AVG) will ignore empty cells, since counting them as zeros would throw off the calculations. By treating blank cells this way, Framework III can speed up some recalculations.

Let's begin now with the statistical functions, which we'll use to create columns of statistical values in the Quarterly Income spreadsheet.

WORKING WITH STATISTICAL FUNCTIONS   The four columns that we added in the Quarterly Income spreadsheet—labeled Totals, Average, Most, and Least—are reserved for computing the statistical values that will help us analyze the four income periods. To compute all these values, we'll use the @SUM, @AVG, @MAX, and @MIN functions, respectively.

Our approach will be as follows: we'll write all four of the statistical functions in the first row of the table, row 5 (Earnings). Then we'll simply copy the formulas into the remainder of the spreadsheet.

You can see in Table 3.3 that all four of the functions we'll be using take *list* or *range* parameters. In the Quarterly Income spreadsheet, we'll want each function to work on a range of values located in columns B to E. For example, to find the total earnings for all four quarters, we'll enter the function

@SUM(B5:E5)

Notice how the colon character is used to express a range of references. This function tells Framework III to find the sum of all the numeric values in row 5, from column B to column E.

Begin by moving the highlight to cell F5; this is where we'll enter the formula for calculating the total earnings for the four quarters. Press the @ character. When you do, you'll notice that Framework III recognizes this character as the beginning of a formula; you'll see this familiar message appear below the desktop:

Formula/number editing; RETURN finishes

Continue entering the name of the function and the opening parenthesis:

@SUM(

Case is not important in function names; you can enter letters in all uppercase, all lowercase, or any combination.

Now is the moment to enter the range parameter for this @SUM function. We'll do so by pointing and extending the highlight over the range. Here are the keystrokes:

↑	(to initiate pointing)
Home	(to position the cursor . . .)
→	(. . . over cell B5)
Extend Select (F6)	(to extend the highlight)
Ctrl-→	(to specify the range, from B5 to E5)
Return	(to finish extending the selection)
Return	(to finish the pointing)

When you press the ↑ key to begin the pointing and then move the highlight to B5, the formula on the edit line will be expanded to

@SUM(B5)

Pressing the Extend Select key (F6) and extending the highlight will result in the formula

@SUM(B5:E5)

The correct range notation is supplied automatically as you extend the highlight; you don't have to enter the colon character from the keyboard.

The final character required to complete the function is a closing parenthesis. Enter the character now, and press the Return key to complete the formula entry. You will see the result of the @SUM function in cell F5:

$29,079.00

This figure represents the total earnings of your business over the four quarters.

Now enter the other three functions, @AVG, @MAX, and @MIN, into cells G5, H5, and I5, respectively. Use the same sequence of steps we followed for the @SUM function:

1. Enter the name of the function, starting with the @ character, along with an open parenthesis.

2. Begin pointing (press ↑), and move the highlight to cell B5.

3. Press Extend Select (F6), and extend the highlight to cell E5.

4. Enter a closing parenthesis, and press Return to complete the formula entry.

Notice that after you extend the highlight over the range, you can avoid a keystroke by simply entering the closing parenthesis. Pressing the Return key to complete the Extend Select process is not required.

Here are the values that the three new functions will display in their respective spreadsheet cells:

Average	Most	Least
$7,269.75	$12,875.44	$2,367.82

You may note that the average earnings for the four quarters fall about halfway between the best and worst quarters' earnings.

Now we can copy the four new formulas down into the remaining rows of the Quarterly Income spreadsheet. Position the highlight at F5, and proceed as follows:

Extend Select (F6)	(to extend the highlight)
Ctrl-→	(to specify the range to be copied: F5 to I5)
Copy (F8)	(to copy the range)

↓	(to specify the beginning of the destination range: row 6)
Extend Select (F6)	(to extend the highlight)
Ctrl-↓	(to specify the entire destination range: rows 6 to 10)
Return	(to complete the Extend Select operation)
Return	(to complete the copying)

Figure 3.11 shows the result of the copy operation. All four statistical values have been successfully calculated in each row of the table. If you move the cursor down a given column of the spreadsheet, you'll find that this was, indeed, a *relative* copy operation. The row numbers in the range references were automatically incremented for each row down the table. For example, here are the formulas you will see in column F:

@SUM(B5:E5)
@SUM(B6:E6)
@SUM(B7:E7)
@SUM(B8:E8)
@SUM(B9:E9)
@SUM(B10:E10)

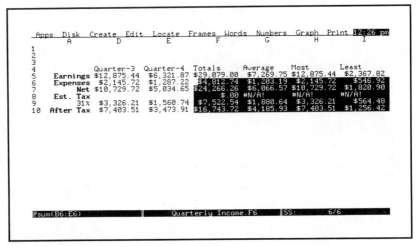

Figure 3.11: Using statistical functions

There is an interesting set of displays in row 8. Since this row has no data in it between columns B and E, the functions we copied have nothing to work with. For @AVG, @MAX, and @MIN, this creates an error situation. Framework III displays the following message in the cells that contain these functions:

#N/A!

This tells us that the values for these cells are *not available*. If you position the highlight over one of these cells, you'll see an additional message below the desktop:

Function requires at least one numeric value

When you create a spreadsheet formula that cannot be calculated, Framework III does its best to tell you what is wrong. You can simply delete the contents of row 8, from columns F to I, by using Extend Select (F6) and the cursor keys to select the row, and then using the Delete key.

The Quarterly Income spreadsheet is now complete. Once again, you may want to try out some "what-if" scenarios on this spreadsheet. For example, change the estimated tax rate or one of the quarterly earnings figures. Each time you change a numeric value on the spreadsheet, all of the formulas will be recalculated, including, of course, the statistical formulas in columns F to I. For example, you can easily find out what happens to the average quarterly after-tax income (in cell G10) as a result of a change in the tax rate.

After all this work, you'll probably be interested in learning about two Framework III operations that will help you keep permanent records of your spreadsheet: saving and printing. We'll look briefly at these operations in the next section.

SAVING AND PRINTING SPREADSHEETS

In Chapter 2, we discussed the Save and Continue operation. This operation lets you save a frame in its current condition and then continue your work with the same frame. All you have to do to execute this operation is press Ctrl-Return. You can perform the Save and Continue operation with the highlight positioned either on the Spreadsheet frame's border or inside the spreadsheet. In either case, Framework III will save a copy of the spreadsheet on the current disk and then return you to the desktop.

Alternatively, you can use the Disk menu's Put Away option to save a file. This option stores the currently selected frame on disk and then removes the frame from the desktop.

To print your spreadsheet, use the Print menu. In many cases, all you will have to do is enter a few keystrokes to print out an entire spreadsheet:

Ctrl-P   (to open the Print menu)

B   (to begin printing)

Again, it doesn't matter where the highlight is located when the printing operation begins; the highlight can be either on the frame's border or inside the spreadsheet. If the highlight is inside the frame and extended over a range of cells, however, that range will print.

When a spreadsheet contains more columns than can be printed with the currently established line length (more on that in Chapter 4), Framework III will print as many columns as possible in one block and then proceed with subsequent columns in a second block; however, how and where these blocks will print depends on the status of the Lock Columns/Rows option found on the Edit menu. If you have toggled the Lock Columns/Rows option on, and if you have locked row 1 and column A, then Framework III will repeat the first column in each block of the printout, and it will continue the printout of extra columns directly below the first set of columns.

Figure 3.12 shows a printout of the Quarterly Income spreadsheet with row 1 and column A locked. You can see that columns A through F were printed in the first block of the printout. The second block repeats column A and then continues with columns G through I. You'll also notice that the first title lines were repeated on the second block of the printout.

If you lock multiple rows and columns, or you turn locking off, then Framework III will print the first columns at the top of the first sheet of paper and will continue the printout on the next sheet with

 Version Note

The presence or absence of column and row labels on spreadsheet printouts may vary from one version to another. The descriptions and figures mentioned here apply to Framework III. If you are using another version, you may want to test your printouts with the first column and row locked to see how they print.

```
Consulting and Speaking Activities
     Quarterly Income Statement

             Quarter-1  Quarter-2  Quarter-3  Quarter-4  Totals
Earnings   $2,367.82   $7,513.87 $12,875.44   $6,321.87 $29,079.00
Expenses     $546.92     $832.88  $2,145.72   $1,287.22  $4,812.74
     Net   $1,820.90   $6,680.99 $10,729.72   $5,034.65 $24,266.26
Est. Tax
     31%     $564.48   $2,071.11  $3,326.21   $1,560.74  $7,522.54
After Tax  $1,256.42   $4,609.88  $7,403.51   $3,473.91 $16,743.72


Consulting and Speaking Activities
     Quarterly Income Statement

             Average    Most        Least
Earnings   $7,269.75  $12,875.44   $2,367.82
Expenses   $1,203.19   $2,145.72     $546.92
     Net   $6,066.57  $10,729.72   $1,820.90
Est. Tax
     31%   $1,880.64   $3,326.21     $564.48
After Tax  $4,185.93   $7,403.51   $1,256.42
```

Figure 3.12: The printed spreadsheet

the remaining columns. It will not repeat the first-column information. You can use this type of printout to physically cut and paste the
extra columns to the end of the first page, creating a long format
printout of the spreadsheet.

You can also print a selected portion of a spreadsheet. To do so,
first select the portion you want to print with Extend Select (F6).
Then, just as you did for printing the entire spreadsheet, press

Ctrl-P   (to open the Print menu)

B   (to begin printing)

If you have locked the first row and column, as we have done in
our exercise, they will be printed along with the selected cells. Figure
3.13 shows a printout of a selected portion of the spreadsheet—the
part containing all the summary figures (cells F4 through I10).
Notice that the row labels from column A appear at the left. The
printout also shows the column labels. To print a selection that
includes these labels, you must include them in the selection, as we
have done in Figure 3.13. They will not print unless they are specifically selected.

If you want to see how your printout is going to look before you
actually send it to paper, you can begin by storing the output as a

```
Consulting and Speaking Activities
                   Totals      Average      Most        Least
      Earnings     $29,079.00   $7,269.75  $12,875.44   $2,367.82
      Expenses      $4,812.74   $1,203.19   $2,145.72     $546.92
      Net          $24,266.26   $6,066.57  $10,729.72   $1,820.90
      Est. Tax
      31%           $7,522.54   $1,880.64   $3,326.21     $564.48
      After Tax    $16,743.72   $4,185.93   $7,403.51   $1,256.42
```

Figure 3.13: Printing a portion of a spreadsheet

print file on disk. The Print menu has a submenu that allows you to specify where the printout will be sent:

Destination of Printout

Select this submenu, and then choose the DOS File option inside the submenu:

Ctrl-P	(to open the Print menu)
D	(to open the Destination submenu)
D	(to select the DOS File option)
Out (−)	(to return to the main Print menu)
B	(to begin ''printing'' to disk)

When you ''print'' the frame, Framework III will send the copy to a file on disk, with the extension name .PRT. To examine this print file, simply load it onto the desktop from the disk.

As a final step in your work with the Quarterly Income spreadsheet, you might want to create some graphs. We'll see how easily this can be done in the next section.

CREATING GRAPHS FROM A SPREADSHEET

Figure 3.14 shows the Graph menu. Using this menu to create graphs from a Framework III spreadsheet is a concise and efficient process.

The steps are simple:

1. Extend the highlight over the block of spreadsheet numbers that you want to graph.

2. Open the Graph menu and select the graph type you want to create.

3. Set options, if necessary, for your graph; for example, specify titles for the x- and y-axes (that is, the horizontal and vertical axes of your graph).

4. Select the appropriate Graph menu option to draw the graph.

5. When you are prompted, tell Framework III where you would like the graph to appear.

Several important aspects of designing the graph are automatically

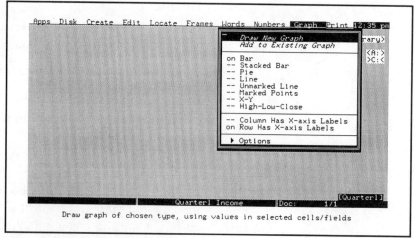

Figure 3.14: The Graph menu

taken over by Framework III; for example:

- The graph is scaled appropriately.

- Labels to identify scaled values along the x- and y-axes of the graph are taken from row 1 and column A of the spreadsheet.

- The title for the graph is copied from the label that you give to the Graph frame.

Framework III also automatically determines the nature of the hardware environment it is working in. Framework III can draw graphs on either a monochrome monitor (controlled by a monochrome display card installed inside your computer) or a color graphics monitor (controlled by a color display card). It will adjust the resolution to the type of display—CGA, EGA, or VGA. The program will also support Hercules-type cards for displaying graphics.

To create monochrome graphs, Framework III makes use of the special "text graphics" characters that are provided at the high end of the ASCII character code used by MS-DOS. (ASCII, an acronym for American Standard Code for Information Interchange, is simply a code that assigns a fixed number, from 0 to 255, to every character that the computer uses or displays on the screen.) You can see the text graphics characters in Appendix C, which displays the entire ASCII code. These characters are just fine for drawing graphs that are by nature horizontally or vertically oriented, such as bar graphs and marked-points graphs. Framework III can create attractive graphs of these types on the monochrome screen. Some other types of graphs, such as the pie graph, will be drawn a little clumsily with text graphics characters.

On a color graphics monitor, Framework III enjoys the advantages of color and high-resolution graphics. On this equipment, Framework III can therefore produce graphs that are more accurate and precise—and often more attractive—than those created on a monochrome monitor. In addition, Framework III can display the graphs in color.

One of Framework III's advantages over other integrated spreadsheet packages is that it works successfully with whatever display hardware you have installed on your computer. Some other spreadsheet and graphing programs will display graphs only on a color graphics monitor.

Once you have highlighted the spreadsheet range that you want to graph and selected a graph type, Framework III gives you two options for creating the display itself. These options are identified at the top of the Graph menu:

Draw New Graph
Add to Existing Graph

If you select the Draw New Graph option, you must then specify the destination of the graph:

- You can put the new graph in an Empty frame that already exists on the desktop; this frame becomes a Graph frame.

- You can let Framework III create a new Graph frame for you.

The other graphing option, Add to Existing Graph, allows you to lay one graph over another inside the same Graph frame. An overlay is restricted to specific types of graphs—you can overlay a line or marked-points graph over another line, marked-points, or bar graph that you have already created.

We'll create two graph examples from the Quarterly Income spreadsheet: a pie graph representing the earnings of the four quarters, each quarter as a wedge of the pie, and a combination bar and marked-points graph, posting quarterly expenses against quarterly after-tax income.

To create these graphs, we'll want to begin by making some changes in the format of the spreadsheet. We've already mentioned that Framework III takes the labels for the graph from column A and row 1 of the spreadsheet. For this reason, we'll want to start with a version of the spreadsheet that begins with the four quarter headings in row 1. (In other words, we'll go back to the version of the Quarterly Income spreadsheet as it appeared before we added the three rows for a spreadsheet title.)

Furthermore, there will not be room on the graph for long labels such as Quarter-1. We'll have to revise these labels to the following abbreviations:

Q1   Q2   Q3   Q4

You may often find yourself going through this process of making small revisions in a spreadsheet before you create graphs. The goal is to make the spreadsheet's format conform as closely as possible to the simple requirements of Framework III's graphing options. You can easily keep two versions of your spreadsheet: one finished version for viewing and printing, and another simplified version for creating graphs.

Make sure you have saved to disk our current version of the Quarterly Income spreadsheet, with the spreadsheet title displayed in rows 1 and 2. Then revise the spreadsheet on the desktop, following these steps:

1. Use the Edit menu to delete the first three rows of the spreadsheet. Extend the highlight over these three rows, open the Edit menu, and select the option

   Rows/Records: Remove

   This deletion cannot be undone, so Framework III will ask you to confirm that you really want to go through with it.

2. Change the quarter headings, now in row 1, to the two-character abbreviations Q1, Q2, Q3, and Q4.

3. Select column A with the Extend Select key (F6), and use the Words menu to change the style of the text from bold to normal. To do so, press

   Ctrl-W   (to open the Words menu)
   N   (to select normal text)

Now let's create our graphs. Begin by extending the highlight over the four numbers representing quarterly earnings, in row 2 of the current spreadsheet. We'll create a pie graph of these values. Here are the necessary keystrokes:

   Ctrl-G   (to open the Graph menu)
   P   (to select the Pie option)
   D   (to draw the new graph)

At this point, Framework III will display the following message below the desktop:

**Press RETURN to draw graph here, or select desired frame
and press RETURN**

We haven't bothered to set aside an Empty frame for the graph, so we'll let Framework III create the frame for us. Simply press the Return key, and the new Graph frame will appear on the desktop.

The Zoom key (F9) is an important tool for viewing Framework III's graphs. You'll find that detail will be superior when you view a graph in full-screen mode rather than inside a frame on the desktop, but if you are working in a high-resolution graphics mode, the graph in the window will be almost as clear. Press Zoom (F9) to look at the pie graph in full-screen mode. Figure 3.15 shows the graph.

A pie graph provides a clear way to compare a few values that make up a whole. In this case, the "whole" is the total earnings for the year; the wedges that make up the pie represent the quarterly earnings. You can see at a glance in which quarters you earned the most and the least.

Now let's try creating a Graph frame that contains two graphs: an original and an overlay. This time, let's begin by creating an Empty frame for our work:

    Zoom (F9)   (to return to the desktop view)

    Ctrl-C   (to open the Create menu)

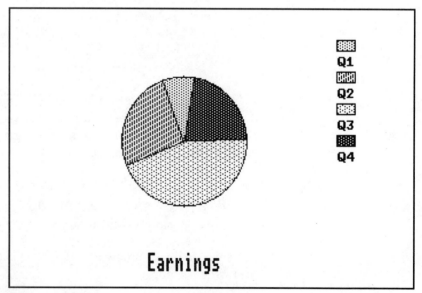

Figure 3.15: A pie graph of quarterly earnings

E   (to create an Empty frame)

Enter the following label into the frame's border:

Income vs. Expenses

Press the Return key to close the frame, putting it aside temporarily in its tray at the corner of the desktop.

Inside the revised Quarterly Income spreadsheet, highlight the four quarterly after-tax income figures in the last row. Then press the following keys:

Ctrl-G   (to open the Graph menu)

B   (to select the Bar option)

O   (to select the Options submenu)

Figure 3.16 shows the Options submenu of the Graph menu. This submenu gives you ways of manually specifying some graph characteristics that Framework III would otherwise determine automatically. It also allows you to enter titles for the x- and y-axes using the following options:

X-axis Title   {}
Y-axis Title   {}

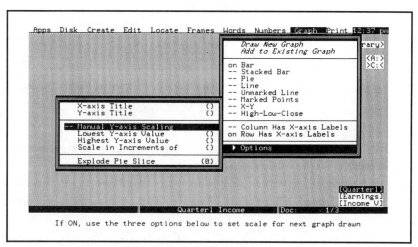

Figure 3.16: The Options submenu of the Graph menu

With the Options submenu open on the desktop, type the following commands and data:

X	(to choose the X-axis option)
Quarters	(the title for the x-axis)
Return	(to enter the title into the menu)
Y	(to choose the Y-axis option)
Amount in $	(the title for the y-axis)
Return	(to enter the title into the menu)
Out (–)	(to return to the main Graph menu)
D	(to draw the graph)

At this point, you will have to select the frame in which you want the graph to appear. Using the ↑ or ↓ key, move the highlight to the frame we have created for this graph. It is in its tray and looks like this:

[Incomev]

Press the Return key to complete the graphing operation.

Before we even look at the graph, let's create the overlay. Return the highlight to the inside of the spreadsheet, and extend the highlight over the four values representing quarterly expenses. Press the following keys:

Ctrl-G	(to open the Graph menu)
M	(to select Marked-points)
A	(to select the Add to Existing Graph option)
↑ or ↓	(to select the Income vs. Expenses Graph frame on the desktop)
Return	(to draw the graph overlay)

Now select the Graph frame again and press the Zoom key (F9). Figure 3.17 shows the graph you have created. The after-tax income figures are represented by bars, and the quarterly expenses by "marked points" inside each bar. The titles that you entered into the

Figure 3.17: A composite graph: After-Tax Income vs. Expenses

Options submenu are displayed below and to the side of the x- and y-axes. Also notice that Framework III has automatically created a legend at the upper right corner of the graph, to identify the various elements.

For exploring "what-if" scenarios, graphs may be as valuable as the spreadsheets they are based on. Framework III will redraw Graph frames in response to changes you make in the numeric data of the original spreadsheet. However, because the graph resides in a different frame than the spreadsheet, the revision of the graph does not occur automatically. If you make changes in the spreadsheet, you must then move the highlight to the Graph frame and press the Recalc key (F5). Recalc makes Framework III redraw the graph according to the new data in the spreadsheet.

Later in this chapter, we'll learn more about using the Recalc key. We'll also discover a way to link two frames explicitly, so that changes in one frame will automatically result in changes in the other frame.

Using a graph that's been saved to disk presents a special problem. To work successfully with a graph, Framework III relies on the presence, on the desktop, of the spreadsheet from which the graph was originally created. If you save a graph and later bring it back to the desktop without its corresponding spreadsheet, Framework III will have no way of redrawing the graph.

For this reason, it is a good idea to create an Empty frame to store a spreadsheet together with all of the graphs that you create from that spreadsheet as an outline. Save this Outline frame on disk under a different name than the original spreadsheet (Quarterly Income); then, when you load the frame back onto the desktop, you can be assured that the Graph frames will have access to the appropriate Spreadsheet frame.

Framework III will print a graph on any printer. The resolution of the paper copy will depend on the graphics capabilities of your printer and on whether you are using a monochrome display card or a color display card. If you have a daisy-wheel printer, which prints only characters, Framework III will use appropriate letters and symbols to build the graph on paper.

We have examined a broad range of Framework III activities, from building Spreadsheet frames to creating Graph frames. Now let's make another visit to The Sophisticated Palate to see how all these features might be put to use.

EXAMPLES

In addition to simple record-keeping tasks, Eileen Wilcox and George Farley use spreadsheets to analyze past business events and project future transactions. In this section, we'll look at three spreadsheets and spreadsheet systems that they have put together for analyzing, projecting, and recording various financial aspects of their business:

- A spreadsheet and graph that help the principals compare and analyze sales revenues over time from the three major activities of their business

- A spreadsheet that they have devised to help them make decisions regarding an upcoming real estate investment

- The outline of expense spreadsheets that we began investigating in Chapter 2

SALES COMPARISONS BY ACTIVITY

George Farley has recently started keeping separate monthly sales records for the three parts of The Sophisticated Palate's business: the catering service, the imported items for which they act as wholesale distributors, and the prepared foods that they distribute wholesale. He wants to begin developing semiannual comparative summaries of these three activities to track their relative growth rates.

Figure 3.18 shows a spreadsheet he has created for the first six months of the year. He has typed in the dollar sales for each of the three activity categories—Catering, Wholesale Imports, and Wholesale Prepared Foods—for each of the months. Then, using the @SUM function, he computed the total sales for January and the total sales for the grocery across the entire six-month period. Finally, he used the Copy key (F8) to copy the monthly total formulas across from January, and the activity-total formulas down from the Deli total.

At this point, he decided he would like to create a graph that would give him a picture of comparative sales for each month. The Stacked Bar option of the Graph menu turned out to be just what he wanted. Figure 3.19 shows the graph that this option produced for him from his spreadsheet data. Each bar of the graph, representing a month of sales, is a composite of three different textural shades, representing the three business activities.

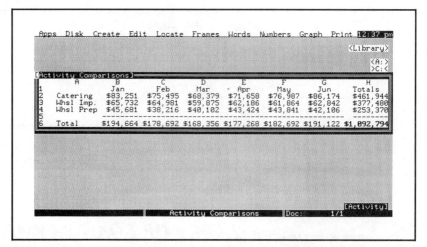

Figure 3.18: The Sophisticated Palate—Sales comparisons by activity

Figure 3.19: A stacked-bar graph of sales revenues

To create the graph, he began by extending the highlight over all of the numeric "raw" data of the spreadsheet: the rectangular block containing the sales figures for all three business activities, over the six-month period. Then he opened the Graph menu and selected first the Stacked Bar option, then the Draw New Graph option. Finally, he pressed the Return key to instruct Framework III to create a new frame for this graph.

To add a title to the graph, he entered the following label into the border of the Graph frame:

Sales by Activity

He had to press the Recalc key (F5) to make Framework III redraw the graph including the new title he had supplied.

He plans to create a graph like this every six months, to keep a continual comparison of sales revenues from the three parts of the business.

A TABLE OF LOAN PAYMENTS

The Sophisticated Palate has been doing extremely well in recent years. In fact, it has experienced increasing demand for its services from neighboring cities. However, since both the wholesale prepared foods and the catering trays must be prepared fresh daily, meeting the demand will require some form of expansion. One possibility is to increase the size of its fleet of trucks and expand the kitchen. However, it seems more sensible to obtain a new building in a neighboring city. This alternative would allow the business to maintain the quality and freshness of its products. Although it would still have to expand the fleet of trucks, the smaller distances they would have to cover would result in lower overall transportation costs.

George and Eileen have found a suitable building in an ideal location. However, it is for sale, rather than for lease, at a price of $320,000. They would like to buy the building, hoping to pay 20 percent down and cover the rest by means of a loan. Adding three new trucks will cost an additional $27,000. They have been negotiating for a business loan, while Ariana Katz, the administrative assistant, has been handling dealings with a real estate agent who believes the price is negotiable.

In the meantime, Eileen has asked Frank, the bookkeeper, to calculate the probable rate of payment, based on the various factors that might affect it.

Framework III has a function, @PMT, that calculates a monthly payment based on three parameters:

- The principal amount of the loan
- The annual interest rate
- The number of months in the term of the loan

Based on the worst-case assumption that they pay the asking price for the building, Frank calculates that they will pay $69,400 down on the building and borrow the remaining $277,600. He has created a small spreadsheet to find the resulting monthly payment:

	A	B
1	principal:	277600
2	rate:	7
3	yrs to pay:	15
4		
5	payment:	2495.15

Cells B1 to B3 contain the raw data: the principal, the annual interest rate, and the term of the loan in years. In cell B5, Frank entered the following formula:

@PMT(B1,B2/1200,B3*12)

As you can see from Table 3.3, the @PMT function computes the payment per period (defined by B3*12) required on a principal loan (B1) at a specified interest rate per period (B2/1200). Frank used the pointing technique to develop the formula. The expression B2/1200 represents the *monthly* interest rate in decimal form. The expression B3*12 represents the number of months in the term of the loan.

Eileen has discovered that she can change the raw data in this spreadsheet to produce an instantly recalculated figure for the payment. For example, if she wants to find out the payment on the same loan over a 30-year term, she can simply move the highlight to cell B3 and enter the number 30.

Finally, she realizes that she could easily use the @PMT function to create an entire two-dimensional table of loan payments, given a range of principals and a range of interest rates. This exactly suits her needs, since neither the principal nor the rate is determined yet. She asks Frank to complete this spreadsheet.

Figure 3.20 shows the spreadsheet he creates. In the upper left corner of the spreadsheet are the input values required for the payment calculation. But now the value in cell B1 represents the starting principal in the table; that is, the first of a range of possible principals. Likewise, the value in cell B2 is the first of a range of possible interest rates. These two values are carried forward to cells A6 and B5, respectively. Row 5 contains a series of interest rates, each incremented by a quarter of a percent. Column A, from cells A6 to A18, contains a range of principals, decremented by $1,000. These rates and principals are used to generate a table of loan payments.

Here are the steps Frank followed to formulate this table:

1. *To create the column of principals:* He entered the following reference into cell A6:

   +B1

```
 Apps  Disk  Create  Edit  Locate  Frames  Words  Numbers  Graph  Print  5 21 am
            A         B         C        D        E        F         G
  1  principal:   277600
  2  rate:             7
  3  yrs to pay:      15
  4
  5                   7      7.25     7.50     7.75        8      8.25
  6       277600  2495.15  2534.11  2573.39  2612.98  2652.89  2693.11
  7       276600  2486.16  2524.98  2564.12  2603.57  2643.33  2683.41
  8       275600  2477.17  2515.85  2554.85  2594.16  2633.78  2673.71
  9       274600  2468.18  2506.72  2545.58  2584.74  2624.22  2664.01
 10       273600  2459.19  2497.59  2536.31  2575.33  2614.66  2654.30
 11       272600  2450.21  2488.46  2527.04  2565.92  2605.11  2644.60
 12       271600  2441.22  2479.34  2517.77  2556.50  2595.55  2634.90
 13       270600  2432.23  2470.21  2508.50  2547.09  2585.99  2625.20
 14       269600  2423.24  2461.08  2499.23  2537.68  2576.44  2615.50
 15       268600  2414.25  2451.95  2489.96  2528.27  2566.88  2605.80
 16       267600  2405.26  2442.82  2480.69  2518.85  2557.32  2596.10
 17       266600  2396.28  2433.69  2471.41  2509.44  2547.77  2586.39
 18       265600  2387.29  2424.56  2462.14  2500.03  2538.21  2576.69

 @Pmt($A6,B$5/1200,$B$3*12)          Payments.B6          SS:         2/6
```

Figure 3.20: A table of loan payments

and the following formula into cell A7:

+A6! – 1000

He then used the Copy key (F8) to copy this decrementing formula down column A into cells A8 to A18.

2. *To create the row of loan rates:* He entered the following reference into cell B5:

+B2

and the following formula into cell C5:

+B5 + .25

He then copied this formula across row 5 into cells D5 to G5.

3. *To create the payment table:* Using the pointing technique, he entered the following formula into cell B6:

@PMT($A6,B$5/1200,$B$3*12)

Replicating this formula required two separate copy operations: first copying the single formula across row 6; then copying all the @PMT formulas of row 6 down into rows 7 to 18.

For the copy operations to be successful, Frank had to distinguish carefully between relative and absolute references in the @PMT formula. In the reference to the principal amounts ($A6), the column, A, is fixed, but the rows, 6 to 18, are relative. In contrast, the interest rate (B$5) has a relative column reference but an absolute row reference. Finally, the "years to pay" ($B$3) is an absolute reference both for the column and the row. No other combination of references would have yielded the desired table.

Because this spreadsheet required something of an effort to prepare, Eileen wanted to protect Frank's work. Looking at the spreadsheet, she realized that the only cells that she would ever want to change would be the three input cells, B1, B2, and B3. Accidental deletions or changes in the values or formulas of any of the other cells would be undesirable and would require some effort to repair.

Conveniently, Framework III offers a way to protect selected cells in a spreadsheet from any accidental changes. This option is controlled from the Edit menu and is called

Protect from Editing

This option protects the current contents of the spreadsheet cells that you have selected from being accidentally revised or deleted. The Edit menu also has an option that removes this protection if you decide to go back and modify a protected cell:

Allow editing

To protect the spreadsheet, then, Eileen extended the highlight over all the values in rows 5 to 18 and pressed the following keys:

Ctrl-E   (to open the Edit menu)

P   (to select the Protect option)

Placing the table in protected mode does not, of course, change the spreadsheet's responsiveness to changes in the input data. A change in any one of the three input values—the starting principal, the starting interest rate, or the term of the loan—results in an immediate recalculation of the entire table.

Unfortunately, the recalculation process is rather slow in this table; Framework III takes a long time to perform so many @PMT functions. This becomes a problem when Eileen wants to change two input values at once. For example, let's say she wants to change the starting principal to $265,000 and the loan term to 30 years. In its current settings, Framework III recalculates the entire table after *each* of these new entries, even though Eileen is interested only in the *final* result, after both entries have been changed. She finds it annoying to have to wait for the recalculation to occur twice.

The Options submenu of the Numbers menu (shown in Figure 3.21) presents a solution to this problem. When you first create a new Spreadsheet frame, Framework III by default goes into Automatic recalculation *mode,* and the default *order* in which it recalculates is called Natural. This means that the spreadsheet will be recalculated whenever you enter a new numeric value that will have an effect on some other value. Using the Options submenu, you can change the recalculation mode to Manual. In this mode, Framework III recalculates the spreadsheet only when you explicitly command it to do so by pressing the Recalc key, F5. (A change in the recalculation mode applies only to the current spreadsheet.)

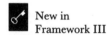
New in
Framework III

In Framework III, you can now recalculate a selected range of cells. This means that you no longer have to recalculate an entire spreadsheet when you want to see how the values have changed. To do so, use

Figure 3.21: The Options submenu of the Numbers menu

Extend Select (F6) to highlight a range of cells, then press Recalc (F5). You'll notice that sometimes cells outside the range will also be recalculated. This is because these cells hold intermediate values necessary for finding the values of cells within the selected range.

Eileen pressed the following keys to change Frank's payment spreadsheet to Manual recalculation:

Ctrl-N   (to open the Numbers menu)

O   (to select the Options submenu)

M   (to switch to Manual recalculation mode)

Now she can change as many of the input values as she wants; when she is ready for the table to be recalculated, she the presses Recalc key (F5).

We'll discuss the other recalculation options, which define the *order* of recalculation, in the next section, as we examine George's business expense Outline frame.

EXPENSE SPREADSHEETS, WITH A SUMMARY

At the end of Chapter 2, we left George organizing a monthly summary of the business's expenses. Figure 3.22 shows the Outline frame he has prepared. The outline holds nine different spreadsheets: seven for the various categories of fixed expenses, one for Cost of Goods Sold, and finally the Summary of Expenses spreadsheet at the bottom of the outline.

George has organized this outline so that it can be reused each month for two purposes: to record fixed and variable expenses in a series of categories, and to yield a summary spreadsheet of all those expenses. Let's examine George's work.

Figure 3.23 shows the Summary of Expenses spreadsheet located at the end of George's outline. This spreadsheet takes one value from each of the other spreadsheets in the outline. These values represent the bottom-line, total expenses in each of the expense categories. The values are transferred from the expense spreadsheets to the Summary of Expenses spreadsheet through references that George has typed into the summary.

Figure 3.22: The Sophisticated Palate—Grocery expense outline

Figure 3.23: The Summary of Expenses spreadsheet

For example, you can see that The Sophisticated Palate spent $3,420 on advertising this month. Figure 3.24 shows the Advertising spreadsheet. It has four columns of data: the date of each expense, a description, the amount of each item, and a total for all the advertising expenses. George computed this total using the @SUM function.

The total amount is in cell D14 of the Advertising spreadsheet. Notice that the top cell of column D and the leftmost cell of row 14

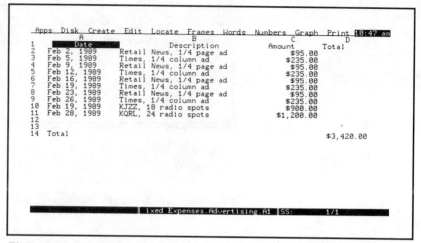

Figure 3.24: The Sophisticated Palate—Advertising expense spreadsheet

both contain the label *Total.* This allows us to call cell D14 by the following English name reference:

Total.Total

Because this reference is inside the Advertising spreadsheet, the cell's expanded English name is

Advertising.Total.Total

But Advertising is a subframe inside the major outline heading *Fixed Expenses.* So, finally, the full name of cell D14 is

Fixed Expenses.Advertising.Total.Total

This name can be used as a reference by any other spreadsheet inside the expenses outline. As a reference, its function will be to transfer the value contained in the Advertising spreadsheet's cell D14 to another spreadsheet location in the outline.

The Summary of Expenses spreadsheet (Figure 3.23) uses a series of references like this one to fetch all the total values from the expense spreadsheets. George has been careful to organize all of the expense spreadsheets so that their totals each have the English name

Total.Total

If you were to look at the references behind the values in column C of the Summary of Expenses spreadsheet, this is what you would find:

```
+ Fixed Expenses.Advertising.Total.Total
+ Fixed Expenses.Equipment Loans.Total.Total
+ Fixed Expenses.Equipment Maint.Total.Total
+ Fixed Expenses.Insurance.Total.Total
+ Fixed Expenses.Rent.Total.Total
+ Fixed Expenses.Utilities.Total.Total
+ Fixed Expenses.Wages.Total.Total
+ Variable Expenses.COGS.Total.Total
```

Each of these references links the Summary of Expenses spreadsheet to one of the expense spreadsheets and transfers a data item.

Finally, in cell C13 of the Summary of Expenses spreadsheet, George has entered the formula that finds the total expenses for the month:

@SUM(C3:C11)

The advantage of this outline organization is this: the format of each expense spreadsheet can be designed independently and need not conform to the organization of the Summary of Expenses spreadsheet. Each expense spreadsheet can be as simple or as complex as necessary. The single requirement is that the cell containing the total of each expense spreadsheet have the same English name reference— Total.Total.

With this outline, Frank can enter the data in the various expense spreadsheets daily. When the expense spreadsheets are complete, the total values will be transferred to the Summary of Expenses spreadsheet.

There is only one small problem with this arrangement. References from one spreadsheet to another often need to be manually recalculated. For example, let's say Frank enters a new set of data into the Advertising spreadsheet and then George wants to open the Summary of Expenses spreadsheet to examine the effect on the total month's expenses. George has to press the Recalc key (F5) from the

Summary spreadsheet before the new Advertising.Total.Total value will be transferred.

LINKING THE EXPENSE SPREADSHEETS TO THE SUMMARY

Framework III provides a solution to this problem. To complete the link between two spreadsheets, you can enter a special kind of reference in the *source* spreadsheet—that is, the spreadsheet that is sending data to a new destination. This special reference begins with the @ symbol.

For example, the Advertising expense total is located in cell C3 of the Summary spreadsheet. To provide an automatic link between the Advertising and Summary spreadsheets, George can enter the following value into a free cell in the Advertising spreadsheet:

@Summary of Expenses.C3

Now, whenever George enters a new numeric value into the Advertising spreadsheet, resulting in a recalculation of the spreadsheet, this @ reference will ensure that the Summary of Expenses spreadsheet's cell C3 will also be recalculated. Transfer of data between the two spreadsheets will thus occur automatically, eliminating the need to use the Recalc key in the Summary of Expenses spreadsheet.

George had to find some out-of-the-way location in the Advertising spreadsheet to store this @ reference. To avoid making a mess of the spreadsheet, he decided to add a new column for this reference. He used the Create menu to add one column at the right side of the spreadsheet—column E. Into cell E14 he entered the necessary linking reference:

@Summary of Expenses.C3

Column E does not contain information that needs to be displayed in the spreadsheet. In fact, its appearance might be a distraction from the real information of the spreadsheet. Fortunately, Framework III provides a little trick that you can use to *hide* any column in a spreadsheet. The trick is performed by the Size key. Here are the steps:

1. Place the highlight in the column you want to hide.

2. Press the Size key (F4).

3. Press the ← key until the column is 0 spaces wide.

4. Press the Return key to complete the operation.

A column thus hidden is still part of the spreadsheet; it simply is not displayed.

George used this technique to hide column E in the Advertising spreadsheet. But he found that one final adjustment was necessary to make the interspreadsheet link functional. Whenever he changed a figure in the Advertising spreadsheet, only the values that depended on that figure were recalculated. The reference linking the total to the Summary of Expenses spreadsheet was not recalculated, because the reference does not depend on any other values. So his new totals did not get transferred automatically. To remedy this, he had to change the order in which Framework III recalculated the values in the Advertising spreadsheet.

The default recalculation order is called *Natural;* when Natural order is on, Framework III recalculates values in the order defined by the spreadsheet's references. For example, if a given formula depends on two other values elsewhere in the spreadsheet, those two values are recalculated before the formula. Significantly, if you change a value that does not affect any other values, no recalculation takes place.

The alternate recalculation order is called *Row-wise.* Under this order, Framework III recalculates every row of the spreadsheet, from the top row to the bottom row, every time you enter a new numeric value. This order ensures that every cell of the spreadsheet will be recalculated, no matter how simple or complex a system of references the spreadsheet contains.

Thus, to make sure the @ reference in cell E14 would be recalculated after each new entry into the Advertising spreadsheet, George pressed the following keys to change the spreadsheet's order of recalculation:

Ctrl-N   (to open the Numbers menu)

O   (to select the Options submenu)

R (to change recalculation to Row-wise)

To summarize, here are the steps George followed to link each of the expense spreadsheets to the Summary of Expenses spreadsheet:

1. Add a column at the right side of each expense spreadsheet.

2. At the new lower right corner of each spreadsheet, enter the appropriate @ reference into the Summary spreadsheet.

3. Hide the new column from view, using the Size key (F4).

4. Change each expense spreadsheet's recalculation order to Row-wise.

This may seem like a lot of trouble to go through; but remember, this outline can now be used as a template for recording and summarizing the company's expense records each month. Thanks to the rather elaborate system for linking spreadsheets inside the outline, George can be certain that his Summary of Expenses spreadsheet will be developed automatically as he enters information into the individual expense spreadsheets.

EXPLORING FURTHER

As you continue to expand your knowledge of Framework III, you will find that its resources for spreadsheet programming go far beyond what we have covered in this chapter. In particular, Framework III and FRED provide a rich collection of functions and facilities that can increase the versatility and power of a spreadsheet. We'll discover many more of these functions in the chapters ahead.

THE DATE FUNCTIONS

One important group of functions consists of the date functions. You can see the @DATE function in action in George's Advertising expense spreadsheet, Figure 3.24. For example, in cell A2, George entered the following formula:

@DATE(1987,2,2)

As you can see, this formula resulted in the display

Feb 2, 1987

George could have entered this date as a label, but he has learned that it's a good idea to enter it through the @DATE function, so that if necessary he can later perform arithmetic on the date. We'll examine the date functions in detail when we study Framework III databases in Chapter 5.

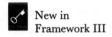 New in Framework III

In Framework III, you can use the Entry Format for Data option from the Numbers menu to preselect a date entry format for a cell or range of cells. The Entry Format for Dates submenu contains seven possible date formats that you can use to enter dates directly into cells without using the @DATE function. You can enter dates as:

- month day year (1/10/89; January 10, 1989)
- day month year (10-1-89; 10 Jan 1989)
- month year (1 89; J 1989)
- year month day (89.1.10; 1989 January 10)
- day month (10-1; 10 Jan)
- month day (1/10; January 10)
- month (January, Jan, Ja, J)

The date entry format has no effect on the date display style that you can set using the styling options on the Numbers menu. Several of the styling options will change the way the date displays on the screen and prints. However, the Entry Format for Dates option is used to determine how you will enter dates into spreadsheets and databases (see Chapter 5).

Before ending this chapter, we'll look briefly at two last topics: sorting a spreadsheet, and a special spreadsheet-navigation command.

SORTING

The Locate menu has two options that allow you to rearrange spreadsheet data:

Ascending Sort
Descending Sort

These options use a selected column or portion of a column as the "key" to rearrange the spreadsheet. The sort will work on text, numbers, or dates, rearranging alphabetically, numerically, or chronologically.

To use these sorting options, follow these steps:

1. Extend the highlight over the column you have selected as the "key" for the sorting operation.

2. Open the Locate menu.

3. Select Ascending Sort or Descending Sort.

Let's use George's Summary of Expenses spreadsheet (Figure 3.23) for a quick example of sorting. Let's say George has decided to sort the fixed expenses in the spreadsheet from the largest to the smallest expense. He extends the highlight over the expense amounts in cells C3 to C11. Then he presses these keys:

Ctrl-L   (to open the Locate menu)

D   (to select the Descending Sort)

As soon as he completes these keystrokes, the fixed expenses reappear in the following order:

Wages	$39,051.00
Insurance	$9,862.00
Equipment Loans	$8,791.00
Rent	$3,600.00
Advertising	$3,420.00
Equipment Maint.	$1,756.00
Utilities	$1,142.00

Notice that the labels in column B are also rearranged to correspond appropriately to the new order of column C. At some point, George might change his mind and decide to rearrange these expenses in alphabetical order, by the name of the expense. To do so, he would extend the highlight over the labels in cells B3 to B11 and press

Ctrl-L   (to open the Locate menu)

A   (to choose the Ascending Sort)

This will put the expenses back in the order in which you see them in Figure 3.23.

New in Framework III

When you sort a range of cells, Framework III will keep formula references accurate for the sorted cells. This means that a formula that references specific cells will be able to continue to reference the same information, even if it is located in a new position due to sorting.

We'll learn more about sorting and the Locate menu in Chapter 5.

REPLACING FORMULAS WITH VALUES

New in Framework III

In Framework III, you can select a cell or range of cells that contains formulas and quickly convert the formulas to values only. To do so, select the range of cells you want to convert, select Copy (F8), and press # instead of Return to complete the copy process.

In earlier versions of Framework, you could accomplish the same result by copying the selected block to another region on the spreadsheet, then copying it back, ending the copy with #. In Framework III, you can perform this task in one step.

THE GOTO COMMAND

An additional command—Goto, on the Locate menu—can be used to speed your movement through spreadsheets. To use it, press

Ctrl-L   (to open the Locate menu)

G   (to invoke the Goto command)

cell name   (to tell Framework III the name of the cell you want to move to)

Return (to record your selection and move to the cell)

You can even use this option to move to a spreadsheet cell in a frame other than the one you are currently using.

George found this command useful when he was working out his Summary of Expenses spreadsheet. He needed to know if the formula he had entered had actually succeeded in placing the summary information in the correct location. With it, he could enter the hidden formula in column E of his Advertising spreadsheet, and then move immediately to cell C3 in the Summary of Expenses spreadsheet, by entering

Summary of Expenses.C3

as the name of the cell to go to.

This command has an additional feature that makes it especially useful for comparing the results of two widely separated frames. After you have moved to the specified cell, you can press the Instruct key, followed by Return, to get back to the cell from which you moved. Thus, you can make repeated adjustments to a formula in one cell and easily check to see that the results in another cell are what you intended. If they are not, two keystrokes return you to the original cell for further editing.

The Goto command is not restricted to spreadsheets. In fact, you can use it to move between any items on the desktop that have names. You can move from one subhead of an outline to another, for example, or from a frame on the desktop to one in the Library cabinet. You can even move from a spreadsheet cell in a frame nested several levels deep in one outline frame to a cell in a spreadsheet in a completely different outline. No matter how far you move, you can always return to your previous location by pressing Instruct Return Return.

SUMMARY

A Spreadsheet frame is designed to help you work with tables of numbers and to relieve you of the tedium of arithmetic. Spreadsheets also help you explore "what-if" scenarios; you can quickly find out what happens to calculated values as a result of new input data.

The rows and columns of a spreadsheet form a grid of cells. Each cell has an address, consisting of its column letter and its row number. This address can be used as a *reference* to the value the cell contains.

Formulas in spreadsheets are designed to calculate new values from already existing values. A formula can contain references to other cells, and it can perform arithmetic operations. Once you have written a formula, you can copy it to other cells in your spreadsheet. For the purposes of copying, references in formulas can be designated as *relative* or *absolute*.

To simplify the process of writing certain kinds of formulas, Framework III provides a considerable set of *functions* for you to work with in spreadsheets.

Using Framework III's menus and function keys, you can control the appearance and organization of a spreadsheet. You can change the display style of numbers and labels. You can insert or delete rows and columns. You can move blocks of data from one place to another. You can even sort data in the spreadsheet by columns.

Producing graphs from spreadsheets is an easy process in Framework III. The Graph menu offers several different types of graphs for you to choose from.

Finally, Framework III offers some rather elaborate techniques for linking spreadsheets, automating the transfer of data from one spreadsheet to another. This can be an important feature when you find yourself creating complex systems of spreadsheets within an Outline frame.

4

Word Processing

OVERVIEW

INTRODUCTION

WORD FRAMES ARE DESIGNED FOR ENTERING, REVISing and formatting pages of text. No matter what kind of writing you do—from business letters, memos, reports, or legal documents to personal letters, essays, or poetry—Framework III's word processing capabilities will allow you to concentrate on the writing itself rather than on the mundane details of producing typewritten paper drafts of your writing.

In this chapter, you'll learn how to begin writing in a Word frame, as well as how to revise your work once you've completed a written document. Here are the major topics we'll explore:

- *Entering text:* Using the keyboard, understanding word wrap, and moving the cursor.

- *Formatting text:* Changing the alignment of the text on the page and setting margins, paragraph indents, and tab stops.

- *Editing a document:* Selecting portions of the text for editing, inserting and deleting, styling text for special printing effects such as boldfacing and underlining, moving blocks of text from one place to another, using the search and replace feature, and correcting spelling errors.

- *Printing a document:* Using the submenus of the Print menu to set margins and pages, incorporate headers and footers into a document, and control the print mode. In addition, we'll look at some special FRED functions used to format a document for printing and to control the printer.

As with other types of frames, your major tools for working in Word frames will be the cursor-movement keys, the special function keys at the left side of the keyboard, and the Framework III menus. The Words and Print menus are particularly important for word processing. We'll also be working with the Locate and Edit menus and, of course, the Create menu. In addition, we will learn how to place FRED functions *behind* a Word frame to control the printing process.

CREATING A WORD FRAME

The option in the Create menu that places a new Word frame on the desktop is called

Empty / Word Frame

Here are the keystrokes that place a Word frame on the desktop:

Ctrl-C   (to open the Create menu)

E   (to create an Empty frame)

You may recall from Chapter 2 that an Empty frame has two main uses. You can move other frames into it, in which case it becomes an Outline (or *containing*) frame. Or you can move inside the frame and begin word processing; it then becomes a Word frame. (You can also use an Empty frame to place a graph in or to conduct a telecommunications session; it then becomes a Graph frame or a Telecommunications frame.)

These two uses are mutually exclusive: once you begin word processing in an Empty frame, Framework III will not allow you to move other frames inside what has become a Word frame. If you want to combine word processed text with other types of frames, you'll have to create a separate Outline frame to contain all of the various document frames you are working with. Near the end of this chapter, we'll explore the use of Word frames in an outline.

As always, the first thing you'll want to do when you create a new frame is to type a label into the frame's border. You'll recall that this label has two purposes: it helps you distinguish among the various frames you might have on the desktop, and it ultimately serves as a file name for your document when you save it on disk.

The In key (+) moves you into the Word frame, at which point you are ready to begin word processing. As soon as you move inside a Word frame, you'll notice the *cursor* that marks your place in the frame. The word processing cursor is the same visual marker that we have worked with so often on the edit line below the desktop: a flashing underscore character, contained within a single reverse-video space.

Up to now, in our work with Outline and Spreadsheet frames, we've distinguished between the cursor, on the edit line, and the *highlight,* inside the frames themselves. The distinction may seem a little less clear in Word frames. In word processing, the cursor (the flashing underscore) always marks the current character position in a document. But the reverse-video highlight that *encloses* the cursor can be extended to block off larger parts of a document: words, sentences, paragraphs, and larger sections of text.

We will see that Framework III gives you convenient keyboard commands for *selecting* these various portions of text by extending the highlight over them. Once you have thus selected the text you want to work with, you can choose any of the word processing operations to modify the text: formatting, styling, moving, copying, deleting, and so on.

But before you can learn to use Framework III's word processing features to *revise* the appearance of text, you have to begin by *entering* some sentences and paragraphs into a frame.

ENTERING TEXT

The sample document we'll be working with in this chapter is a two-page office memorandum. Imagine yourself as the executive in charge of purchasing computer hardware and software, in a company that has recently placed a new personal computer on the desk of every manager. After considering several integrated software packages, you have just bought copies of Framework III for use on these PCs. You've decided to distribute a memo to all your managers, encouraging them to start using Framework III and describing some of the program's features.

Figure 4.1 is a printout of the first draft of your memo. To gain some hands-on experience with Framework III word processing, you type the memo into your own PC. Once you have finished entering the first draft into a Word frame, you plan to begin revisions, exploring several of Framework III's formatting and editing features along the way. Don't worry if you make some mistakes in typing. You'll see in a little while how easy it is to make corrections on the screen before you print your document, and you'll also use Framework III's built-in spelling checker to catch and correct any errors you might not have noticed along the way. (If you want a preview of the final product of your work with this memo, take a look at Figure 4.11.)

```
Date:  March 3, 1989

To: All Managers
From: B.B.

RE: Using Framework III in the Office

We have recently purchased several copies of the integrated
software package called Framework III. I would like all of you to
begin working with this program as soon as possible, evaluating
its effectiveness for your own data processing tasks.

In Framework III you do all your work in special-purpose frames
that appear on the display screne. The screen becomes your
"desktop," the palce where all the action of the program takes
place. You can control exactly what part of your current work is
displayed on the desktop at a given time. You may want to work
with several frames at a time,m in which case they can all be
present on the desktop at once. Frames on the desktop are either
open--displaying their contents--or closed--temporarily placed in
a special "tray" at the side of the desktop.

You can crteate several different types of frames. Here are brief
descriptions of the frames you'll probably be working with the
most frequently:

Spreadsheet frames are designed to help you work with tables of
numbers. Any time you organize numbers and labels into columns
and rows for the purpose of calcualting totals, averages, or
other statistical values, a spreadsheet frame will simplify the
task and increase your ability to analyze the data itself. In
addition to numbers, you can enter formulas into your
spreadsheets, to take over the more tedious arithmetic tasks
involved iwth numeric record keepint. Formulas can be copied
across rows or down columns of your spreadsheet, alowying you to
perform, in minutes, what might otherwise turn into hours and
hours of complex aritmentic tasks.

A spreadsheet is also a projection tool, allowing you to find
answers to "what-if" questions. Change a single number on ;your
spreadsheet, and all formulas that rely on that number will be
recalculated, automatically. Those of you who do cost projections
will particularly appreciate this feature.

Graph frames give you presentation-quality graphs from the tables
of numbers that you enter into a spreadsheet frame. Framework III
can draw a variety of different types of graphs: bar, stacked
bar, pie, mark points, line, x-y, and high-low-close. Graphs are
simple to draw, and you can even print them out ont paper, using
the printer attached to yoru PC.

Database frames allow you to organize, sotre, and work with
groups of data. You may want to create databases to handle
employee records, client information, sales records, and
inventories.

Word frames are used for working with Framework III's easy but
powerful word processor. Those of you who are used to typing your
own memos will find this to be a refreshing new way to create
documents. You can even store frequently used forms in a library
on the desktop, so that you don't have to create them from
scratch every time. You may also want to introduce your
secretaries to Framework III word processing, if you can stand
the thought of sharing your desktop computers with another
person.
```

Figure 4.1: Office memorandum, first draft

```
If you can't, Framework III also has telecommunications frames,
which you can use not only for conventional telecommunications
purposes--logging on to the Central Data Processing department's
mainframe to read information processed there, for example-- but
to hook your computer directly to others in the building, and
share your work instantly with those who need to use the results
of your analyses, or the information in your files.

Please begin working with Framework III as soon as you can; ;I
think you'll find that the effort you put into learing to use the
program will pay off almost immediately. Let me know your
thoughts within a couple of weeks.

                                        B.B.
```

Figure 4.1 (continued): Office memorandum, first draft

Create a Word frame on the desktop, and enter the following label into the border of the frame:

Memo to Managers

 New in Framework III

Press the In key (+) to move the cursor into the frame.

In Framework III, word frames can now contain a *ruler line*, which displays the left and right margins, paragraph indentations, and tab locations. You can turn the ruler line on or off using Display Ruler on the Word Options submenu of the Words menu. You'll learn more about this new feature later in this chapter.

The first several lines of our office memorandum comprise the heading, which specifies whom the memo is addressed to and who wrote it, as well as the date and the subject of the memo. After you type each line, press the Return key to move the cursor to the beginning of the next line. To place a blank space between two lines, press Return a second time.

When you begin entering the first paragraph of the text (beginning "We have recently purchased . . ."), you'll find that you do *not* have to press the Return key when you come to the end of a line. When the appropriate moment arrives, Framework III automatically moves the cursor down to the beginning of the following line on the screen. If you are in the middle of a word when you reach the end of the line, Framework III will carry that word down to the next line.

This feature is called *word wrap*. Thanks to word wrap, you need to press the Return key only when you have completed a paragraph. In fact, you should *avoid* pressing the Return key at the end of a line inside a paragraph. Otherwise, you will have unwanted *carriage-return characters* inside what you consider a paragraph, and later on you'll have trouble using Framework III's formatting tools to change the format of the paragraph.

Another important key in a Word frame is the Backspace key. Backspace does two things. It moves the cursor backward by one space, and it erases the character you had typed into that space. Backspace is a convenient key to use when you make a typing mistake and you want to move back and correct it.

Hold down the Backspace key for several seconds, and the cursor will move backward quickly, erasing several characters of the current line. If you backspace to the beginning of a line and then press Backspace again, the cursor will move up to the end of the previous line, a process that is the reverse of word wrap.

As you enter text into a Word frame, you will see a message like the following in the third section of the status panel:

Char: 36/7

This particular pair of numbers means that you are at the 36th character of the 7th line of your text. The first of these two numbers increases by 1 every time you press a key, adding a character to your line; it starts over from 0 with every new line. The second number increases whenever the cursor moves down a line. When you first create a Word frame, Framework III sets the default line length at 65 characters. We will see later how you can change that length when you want longer or shorter lines.

That's really all you need to know for the most basic word processing skill: entering text into a frame. Before you read further, spend some time entering the entire text of the memo shown in Figure 4.1. Painful a task though this may seem, you'll be glad to have this document to experiment with as we begin discussing some of the more exciting word processing features.

MOVING THE CURSOR

Once you've begun to create a document, you may find yourself wanting to move backward and forward within it, to insert, delete, or revise. Two kinds of cursor and highlight movement are possible in Word frames; both make use of the cursor-movement keys at the right side of your keyboard.

Simple cursor movement involves moving the cursor from one part of the document to another. You can move the cursor in any direction inside the document. You can also make the cursor jump a distance, from one location to another:

- To the beginning or end of the current line
- To the beginning or end of the entire document
- Up one frame or down one frame

Table 4.1 describes the cursor-movement keys that you will want to master for word processing in Framework III.

These cursor-movement operations do not extend the highlight; they simply move the cursor to a new character position inside the

Table 4.1: Cursor-Movement Keys in Word Frames

KEYS	ACTION
↑, ↓	Moves the cursor up or down one line in the text.
←, →	Moves the cursor one character to the left or right in the text.
Home	Moves the cursor to the first character position in the current line.
End	Moves the cursor to the last character position in the current line.
Ctrl-Home	Moves the cursor to the beginning of the entire document.
Ctrl-End	Moves the cursor to the end of the entire document.
PgUp	Moves the cursor to the top of the current frame, or scrolls one frame up.
PgDn	Moves the cursor to the bottom of the current frame, or scrolls one frame down.

text. But for many word processing functions you'll want to use the highlight to *select* a portion of your document as the target for a certain activity. For these operations, the Ctrl key works with the cursor-movement keys to extend the highlight over the text you want to select.

SELECTING BLOCKS OF TEXT

By extending the highlight over a range of text, in much the same way that you learned to extend the spreadsheet highlight over a range of cells, you select a portion of your document as the object of a Framework III activity. Framework III gives you pairs of keystrokes for selecting the following portions of text:

- A word
- A sentence
- A paragraph

Table 4.2 describes the selection keys that extend the cursor in these three ways. To help you understand the effects of these keys,

Table 4.2: Text-Selection Keys in Word Frames

KEY	ACTION
Ctrl-→	Selects the word or portion of a word immediately following, and including, the cursor position.
Ctrl-←	Selects the word or portion of a word immediately preceding, and including, the cursor position.
Ctrl-↑	Selects the sentence or portion of a sentence immediately preceding, and including, the cursor position.
Ctrl-↓	Selects the sentence or portion of a sentence immediately following, and including, the cursor position.
Ctrl-PgUp	Selects the paragraph or portion of a paragraph immediately preceding the cursor position.
Ctrl-PgDn	Selects the paragraph or portion of a paragraph immediately following the cursor position.

Figures 4.2 to 4.4 show examples of word, sentence, and paragraph selection, in a portion of the office memorandum that you have now entered into your Word frame.

Of course, if you want to select *several* words, sentences, or paragraphs, you should use the Extend Select key (F6). Press the key, and then use the Ctrl-key combinations described in Table 4.2 to extend the highlight over the exact block of text you want to work with.

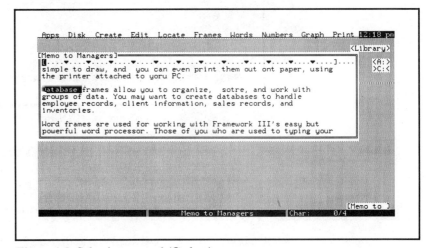

Figure 4.2: Selecting a word (Ctrl-→)

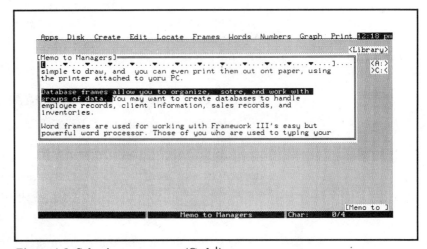

Figure 4.3: Selecting a sentence (Ctrl-↓)

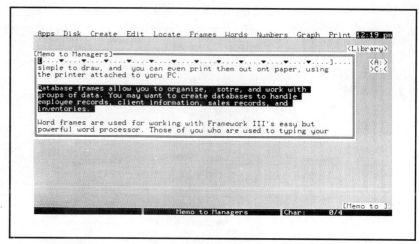

Figure 4.4: Selecting a paragraph (Ctrl-PgDn)

Now we're going to look at the tools Framework III provides to help you change the appearance of your word processed document.

FORMATTING YOUR DOCUMENT

Figure 4.5 shows the Words menu. It is divided into four parts, dealing with printing styles, text alignment, margins and tabs, and the Word Options submenu. Here we'll look at text alignment and margins and tabs, as well as some of the Word Options features. A little later in the chapter we'll examine styling, which occupies the first part of this menu.

GLOBAL VERSUS LOCAL FORMATTING

In the sections ahead, we'll be examining the variety of formatting and styling options available in Framework III word processing. All of these options can be used either globally—affecting the entire document—or locally—affecting only a selected portion of the document. Here are the two techniques for distinguishing between these modes of operation:

- To assign a global format or style, move the highlight to the border of the Word frame (Out key, –) and select the appropriate option from the Words menu.

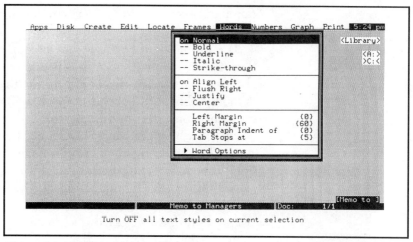

Figure 4.5: The Words menu

- To assign a local format or style, move the cursor into the Word frame, extend the highlight over the block of text that you want to work with, and select the appropriate option from the Words menu.

We'll begin by performing some global operations on our office memorandum document. Then we'll do some local operations on certain portions of the text.

TEXT ALIGNMENT

The *format* of your document refers to the alignment of the left and right sides of the text in relation to the margins. Framework III offers four different alignment options. As we just mentioned, these can be assigned either globally or locally.

The Align Left option is the default condition for a Word frame. Under this option, the left side of the text is justified—that is, arranged in a straight line along the left margin. The Align Left option leaves the document in a *ragged-right* format. This means that each line simply ends randomly at or near the right margin, depending on the length of the line's last word. The version of our memorandum shown in Figure 4.1 is arranged under the Align Left option, as are the displays in Figures 4.2 to 4.4. This format should seem familiar, because most typewritten documents end up in this condition by default.

The Flush Right option is just the opposite. The right side of the document is aligned, and the left side becomes ragged. Figure 4.6 shows a paragraph displayed under the control of this option. Although this unusual format appears only rarely in print, you will find a use for it later in this chapter.

The Justify option aligns both the left and right sides of the document. The final version of the office memorandum, shown in Figure 4.11, is both left- and right-justified. To achieve this kind of justification, Framework III carefully inserts spaces inside the text, so that each line will end at exactly the same point at the right margin. Many people find that a justified document is more appealing to the eye than one that has a ragged-right edge.

Finally, the Center option of the Words menu centers each line of text that you enter into a Word frame. We'll be using this option locally inside the office memorandum to center the lines of the memo's heading.

First, let's try using the Justify option globally on the memorandum. Actually, you can specify a text alignment either before you begin entering text into your document or after the document is already complete. If you specify the format before you enter any text, each new line you type will be automatically aligned according to

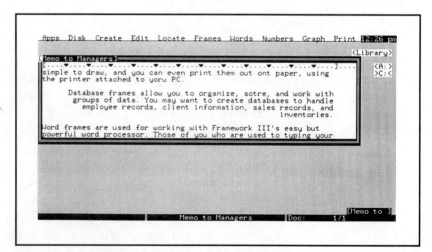

Figure 4.6: A paragraph displayed in flush-right format

your specification. If you wait until after the document is complete to specify a format, Framework III will quickly reformat your document, briefly displaying the following message at the bottom of the screen:

FORMATTING

Because our memorandum is already completely entered into the frame, we'll have to begin by moving the highlight to the frame's border to perform a global format operation. Here are the keystrokes:

Out (–)   (to move the highlight to the border)

Ctrl-W   (to open the Words menu)

J   (to justify the document)

In response, Framework III will reformat the entire document so that each paragraph is both left- and right-justified.

MARGINS, INDENTS, AND TABS

 Version Note

There are actually two ways to set margins and tabs. One method is from the menus; the other uses the new ruler line. In the examples that follow, we will use both methods. If you are using a version of Framework earlier than version III, you will have to use the menu method in all examples. The result will be exactly the same, regardless of the method used.

Formatting a document also involves several other characteristics: selecting numeric values for the left and right margins, thus determining the maximum length in characters of each line; specifying paragraph indents; and defining tab stops. The third section of the Words menu deals with these options.

The default left margin is set at 0, and the default right margin at 65. This means that each line can have a maximum of 65 characters. (The actual horizontal positioning of the text on the printed page is determined by other Framework III tools, which we will examine later.)

If you reset the margins of a Word frame before you enter any text into the frame, each line of text that you enter will be correctly formatted within the margins you have specified.

When you change the margins of an already existing document or part of a document, Framework III automatically reformats the text within the new margins. In reformatting the document, Framework III also follows the alignment option that you have selected.

Let's look at an example. The office memorandum contains six paragraphs that describe the various components of Framework III.

Let's say you decide to emphasize these paragraphs by printing them with narrower widths than the other paragraphs of the document.

To make this *local* change in the document, you begin by moving inside the Word frame. Then you move the cursor to the beginning of the first target paragraph, which reads, "Spreadsheet frames are designed . . .". We'll use the menu method to change the margins for the first three paragraphs. To begin, press the following keys:

Extend Select (F6)	(to extend the highlight)
Ctrl-PgDn, three times	(to select the first three target paragraphs)
Ctrl-W	(to open the Words menu)
L	(to change the left margin)
11	(the new left margin)
Return	(to enter the value into the menu)
Ctrl-W	(to open the Words menu again)
R	(to change the right margin)
60	(the new right margin)
Return	(to enter the value into the menu)

Now the first three paragraphs describing the components of Framework III are displayed within the margins 11 to 60. These paragraphs are also justified within the new margins, because we have already chosen justification for the entire document.

Now let's change the margins for the next three paragraphs using the ruler method. (Note that it doesn't matter if the ruler is currently displayed or not. You can edit the ruler settings even if the Display Ruler option is turned off.) Move the cursor to the next paragraph (the one beginning "Database frames allow you to...") and press the following keys:

Extend Select (F6)	(to extend the highlight)
Ctrl-PgDn, three times	(to select the next three target paragraphs)
Ctrl-W	(to open the Words menu)

W   (to open the Word Options
                           submenu)

M   (to select Modify Ruler)

After you select Modify Ruler, you will be in the ruler edit mode. Your document will display on the screen, with the cursor inside the ruler line. At the bottom of the screen, a list of options displays.

In this example, you will simply set new margins for the three selected paragraphs. To do so, move the cursor to column 11. Notice that the default tab markers (represented by downward-pointing triangles) are placed every five spaces. Therefore, move the cursor one space past the second tab. Now press the left square-bracket key ([). This will set the new margin to 11.

Next, move the cursor to position 60. You can move the cursor using many of the familiar cursor-movement keys, including the → and ← keys, the spacebar, Home (to move to the left edge of the screen), End (to move to the right edge of the screen), and Tab and Shift-Tab to move one tab at a time (Tab also stops on margin markers and indentation marks, #). For a complete list of available keys in the ruler line, see Table 4.3.

Table 4.3: Ruler-Line Key Options

KEY	ACTION
[	Sets the left margin at the cursor
]	Sets the right margin at the cursor
#	Sets the paragraph indent at the cursor (the indent is relative to the left margin, so if you move the left margin, the indent also moves)

The easiest way to place the right margin at 60 is to realize that it is currently set at 65 and is marked by the right square bracket (]). Move the cursor to the tab stop before the current right-margin location, and press].

When you are finished setting the new margins on the ruler line, press Return to complete the process and return to the document.

Another convenient Framework III word processing feature is automatic paragraph indentation. By default, this option is set at zero:

Paragraph Indent   {0}

If you would like each new paragraph in your text to be indented by a certain number of spaces, you can assign a nonzero value to this menu option. Let's try globally indenting the paragraphs of the memorandum. Place the highlight at the frame's border again, and press

Ctrl-W   (to open the Words menu)

P   (to select the Paragraph Indent option)

8   (to indent by eight characters)

Return   (to complete the operation)

When Framework III's reformatting is complete, each paragraph in the memorandum will be indented by eight characters.

If you were now to add new paragraphs to the document, you would see how the Paragraph Indent option works on newly entered text. Whenever you press the Return key to begin a new paragraph, Framework III automatically places the cursor at the indent setting rather than at the left-margin setting. The rest of the lines of each paragraph will begin at the left margin.

Framework III also allows you to create *negative indents* at the beginnings of paragraphs whose left margins are greater than zero. This means that the first line of the paragraph will begin to the left of the paragraph's own left margin. To create a negative indent, simply specify a negative number for the Paragraph Indent option. Let's try this feature out on the memorandum document.

We have set new, larger margins for the six paragraphs in the memorandum that describe the components of Framework III. To further emphasize the importance of this information, we'll make the first line of each paragraph hang into that paragraph's left margin. Begin by entering the frame and extending the highlight over the six paragraphs again. Begin with the section that reads, "Spreadsheet frames are designed to..." and press the following keys:

Extend Select (F6)   (to extend the highlight)

Ctrl-PgDn, six times   (to select the six target paragraphs)

Ctrl-W	(to open the Words menu)
W	(to select the Word Options submenu)
M	(to select Modify Ruler)

Once you select Modify Ruler, you will once again see the ruler line you saw in the last section. This time, move the cursor three spaces to the left of the left-margin marker ([) and press #. This has the same effect as using the menu method we used above and entering a value of – 3. When you are finished, press Return. You can see the effect of this change in Figure 4.11. Finally, Framework III allows you to set tab stops at regular intervals.

New in
Framework III

In Framework III, you can also set irregular tab stops using the ruler line. The Tab key, located near the upper left corner of your keyboard, is labeled with two arrows, pointing left and right. Each time you press the Tab key inside a Word frame, the cursor will move forward to the next tab stop.

You can see on the Words menu that the default tab stops occur every five spaces. To change this default, select the Tab Size option and enter a new value.

To change Tab stops using the ruler line, you can press the equals key (=) to create regular tab stops, duplicating the function of the Tab Size menu selection, or you can place tabs at any selected location on the ruler line. Use Ctrl-Tab or ! to enter a new tab at the cursor location. Or use Delete to remove any tab stop. Ctrl-Delete will remove all tab stops, and Backspace will remove tab stops, margins, and indentations to the left of the cursor.

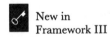
New in
Framework III

In Framework III, you can also change the *displayed* line spacing in individual paragraphs. This affects the way the paragraph displays on screen as well as how it prints. To do so, select Spacing Between Lines from the Word Options submenu.

Be aware, however, that the effect of this command combines with the effect of the Spacing option on the Print menu's Format Options submenu. Spacing affects the whole document, so if you set the Format Options Spacing command to double spacing (2), and you also set a paragraph to double spacing using Spacing Between Lines, the net effect will be quadruple spacing.

Suppose you want to double-space your memo, but to single-space the six paragraphs you indented. Using Spacing Between Lines, you would set all other paragraphs to double spacing, then use Spacing from the Format Options submenu to set the document at single spacing. That way, the six paragraphs that weren't explicitly set to double spacing will print as single-spaced, but the rest of the document will print double-spaced.

CREATING BULLETED LISTS

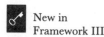
New in
Framework III

Often, you will want to create bulleted lists with sublevels of the list automatically indented with new margins. In Framework III, you can use the Ctrl-Tab key combination to create bulleted lists quickly and easily. To see how to do so, return to the sample memo and move to the end of the first paragraph (following "for your own data processing tasks.").

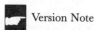
Version Note

If you are not using Framework III, you can still create formatted lists by changing the settings of the left-margin and paragraph indents by hand. Though it isn't as streamlined, the effect will be the same.

Now press Return twice to make a space, and enter:

Framework has three main components that I feel will be useful to you in the following activities:

Then press the following keys:

Return, two times   (to end the paragraph and insert a line space)

*   (to create a bullet point)

Ctrl-Tab   (to set the margin indentation to the next tab stop, leaving the paragraph indent at the previous tab position)

Enter the following text, pressing Tab after each *, and pressing Return twice between paragraphs:

performing evaluations of incoming data and projections of future earnings and capitalization projects,

* maintaining records and databases, particularly in the areas of inventory management and personnel updates,

* creating documents for distribution and for publication company-wide, memos (like this one), and other correspondence.

Be sure to press Return twice after the last paragraph to separate it from the rest of the memo.

Instead of asterisks, you could type numbers for a numbered list. You can also create sublevels by pressing Ctrl-Tab at subsequent levels. To return the margins and indents to the previous level, press Shift-Tab.

INSERTING SOFT HYPHENS

Now that your document has been fully formatted, with both margins justified, you may find that some of the lines appear to have too much space between the words. You can correct this condition with a special character called a *soft hyphen*. A soft hyphen will cause a word to break at the right margin if there is enough room for the portion of the word that precedes the hyphen on the line before it. A regular— or *hard*—hyphen is always printed on paper; a soft hyphen is printed only if the word does break. If you add text and reformat your paragraphs, the soft hyphen will disappear. The soft hyphens are found on the Edit menu.

 New in Framework III

Before Framework III, you could insert soft hyphens from the Edit menu selection Insert Hyphen. However, in Framework III, the hyphenation options are located on the Hyphens submenu of the Edit menu, which contains two choices: Hyphenate Selection (to insert soft hyphens in any selected block of text) and Insert Soft Hyphen (to insert a soft hyphen at the current cursor location).

To start with, let's look at the telecommunications paragraph, which has a lot of "white space," particularly in the first line. It appears in Figure 4.7. Move the cursor to the first c in *Telecommunications* on the first line of the paragraph. Press

Ctrl-E	(to open the Edit menu)
H	(to open the Hyphens submenu)
I	(to insert a soft hyphen)

The letters *Tele* immediately move to the end of the first line, followed by a hyphen. There's still quite a bit of white space on the first line, and now there's even more on the second. Move the cursor to the first i in *Telecommunications*. Press Instruct (Ins) three times to insert another soft

```
If   you   can't,   FRAMEWORK   III   also   has
Telecommunications frames,  which you can use not
only    for    conventional    telecommunications
purposes--logging    onto    the    Central   Data
Processing   department's   mainframe   to    read
information processed there,  for example--but to
hook your   computer   directly   to   others   in the
building,   and  share  your  work  instantly with
those  who  need  to  use  the  results  of  your
analyses, or the information in your files.
```

Figure 4.7: The telecommunications paragraph of the memo, right-justified

hyphen. The letters *commun* now move to the first line, the first hyphen you inserted disappears from view, and a new hyphen appears after the *n*. The paragraph reformats automatically. You can work through the rest of the document, inserting soft hyphens where they are appropriate.

The telecommunications paragraph still has too much white space, however. To hyphenate the entire paragraph, position the cursor at the beginning of the paragraph and press:

Ctrl-PgDn   (to select the paragraph)

Ctrl-E   (to select the Edit menu)

H   (to open the Hyphens submenu)

H   (to select Hyphenate Selection)

Moments later, Framework III will display the entire paragraph with soft hyphens, as shown in Figure 4.8. Notice that much of the white space is gone.

```
If   you   can't,   FRAMEWORK   III   also  has  Telecommun-
ications frames,   which you can  use  not only for
conventional  telecommunications  purposes--logging
onto   the   Central   Data   Processing department's
mainframe   to   read   information   processed there,
for example--but  to hook your  computer directly
to   others  in the  building,   and   share your work
instantly with those who need to use  the results
of  your   analyses,   or   the   information  in  your
files.
```

Figure 4.8: The telecommunications paragraph with soft hyphens

Finally, having seen how successful that one paragraph was, you decide to hyphenate the entire document. To do so, use the Out key (–) to move to the frame border, and then select Hyphenate Selection from the Hyphens submenu. The entire document will be hyphenated in seconds.

DISPLAYING HIDDEN CHARACTERS

Tabs, spaces, and carriage-return characters inside your document are called *hidden characters*, because they are not normally displayed on the screen. From time to time, you may want to examine these hidden characters in a document you are producing. Seeing where they are located may occasionally help you in formatting your document. The Edit menu has a *toggle* option that alternately displays and hides these characters. The option is called

– – Display Hidden Characters

To choose this option, press the following keys:

Ctrl-E   (to open the Edit menu)

D   (to display hidden characters)

Figure 4.9 shows a sample display of these hidden characters. The space character is represented by a small dot, the carriage-return by a paragraph symbol, the left hyphen by a double tilde, and the tab character by a line of hyphens with arrows at either end. Justified paragraphs use a large dot to represent "soft" spaces. To hide these characters once again, open the Edit menu and select the Display option.

We have examined the Words menu's formatting options, which control alignment, margins, paragraph indents, and tabs. Together, these options determine much about the ultimate shape and size of the document on the printed page. Keep in mind that you can set all of these options either before you begin entering text into a frame or after you have finished typing your document. For a final formatting exercise, let's center the heading lines at the top of the office memorandum document.

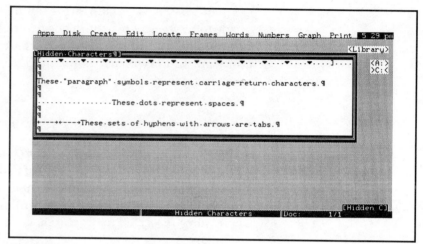

Figure 4.9: Displaying hidden characters

CENTERING A HEADING

Begin by moving the cursor to the top of the document and highlighting all four lines:

Ctrl-Home	(to move the cursor to the beginning of the document)
Extend Select (F6)	(to extend the highlight)
Ctrl-PgDn, four times	(to select all the lines of the memo heading)
Ctrl-W	(to open the Words menu)
C	(to center the heading)

Once again, check Figure 4.11 to see how this operation changes the document.

EXPANDING ABBREVIATIONS

New in
Framework III

In Chapter 7, we'll introduce FRED programming and some of the powerful things you can do with Framework. However, one new Framework III feature is worthy of note in this chapter. It has to do with abbreviations.

Briefly, as you will learn in Chapter 7, you can create special abbreviations that automatically expand when you type Alt-Backspace. For instance, you can type *fw*, and then press Alt-Backspace to expand the abbreviation to *Framework*.

In Framework III, you can now set abbreviation expansion on automatically. If you select Expand Abbreviations from the Word Options submenu (found on the Words menu), Framework III will automatically expand any abbreviations you have defined as you type. You won't have to press Alt-Backspace.

USING A WORD FRAME

In this section, we'll discuss a variety of techniques for changing the appearance and content of your document, including inserting, replacing, and deleting text; styling the text; moving blocks of text; and searching for and replacing words or phrases. We'll also see how to save and print the document.

INSERTING, REPLACING, AND DELETING TEXT

Revising your text electronically, within the computer's memory, saves you the aggravation of going through multiple paper drafts of a document. These are the most basic kinds of revisions:

- Inserting new words

- Replacing parts of the document with new text

- Deleting portions of the document

- Moving blocks of text from one point in the document to another

Framework III actually has two different text entry modes for Word frames: *insert* and *typeover*. The insert mode is Framework III's default text entry mode. In the insert mode, any characters you enter from the keyboard are inserted into the document at the current cursor location. For example, let's say you have entered the following sentence into your document:

You can create different types of frames.

You decide to insert the word *several* between the words *create* and *different*. Move the cursor to the *d* of *different*, and begin typing the new word. As you type each character, the latter part of the sentence moves to the right to make room for the new word:

You can create several different types of frames.

In the typeover mode, the characters you type at the keyboard will *replace* the current characters in your text. To switch into the typeover mode, use the Typeover option of the Edit menu:

Ctrl-E   (to open the Edit menu)

T   (to switch to Typeover mode)

Let's look at what happens to the above sentence as we enter the word *several* in the typeover mode. Again, position the cursor at the *d* of *different* in the original sentence, and type *several*. Here is what you'll see:

You can create severalnt types of frames.

The first seven characters of *different* have been replaced by *several*. Now, to delete the final two characters, *nt*, you press the Delete key twice. Here is the result:

You can create several types of frames.

Normally, you'll probably want to enter text in the insert mode. But keep in mind that through the Edit menu you also have the option of switching into the typeover mode. To toggle back into the insert mode, open the Edit menu and select the Typeover option a second time.

We have just seen how the Delete key erases characters from the Word frame. You can also delete blocks of text. The Delete key erases whatever portion of text is currently selected by the highlight. To delete a word, press the following keys:

Ctrl-→ or Ctrl-←   (to highlight the word)

Delete   (to delete the word)

To delete a sentence, press

Ctrl-↓ or Ctrl-↑   (to highlight a sentence)

Delete   (to delete the sentence)

Finally, to delete an entire paragraph, press

Ctrl-PgDn or   (to highlight a paragraph)
Ctrl-PgUp

Delete   (to delete the paragraph)

(You can review these Ctrl-key combinations by looking back at Table 4.2.) Always keep in mind that Framework III has an Undo option that can bring back accidental deletions:

Ctrl-E   (to open the Edit menu)

U   (to select the Undo option)

Next, we'll look at some of the more sophisticated word processing features that Framework III offers.

STYLING TEXT

The first section of the Words menu offers you five different text styles: Normal, Bold, Underline, Italic, and (new in Framework III) Strike-through.

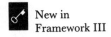
New in
Framework III

In addition to the five text styles on the Words menu, the Word Options submenu contains five more text-style settings that are new in Framework III: All Capitals, No Capitals, Initial Capitals, Raised (Superscript), and Lowered (Subscript).

The default style is Normal. To change to one of the other styles, extend the highlight over the target block of text and select the appropriate Words menu option.

Use the office memorandum document (Figure 4.1) to experiment with styling. Begin with the first line of the document, the memo's date:

Date: March 3, 1989

Put the word *Date* in boldface, and then underline the date itself:

Ctrl-Home   (to move to the beginning of the document)

Ctrl-→   (to select the word *Date*)

Ctrl-W   (to open the Words menu)

B   (to select the Bold option)

To perform these operations on the rest of the headings, you can take advantage of a shortcut Framework III provides. Whenever you select an option from the menu, the menu highlight remains on the last option you selected. Therefore, if you've pressed the Instruct key to select an option, all you have to do is press Instruct again to repeat the option. We'll use this technique now. Use the cursor keys with Ctrl-→ or Ctrl-← to select *To*, *From*, and *RE*, and press Instruct twice after each selection.

Next, use the Extend Select key (F6) to select the rest of each heading in turn. Begin by placing the cursor on the M in the word *March*. Then press

Ctrl-↓   (to select the date itself)

Ctrl-W   (to open the Words menu)

U   (to select the Underline option)

Here is the result:

Date: March 3, 1989

After that, all you have to do is select the appropriate part of each headline, and press Instruct twice.

The final version of the memorandum (Figure 4.11) has additional boldfacing: the three isolated lines below the second paragraph, and the first two words in each of the paragraphs that describe the Framework III components. Make all of these style changes in your own Word frame.

The use of the Italics option in the Words menu depends on the capabilities of the hardware in your computer system. On a monochrome monitor and on many printers, italics will be identical to underlining. However, if you have a color graphics monitor, you will see text displayed in true italics. Likewise, a printer that has an italics mode will be able to use this option properly.

Often, you will find yourself setting more than one attribute to the same text. For instance, you might select Bold and Italic, or Underline and Bold. In Framework III, you can turn off any individual attribute by first selecting the text to change, then opening the Words menu, moving the cursor to the attribute you want to turn off, and then pressing Delete.

 New in Framework III

In Framework III, you can also select Strike-through, All Capitals, No Capitals, Initial Capitals, Raised (Superscripts), and Lowered (Subscripts). These new text styles all work the same way as the others already mentioned in this section.

- All Capitals changes the selected text to all capital letters

- No Capitals changes selected text to all lowercase letters

- Initial Capitals changes selected text so that the first letter of each word is capitalized

- Raised creates superscripts, as in footnotes and mathematical notation

- Lowered creates subscripted characters, as in chemical formulas

Styling can also be performed globally. For example, you can have an entire Word frame styled in all caps. To assign a global style, place the highlight on the frame's border before you open the Words menu. Then select the style you want for the contents of the frame.

MOVING AND COPYING BLOCKS OF TEXT

You can use the Move and Copy keys (F7 and F8, respectively) when you want to move or copy a section of text from one point to another inside your document. There are three simple steps required to perform a move or copy operation:

1. Extend the highlight over the block of text that you want to move or copy.

2. Press the Move (F7) or Copy (F8) key.

3. Move the cursor to the point in the document where you want to move or copy the text you have selected; press Return to complete the operation.

To practice with a move operation, let's turn once again to the memorandum document. We'll move the paragraph that begins "Graph frames give you . . ." to a new position, just before the last paragraph of the memo. Begin by moving the cursor to the first character of the target paragraph. Press Ctrl-PgDn to select the entire paragraph; then press the Move key (F7) to begin the move operation. Navigate the cursor to the new position, the blank line just above "Please begin working with Framework III . . .". Finally, press Return. Framework III will move the paragraph to the new location you have chosen for it.

After this paragraph move, you may have to correct the spacing between paragraphs. Press Return to insert an additional blank line, or press Delete to close up an unwanted blank line.

New in
Framework III

THE CLIPBOARD   In Framework III, you can use Cut (Shift-F7) and Paste (Shift-F8) to make copies of text selections. When you select a block of text and press Cut (Shift-F7), the contents of the block are stored in Framework III's electronic clipboard, a memory buffer. Actually, the selected text is unaffected by the operation, so to perform a true cut operation, you would want to press Delete after pressing Cut (Shift-F7).

Once the information is in the clipboard memory, you can use Paste (Shift-F8) to insert it into any document as many times as you wish. Furthermore, you can view and edit the contents of the clipboard by pressing Edit Cut Text (Shift-F2). Initially, you will see the contents of the clipboard at the bottom of the screen, one line at a time. However, you can press Zoom (F9) to open an edit window, where you can use normal word processing techniques to edit the clipboard contents prior to pasting.

This new feature can come in handy when you keep a library of document templates that require minor changes before being used. Use Cut (Shift-F7) to pull the template text from the original document, edit it (using Shift-F2) in the clipboard, then use Paste (Shift-F8) to insert it into the new document. You might also use this technique to modify FRED programs that contain similar blocks of commands.

FOOTNOTES

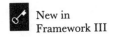
New in
Framework III

In Framework III, you can now create footnotes. Footnotes are used to expand or clarify information in text, and they are usually placed at the bottom of the current page or at the end of a document. Framework III will automatically number or renumber footnotes, and it can mark them with a symbol of your choice.

To create a new footnote, select the Footnotes submenu from the Edit menu, then select Create Note.

For instance, let's add a footnote to the memo we've been writing. To begin with, place the cursor just after the words FRAMEWORK III in the first paragraph. Now press

Ctrl-E	(to open the Edit menu)
F	(to open the Footnotes submenu)
C	(to select Create Note)
product of Ashton-Tate Corporation	(text to enter on the edit line)
Return	(to end the entry)

For longer footnotes, you can press Zoom (F9) to add multiple lines, using normal word processing techniques, then press Escape to end the footnote creation or editing.

Ordinarily, Framework III will number footnotes automatically and place them at the bottom of the current page. However, you can change many of the settings and affect how the notes are marked, and where they print. For instance, you can choose Marker for Note from the Footnotes submenu to change the kind of marker used. You could use a symbol such as the asterisk (*) or the caret (^). Also, you can use numbers with characters. For instance, if you select Numeric note markers and enclose the number with markers (for example, ##1##), Framework III will print the markers and will also increase the enclosed number sequentially. You can determine the starting footnote number by selecting Marker for Note, selecting Numeric, and entering the starting number.

Framework III will renumber notes *as you add them*, regardless of their position within the text. Therefore, if you skip around in your text, placing footnotes out of sequence, the numbers will not be correct. There are several ways to renumber the markers, all using the *Renumber Notes Starting at* option found on the Footnotes submenu:

- To renumber the entire document, you can place the cursor on the document frame or on a single footnote occurrence.

- To renumber a group of footnotes, use Extend Select (F6) to select the text containing the footnotes to renumber, and select *Renumber Notes Starting at* from the Footnotes submenu.

- You can extend footnotes over several Word frames. To renumber them through a whole series of frames, either select all frames to renumber, or place the highlight on a frame that contains the ones you want to renumber.

In all cases, once you have chosen Renumber Notes Starting at, you will enter the number to use as the starting number. If you enter a symbol, all footnote markers will be changed to display that symbol. To change back to numbers again, simply reselect the option and enter an appropriate numeric marker.

To edit a footnote, place the cursor on the footnote marker, then select Edit Note from the Footnotes submenu. You can edit on the edit line, or press Zoom (F9) to edit a longer note on the full screen. Another way to edit a note is to place the cursor on the marker and press the In key (+).

There are several ways to print footnotes. By default, footnotes appear at the bottom of the current page. This is set on the Footnotes submenu with the Bottom of Page option. If you set the After Frame Contents (Endnotes) option, Framework III will print the notes at the end of the current frame. Instead, you can have Framework III accumulate endnotes and print them all at the end of a particular frame. For instance, suppose you have a containing frame with several Word frames inside. In each Word frame, you select After Frame Contents. Then, on the containing frame, select Print Endnotes after This Frame from the Footnotes submenu. All footnotes will print at the end of the document.

You can also mix types of notes. For instance, in the preceding example, suppose you wanted normal footnotes in one of the Word frames. Just select that frame border, and select Bottom of Page from the Footnotes submenu.

SEARCHING FOR
AND REPLACING WORDS OR PHRASES

In Chapter 3, we explored the use of the Locate menu for sorting columns of data. You can't use the sorting option in Word frames, but the Locate menu does present two other important functions that *are* designed for word processing: searching and replacing. These options appear as follows in the menu:

Search   {}
Replace   {}

Actually, these options can be used in *any* type of frame. In Chapter 5, we'll look at them again in the context of Database frames.

The Search option allows you to locate a specific string of characters, if it exists in your document. Framework III moves the highlight to the string as soon as it is found. In fact, Search is a repeating function; you can continue searching for your target string of characters for as many times as the string occurs in the document. The Search option is particularly valuable for finding specific information in long documents.

The Replace option carries the process one step further. Replace also searches for a string of characters that you specify, and then it prepares to replace that string with a second string of characters that you also specify. Once again, Replace is a process that can be performed throughout the document, offering you the opportunity to replace every occurrence of the target string. You can replace selectively or globally.

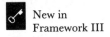 New in Framework III

In Framework III, if you want the contents of footnotes to be searched, you need to be sure that the Notes Included option, found on the Locate menu, is on.

We'll see that both the Search and Replace operations display important messages at the bottom of the screen. To try them out, we'll first search for the word *Framework* in the office memorandum; then we'll replace it with its uppercase equivalent, FRAMEWORK.

You can begin the Search or Replace option from any point within your document. Let's begin with the Search operation:

Ctrl-L   (to open the Locate menu)

S   (to select Search)

At this point, Framework III moves the cursor down to the edit line and displays the following message:

Enter text to find; press RETURN to accept or ESC to exit

Enter the word *Framework* on the edit line; as you do, the word will also appear in the Locate menu:

Search: **{Framework}**

Press the Return key to begin the search. The highlight will immediately move to the first place *Framework* occurs after your cursor position. If you moved your cursor to the top of the document (using Ctrl-Home) before you began the search, your screen will look like Figure 4.10. Below the desktop, you see the following messages:

TEXT FOUND

↓ – – Find Next ↑ – – Find Previous Any other key exits.

Following these instructions, you can press the ↓ key to move the highlight to the next occurrence of the word. If you press the ↑ key, the highlight will move backwards and find a previous occurrence of *Framework* in the document. If the highlight is currently at the first occurrence, this means that the highlight will cycle to the *end* of the document. Similarly, if your cursor is positioned after the first occurrence of *Framework* when the search begins, pressing ↓ will continue cycling the highlight through the document, from the end back to the beginning, until it returns to your cursor position. Press any other key to end the operation.

Framework III will also tell you how many times it has found the word in the document; for example, you may see a message like this:

TEXT FOUND: 3 TIMES

If you press the ↓ key after Framework III has found the last occurrence, the following message will appear on the screen:

NOT FOUND AGAIN

At this point, Framework III automatically exits from the Search operation.

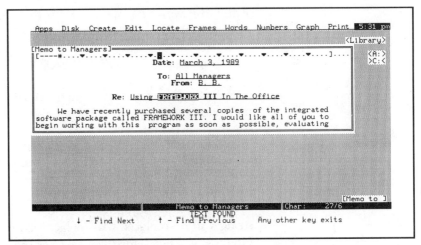

Figure 4.10: The Search operation

After completing a search, you may sometimes decide that you want to repeat that same search. The Locate menu retains the last string you searched for, so you can simply return to the menu to begin the process again.

To use the Replace option, you must specify both a target string of characters and a replacement string. Begin by selecting the option:

Ctrl-L   (to open the Locate menu)

R   (to select Replace)

The cursor will move to the edit line, and you will first see the same message you saw for the Search operation:

Enter text to find; press RETURN to accept or ESC to exit

Because we have just searched for the word *Framework* in the memorandum document, this target word will still be in the Locate menu and will automatically appear on the edit line. Just press Return to accept it.

Next, you will see the message

Enter Replacement text; press RETURN to accept or ESC to exit

Enter the word *FRAMEWORK* on the edit line; the word will also appear in the Locate menu:

Replace   {FRAMEWORK}

Press the Return key to begin the replacement process. A message at the bottom of the screen offers you five different options at this point:

RETURN – – Replace and Find Next   ↓ – – Find Next
HOME – – Replace and Stay   END – – Replace All
ESC to exit

To replace globally, press the End key. Every occurrence of the target string will be replaced. To replace selectively, use the Return, ↓, or Home key. The Return key replaces the currently highlighted occurrence and moves the highlight to the next occurrence. The ↓ key moves the highlight forward *without* replacing the current selection. Home replaces the current selection but does not move the highlight forward. Finally, the Escape key drops you out of the operation altogether.

In the memorandum document, replace all occurrences of *Framework* with *FRAMEWORK*. You'll find that the underlining under the first appearance of *FRAMEWORK* has disappeared. Go back to the Words menu and choose the Underline option again, to apply to *FRAMEWORK*. You can see the result in Figure 4.11, the printout of the final draft of the office memorandum.

```
          Date: March 3, 1989

          To: All Managers
          From: B.B.

          RE: Using FRAMEWORK III in the Office

               We have recently purchased several copies of the in-
          tegrated software package called FRAMEWORK III. I would like all
          of you to begin working with this program as soon as possible,
          evaluating its effectiveness for your own data processing tasks.

               FRAMEWORK III has several components that I feel will be
          useful to you in the following activities:

               * performing evaluations and projections,
               * maintaining records and databases, and
               * creating documents.
```

Figure 4.11: Office memorandum, final draft

In FRAMEWORK III you do all your work in special-purpose frames that appear on the display screen. The screen becomes your "desktop," the place where all the action of the program takes place. You can control exactly what part of your current work is displayed on the desktop at a given time. You may want to work with several frames at a time, in which case they can all be present on the desktop at once. Frames on the desktop are either open--displaying their contents--or closed--temporarily placed in a special "tray" at the side of the desktop.

You can create several different types of frames. Here are brief descriptions of the frames you'll probably be working with the most frequently:

Spreadsheet frames are designed to help you work with tables of numbers. Any time you organize numbers and labels into columns and rows for the purpose of calculating totals, averages, or other statistical values, a spreadsheet frame will simplify the task and increase your ability to analyze the data itself. In addition to numbers, you can enter formulas into your spreadsheets, to take over the more tedious arithmetic tasks involved with numeric record keeping. Formulas can be copied across rows or down columns of your spreadsheet, allowing you to perform, in minutes, what might otherwise turn into hours and hours of complex arithmetic tasks.

A spreadsheet is also a projection tool, allowing you to find answers to "what-if" questions. Change a single number on your spreadsheet, and all formulas that rely on that number will be re-calculated, automatically. Those of you who do cost projections will particularly appreciate this feature.

Graph frames give you presentation-quality graphs from the tables of numbers that you enter into a spreadsheet frame. FRAMEWORK III can draw a variety of different types of graphs: bar, stacked bar, pie, marked points, line, x-y, and high-low-close. Graphs are simple to draw, and you can even print them out on paper, using the printer attached to your PC.

Database frames allow you to organize, store, and work with groups of data. You may want to create databases to handle employee records, client information, sales records, and inventories.

Word frames are used for working with FRAMEWORK III's easy but powerful word processor. Those of you who are used to typing your own memos will find this to be a refreshing new way to create documents. You can even store frequently used forms in a library on the desktop, so that you don't have to create them from scratch every time. You may also want to introduce your secretaries to FRAMEWORK III word processing, if you can stand the thought of sharing your desktop computers with another person.

If you can't, FRAMEWORK III also has **Telecommunications frames**, which you can use not only for conventional telecommunications purposes--logging onto the Central Data Processing department's mainframe to read information processed there,

Figure 4.11 (continued): Office memorandum, final draft

```
                    for example--but to hook your computer directly
                    to others in the building, and share your work
                    instantly with those who need to use the results
                    of your analyses, or the information in your
                    files.

                        Please begin working with FRAMEWORK III as soon as you
                    can; I think you'll find that the effort you put into learning to
                    use the program will pay off almost immediately. Let me know your
                    impressions within a couple of weeks.

                             B.B.
```

Figure 4.11: Office memorandum, final draft (continued)

CHECKING YOUR SPELLING

Now that you've made your final format changes to the document, it's time to check your spelling. Framework III has a powerful spelling checker, located on the Apps menu. The Spelling Check submenu is shown in Figure 4.12. With the document that you want to check selected, press

Ctrl-A   (to open the Apps menu)

S   (to choose the Spelling Check submenu)

B   (to begin the spelling check)

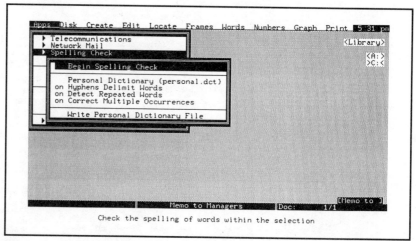

Figure 4.12: The Spelling Check submenu

If you are using a floppy disk system, you will be prompted to insert the Spell disk in drive A.

Framework III will scan your document, checking each word against an 80,000-word dictionary. As it finds a suspect word, it displays something like this in the message area:

Word: B.B.   Suggest   Edit   Go On   Add Word

As you can see, you have four choices:

- Ask Framework III to suggest an alternative—which is selected, resulting in the message

   List suggested correct spellings—ESC to exit

- Edit the word

- Ignore the (apparent) misspelling

- Leave the spelling-check function

Let's assume that you habitually sign your memos *B.B.* If so, it would be useful to have Framework III regard that as a legitimate word, and ignore it during spelling checks. To accomplish this, press A. This selects the Add Word option, and displays the message

   Add the selected word to your Personal Dictionary—ESC to exit

The word will then be added to a file called PERSONAL.DCT, one of the dictionary files Framework III may scan during a spelling check.

If you want to edit the error, press E, and the suspect word will appear on the edit line. The message area will display

   Edit the selected word—ESC to exit

When you have made your corrections, press Return, and the corrected word will replace the error in the document.

If you have used a word frequently in a document, but don't want to add it to your dictionary, choose Go On by pressing G. The message

   Skip the selected word and continue spell checking—ESC to exit

will appear, and any other instances of the word in the document will be ignored.

If you're not sure of the correct spelling, or if you just want to see exactly how smart Framework III is, choose Suggest by pressing S. Framework III will look in its dictionaries for words that resemble the suspect word, and display several of them. More often than not, the correct word will appear among the choices. For example, on discovering the misspelling *screne* in the document, Framework III displayed the following:

```
Word: screne         Choose correction or ESC to previous menu
screen scene scream strewn scrounge screwing scram
strain
```

Move the highlight to the correct word, *screen*, press Return, and Framework III will replace the error in the text. Sometimes, however, you are not so lucky. On encountering the misspelling *aritmentic*, Framework III offered the suggestions

```
arraignments arraignment aerodynamic regimented
aerodynamics
```

When a word appears twice in a row, the second occurrence will be highlighted, with the following options displayed:

```
Repeated: to      Delete   Edit   Go On
            Delete the selected word—ESC to exit
```

You can turn off this feature before the spelling check starts by selecting

```
on Detect Repeated Words
```

from the Spelling Check menu and pressing Return.

Finally, if the program finds an error that has previously been detected, you are offered the chance to correct it globally:

```
wil – – > will ?      Replace   Auto Replace   Edit   Go On
            Replace the selected word with the suggestion—ESC to exit
```

Choose Auto Replace, and every instance of *wil* will be replaced by *will*.

EDITING YOUR DICTIONARIES

Framework III includes four dictionaries. In addition to the main dictionary are a dictionary of computer terms, a dictionary of business terms, and an empty dictionary. They are called COMPUTER.DCT, BUSINESS.DCT, and PERSONAL.DCT, respectively. You can use any one of them in addition to the main dictionary as a source of correctly spelled words. The default dictionary is PERSONAL.DCT. To choose another one, press

Ctrl-A	(to open the Apps menu)
S	(to choose the Spelling Check submenu)
P	(to bring the Personal Dictionary option to the edit line)
dictionary name	(enter the name of the dictionary you want to use)
Return	(to record your selection)

Whichever one you choose will be scanned during a spelling check. It will also be the dictionary to which words are added when you choose the Add Word option.

You can edit the existing dictionaries, or even create new ones. To edit any of the dictionaries, bring it to the desktop, and edit the contents as you would any Word frame. Don't be disturbed by the apparently random order of the words. Framework III optimizes the order to make it easy to search each time you bring a dictionary to the desktop.

When editing a dictionary, you must be careful to use capitalization and periods exactly as you would use them in text. If you add a word that begins with a capital letter to the dictionary, Framework III will consider the word correctly spelled in the document only if it begins with a capital letter. You may inadvertently add such a word by using the Add Word option when the word is the first word of a sentence. Similarly, if you add the abbreviation *a.m.* to your dictionary, *a. m.* will not be regarded as correct.

While editing, you can add words in any order. Framework III will sort the words into optimum searching order when you save your additions.

When you have finished editing your dictionary, press

Ctrl-A   (to open the Apps menu)

S   (to choose the Spelling Check submenu)

W   (to write to the dictionary file)

If there is already a dictionary by the same name, you will be asked for permission to replace the old dictionary with the new one.

Similarly, you can create a new dictionary with any name you choose, provided the name has no more than eight characters. You may want separate dictionaries for different types of projects, or for correspondence with different organizations, each one containing personal names and technical terms appropriate to the subject. To create a new dictionary, simply enter the words in a Word frame, one to a line, then move the highlight to the label, and choose the Write Personal Dictionary File option from the Spelling Check submenu.

New in
Framework III

In Framework III, you can use foreign dictionaries available from Ashton-Tate. If you have purchased one of the alternate language dictionaries, you can select the Language option from the Global Options submenu found on the Apps menu.

FINDING SYNONYMS

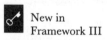
New in
Framework III

Sometimes you're looking for exactly the right word to use, but you just can't think of it. In Framework III, you can select List Synonyms (or Shift-F6) to use Framework's built-in thesaurus. To do so, first place the cursor somewhere on the word you want to look up. Next, select List Synonyms from the Apps menu. Framework III will display the meaning and part of speech of the word. If there is more than one meaning, several definitions and parts of speech will be shown. You then choose the appropriate meaning and press Return to display the synonyms. Finally, if you see a synonym that you prefer, select it using the arrow keys and press Return to replace the original word directly in your text.

Let's look at the memo we've been writing. You'll notice at the end of the document, you wrote, "...let me know your thoughts within a couple of weeks." Perhaps there is a better word than *thoughts*.

Place the cursor anywhere within the word *thoughts*, and then open the Apps menu and select List Synonyms.

Almost immediately, Framework III will display two possible meanings for the selected word, as shown in Figure 4.13. In this case, the second meaning is closer to what you mean to say, so press the ↓ key once, and then press Return.

A list of possible synonyms displays, as shown in Figure 4.14. Now you can confirm your original decision to select the second set of synonyms by pressing PgUp to see the synonyms for the other definition. You'll see that they aren't what you are seeking, so press PgDn to return to the other set.

Now look at the words listed. You'll see that one of the options is *impressions*. That looks like a good choice, so you can use the arrow keys to place the highlight on it, and press Return to replace the word *thoughts* with the word *impressions* directly in the document. You can also press Thesaurus (Shift-F6) to look up *impressions* and see what synonyms it has. In this way, you can continue looking up words to seek more meanings and more ideas.

If you change your mind, or you want to back up a screen (perhaps to view the meanings once again), press Escape. For this example,

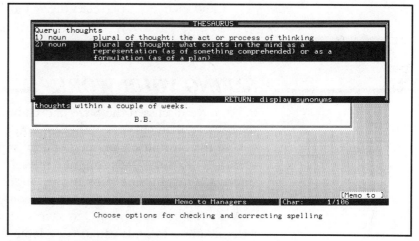

Figure 4.13: Looking at definitions

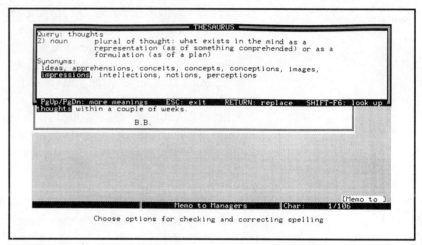

```
╔═══════════════════════════ THESAURUS ═══════════════════════════╗
║Query: thoughts                                                   ║
║2) noun      plural of thought: what exists in the mind as a      ║
║             representation (as of something comprehended) or as a║
║             formulation (as of a plan)                           ║
║Synonyms:                                                         ║
║ ideas, apprehensions, conceits, concepts, conceptions, images,   ║
║ impressions, intellections, notions, perceptions                 ║
║                                                                  ║
║ PgUp/PgDn: more meanings    ESC: exit    RETURN: replace   SHIFT-F6: look up ║
║thoughts within a couple of weeks.                                ║
║                        B.B.                                      ║
║                                                                  ║
║                                                       [Memo to ] ║
║              Memo to Managers       Char:      1/106             ║
╚══════════════════════════════════════════════════════════════════╝
      Choose options for checking and correcting spelling
```

Figure 4.14: Looking at synonyms

place the cursor inside the word *thoughts*, and press

Ctrl-A	(to open the Apps menu)
L	(to select List Synonyms)
↓	(to select the second definition)
↓ and then →	(to select the synonym, *impressions*)
Return	(to replace *thoughts* with *impressions*)

SAVING YOUR WORK

We have discussed the Save and Continue operation already, in the context of other types of frames. You'll recall that you can either choose the Save and Continue option from the Disk menu or just press Ctrl-Return. This command saves the current frame to disk under the label name supplied in the frame's border. If the file already exists on disk, it will be replaced by this new version.

A good piece of advice is to save your Word frame about once every 20 minutes while you are developing the document it contains. This will prevent any significant accidental loss of time and effort. If something goes wrong, the most you can lose is 20 minutes of work.

PRINTING THE DOCUMENT

The Print menu takes charge of sending the contents of a Word frame to the printer:

Ctrl-P   (to open the Print menu)

B   (to begin printing)

But before you print a word processed document, you will often want to define precisely how Framework III will carry out the printing task.

The Print menu contains several submenus to help you control many characteristics of printing. The submenu you will probably use most often is the Format Options submenu, shown in Figure 4.15. These options can be used for printing any type of frame, but many of them are especially relevant to Word frames.

POSITIONING THE DOCUMENT

The leftmost menu on the Format Options submenu helps you to lay out the printed page by allowing you to establish the offset from

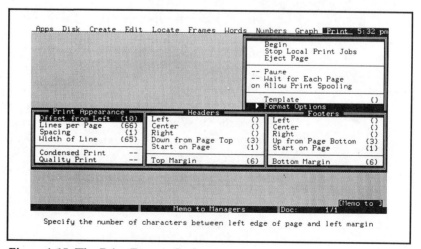

Figure 4.15: The Print Format Options menu

the left edge of the page and the length of each line. These options must be coordinated with the margins you have already established inside the document (in the Words menu). If your paper is longer or shorter than the standard 11 inches, you can also change the number of lines per page. In addition, the last options on the center and rightmost portions of the menu allow you to set a top and bottom margin.

The offset is actually the size of the left margin on the printed page. The default value is 10, but you can change it from this menu. In conjunction with the default margins for Word frames (0 on the left and 65 on the right), this value results in a page that is reasonably well centered on standard 8½-inch-wide paper.

There are two ways to control the left-to-right positioning of text as it is printed. As mentioned, you can set the left margin inside the Word frame. For example, if you are using standard 8½ × 11-inch paper and an 80-column printer, you could establish margins inside your Word frame of 10 and 70, and print with no offset. It is more common, however (and easier to visualize your documents), to set the left margin so that the text you want to appear farthest to the left in the document is at a margin of 0, and to establish a right margin that formats your text as you want it to appear. In any case, you should be careful that you don't give Framework III conflicting instructions, even though it will do its best to accommodate you. If you choose an offset of 40 and a line length of 30 for a document with margins of 0 and 65, each line will break at the right margin, after 30 characters have been printed, and the rest of the line as it appeared in the Word frame will appear at the left edge of the paper on a separate line.

Let's say, for example, that you have an especially wide document—75 characters wide. You want it to be centered on the paper. You establish margins of 0 and 75 in the Word frame. When the time comes to print, you press

Ctrl-P	(to open the Print menu)
F	(to select Format Options)
O	(to select the Offset option)
Return	(to enter your Offset selection)

2	(to set the left margin for printing two characters wide)
Return	(to record your selection)
Out (–)	(to return to the main Print menu)
B	(to begin printing)

By default, Framework III prints documents using single spacing, but you can use the Spacing option on the Format Options submenu to change to double or triple spacing, or even wider intervals. As with all menu options that require a value to be entered, you press Return to bring the selection to the edit line, enter the value of your choice, and press Return again.

If your paper is longer or shorter than 11 inches, you can adjust to your paper size by selecting the Lines per Page option. Most printers print six lines per inch (although some printers allow you to change this value; we'll see how to do so shortly). If your printer does print six lines per inch, you must multiply the length of your paper (in inches) by six.

The last options on the center and right menus are used to set a top and bottom margin, respectively. Framework III uses default values of six lines, or one inch, but you can enter different values.

PROVIDING HEADERS OR FOOTERS

A header or footer is an identifying item of information that appears on every page of your document, either at the top of the page (header) or at the bottom (footer). Headers or footers might consist of the title of the document, the date, the page number, the author's name, or some combination of these and other items. You can enter any or all of them, and position the headers or footers on the page, by using the Format Options submenu (Figure 4.15).

The central portion of the menu is for headers, and the right portion is for footers. In each section, you will see the options

Left	{}
Center	{}
Right	{}

These options determine the location for the information.

To enter the information, choose the position where you want it to appear (at the top or the bottom of the page, at the left margin, the right margin, or the center), press Return, and enter the text you want to use. If the entries are not too long, you can have separate information appearing in each of the six positions.

To have Framework III print page numbers on your document, enter the text

<page>

in one of the six header or footer positions on the menu. To include a date, you must include the name of one of the FRED date-formatting functions (without the @ symbol, and enclosed in triangular brackets, as with page numbers), which you will learn about later in this chapter. For example, if the date were May 5, 1989, entering

<date4>

would print

May 5, 1989

at the specified location.

You can also choose the position of the header or footer on the page. In the center section, the option

Down from Page Top   {3}

indicates that the default position for a header is three lines from the top of the page. This is well within the default top margin of six spaces. If you change either the top margin or the vertical position of the header, be sure the values you choose don't conflict. Similarly,

Up from Page Bottom   {3}

sets a default position for a footer at three lines from the bottom, and allows you to change it.

Figure 4.16 shows a Format Options submenu filled in. When the page is printed, it will appear with the header

Memo to Managers   March 3, 1989   Page 2

and the footer

Framework in the Office

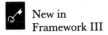

New in
Framework III

In Framework III, you can add special effects to headers and footers in the Format Options submenu. To do so, first highlight the text you want to modify, then press Ctrl-W to open a special menu of effects. To add multiple effects, press Ctrl-W additional times. Figure 4.17 displays the options that are available.

Although you can do more with the print options from the menus in Framework III than you could in earlier versions, you may still want to know how to add printer codes to your documents and frames. Therefore, we have included a section on Fine-Tuning Your

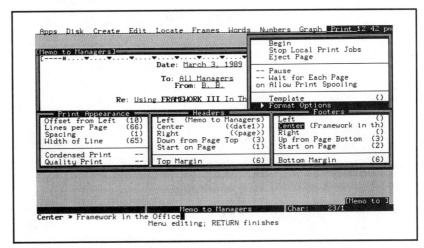

Figure 4.16: Selecting headers and footers

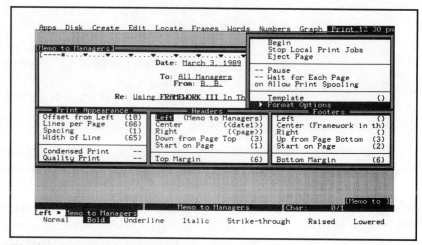

Figure 4.17: Adding effects to the header

Printout, later in this chapter, where you will learn how to use embedded printer codes to further control your documents.

The final option regarding headers and footers controls the page they start on. You may want your opening page, for example, to have no header, as the document's title and opening remarks will contain most of the information that would ordinarily appear in a header. To have Framework III begin placing headers on page 2, select the option

   Start on Page   {1}

from the central portion of the menu, press Return, enter the value 2, and press Return again. Similarly, you can have footers begin appearing on any page you choose by entering a value in the same option on the Footers portion of the menu.

STYLING YOUR TEXT

Most printers can print text in various sizes and styles. The Format Options menu provides for three different styles and sizes—normal printing, quality printing, and condensed printing. At the bottom of the leftmost portion of the Format Options menu are two choices:

Condensed Print   – –
Quality Print   – –

The default print style is normal printing. If your printer offers near-letter-quality or correspondence-quality print style, and you have installed your printer correctly (see Appendix A), you can choose the Quality Print option. Condensed print has more than 12 characters per inch (the exact number—generally between 15 and 18—depends on your printer). If you choose Condensed Print, and your printer can handle it, your entire document is printed in this style.

FINE-TUNING YOUR PRINTOUT

Any settings you choose from the Print menu will affect the entire document. Settings chosen for a containing frame will automatically be applied to all the frames within it, unless you have previously selected settings from the Print menu for individual subframes. But what if you want more precise control over the appearance of your document? What if you want to use several type styles or print pitches in the same document? These aspects of printing are generally controlled by *printer escape sequences*. Printer escape sequences are series of characters, generally beginning with the Escape character (ASCII 27), that send instructions directly to the printer. The Escape character tells the printer that what follows is to be interpreted as instructions, rather than as characters to be printed.

There are two ways to send escape sequences to your printer through Framework III: directly in text, and through the FRED printing functions. For various purposes, you might want to combine both strategies. If you want to set a few words in a different type style— one that is not among the menu choices—you are better off inserting the escape sequence into the text. This has certain pitfalls, however. On the other hand, if you want to style a whole section differently from the body of the document, you should use the FRED printing functions. In either case, you must first consult the manual that came with your printer to see what characters have what effects. We'll look first at how to insert escape sequences into text, and then examine some of the FRED printing functions.

INSERTING ESCAPE SEQUENCES INTO TEXT One of the powerful features of Framework III is its ability to accept graphics characters in text. Table C.1 in Appendix C is a complete table of all the graphics characters that you can produce in Framework III. For our present purposes, however, the most important of these are the first 32, which represent the control characters, summarized in Table C.2. The characters that affect the printer are generally among these characters. The most important of them, the Escape character (ASCII 27), can be entered by pressing Ctrl-{. This produces a small ← on your screen. If, for example, your printer expects Escape-S to print a subscript, you can cause it to make this change by typing Ctrl-{S just before the characters to be printed as a subscript. After those characters, enter the code to return to normal printing.

Some control characters, such as Ctrl-X or any of the control characters that open menus, cannot be entered by pressing a Ctrl-key combination. To enter these characters, you must use a different technique. You can see in Table C.2 that Ctrl-X has an ASCII code of 24. To enter any character that cannot be entered directly, hold down the Alt and Shift keys while entering the digits of the ASCII code on the numeric keypad. Thus, to enter Ctrl-X, hold down Alt and Shift while pressing 2 4 on the keypad. When you release the keys, a ↑ symbol, the graphic equivalent of ASCII 24 (see Table C.1), will appear on your screen. For many printers, this character cancels all previous print settings.

The danger with this approach is that it may distort the length of your lines. When counting the number of characters per line, Framework III will treat the characters in an escape sequence just like any other character; two two-character escape sequences on a line will make that line four characters too short. It requires a great deal of experimentation with sample printouts to get the spacing exactly the way you want it.

THE FRED PRINTING FUNCTIONS Another way to mix different styles of text is to put each block of text that you want to appear in a different style in a separate frame, and place a FRED printing function in the formula area *behind* the frame. This is the normal location for any FRED formula or program, as we discussed in Chapter 1. Although Framework III will normally ignore such formulas when printing, you can force it to act on them with a Print menu option. To use a FRED printing function, press

Ctrl-P	(to open the Print menu)
C	(to open the Control Options submenu)
R	(to choose Recalc Formula during Printing)

This tells Framework III that any printing formulas anywhere among the frames to be printed should be acted upon.

From our work with spreadsheet functions in Chapter 3, you'll recall the three characteristics of FRED functions:

- Every function name begins with the @ character. You can type the name itself either in uppercase or lowercase, or in some combination of both.

- Most functions require one or more *parameters,* values that you send to define the action of the function. You place the parameters between parentheses, after the function's name.

- Functions return a value or produce some programmed result. In the case of the printing functions, the result is a specific characteristic of the printed page.

Let's first look at some of the kinds of printing functions that FRED offers; then we'll see exactly how to incorporate them into a Word frame.

Although you can accomplish everything on the Print menu through FRED functions (and there may be times when you want to do so), it is generally easier to use the menu options when they are available. There are circumstances, however, when the menu options do not go far enough. For this reason, Framework III contains several FRED printing functions.

Suppose, for example, that you want the header on the Memo to Managers to be in boldface. You can use a FRED function to enter such a header. Instead of placing *Memo to Managers* in the left-header section of the Format Options submenu, we'll see shortly how to use the function @HL to create this left header.

In particular, there are two functions you can use to select other type styles that are not available on the menus—say, double-wide enhanced type, or eight lines per inch instead of six. To enter the control codes or escape sequences that turn on these effects, use the printer setup function, @ST. This function takes as its *argument,* or *parameter,* the control code or escape sequence. There are two ways to enter it. You can enter it by name; for example, if your printer uses Escape-8 to switch to eight lines per inch, you can use the formula

> @ST("{Esc}8")

If your printer uses ASCII 31, Ctrl-, to switch to double-wide print, you could use either of the following formulas:

> @ST("{Ctrl-}")
>
> @ST(@CHR(31))

Now we'll look at how to install FRED printing functions behind a Word frame.

USING THE PRINTING FUNCTIONS IN A WORD FRAME

To place printing functions behind a Word frame, you must first move the highlight to the frame's border and then press the Edit key:

Out (–)	(to select the frame's border)
Edit (F2)	(to place a formula or function behind the frame)

You will see the following message appear below the desktop:

Formula/Number editing; RETURN finishes

We saw this message many times in Chapter 3, as we entered formulas and functions into spreadsheet cells. Now we are beginning an equivalent process; the only difference is that we are placing a formula behind a frame rather than behind a cell.

In this chapter, we'll be working only with the printing functions, placed behind Word frames. In Chapters 5 and 7, we'll use functions in still other contexts. The process of placing the functions behind a frame will be the same.

When you press the Edit key (F2) at the frame's border, you'll be able to begin typing the function on the edit line. Let's enter a function behind the office memorandum frame. We'll now produce the same left-justified *Memo to Managers* header, but we'll use the FRED function to do so. Here are the keystrokes you'll type to produce this header:

Out (–)	(to select the frame's border)
Edit (F2)	(to enter a formula behind the frame)
@hl("Memo to Managers. Page " & @pn)	(to create a left-justified header including a page number)
Home	(to move the edit cursor to the beginning of the function)
→, five times	(to move the cursor forward to the M in *Memo*)
Ctrl-↓	(to select the first sentence of the header)
Ctrl-W	(to open the Words menu)
B	(to select the Bold option)
Return	(to place the finished function behind the Word frame)

Before actually entering the formula into the frame, we have taken the necessary steps to style the header in boldface.

In the first section of the status panel, below the desktop, you'll be able to see part of the function you have just placed behind the frame. As always, this panel shows you when a frame or a cell has a formula behind it. When you print the frame, this @HL printing function will print a header and page number at the top of each page.

Framework III also allows you to enter more than one line of functions and formulas into the area behind a frame. For example, you may want to place several printing functions behind a Word frame, to control more than one characteristic of the final printed version.

To create a multiple-line formula behind a frame, you use the Zoom key. In effect, this puts the edit line in full-screen mode, allowing you to enter any number of lines into the formula behind the frame. Here are the necessary keystrokes to begin this process:

Out (–)   (to select the frame's border)

Edit (F2)   (to enter a formula)

Zoom (F9)   (to enter a multiple-line formula)

Let's say you want to print the memo at eight lines to the inch instead of six, in addition to having a boldface header. Once you've used the Zoom key to bring the edit line into full-screen mode, you can enter each function on a separate line, typing a comma to separate each function from the next. For example:

@hl(**Memo to Managers**),
@st("{Esc}"8")

Note that if the formula area already contains a FRED program, place the printing formulas first, and follow them with the function @PRINTRETURN to keep the rest of the formula from being recalculated while the frame is being printed. To complete the process, press the Zoom key (F9) again to drop out of full-screen mode. Finally, press the Return key to enter the multiple-line formula into the frame. These two functions will produce the desired result.

In preparing the final printed version of our office memorandum, we've seen the full range of Framework III word processing features at work. The next step is to investigate the process of coordinating Word frames with other types of frames, using an Outline frame as the tool for combining these various documents. This is exactly what

The Sophisticated Palate is doing to produce an invoice form, as we will see in the next section of this chapter. We'll also see some creative use of the FRED printing functions, and learn a new technique—free dragging of frames.

EXAMPLES

OUTLINING AN INVOICE FORM

The prepared trays that The Sophisticated Palate has been offering as part of its catering service for some time have been a great success. Lately, the company has been receiving increasing numbers of calls from families in the neighborhood, who want to purchase them as take-out items for cocktail parties, and from businesses, who want to serve them at conference-room luncheons during work. Eileen and George had not anticipated such business, and they want to encourage it. Therefore, they have had Frank Osawa, the book-keeper, develop monthly accounts for regular customers, and they have asked Ariana Katz, the administrative assistant, to develop an invoice form for the purpose. Because the invoice form is an odd combination of numbers and text, it is an ideal application for an Outline frame—combining a Spreadsheet frame and some Word frames.

Figure 4.18 shows a filled-in example of the invoice that she has developed, using Framework III spreadsheet programming and word processing. The top half of the invoice is the customer's copy, with itemized orders and a total bill amount. The lower half is to be returned to the grocery with the customer's payment. Ariana decided to include a short survey at the bottom of the invoice, to see if she could elicit some information on customer satisfaction.

The invoice actually consists of four different frames, held inside an Outline frame that Ariana calls *Corporate Invoice and Survey*. Figure 4.19 shows the containing frame, in Outline view.

THE INVOICE SPREADSHEET

The first frame in the outline is a spreadsheet, called *Invoice*, which contains all the numeric calculations of the invoice. The spreadsheet

```
INVOICE                Customer Copy

The Sophisticated Palate, Inc.          This Bill Date:
3435 Seventh Street                         May 23, 1989
San Francisco, CA 94109                 Payment due by:
                                            Jun 22, 1989
(415) 555-1224
------------------------------------------------------------
To:

Chasen-Ketcham Co.
83 Colma Street                      Invoice #602-83045
Suite 6
South San Francisco, CA 94597
------------------------------------------------------------
         Description        Quantity   Unit Price      Amount
Party Tray 6, 4/15              3        $86.00       $258.00
Buffet Tray 2, 4/21            1       $108.00       $108.00
Party Tray 8, 5/12             2        $94.00       $188.00


------------------------------------------------------------
TOTAL===============>                                 $554.00

       (Please retain this portion for your records)
============================================================
       (Please return this portion with your check)
Chasen-Ketcham Co.
83 Colma Street                      Invoice #602-83045
Suite 6                          Total Due:      $554.00
South San Francisco, CA 94597    Amount Enclosed:
```

Note: Please make check payable to The Sophisticated Palate, Inc. If you have a billing question please call the number above between 10 a.m. and 5 p.m. Monday through Friday. Terms 2/10, n/30 unless other arrangements have been made.

*** To help us serve you better, we ask that you answer the following questions:

1. Were You satisfied with our service? __Yes __No
2. Were you satisfied with the quality of our foods? __Yes __No
3. If you ordered out fixed-menu party trays:
   a: Was the amount of food sufficient for the number of guests? __Yes __No
   b: Were you happy with the menu offered on each tray? __Yes __No
4. Would you use this service again, or recommend it to your associates? __Yes __No

We welcome your comments and suggestions.

Figure 4.18: A corporate invoice form

actually takes up a little more than half of the final invoice page, down to the line that is just above the invoice's fine print (see Figure 4.18). The first part of the Spreadsheet frame, zoomed to full-screen view, is shown in Figure 4.20. Let's review it briefly.

Ariana has written formulas into the spreadsheet to calculate the total amount of each order (the quantity multiplied by the price) and the total for all the orders itemized on the bill. For this total, she

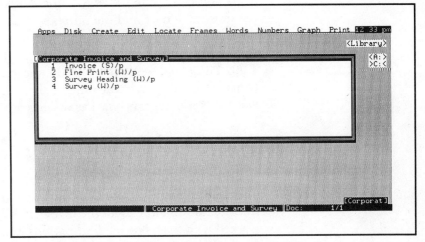

Figure 4.19: The Outline frame for the corporate invoice form

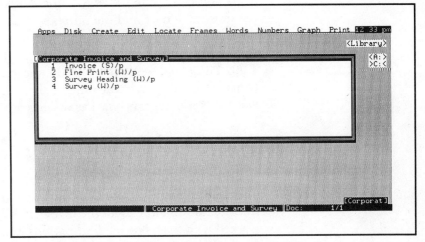

Figure 4.20: The Sophisticated Palate's invoice spreadsheet

used the @SUM function. To display the invoice date in cell D4, she has used the @TODAY function, which provides today's date. Since all payments are due 30 days after billing, Ariana has also taken advantage of Framework III's @SUMDATE function, to add 30 days to the date in cell D4. She entered the following formula into cell D6:

@sumdate(D4,30)

As you can see in Table 3.3, the @SUMDATE function takes two parameters, a date and the number of days you want to add to the date. Ariana uses this function to determine the date payment is due.

Notice the graphics symbols in cell A1 of the spreadsheet in Figure 4.20. These represent control codes for the printer. The first symbol turns double-wide printing on, and the second turns it off, so that the word *INVOICE* appears twice as wide as any other text.

THE INVOICE WORD FRAMES

Below the Spreadsheet frame are three Word frames. The first of these, called *Fine Print*, contains payment instructions and some contractual information about the invoice. To format this frame, Ariana worked with the following four options in the Words menu:

on Bold
on Justify
    on Left Margin   {19}
    on Right Margin   {108}

She also selected

Condensed Print on

from the Print Format Options submenu. When she prints this frame on a dot-matrix printer, the result is the condensed, boldface paragraph that you can see in Figure 4.18.

The second of the Word frames, called *Survey Heading*, simply contains a two-line title for the survey at the bottom of the invoice. Ariana retained the default margins for this frame, but she changed the following two Words menu options:

on Underline
on Center

Because neither Quality Print nor Condensed Print was turned on
for the containing frame, both the Invoice and Survey heading
frames will be printed in normal print.

Finally, the last of the three frames, *Survey*, has the same margins as
Fine Print. It also requires the Condensed Print menu option to switch
the printer once again into condensed mode. Figure 4.21 shows the
Format Options submenu for the containing frame, with Ariana's
chosen settings.

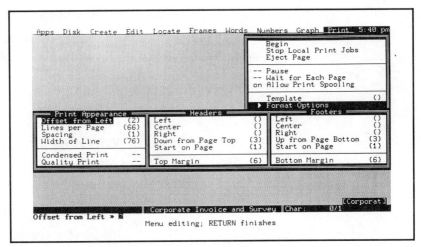

Figure 4.21: A filled-in Format Options menu

PRINTING AND SAVING
THE INVOICE AND SURVEY OUTLINE

Several interesting steps are required to print this outlined document properly. First, Ariana moves the highlight to the outer border
of the outline and presses the View key (F10) to place the outline in
Frames view.

Normally, when you print an entire outline of documents, Framework III also prints the labels of the frames contained in the outline. Ariana does not, of course, want the labels of the various frames of her Invoice and Survey outline to appear in the printed invoice form. To prevent Framework III from printing the labels, Ariana has to go into the Output Options submenu of the Print menu (shown in Figure 4.22) and disable the following option:

    – – Print Frame Labels

Next, she has to go to the Control Options submenu of the Print menu and choose one of these two options:

    – – Keep Frame on One Page
    – – Begin Frame on New Page

Ariana chooses Keep Frame on One Page, so that all the subframes will be printed one after the other on the same sheet. The result is shown in Figure 4.23.

Once the format options have been selected, the entire process of printing the invoice requires the following sequence of keystrokes:

Ctrl-Out (–)	(to select the outer border of the Outline frame)
View (F10)	(to place the outline in Frames view)
Ctrl-P	(to open the Print menu)
O	(to open the Output Options submenu)
P	(to disable the Print Frame Labels option)
Out (–)	(to move back into the main part of the Print menu)
C	(to open the Control Options submenu)
Out (–)	(to return to the Print menu)
B	(to begin printing)

Ariana finds that she can easily use this Outline frame again and again, each time she has a new invoice to send. She simply changes the customer address, the invoice number, and the order information

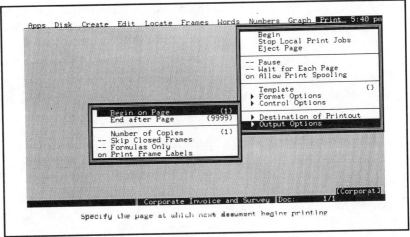

Figure 4.22: Output Options submenu of the Print menu

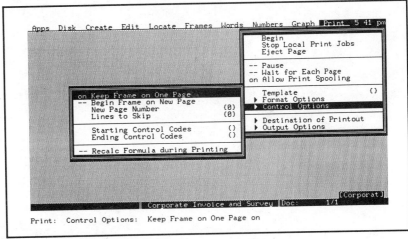

Figure 4.23: Control Options submenu of the Print menu

in the original Spreadsheet frame. Then she prints out the new invoice.

There are a few final steps to take. First, she creates an Empty frame, and labels it with the customer's name. Next, she changes the label of the Outline frame to the current date, and moves the Outline frame into the frame with the date label. Third, she creates another Empty frame labeled *Invoices*, moves all the customer frames into it, selects it, and uses the Ascending Sort option of the Locate menu to place the customer names in alphabetical order. Now she can have a single file of customer invoices, conveniently arranged in order by date. This is the form in which she will save the information on disk.

EXPLORING FURTHER

STORING TEMPLATES IN THE LIBRARY

Ariana realized that she would need several blank invoice forms every month, so she made use of the Library to keep a blank on hand. First, she copied a completed invoice. Next, she blanked out all the values, such as dates, invoice numbers, customer names, and dollar amounts, that change from one invoice to the next. Here are the keystrokes she used to place the blank invoice in the Library:

Shuttle (Scroll Lock)	(to select the Library)
Return	(to open the Library cabinet)
In (+)	(to enter the Library cabinet)
↓, seven times	(to place the cursor below {Alt-F6}, the Memos and Letters macro)
Shuttle (Scroll Lock)	(to return to the desktop)
↑, several times	(to select the blank invoice)
Move (F7)	(to invoke the move function)
Shuttle (Scroll Lock)	(to return to her location in the Library cabinet)
Return	(to complete the move)

You can use a similar procedure to store printing templates, as well as blank forms. Once you have created a frame with format and control options that you want to use again, press

Ctrl-F	(to open the Frames menu)
B	(to select the Blank All option)

This will erase all the text from the frame. Framework III will remember the printing options you selected, however, even if the frame is empty. Give the frame an appropriate name (one that you will remember) and move it into the Library cabinet under the Printing Templates heading. Next time you want to use the same print options, press

Ctrl-P	(to open the Print menu)
T	(to select the Template option)
template name	(enter the name of the template)
Return	(to record your selection)
B	(to begin printing)

That way, once you have a set of satisfactory settings, you don't have to go through the tedium of reentering them every time you want to use them.

PAGE BREAKS

Normally, Framework III will print two blank lines between frames, unless you specify otherwise in the Print Control Options submenu. There are, however, several ways to control the spacing between frames. First, the Print Control Options submenu includes these options:

- – Keep Frame on One Page
- – Begin Frame on New Page
- – Lines to Skip   {0}

The first two options can be applied to a containing frame with many subframes, or to any frame within a containing frame. For example, if you have an outline that includes a graph, you will not want to break the graph across pages. If you select the Graph frame and then select Keep Frame on One page, the graph will not be printed on the current page if there is not enough space left to hold it. If you select Begin Frame on New Page, the graph will begin on a separate page whether or not it could fit on the previous page.

If you choose Begin Frame on New Page for a containing frame, every frame will begin on a new page. This may be useful when you are printing an outline that contains many different types of frames— Graph and Spreadsheet frames intermixed with Word frames, for example.

If you want more than the normal three lines between frames, select Lines to Skip, and enter the number of lines you want skipped between frames.

Yet another way of controlling the appearance of the printed page is to select Hide Borders from the Frames menu. Normally, Framework III inserts a line for each top and bottom frame border. If the borders are hidden, you can overlap them, and no space will be skipped between frames. With this option selected, frame labels will also not be printed. This may be useful if you are setting up a document in outline form and want to use the outline headings to keep track of your work, but want to print the document as a continuous piece of text.

On the other hand, if you are creating a rather long document in a Word frame, you may want certain parts of the text to begin on new pages. First, you might want to find out where the page breaks will fall. To do so, press

Ctrl-F   (to open the Frames Menu)

V   (to choose the View Pagination option)

The message area will display

CALCULATING PAGE NUMBERS

and after the screen scrolls a bit, your text will be broken up by lines that look like this:

– – – – – – – – – – – – – 24 – – – – – – – – – – – – – –

As you insert text at various points in your document, these lines will adjust themselves to the text. Each of these lines represents the beginning of a new page, and the number tells you the page number.

If these lines do not fall where you want them, Framework III allows you to insert a *hard page break*. To do so, press

Ctrl-E   (to open the Edit menu)

B   (to select the Begin New Page option)

A heavy line will appear across the screen. The text immediately following that line will begin on a new page.

PRINTING PARTS OF FRAMES

Sometimes you don't want to print all of a document. Framework III provides several ways for you to print only part of a document. First, if your document has many subframes and you want to print only some of them, select and open the containing frame, and follow these keystrokes:

In (+)   (to enter the frame)

↑ or ↓   (to select the frames that you don't want to print)

Return   (to close those frames)

Ctrl-Out (−)   (to select the containing frame)

Ctrl-P   (to open the Print menu)

O   (to open the Output Options submenu)

S   (to turn on the Skip Closed Frames option)

If you want to print only one of several subframes, all you have to do is make sure that that frame is selected before you go to the Print menu. As with so many other features of Framework III, the Print menu commands operate only on what is selected. Therefore, if you are inside a Word frame, you can print part of the frame just by using Extend Select (F6) to highlight the part of the frame that you want to print, and then using whatever print options you choose.

If you have turned on the View Pagination option, you can also print a specific series of pages within the document. This is useful especially if you have made a small change to a single page, and you don't need to reprint the rest of the document. To do so, press

Ctrl-P   (to open the Print menu)

O   (to open the Output Options submenu)

B	(to choose Begin on Page)
number	(enter the starting page number)
Return	(to record your selection)
E	(to choose End after Page)
number	(enter the ending page number)
Return	(to record your selection)
Out (–)	(to return to the main Print menu)

You can then go on and choose any other options you want to use.

SPECIAL EFFECTS IN HEADERS AND FOOTERS

There are several more special effects that can be used in headers and footers. In this section, we'll take a brief look at ways to use multiple-line headers and footers and alternate headers or footers on opposite pages, and explore a bit further the method of inserting dates into headers and footers.

DATE STRINGS

In Chapter 3, we learned how to use the @DATE function to put dates into a spreadsheet, and a few pages ago we learned how Ariana used the @TODAY function in the same way. The result of these two functions is a *date value,* on which you can ultimately perform two kinds of *date arithmetic:*

- You can find the number of days between two dates (using the @DIFFDATE function, which we'll examine in more detail in Chapter 5).

- You can add a number of days to a given date (using the @SUMDATE function).

You cannot use @DATE or @TODAY in a context that requires a *text value;* the result of these two functions is not text. However, Framework III does provide four different functions for converting date values into text, or *string values*. These functions are called @DATE1, @DATE2, @DATE3, and @DATE4, and they all require date-value parameters. Each displays the date in a different format. Here are examples of the formats:

Function	Result
@date1(@date(1989,6,20))	Jun 20, 1989
@date2(@date(1989,6,20))	Jun 1989
@date3(@date(1989,6,20))	Jun 20
@date4(@date(1989,6,20))	June 20, 1989

To insert today's date into a header, we don't actually have to use these FRED functions; just their names. Thus, if today's date were July 4, 1999, entering

<date4>

in any of the six menu options that place headers or footers on a page would result in

July 4, 1999

being displayed at the chosen location. A similar series of functions allows you to print the time in various formats. We'll look at these functions in Chapter 5.

MULTIPLE-LINE HEADERS AND FOOTERS

To create a header or footer that continues on an additional line, include the symbol

<return>

within the text that you enter in the menu option. Anything following this symbol will be printed on a separate line. You can create headers or footers that are several lines long by using more than one such symbol in your text. Be sure that your margin and your placement of the header or footer allow for the number of lines you want to use.

ALTERNATING HEADERS AND FOOTERS

An additional symbol lets you place different headers and footers on opposing pages. Suppose, for example, that you were printing out this book, and you wanted the book title as the header on left-hand pages and the chapter title on right-hand pages. Framework III makes the distinction with respect to even- and odd-numbered pages, however, rather than left and right. To separate the text appropriately, the symbol

<even/odd>

is used. Since odd-numbered pages traditionally fall on the right, choosing the center position for headers and entering the text

Word Processing<even/odd>Mastering Framework III

would give you the result you want.

PAGE LAYOUT

A special technique allows you to lay out your pages in a "what you see is what you get" fashion. This technique is called *free dragging*. To use it, choose the containing frame, and press

Ctrl-F   (to open the Frames menu)

A   (to select Allow Free Dragging)

You can then drag the frames to any position on the screen, and the printout will reflect their relative position. There are several important limitations to this technique:

- Only the text that actually appears in the frame will be printed; if the text extends beyond the frame border, any text that does not appear will not be printed. The only exception to this rule is that printing starts at the upper left corner of the frame. Thus, if the frame contains 16 lines, and it is set at 14 lines in length, the last two lines will not be printed.

- Any print options that have been selected for the subframes will be ignored; only those for the containing frame will have any effect. Therefore, any styling of text in subframes must be done by inserting escape sequences directly in text.

- No FRED printing formulas will be executed.

- If any open frames overlap physically, their text will be intermixed in the printout.

In this connection, we can see a use for the Flush Right option in the Words menu. Figure 4.24 shows another way of laying out part of Ariana's invoice. The Hide Borders option from the Frames menu has been selected, and the frame near the upper right corner of the screen has the following options selected from the Words menu:

on Flush Right
on Right Margin   {0}

The right margin of 0 is necessary to make sure that there is no irrelevant "white space" that is theoretically inside the frame to the left of the text. To see the trouble you can get into, try setting the right margin of such a frame to 65, entering the frame, and pressing Ctrl-Home. You will find that all the text will be pushed to the right, out of view of the frame; it will therefore not be printed at all.

The Free Dragging option is one of the most complex print options available. Be aware that it may take numerous printouts to have everything appear exactly as you want it.

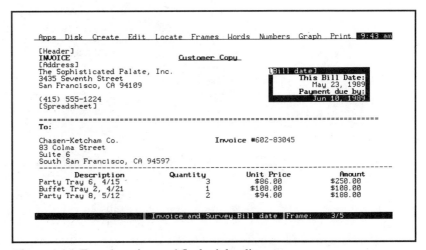

Figure 4.24: Free dragging and flush-right alignment

When you have repositioned frames through free dragging, you may find that, when you revert to Outline view, they appear to be in the wrong order. You can use the Move key (F7) to move the outline headings into the correct order without affecting the layout in Frames view. Thus, you can have the advantages of both an orderly outline and a precise page layout.

PRINTING A FRAME TO DISK

We have learned several ways to format and control the final printed appearance of a document. Not all of these characteristics show up in the Word frame on the screen. For example, if you enter a header or footer function in the Format Options submenu, you won't be able to see the result of that function until you actually print the frame.

Sometimes, you may want to check to see if a document looks the way you want it to before you go to the trouble of putting it on paper.

The Destination submenu of Framework III's Print menu (shown in Figure 4.25) gives you an option that allows you to create a *print file* on disk. This file will contain the same information that Framework III will send to your printer when you ultimately print the file.

Figure 4.25: Destination submenu of the Print menu

To create a print file, follow these steps:

Out (−)   (to select the frame border)

Ctrl-P   (to open the Print menu)

D   (to open the Destination submenu)

D   (to select the DOS File option)

Out (−)   (to move back to the main Print menu)

B   (to begin printing)

These commands produce a print file on disk, using the frame's label as the file name. The extension name of a print file is .PRT. So, for example, if the frame you are printing is called *Invoice*, the name of the print file will be

INVOICE.PRT

To see exactly how your document will look when you print it onto paper, just load this print file onto the desktop. If you have included any styling, it will be represented in this file by printer escape sequences. Similarly, any format options you have selected—such as headers, footers, and margins—will be reflected in the layout of text in the file. Page breaks will be represented by a female symbol, which is the displayable version of the form-feed character (ASCII 12).

COUNTING YOUR WORDS

An additional feature on the Edit menu is especially useful if you need to know how many words a Word frame contains. Word Count will count the number of words in a frame, displaying

WORD COUNTING

in the message area while the process proceeds, and then displaying a count of the number of words in the frame.

SUMMARY

Framework III's word processing tools include keyboard functions, menu options, and special frames in the Library cabinet. Here is an inventory of these tools:

- *Cursor-movement keys.* You can use the four arrow keys to move the cursor backward, forward, up, and down inside your document. Ctrl-Home and Ctrl-End move the cursor to the beginning and the end of the document, and PgUp and PgDn move up and down one screen at a time, respectively.

- *Text-selection keys.* You can select a word (Ctrl-→), a sentence (Ctrl-↓), or an entire paragraph (Ctrl-PgDn) for some subsequent activity in a Word frame. Similarly, you can select the same units going upward or backward using Ctrl-←, Ctrl-↑, and Ctrl-PgUp, respectively. You can also use the Extend Select key (F6) for extending the highlight over larger portions of text.

- *Other function keys.* The Move (F7) and Copy (F8) keys will move or copy a selected block of text from one location to another inside your document. Cut (Shift-F7) and Paste (Shift-F8) will place a copy of a selected block of text in the electronic clipboard, and Edit Cut Text (Shift-F2) will let you edit the contents of the clipboard. The Thesaurus key (Shift-F6) will allow you to look up synonyms at any time.

- *The Apps menu.* This menu contains the Spelling Check submenu and the List Synonyms option. Under Global Options it allows you to select foreign dictionaries if you have them.

- *The Words menu.* This menu controls styling, text alignment, margins, paragraph indentation, and tabs in a Word frame. You can assign style and format specifications globally or locally. The Word Options submenu contains additional features, including Display Ruler and Modify Ruler.

- *The Edit menu.* This menu includes six functions and two submenus that are important in word processing. Four of the options are used almost exclusively in Word frames: switching between insert mode and typeover mode; displaying the "hidden" characters—space, tab, paragraph beginning, carriage return, and soft hyphen; inserting soft hyphens; and inserting hard page breaks. In addition, the Undo option lets you restore text that has been deleted, or restore text that has been moved to its former position; and the Word Count option displays a count of the number of words in a frame. The Footnotes submenu allows you to create and edit footnotes or endnotes, and other options allow you to customize the way the footnotes are marked and where they will print. The Hyphens submenu contains options to add soft hyphens or to hyphenate an entire selection of text.

- *The Locate menu.* Through this menu, you can search for specific strings of text inside your document, or you can replace one string with another throughout the document.

- *The Print menu.* This menu prints your document, either on paper or to a print file on disk. It also allows you to specify many aspects of the final printed version of your document: the paper margins and dimensions, the spacing, the headers and footers, the printing mode of the printer, and the relationship between frames and pages. If these options do not give you all the printing features you want, special FRED printing functions can be placed in the formula area behind a Word frame (which you reach by pressing the Edit key, F2), and you can also insert printer escape sequences directly into your frame.

- *Printing templates.* A frame that has been formatted for printing can be stored in the Library cabinet with its text deleted. Entering the name of this frame in the Printing Template option of the Print menu when you print a frame will automatically cause the frame to be printed with the formats you have stored in the Library.

- *Document templates.* You can store a partially completed frame, containing text in a form that you use regularly, as a document template in the Library. To do so, copy the frame to the

Library cabinet, beneath the heading for the macro labeled {Alt-F6}.

Finally, we have seen how the effectiveness of word processing can be combined with other Framework III components to produce mixed documents. Framework III outlining is the tool that makes this kind of integration possible.

Databases

OVERVIEW

INTRODUCTION

A DATABASE FRAME IS DESIGNED FOR ORGANIZING, storing, and working with information. The primary unit of information in a database is called a *record*. A record consists of all the relevant information describing one event, one asset, one employee, one sales transaction, one client, one inventory category—or one item of whatever kind of information you are working with. A *database* is a collection of many such records, all organized in the same way.

Framework III's database management capabilities are designed to simplify the process of working with records of information. Specifically, Framework III gives you these capabilities:

- You can add new records to your database.
- You can delete records.
- You can change the information contained in records.
- You can change the structure of the database.
- You can search for a specific record.
- You can sort the records of the database in any order that you specify.
- You can calculate values for each record in the database.
- You can find groups of records that have certain characteristics in common.

These are the activities that we'll be studying in this chapter. Before we start, however, we should discuss a few general database characteristics.

THE STRUCTURE OF A DATABASE

When you set out to organize a new database, Framework III does not dictate the *structure* of the records you'll be working with. Because each different data processing job has its own particular requirements, Framework III leaves you with the task of deciding how to organize the database. You will determine the specific items of information that each record will contain. These items are called *fields*.

Figure 5.1 shows a database that we are going to be working with in this chapter; it stores information about a group of salespeople and summarizes their sales activities over a half-year period. Each record, or *row,* in the database contains six fields of information, one field for each of the six columns of the table. Together, these six fields in a given row describe one salesperson: the employee number (EmpNo), the last name (Last), the first name (First), the region in which the person works (Reg), the person's total sales for the half-year period (SixMoSales), and finally, the date the person was hired (Hired).

This example illustrates Framework III's normal way of organizing and displaying a database—in Table format. Each row of the database table contains one record; each column, one field category. A database is similar to a spreadsheet in many ways, but there are some essential differences. Whereas a spreadsheet has a free structure, the design of a database requires that rows represent records and columns represent field categories.

When you design a Database frame, one of your first jobs will be to determine the characteristics of each field in the database. Field

Figure 5.1: The Sales People database

categories are normally defined by three elements:

1. A name
2. A width, in characters
3. A data type

Notice in Figure 5.1 that the top row of the frame is reserved for the *field names*. These names express, in an abbreviated way, the nature of the data contained in each field category. Framework III draws a line below this row of names, to separate the names from the actual data. The importance of these names will become clear as soon as we begin working with databases: names give you a way of identifying the field or fields upon which you want to perform specific database operations.

The column widths in a database table determine the maximum number of characters that can be displayed in the field categories. Just as in a spreadsheet, the width of each column can be controlled independently. Using the Size key (F4), you can increase or decrease the width of the database columns. You'll generally want to arrange the size of each column in the table to accommodate the maximum number of characters that you anticipate in a given field.

For example, consider the field called *First* in Figure 5.1; this field contains the salespeople's first names. If the longest first name in your database contains seven characters, you might set this column at a width of 8, allowing an extra space to separate this field from the next one to the right.

Near the end of this chapter, we'll find that the length of a field is not truly limited by the width of the column in the database table. Framework III offers you three ways of looking at a database: the Table format displayed in Figure 5.1, a special *Forms* view, and a view similar to the one used in Ashton-Tate's dBASE products. In the Table format, your concern will be to design a frame that will display all the important information for each record; in this context, the column widths are significant. In the Forms view, however, you look at only one record at a time on the screen. This format allows you to work with fields that contain more than one line of text. In effect, the Forms view allows you to incorporate a small word-processed document as a field in each record of your database. We'll look at examples of the Forms and dBASE views later. In the meantime, as we work with databases in the Table format, we'll think of the column width as the limiting factor on the width of a field.

The final characteristic of a field is its data type. You are responsible for making sure that all the information in a given column, or field, of your database is of the same type. We'll be working with four data types in this chapter: text, numbers, dates, and logical values. When you define a field, you will determine the type of data the field will contain; this data type should remain constant from one record to the next.

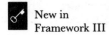
New in
Framework III

In Framework III, you can use the Entry Format for Data option on the Numbers menu to set or change the data type for any field, as you'll see later in this chapter.

Once you have organized the structure of your database, you can begin entering the actual data. You can enter field values manually, or you can have them calculated. When you devise a formula for a calculated field, the entire column that represents that field is filled in at once. We'll find out exactly how to work with calculated fields later in this chapter.

You may need to increase or decrease the number of records and fields in your database during the course of your work with the information in the database. The total size of your database is limited by the amount of memory in your computer. Let's briefly discuss this issue before we begin looking at the details of Framework III database management.

MEMORY CONSIDERATIONS WITH DATABASES

A frame that is currently on your desktop is stored entirely in the computer's random access memory (RAM) if there is room for it. (The largest frame on your desktop is *always* stored in RAM.) Of course, a frame can also be saved as a file on disk; during the course of your work with a frame, however, the whole frame must reside in the computer's memory.

This arrangement contrasts with some other personal computer programs that automatically take care of shifting portions of a long file between the computer's memory and a storage area on disk. This shifting back and forth may take place whenever you work with a long file; only the portion of the file that you are currently working with needs to reside in RAM at any one time. When this automatic shifting procedure is included in a database management program, the result is a potential for larger databases: the size of a database is limited by the storage area available on your disk rather than by the amount of RAM in your computer. If your computer has a hard disk, with storage capacity measured in megabytes, this kind of database management program will allow you to work with very large databases, containing thousands of records.

Framework III, however, always keeps the largest frame on the desktop entirely in RAM. This has serious implications for the size of a database. Database frames require more memory than other types of frames (even Spreadsheet frames that have the same number of cells), so they tend to be large. Second, even empty cells in a Database frame take up a significant amount of memory. The implications are two-fold: first, you can assume that Framework III will want to keep Database frames entirely in RAM; second, this means that the dimensions of a database in Framework III are limited by the amount of memory you have installed in your computer.

This arrangement has advantages and disadvantages. The main disadvantage is, as noted, that although the theoretical limit on the dimensions of a database is 32,000 columns by 32,000 rows, as a practical matter Framework III limits the size of your database to what will fit in your available memory—a maximum of about 32,000 cells. (However, as a consolation, Framework III can be configured to take advantage of any memory resources you have available: expanded or extended memory up to 16 megabytes, RAM disks, or even, if all else fails, your hard disk. The latter is not recommended, however. See Appendix A for details on setting up the program to match your hardware configuration.)

On the other hand, given an appropriate small- to medium-size project, Framework III database management has two advantages over other database programs: simplicity and efficiency. You'll be able to master Framework III's database operations in a short time, yet these operations will allow you as much flexibility with your data as you would expect with more complex programs. Furthermore, because all your data are stored in memory, the Framework III database operations will be performed quickly. In particular, during sorting and searching operations, you won't have to wait for the computer to shift various parts of your database between disk and RAM to complete the operation.

Now let's begin creating a database and finding out how to work with it.

CREATING A DATABASE

The Database option of the Create menu places a new Database frame on the desktop:

Ctrl-C   (to open the Create menu)

D   (to create a Database frame)

However, before you create a Database frame, you should determine the dimensions you want to begin with: the number of fields and the number of records your database will initially contain. The Create menu options that allow you to specify these dimensions are the same as those used for creating a Spreadsheet frame:

Width	(#Cols/Fields)	{50}
Height	(#Rows/Records)	{100}

As we saw in Chapter 3, the default dimensions of a new Database (or Spreadsheet) frame are 50 columns by 100 rows. If you want to change these dimensions, you should select the Width and Height options and enter new numeric values to match your own specifications.

The Sales People database that we have been examining has 6 columns and 18 rows, although only 13 rows are shown in Figure 5.1. In working with this database, you'll imagine yourself the manager of a national sales force, with salespeople stationed in six regions: northeast, southeast, midwest, south, northwest, and southwest (abbreviated NE, SE, M, S, NW, and SW, respectively, in the database itself). You have accumulated total sales figures for each of your salespeople over the last six months. You are creating this database to store the information and to provide a tool for analyzing the relative merits of your employees' performances over this half-year period.

Your first task is to create a frame for the database; here are the necessary keystrokes:

Ctrl-C   (to open the Create menu)

W   (to select the Width option)

6   (to specify six fields)

Return   (to enter this value into the Create menu)

H	(to select the Height option)
18	(to specify 18 records)
Return	(to enter this value into the Create menu)
D	(to create the Database frame)

The resulting frame appears in Figure 5.2. You can see that Framework III automatically supplies a row at the top of the frame for the field names. (This row is not considered one of the 18 record rows of your database.) A double line separates this row from the data section of the frame.

Enter the following title into the frame's border:

Sales People

Then press the In key (+) to move the highlight into the frame. The highlight will initially land in the upper left corner of the frame. Just as in a Spreadsheet frame, you can use the four arrow keys—↑, ↓, ←, and →—to move the highlight, one row or column at a time, inside the Database frame. Unlike a Spreadsheet frame, however, a Database frame does not contain column letters and row numbers. The actual organization of a Database frame is invisible until you begin entering field names and data into the frame, although the status

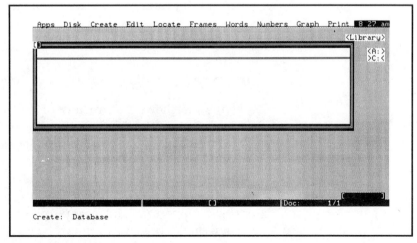

Figure 5.2: A new Database frame

Version Note

In Framework II, the letters at the bottom of the screen showed the number of records currently in the database, and the total number of rows. However, in Framework III, those numbers now show the current record (the one the cursor is in) and the total number of currently filtered selected records.

panel does tell you how many record rows the frame contains:

        Recs: 0/18

We will see later in this chapter how to *filter* a database to limit the number of records it displays.

Press the → and ↓ keys several times now, and you will see that the frame is indeed organized into columns and rows. Each time you press →, the highlight moves one column to the right. The first ↓ keystroke moves the highlight from the field-name row into the data section of the frame; subsequently, ↓ continues to move the highlight down the rows of the frame.

Table 5.1 reviews the keys and keystroke combinations that you can use to move the highlight from one place to another inside the Database frame. These keystrokes should seem quite familiar to you after your work with Spreadsheet frames.

The next step is to prepare the frame to conform to the specifications of your database. You do this in three stages:

1. First, enter the field names.

2. Then size the columns appropriately.

3. Finally, assign data display styles, where necessary, corresponding to the fields' data types and appropriate to the overall appearance of the database table.

We'll work on all of these details in the next section.

PREPARING THE DATABASE FRAME

Figure 5.3 shows the structure of the Sales People database as a spreadsheet containing the name of each field, the width of each column, the type of data that will go into each field, and the purpose of each field. You may find it useful to set up a spreadsheet containing a table similar to this one for each Database frame that you create in Framework III; the table reminds you at a glance exactly how your database is organized and what purposes it serves. You can store the two in a single containing frame.

Table 5.1: Keys for Moving the Database Highlight

KEYS	ACTION
←, →, ↑, ↓	Moves the highlight one field or record in the direction indicated.
Home	Moves the highlight to the first field of the current record.
End	Moves the highlight to the last field of the current record.
Ctrl-↑	Moves the highlight up to the first row (the field-name row) in the current field column.
Ctrl-↓	Moves the highlight down to the last record in the current field column.
PgUp	Scrolls one frame up.
PgDn	Scrolls one frame down.
Ctrl-Home	Moves the highlight to the first field name, in the top row of the frame.
Ctrl-End	Moves the highlight to the last field in the last record of the frame.
Return	Enters data, or moves the highlight one record down.
Tab	Enters data and/or moves the highlight one field to the right.
Shift-Tab	Enters data and/or moves the highlight one field to the left.

With only 6 fields and 18 records, Sales People is a very small example of a database. But imagine a database that has, say, 20 fields of information and a few thousand records; you can see how a table like the one shown in Figure 5.3 could become an essential tool for reminding you exactly what kind of information your database contains. Throughout this chapter, keep in mind that all the database management operations we examine will work effectively on much larger databases than Sales People.

Following the specifications in Figure 5.3, you need to prepare each column of the Database frame for the field information that the

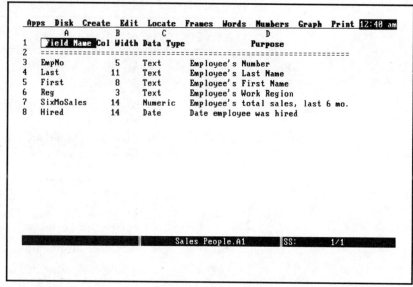

```
 Apps  Disk  Create  Edit  Locate  Frames  Words  Numbers  Graph  Print 12:40 am
            A           B        C                    D
1    Field Name Col Width Data Type            Purpose
2    ====================================================================
3    EmpNo           5     Text       Employee's Number
4    Last           11     Text       Employee's Last Name
5    First           8     Text       Employee's First Name
6    Reg             3     Text       Employee's Work Region
7    SixMoSales     14     Numeric    Employee's total sales, last 6 mo.
8    Hired          14     Date       Date employee was hired







                                    Sales People.A1      SS:        1/1
```

Figure 5.3: Structure of the Sales People database

column will ultimately contain. Let's begin with the first column. Press Ctrl-Home to move the highlight to the upper left corner of the frame, and type the field name

    EmpNo

The name appears in the top row of the database table as you type it. Press Return to enter the name. Now press the Size key (F4) to adjust the width of the column. This first column is to have a width of 5 spaces. Because the default width of database columns is 9 spaces, you'll press the ← key four times to reduce the width of the first column appropriately. A message in the right section of the status panel will tell you the current width of the column; this is how it will look when the column is correctly sized:

    Size: 5/1

Press Return to end the sizing operation.
    Continue this process for each column of the Database frame: first enter the field name; then size the column. When all the field names are in place, you may want to center them inside their respective column

widths. To do so, use the Middle option of the Numbers menu:

Ctrl-Home	(to move the highlight to the first field)
Extend Select (F6)	(to extend the highlight)
End	(to extend across the entire row)
Ctrl-N	(to open the Numbers menu)
M	(to select the Middle option)

Figure 5.4 shows what your frame should look like at this point. Notice that we use the Numbers menu, not the Words menu, to align text entries in the Table format of a database.

Finally, before you begin entering the actual data into the frame, you may want to specify display styles. In Figure 5.1, you can see that the numbers in the SixMoSales field are displayed as currency values, and the dates in the Hired field are right-justified, to allow a little more space between the figures in SixMoSales and the dates. To select Currency style, you'll extend the highlight over the entire SixMoSales column and once again use the Numbers menu. To right-justify the Hired column, follow the same process. Begin by moving the highlight to the field name SixMoSales. Then press the following keys:

Extend Select (F6)   (to extend the highlight)

Version Note

The procedures described in this section will work with *any* version of Framework. If you have Framework III, however, you will probably prefer to use the Entry Format for Data option on the Numbers menu.

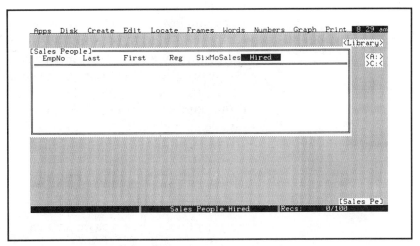

Figure 5.4: Entering field names into the Database frame

Ctrl-↓	(to extend down the entire column)
Ctrl-N	(to open the Numbers menu)
C	(to select the Currency option)
→	(to move the highlight to the Hired column)
Ctrl-N	(to open the Numbers menu)
R	(to select the Right option)

Now when you enter numbers into the SixMoSales column, they will automatically be displayed in Currency style, with dollar signs and commas. And the dates in the Hired column will automatically be right-justified within the column width.

Now we are ready to begin the data entry process.

ENTERING DATA INTO THE DATABASE FRAME

Figure 5.3 shows that the Sales People database contains three types of data: text, numbers, and dates. As we enter the data for each record and field, we have to make sure that Framework III is accepting the data as the correct type. The techniques we learned in Chapter 3 for spreadsheet data entry also apply to Database frames. Let's review those techniques as we enter the first record of the Sales People database.

The employee-number field, EmpNo, contains a four-character identification code for each employee. Notice, though, that these are actually text values—because they contain a mix of digits and letters, Framework III would not be able to accept them as numeric values.

The format of these values, however, imposes a small complication on the data entry process. Each value begins with a digit; for example:

82M1

We know from Chapter 3 that the first keystroke of a data entry determines Framework III's reading of the data type. In this case, if you were to enter the digit 8 as the first character, the following message would be displayed at the bottom of the screen:

Formula/Number editing; RETURN finishes

But numeric entry is not the correct mode for the EmpNo field. You may recall the solution to this problem. Press the spacebar before you enter the number. As soon as you do, you will see the correct data entry message:

Text editing; RETURN finishes

Use the spacebar to begin text data entry whenever the text begins with a digit (or other character) that Framework III would normally read as the beginning of a numeric data entry. Each time you enter one of the employee numbers in the database, use the spacebar to indicate that this code is a text value.

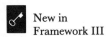 New in
Framework III

    In Framework III, there is an easier method of determining the data type. Using the new Entry Format for Data option on the Numbers menu, you can predetermine the data type for any field. If you remember this command from Chapter 3, you'll already know how it works, but we'll repeat the explanation here.

    In this case, where you want to enter text, but begin it with a number, you select the EmpNo field and choose Entry Format for Data from the Numbers menu. You'll see a list of possible entry formats, as shown in Figure 5.5.

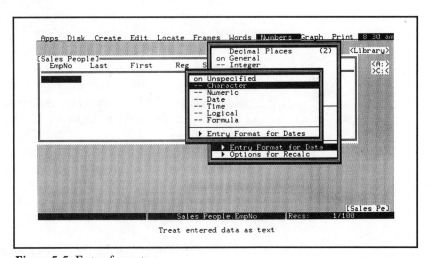

Figure 5.5: Entry formats

Choose Character as the entry format for the EmpNo field. Now when you enter the employee numbers, you won't have to press the spacebar before typing the first part of the field value.

You can select an entry format for more than one field by using Extend Select (F6) to highlight the fields you want to set. Or, if all or most fields will be the same format, you can use the Out key (–) to select the frame border and choose an entry format for all fields. You can still change the format for any individual field or group of fields.

In the examples that follow, we'll see how to apply entry formats to other types of fields.

After typing a field value, you can use the Tab key to perform two functions: to complete the data entry and to move the highlight one field to the right. This is the equivalent of pressing

Return   (to complete the entry)

→   (to move the highlight)

The next three fields—Last, First, and Reg—are simple text values. Here, you can enter the last name, first name, and region of the first salesperson:

Waterman   Pearl   M

Because each of these values begins with a letter, Framework III will put you immediately in the correct data entry mode as you enter them. You do not need to preface the data entry by pressing the spacebar. And, although you could use the Entry Format for Data option to define them as Character fields, the default value of Unspecified is fine, since each of these fields will contain only text entries anyway. If you do use the Character entry format, you can avoid bizarre results from numeric typographical errors.

The SixMoSales field is numeric. Enter the value for the first record as follows:

85977.83

Upon reading the first digit, 8, Framework III will display the correct data entry message:

Formula/number editing; RETURN finishes

When you press the Tab key to complete the data entry, you will see the following value in the SixMoSales field:

$85,977.83

Notice that the dollar sign is added to the entry. The Currency style that you specified earlier determines the display style of the new value.

Again, you could use the Entry Format for Data option on the Numbers menu to predefine the SixMoSales field as a Numeric entry, but it isn't necessary. However, the Numeric data type does present some specific possibilities. If a field is defined as Numeric, it will use the first number it encounters as the field value. For instance, if you enter

One pound and 6 ounces

in a Numeric field, Framework III will interpret that entry as 6. The text is ignored. On the other hand, if you enter

1 or 2 pounds

then the value Framework III will use is 1.

The last field, Hired, is a date value. To enter it, we can use the FRED function called @DATE. Enter the following formula into the Hired field of the first record:

@date(1982,9,29)

When Framework III reads the @ character, you will once again see the *Formula/number editing* message at the bottom of the screen. The result of entering this function will be a display of the following date:

Sep 29, 1982

You can also use the Entry Format for Data submenu to define the Hired field as a Date field. If you do so, you can choose from several Date entry formats by choosing the Entry Format for Dates submenu (see Figure 5.6).

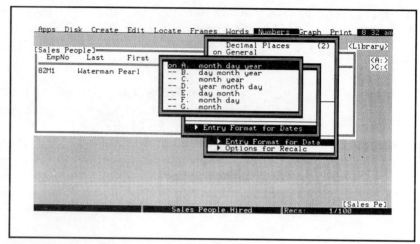

Figure 5.6: Date formats

The Entry Format for Dates submenu contains seven Date formats, which you can use to enter dates directly into cells without using the @DATE function. You can enter dates as:

Format	Examples
month day year	1/10/89; January 10, 1989
day month year	10-1-89, 10 Jan 1989
month year	1 89, J 1989
year month day	89.1.10, 1989 January 10
day month	10-1, 10 Jan
month day	1/10, January 10
month	January, Jan, Ja, J

The Date entry format has no effect on the date display style, which you can set using the styling options on the Numbers menu. Several of the styling options will change the way the date displays on the screen and prints. However, the Entry Format for Dates option is used to determine how you will enter dates into spreadsheets and databases.

You may wonder why you can't simply enter a date as a text value rather than use the @DATE function or the Date entry format. The answer is that you can, if you never intend to perform any special operations involving this date. The @DATE function and the Date entry format, while *displaying* the date themselves, privately record a *numeric* version of the date. This numeric version, sometimes called a *scalar date,* allows you to use the date information in these ways:

1. You can find the difference, in days, between two dates.

2. You can add several days to one date, yielding a second date.

3. You can sort dates in chronological order.

We'll see examples of these activities later in the chapter.

You have now entered one entire record. Before reading further in this chapter, finish entering the entire database—the six fields of information for all 18 salespeople. Press the Zoom key (F9) to shift into full-screen mode; you'll be able to see all 18 rows of the database table at once.

You'll need the complete database for the exercises that follow. Once you have finished the data entry, you should save the database on disk, using the shortcut Save and Continue command:

Ctrl-Return   (to save and continue)

Now we'll begin learning how to work with this database.

USING THE DATABASE

In the sections ahead, we'll study several database management operations, including sorting, searching, changing the structure of the database, writing formulas to calculate field values, and writing "filter" formulas to select groups of records that have specific characteristics in common. In the course of this discussion, we'll find ourselves expanding the contents—and the usefulness—of the Sales People database.

SORTING

We saw in Chapter 3 that sorting means rearranging information in some specified order: alphabetical, numerical, or chronological. The Locate menu offers two sorting orders: ascending or descending.

Sorting a Framework III database is remarkably easy and fast. You always begin by selecting a field in the database that will act as a *key* for the sort. For example, you might choose to sort the Sales People database in any of the following ways:

- Placing the records in alphabetical order by the employees' last names (using the Last field as the key for the sort)

- Placing the records in numerical order by the total sales for the six-month period (with SixMoSales as the key field)

- Placing the records in chronological order by the date employees were hired (using Hired as the key field)

 Version Note

In versions of Framework before Framework III, sort order was straight ASCII order. However, beginning with Framework III, the default sort order is by dictionary order.

Framework III can sort any type of data. By default, an alphabetical sort follows dictionary order, using the following rules:

1. Punctuation characters

2. Lowercase letters, a to z

3. Uppercase letters, A to Z

4. Digits

Since the default is to ignore capitalization, however, uppercase and lowercase letters will not be segregated unless you toggle off the Ignore Capitalization option on the Locate menu. An *ascending* alphabetical sort follows this order; a *descending* alphabetical sort goes in the opposite order.

You can change the sort to ASCII code order using the Setup program option number 4 (Other Options). In ASCII order, punctuation characters and digits are followed by uppercase letters, then lowercase letters. See Appendix C for a chart of ASCII codes. You can also create your own drivers to alter the sort order. This is mostly used to accommodate the need for special sorts in foreign-language versions of Framework.

To perform a sort operation, follow these three steps:

1. Move the highlight to the name of the field that you wish to sort by (that is, the *key* for the sort).

2. Open the Locate menu.

3. Select either the Ascending or Descending sort option.

Notice that you do not have to extend the highlight over the entire field column; it is sufficient to place the highlight anywhere in the first row of the database table.

Let's try a few sorting operations. First we'll sort by the total sales for the period, from best to worst. Begin by moving the highlight to the SixMoSales column, and then press the following keys:

Ctrl-L (to open the Locate menu)

D   (to sort in descending order)

The result will be an instant rearranging of the entire database table in order of total sales—starting from the best record of $117,632.48, down to the worst record of $47,256.70.

Now let's sort by the dates the employees were hired, from the oldest to the newest employee. Move the highlight to the Hired column, and press

Ctrl-L (to open the Locate menu)

A   (to sort in ascending order)

You can see the result of this sort in Figure 5.7.

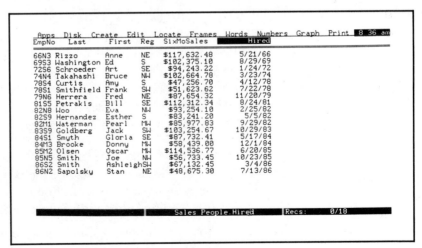

Figure 5.7: Sorting by dates

Finally, let's sort by the employees' last names. Move the highlight to the Last field, and press

Ctrl-L   (to open the Locate menu)

A   (to sort in ascending order)

The records will be reordered by last names, from Brooke to Woo. But there is a problem with this particular operation. You have two salespeople named Smith on your staff, and this sort has left them in the wrong alphabetical order:

Smith   Joe
Smith   Ashleigh

You need some way of making sure that Framework III will sort by first names when two or more last names are identical.

The solution to this problem is simple. You will have to sort the database twice: first by first names, then by last names. When you complete these two operations, the Smiths will be in the correct order:

Smith   Ashleigh
Smith   Joe

In this case, we say that the Last field is the *primary* key and the First field is the *secondary* key for the sort. It may seem that the terminology is backward, but the secondary sort must be performed *before* the primary sort.

You may think of other situations in which it would be appropriate to sort by more than one key. For example, consider the following two problems, and try performing the suggested solutions:

1. You would like to separate the salespeople by region, and, within the regions, arrange the people in order of their total sales, from best to worst. Solution: sort first by SixMoSales (descending), then by Reg (ascending).

2. You want to arrange the salespeople by employee number, within each region. Solution: sort first by EmpNo (ascending), then by Reg (ascending).

SEARCHING AND REPLACING

In Chapter 4, we saw how the Locate menu's Search and Replace options work in Word frames. Search helps you find every occurrence of a specified string of characters. Replace will change every occurrence of a specified string to a new string of characters. The options work almost the same way in Database frames, except that they operate exclusively within the field you have selected.

For example, let's say you want to find all the Smiths in your database. Begin by placing the highlight over the field name Last, and then press the following keys:

Ctrl-L   (to open the Locate menu)

S   (to select the Search option)

Smith   (specify the text you want to search for)

Return   (to begin the search)

You'll recall that Framework III supplies you with a message below the desktop, explaining how to use the Search operation. In brief, you can press the ↓ key to move down to the next occurrence of the text you are searching for, or the ↑ key to move up to the previous occurrence.

If you try this particular search operation, you'll discover that Framework III finds the two Smiths in your database, but it does *not* find the person named Smyth. To help you find related words, or variant spellings, Framework III allows you to use wildcards in both Search and Replace operations. As with the computer's operating system, the character ? will stand for any character in the position it occupies, and the character * for any group of characters in the name. Thus, if you wanted to find Smyth as well as Smith, you would enter

Search   {Sm?th}

in the Search option in the Locate menu. You can use wildcards while searching in *any* type of frame. Thus, to search for any day of the week, you could enter

Search   {*day}

in the Locate menu.

At the same time, you may have noticed that your search operation turned up not only the two Smiths, but also a person named Smithfield. To search only for the name *Smith*, ignoring any names that *begin with* Smith, include a space (press the spacebar) as the last character of the target text, so that the Search option in the Locate menu will look like this:

Search   {Smith }

You can also use this little trick for specifying a precise target text for the Replace operation.

The Replace option requires that you first enter a text for which Framework III will search in the field column you have selected. Then you enter a string to replace the text you're searching for. You'll recall from Chapter 4 that Framework III allows you either to replace all occurrences at once or to step through the occurrences one by one, making individual decisions to replace or not to replace. (Detailed instructions are supplied below the desktop.) Pressing the End key results in the replacement of every occurrence.

Try using the Replace operation on the column that contains the salespeople's work regions. Let's say you've decided to change the abbreviation for the midwestern region from M to MW. Move the highlight to Reg, and press these keys:

Ctrl-L	(to open the Locate menu)
R	(to select the Replace option)
M	(specify the target text)
Return	(to enter the target text into the Locate menu)
MW	(specify the replacement text)
Return	(to enter the replacement text into the Locate menu)
End	(to replace all occurrences)

The results of this particular Replace operation are not dramatic; there are only three occurrences to be replaced. But keep in mind that this operation, like the sort and search operations, works as well on a database containing thousands of records as it does on a small database like this one.

ADDING RECORDS OR FIELDS

At various points in your work with a database, you may want to increase the dimensions of the database table. The Create menu contains two options that allow you to do so; these are the same options that we used in Chapter 3 to increase the size of a spreadsheet:

Columns/Fields:	Add
Rows/Records:	Add

Adding rows to the database table is simply a way of making room for more records. In the case of the Sales People database, you'd want to add a row whenever you hire a new salesperson. In the event that you open up a new sales region, you might have to add several rows at a time, to accommodate all the salespeople in the new region.

Adding a column, however, means changing the *structure* of the database. You may discover that there is some new piece of information that you want to keep about each record in your database. This information will become a new field in the structure of the database.

In some database management programs, changing the structure of an already existing database (by adding new fields) can be a difficult operation, if it is possible at all. Framework III simplifies the operation, again partly because the entire database is held in the computer's active memory during your work.

Despite the simplicity of the operation itself, the addition of a new field into your database is an event you may have to prepare for carefully. First, if you are keeping a structure table for your database (see Figure 5.3), you will want to revise it, adding a description of the new field. Second, you'll have to decide exactly how you are going to fill the new field with data. There are two possibilities:

1. You can enter the data manually, typing a new field value for each record in the database.

2. You can instruct Framework III to enter *calculated* values into the new field.

Your choice between these two approaches will, of course, depend on the nature of the data itself.

We are going to add three new fields to the Sales People database, which we'll call AvgPerMo, Pbn, and Yrs. Here are the descriptions of the new fields:

- AvgPerMo will contain the average monthly sales for each salesperson, during the six-month period covered by the database.

- Pbn will indicate whether a given salesperson has been placed on probation, based on the sales for the period.

- Yrs will show how many years each salesperson has worked for the company.

All three of these will be *calculated* fields; no new manual data entry will be necessary.

Figure 5.8 shows a new structure table for the expanded database. (You will have to add rows to the database to complete this table.) Our first step in changing the structure is to add columns for the new fields. The first two fields, AvgPerMo and Pbn, will be located immediately after SixMoSales. The field Yrs will become the final field of the database, located after Hired. Adding the three new columns will thus be a two-step operation.

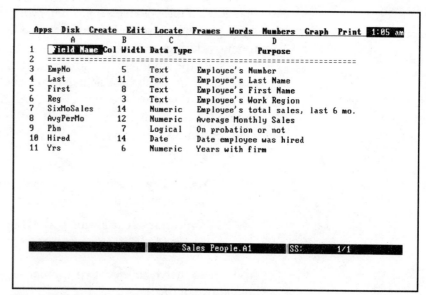

Figure 5.8: Structure of the expanded database

Begin by placing the highlight in the SixMoSales column. Press the following keys to add two new columns to the right of the SixMo-Sales column:

Ctrl-C	(to open the Create menu)
C	(to add new columns)
2	(to specify two columns)
Return	(to complete the operation)

Now place the highlight in the Hired column, and press

Ctrl-C	(to open the Create menu)
C	(to add new columns)
1	(to specify one column)
Return	(to complete the operation)

You now have three empty columns in your database, for three new fields of information. In the next section of this chapter, we'll learn how to write formulas that will fill these columns with data. But first we need to prepare the columns properly for the data they will contain. In making these preparations, we'll follow the specifications outlined in Figure 5.8. Here are the steps:

1. Enter the three field names into the first row of the database table: AvgPerMo, Pbn, and Yrs.

2. Revise the column sizes. Use the Size key (F4) to initiate the procedure and the → or ← key to increase or decrease the size of the column. The AvgPerMo column should be 12 spaces wide; Pbn, 7 spaces; and Yrs, 6 spaces. Use the Middle option of the Numbers menu to center the field names inside their column widths.

3. Select appropriate styles for the two numeric fields. Assign the Currency style to the AvgPerMo column. Extend the highlight over the entire column, and select the Currency option of the

Numbers menu. For the Yrs column, specify the Fixed Decimal style, with one decimal place. Extend the highlight over the entire Yrs column, and press the following keys:

Ctrl-N	(to open the Numbers menu)
D	(to select the Decimal Places option)
1	(to specify one decimal place)
Return	(to enter the value into the Numbers menu)
Ctrl-N	(to open the Numbers menu again)
F	(to select the Fixed Decimal style)

Figure 5.9 shows what the database should look like at this point in your work.

WRITING FORMULAS TO CALCULATE FIELD VALUES

One of the most useful features of Framework III database management is its ability to calculate values for a field column, based on a defining formula that you supply. In a way, this feature has the same effect as the process of writing and copying formulas in a spreadsheet.

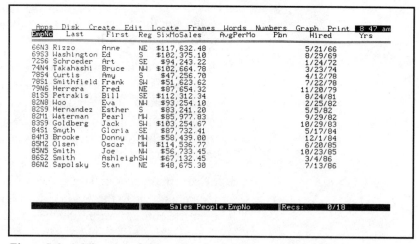

Figure 5.9: Adding new fields to the database

But the procedure is even simpler in a Database frame, because you need to enter only one formula to define an entire calculated field category.

The top row of the database table, which up to now we have used exclusively for displaying field names, is also the correct location for formulas that calculate field columns. Formulas that you enter into this row will reside *behind* the field names. In Chapter 4, we saw how a formula can reside behind a frame; we used the Edit key to place FRED printing functions behind our Word frames. Likewise, the Edit key (F2) will also give us access to the area behind the field names in a Database frame. Entering such a formula does not affect the display of the field name itself, because the result of the formula appears in the data portion of the frame, as a column of calculated field values.

Database formulas for calculating fields can be written in one of two formats. The result of these two formats is identical; you can use whichever format seems clearer and easier to you. Both formats have two essential parts: first, the name of the field category that will be calculated, and second, the formula that defines the calculation.

The first format uses a FRED function called @SET to establish a defining formula for a given field:

@set(*field, formula*)

You might read this function as, "Set each value in the *field* column to the result of *formula*." The second format uses a special symbol (: =) to *assign* a formula to a field:

field : = *formula*

This statement could be read as, "Assign the result of *formula* to each value in the *field* column." This is the format we will use in this chapter. Remember, the two formats perform exactly the same task.

You can place defining formulas behind any field name in the top row of the database. A formula does not necessarily have to reside behind the name of the field that it defines; but usually the most convenient place to write a formula will be in the column that actually receives the resulting calculated values.

Here are the steps involved in writing a defining formula:

1. Move the highlight to the field name where you want the formula to reside.

2. Press the Edit key (F2).

3. Type the formula itself, on the edit line, in either of the two legal formats.

4. Press the Return key to enter the formula into the area behind the field name.

When you complete this process, assuming you have written a valid formula, Framework III will immediately begin calculating results for the entire field category that you have defined. You will also see the formula itself displayed in the left section of the status panel. (You can always review the formula by placing the highlight over the field name where the formula resides; the formula will appear in the status panel.)

We're going to enter three formulas to calculate values for the three new field categories of the Sales People database: AvgPerMo, Pbn, and Yrs. Figure 5.10 shows the database after these three formulas have been entered. As we write each formula, you should examine this final version of the database and make sure you can find the specific calculated values that result from the formulas.

The simplest of the three formulas is for the field category AvgPerMo. We know that the field SixMoSales contains total sales amounts for a six-month period. So to calculate the average monthly

```
 Apps  Disk  Create  Edit  Locate  Frames  Words  Numbers  Graph  Print  8:53 am
 EmpNo    Last      First     Reg   SixMoSales   AvgPerMo     Pbn      Hired      Yrs
 86N2  Sapolsky   Stan      NE    $48,675.30    8112.55   #TRUE    7/13/86    2.41
 82M1  Waterman   Pearl     MW    $85,977.83   14329.64  #FALSE    9/29/82    6.20
 85M2  Olsen      Oscar     MW   $114,536.77   19089.46  #FALSE    6/20/85    3.47
 85N5  Smith      Joe       NW    $56,733.45    9455.58   #TRUE   10/23/85    3.13
 83S9  Goldberg   Jack      SW   $103,254.67   17209.11  #FALSE   10/29/83    5.12
 84S1  Smyth      Gloria    SE    $87,732.41   14622.07  #FALSE    5/17/84    4.57
 79N6  Herrera    Fred      NE    $87,654.32   14609.05  #FALSE   11/20/79    9.06
 78S1  Smithfield Frank     SW    $51,623.62    8603.94   #TRUE    7/22/78   10.39
 82N8  Woo        Eva       NW    $93,254.10   15542.35  #FALSE    2/25/82    6.79
 82S9  Hernandez  Esther    S     $83,241.20   13873.53  #FALSE    5/5/82     6.60
 69S3  Washington Ed        S    $102,375.10   17062.52  #FALSE    8/29/69   19.29
 84M3  Brooke     Donny     MW    $58,439.00    9739.83   #TRUE   12/1/84     4.02
 74N4  Takahashi  Bruce     NW   $102,664.78   17110.80  #FALSE    3/23/74   14.73
 81S5  Petrakis   Bill      SE   $112,312.34   18718.72  #FALSE    8/24/81    7.30
 86S2  Smith      AshleighSW    $67,132.45    11188.74  #FALSE    3/4/86     2.77
 72S6  Schroeder  Art       SE    $94,243.22   15707.20  #FALSE    1/24/72   16.89
 66N3  Rizzo      Anne      NE   $117,632.48   19605.41  #FALSE    5/21/66   22.57
 78S4  Curtis     Amy       S     $47,256.70    7876.12   #TRUE    4/12/78   10.67

                                    Sales People.EmpNo        Recs:      0/18
```

Figure 5.10: Placing calculated field values in the database sales for each employee, we will simply divide the SixMoSales value by 6.

Move the highlight to the AvgPerMo field name. Press the Edit key (F2), and enter the following formula onto the edit line:

AvgPerMo : = SixMoSales/6

The : = symbol assigns the formula to AvgPerMo, and the / symbol performs the division in the formula itself. Press the Return key to enter the formula into the database. As soon as you do so, the AvgPerMo column will be filled with dollars-and-cents values. (Recall that we have already specified the Currency display style for this column.)

If you wanted to use the alternative format for this defining formula, this is what it would look like:

@set(AvgPerMo, SixMoSales/6)

You may find a small advantage in using this format: you need not press the Edit key before you begin entering the formula. Framework III reads the @ symbol as the beginning of a formula, and therefore automatically puts you in the correct data entry mode.

Next, we'll enter the formula for calculating the number of years each employee has worked for the firm. This formula will go into the last column of the database, the field named Yrs. To compute the values for this field, we'll use the FRED function @DIFFDATE, which supplies the number of days between any two dates. The @DIFFDATE function takes the following format:

@diffdate(*date1, date2*)

Assuming that *date1* is later in time than *date2,* @DIFFDATE yields the positive number of days that separate the two dates. Both *date1* and *date2* have to be Framework III date values, not text expressions that represent dates.

We saw in Chapter 4 that the @TODAY function supplies today's date, which is read from the DOS system calendar. For each employee in the Sales People database, we want to find out how much time has elapsed between the date the person was hired and today's date. Here is the @DIFFDATE function that will supply the information:

@diffdate(@today, Hired)

But this expression yields the difference between the two dates in days. Because we want the value to be expressed in years, we'll have to divide the result by 365, the number of days in a year:

@diffdate(@today, Hired)/365

So, finally, here is the defining formula that we'll enter into the area behind the Yrs field name:

Yrs : = @diffdate(@today, Hired)/365

You can see the result of this formula in the last column of the final version of the database, in Figure 5.10. (Actually, because these values depend on the value of @TODAY, the Yrs column you produce on your own computer will undoubtedly display larger values than those in Figure 5.10.)

The last of the three formulas that we'll enter into the Sales People database will result in a field of *logical values* for Pbn. You'll recall the purpose of the Pbn field: to indicate whether a given salesperson is on probation. As manager of the sales force, you have decided to place on probation any employee whose average monthly sales level was less than $10,000 for the six-month period covered by the database.

The FRED programming language supplies Framework III with a pair of *logical constants* for the conditions *true* and *false*. These constants are expressed as the values

#TRUE

and

#FALSE

(The # symbol designates any of several categories of special built-in constants in Framework III and FRED.)

Up to now, we have written formulas that result in numeric values. In these formulas, Framework III evaluates the calculation expressed in the formula and produces the resulting numeric values for the field category. In the Pbn formula, we will see that Framework III can also accept a logical expression as part of a formula. A logical expression is simply a statement that Framework III evaluates as either #TRUE or #FALSE.

Logical expressions are easy to write in Framework III, because they correspond exactly to statements we might make in plain English. For example, consider the following statement:

The average monthly sales level is less than $10,000.

For each one of your salespeople, this statement will be either true or false. If the statement is true, the salesperson will be placed on probation. If the statement is false, that is, if the person's sales level is greater than or equal to $10,000, the employee will remain in good standing with the company.

In the context of the Sales People database, we would express this logical statement as follows:

AvgPerMo < 10000

The < symbol means "is less than." This symbol is called a *relational operator,* because it expresses a relation between two values. Framework III uses a set of six relational operators:

<	(is less than)
>	(is greater than)
=	(is equal to)
< =	(is less than or equal to)
> =	(is greater than or equal to)
< >	(is not equal to)

Any time you write a statement with one of these relational operators, Framework III will evaluate the statement as either true or false.

If you enter such a statement into a spreadsheet cell or a database field, Framework III will display one of the two logical constants, #TRUE or #FALSE.

So, to place logical values into the Pbn field of the Sales People database, here is the formula we'll enter:

Pbn : = AvgPerMo < 10000

This formula tells Framework III to examine the AvgPerMo field in every record of the database. If the AvgPerMo field is less than 10,000, the record's Pbn field will receive the value #TRUE; if the AvgPerMo field is greater than or equal to 10,000, the record's Pbn field will receive the value #FALSE.

Enter the formula into the database, behind the field name Pbn. The resulting column of logical values is shown in Figure 5.10. Looking down the database, you can tell exactly who is on probation (Pbn is #TRUE) and who is not (Pbn is #FALSE).

Actually, Framework III has not one but two pairs of logical values. The two pairs are simply different ways of saying the same thing. By default, Framework III uses #TRUE and #FALSE to evaluate the result of a logical statement. But you can also use the constants #YES and #NO to express the same meaning:

#YES is equivalent to #TRUE.

#NO is equivalent to #FALSE.

In the case of the Pbn field, you might actually prefer to use #YES and #NO to express the status of each employee. In response to the question, "Is this person on probation?", the #YES and #NO values make a little more sense than #TRUE and #FALSE.

As a quick but optional exercise in formula writing, let's change the Pbn values to the alternative logical constants #YES and #NO. The exercise will lead us to yet another important FRED function, one that deals specifically with the results of logical statements. The function is named @IF; its role in spreadsheets, databases, and FRED programs is to provide a decision-making tool.

The @IF function takes three parameters, in the following format:

@if(*logical statement, expression1, expression2*)

The @IF function evaluates its first parameter, *logical statement,* as either true or false. The result of the function depends upon this evaluation:

- If *logical statement* is true, @IF returns the value of *expression1.*
- If *logical statement* is false, @IF returns the value of *expression2.*

The @IF function is valuable in any Framework III task that needs to choose between two values, depending on the result of a logical statement.

Perhaps you've already figured out how we are going to use @IF in the new version of our Pbn formula. To replace the #TRUE and #FALSE values with #YES and #NO values, we'll replace the former Pbn formula with the following one:

Pbn : = @if(AvgPerMo < 10000, #YES, #NO)

Examine the three parameters in the @IF function. The logical statement is the same as before:

AvgPerMo < 10000

If, for any given record in the database, this statement is true, the Pbn field of that record will receive the value #YES. Otherwise (if the logical statement is false), the Pbn field will receive the value #NO.

To revise the Pbn formula, you need only move the highlight to the field name Pbn and press the Edit key (F2). You can either delete the previous formula and then enter the new one, or you can insert the necessary characters of the new formula into the original version. Press Return when the revision is complete, and you will see the Pbn values begin changing immediately. Figure 5.11 shows the resulting revised database.

Because we have added three columns of new information to the database, now is a good time to perform the Save and Continue operation again, to produce a disk copy of the new version of the database. In the next section of this chapter, we'll continue to gain experience with using logical statements and relational operators.

```
 Apps  Disk  Create  Edit  Locate  Frames  Words  Numbers  Graph  Print  8:53 am
 EmpNo  Last        First     Reg  SixMoSales     AvgPerMo   Pbn    Hired      Yrs
 86N2 Sapolsky    Stan      NE   $48,675.30     8112.55  #YES   7/13/86    2.41
 82M1 Waterman    Pearl     MW   $85,977.83    14329.64  #NO    9/29/82    6.20
 85M2 Olsen       Oscar     MW   $114,536.77   19089.46  #NO    6/20/85    3.47
 85N5 Smith       Joe       NW   $56,733.45     9455.58  #YES  10/23/85    3.13
 83S9 Goldberg    Jack      SW   $103,254.67   17209.11  #NO   10/29/83    5.12
 84S1 Smyth       Gloria    SE   $87,732.41    14622.07  #NO    5/17/84    4.57
 79N6 Herrera     Fred      NE   $87,654.32    14609.05  #NO   11/20/79    9.06
 78S1 Smithfield  Frank     SW   $51,623.62     8603.94  #YES   7/22/78   10.39
 82N8 Woo         Eva       NW   $93,254.10    15542.35  #NO    2/25/82    6.79
 82S9 Hernandez   Esther    S    $83,241.20    13873.53  #NO    5/5/82     6.60
 69S3 Washington  Ed        S    $102,375.10   17062.52  #NO    8/29/69   19.29
 84M3 Brooke      Donny     MW   $58,439.00     9739.83  #YES  12/1/84     4.02
 74N4 Takahashi   Bruce     NW   $102,664.78   17110.80  #NO    3/23/74   14.73
 81S5 Petrakis    Bill      SE   $112,312.34   18718.72  #NO    8/24/81    7.30
 86S2 Smith       AshleighSW     $67,132.45    11188.74  #NO    3/4/86     2.77
 72S6 Schroeder   Art       SE   $94,243.22    15707.20  #NO    1/24/72   16.89
 66N3 Rizzo       Anne      NE   $117,632.48   19605.41  #NO    5/21/66   22.57
 78S4 Curtis      Amy       S    $47,256.70     7876.12  #YES   4/12/78   10.67



 Pbn := @if(AvgPerMo < 10)        Sales People.Pbn        Recs:      0/18
```

Figure 5.11: Using #YES and #NO

FILTERING THE DATABASE

One of the most commonly used features of any database management program is called *filtering*. Filtering gives you the power to isolate specific groups of records that have one or more characteristics in common. You can then perform operations on this subset of records as though it constituted an independent database. Framework III's database filtering mechanism is simple and efficient.

To filter a database, you must first determine at least one criterion that Framework III can use to select a subset of records from the entire database. You then translate your criterion into a logical statement, which in this context becomes a *filtering formula*. You must enter this formula into the area behind the Database frame. When you do, Framework III instantly filters the database for you and displays the subset of records that match your criterion.

Before we start writing filtering formulas, let's examine five different examples of selection criteria that you might want to try on the Sales People database. These examples identify five different groups of records, selected from the entire database. The purpose of each of the following expressions is to identify the characteristic (or characteristics) that each record in a selected group will have in common:

1. All the salespeople who have achieved total half-year sales of over $100,000

2. All the employees who have worked for the company for five years or less

3. Everyone who is currently on probation

4. All the people who work in the eastern regions (northeast or southeast)

5. All probationary employees who have worked more than four years for the company

Given the small size of the Sales People database, you might easily be able to pick out the groups of records that each of these criteria represent. But once again, imagine working with a database of several hundred records, only a score of which can fit on the display screen at a time. Scrolling screen by screen through the database to pick out a specific group of records would be a time-consuming process. The larger your database, the more useful Framework III's automatic filtering feature will become to you.

To translate the above criteria into filtering formulas, we'll make use of what we've learned about logical statements and relational operators. For example, consider the first example: employees with total half-year sales over $100,000. Here is the formula that expresses the criterion for selecting this group:

SixMoSales > 100000

For each record in the database, this statement will be either true or false. Only those records for which the statement is true will appear in the filtered database. As a first experiment with filtering, then, let's enter this formula into the area behind the Database frame.

You may recall from Chapter 4 that the first step for entering a formula behind a frame is to move the highlight to the frame's border. Here are the keystrokes for entering the filtering formula:

Out (–)	(to move the highlight to the border of the Database frame)
Edit (F2)	(to place a formula behind the frame)
SixMoSales > *100000*	(the formula itself)
Return	(to complete the formula entry)

Version Note

In Framework II, the numbers after *Recs:* had a different meaning. The first number showed the number of filtered records, and the second number showed the total number of records in the *unfiltered* database. For instance, in this example, they would have read 6/18.

That's all there is to it. When you complete these steps, Framework III will instantly filter the database according to your criterion. Only those records that pass the criterion will be displayed in the Database frame. Figure 5.12 shows the filtered database; you can see the six salespeople who achieved total sales of over $100,000.

When you move the highlight inside a filtered database, the right side of the status panel will tell you both the current position of the cursor and the number of records that were selected by the filtering formula; for example:

Recs: 3/6

This message means that you are examining a filtered subset of six records and that the cursor is currently on the third record. Notice also that the 6 is highlighted, meaning that it is a filtered subset of the total database. Normally, in an unfiltered database, the second number would not be highlighted.

Where are the rest of the records, the ones that didn't make it into the filtered group? They are still in the computer's memory, temporarily hidden from view. They must be retrieved before you impose a new filtering formula, or the formula will work only on the filtered

```
 Apps  Disk  Create  Edit  Locate  Frames  Words  Numbers  Graph  Print  8:54 am
                                                                    <Library>
                                                                         <A:>
                                                                         >C:<
 [Sales People]
 EmpNo  Last        First  Reg  SixMoSales    AvgPerMo   Pbn    Hired
 85M2 Olsen         Oscar   MW   $114,536.77   19089.46  #NO    6/20/85
 83S9 Goldberg      Jack    SW   $103,254.67   17209.11  #NO   10/29/83
 69S3 Washington    Ed      S    $102,375.10   17062.52  #NO    8/29/69
 74N4 Takahashi     Bruce   NW   $102,664.78   17110.80  #NO    3/23/74
 81S5 Petrakis      Bill    SE   $112,312.34   18718.72  #NO    8/24/81
 66N3 Rizzo         Anne    NE   $117,632.48   19605.41  #NO    5/21/66



 SixMoSales > 100000                   Sales People     Doc:       1/1  [Sales Pe]
```

Figure 5.12: Filtering the database

subset. There are two ways to get the hidden records back:

1. Move the highlight back to the frame's border, and press the Edit key (F2). Delete the filtering formula from the edit line. When you press the Return key, the frame will be "recalculated," without the filtering effect, and all the previously hidden records will return.

2. Use the Open All option in the Frames menu, while the highlight is positioned on the border of the frame. This option will result once again in a display of the complete database, without eliminating the filtering formula from behind the frame. If you want to refilter the database, move the highlight to the frame's border and press the Recalc key (F5).

Note that when you bring back hidden records, the group of previously filtered records remains at the top of the database, and the previously hidden records follow. If you want to return your database to some other order, use either the Ascending or Descending sort option of the Locate menu.

Now let's write formulas for the other criterion examples we discussed. Try entering each of these formulas, one at a time, into the area behind the Database frame. Make sure you delete the previous filtering formula and bring back all the hidden records before you enter each new formula.

In the second example, we want to find all the employees who have worked for the company for five years or less. Here is the filtering formula:

Yrs < = 5

Notice the use of the relational operator that means "less than or equal to." In the filtered database resulting from this formula, you'll see that several employees meet this criterion.

The third example is to find all the employees who are currently on probation. The filtering formula for this example is surprisingly simple. It consists of a lone reference to the field name itself:

Pbn

Recall that the Pbn field contains logical values. For this reason, the field reference itself stands as a logical statement, which Framework III will evaluate as either true or false for each record. Figure 5.13 shows the filtered database. You can see that Framework III has selected all the records that contain a value of #YES in the Pbn field.

By the way, this filtering formula, consisting of only the name Pbn, will work correctly with either pair of logical constants: #TRUE and #FALSE or #YES and #NO. It doesn't matter which of these values you currently have in the Pbn field. Framework III selects either all the #TRUE values or all the #YES values.

USING @OR AND @AND TO FILTER

Our final two criterion examples involve *compound* logical statements. Let's review the original expressions of these final two examples:

4. All the people who work in the eastern regions (northeast or southeast)

5. All probationary employees who have worked more than four years for the company

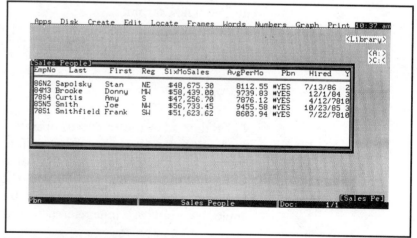

Figure 5.13: Filtering on a logical field

We could rephrase these examples as pairs of criteria, connected by the words *or* or *and*:

4. People who work either in the northeast region *or* in the southeast region

5. People who are on probation *and* have worked more than four years for the company

Translating these criteria into pairs of Framework III formulas, we might write them as follows:

4. Reg = "NE"   *or*   Reg = "SE"

5. Pbn   *and*   Yrs > 4

Clearly, we need some way of expressing two selection criteria at once for filtering the database.

The solution to these problems comes in the form of a pair of FRED functions, called

    @or

and

    @and

Along with @IF, we call these *logical functions,* because they deal primarily with logical expressions. The two functions @OR and @AND take, as parameters, a series of logical expressions. We can describe the format of the functions as follows:

    @or(expression1, expression2, expression3, . . .)
    @and(expression1, expression2, expression3, . . .)

Both @OR and @AND return a logical value, #TRUE or #FALSE. Here is how the two functions operate:

- @OR returns a value of #TRUE if any one of its parameters is evaluated as true. Only if *all* of its parameters are false does @OR return a value of #FALSE.

- @AND returns a value of #TRUE if *all* of its parameters are evaluated as true. If any one of its parameters is false, @AND returns a value of #FALSE.

Given these two functions, we can easily express compound filtering formulas for the last two examples. The following formula will select all the eastern salespeople:

@or(Reg = "NE", Reg = "SE")

Enter this formula into the area behind the Database frame, and Framework III will display the six eastern employees, as shown in Figure 5.14.

The following formula will find any employee who is on probation and has worked more than four years for the company:

@and(Pbn, Yrs > 4)

Enter this formula into the area behind the Database frame, and you will find that there are only three employees who meet both these criteria. You can examine the filtered database in Figure 5.15.

In summary, the @OR and @AND functions allow you to create compound filtering formulas for a Database frame. When you want

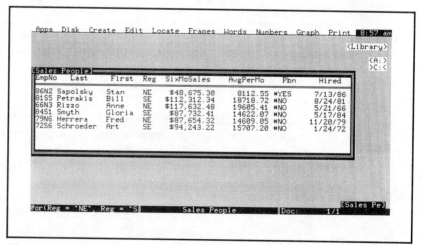

Figure 5.14: Using @OR in a compound filter formula

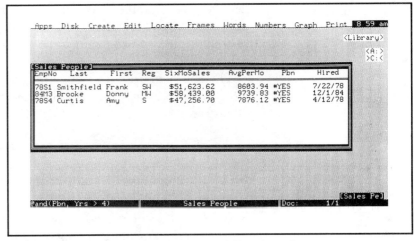

Figure 5.15: Using @AND in a compound filter formula

to find all the records that match *any one or more* elements of a set of criteria, use the @OR function. When you want to find the records that match *all* elements of a set of criteria, use the @AND function.

USING FILTERED DATABASES

Once you have created a filtering formula to select a group of records from your database, you can treat the group of selected records as a database in its own right. You can perform any of the following database management activities on the selected records:

- Sorting by fields
- Searching for field values
- Replacing field values
- Deleting records
- Filtering the database
- Printing the database table

None of these operations will include or have any effect on the records that have been temporarily hidden by the filter operation.

For example, let's say you want to delete a set of records that you have isolated through a filter operation. First use the Extend Select key (F6) to extend the highlight over the filtered records. Then press the Delete key. At that point, you can bring back the hidden records to restore the database, minus the group of records that you have deleted.

The ability to print a group of filtered records can also be important. The process of printing a database is the same as printing any other frame:

Ctrl-P   (to open the Print menu)

B   (to begin printing)

If the database has been filtered, the Print menu will print only the records that are currently displayed in the frame.

You can use any of the styling options from the Words menu, and any of the submenus to the Print menu, as well as the FRED printing functions, to control the way the frame is sent to the printer. There are several factors to be aware of, however:

- If the data in any field exceed the column width allowed for it, only the data that are visible on the screen will be printed.

- If the entire database exceeds your page width, additional columns will be printed separately, just as they are with a spreadsheet.

- If a record contains numeric data that exceed the column width, asterisks will be printed.

As we'll see later, you can use the other two views of a database—Forms and dBASE—to overcome these limitations.

There are also other ways to control the way a database is printed. As with any other type of frame, you can print only part of a database by selecting the portion you want to print and then beginning the printing process. You can also make special adjustments to a database just for printing purposes. For example, you can widen frames that are too narrow to display their entire contents. If there are particular fields that you *don't* want to print, you can use the Size key (F4) to reduce their width to 0. Moreover, if the database is to be part of a larger document, you can use the Allow Free Dragging option discussed in Chapter 4 to center a narrow database on the page, for a more pleasing appearance.

We have examined Framework III's impressive database management facilities; now it is time to turn once again to The Sophisticated Palate to look for an example of these facilities in action.

EXAMPLES

CREATING AN INVENTORY DATABASE

Eileen Wilcox is in charge of tracking the inventory of packaged wholesale goods in the warehouse portion of the business. Her main problem with inventory has always been to determine when it is time to reorder a given item. The warehouse space is limited, so Eileen reorders packaged goods once every two weeks. She wants neither to run out of popular items nor to build up too large a stock of any one product.

A secondary problem is determining wholesale pricing. The wholesale division calculates a 45 percent markup on all packaged goods. However, after this calculation, Eileen likes to adjust prices to retailers slightly, to introduce an "attractiveness" factor. Her adjustment simply assures that the last digit of each price will be either a 5 or a 9. For example, rather than marking the price of an item as $12.37, she increases the price by two cents, to $12.39.

Eileen has created a Database frame called Inventory. The database has seven field categories, with the following field names:

Stock No
Description
CostPerCase
Whsl Pr
Units Avail
Reorder
Supplier

Each record in the database describes one inventory item; Eileen has initially made room for 50 items. Before actually creating the database, she took the time to prepare a structure table, which you can examine in Figure 5.16.

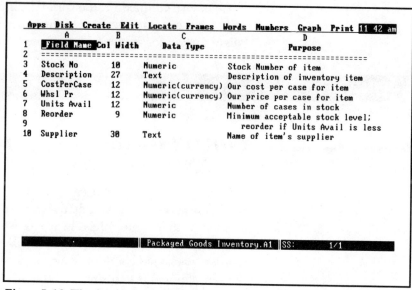

Figure 5.16: The Sophisticated Palate's Inventory database structure

A printout of the Inventory database that Eileen created is shown in Figure 5.17. Because this database is relatively long, Eileen was interested in finding as many shortcuts as possible for the data entry process. For some of the field categories there was no alternative to manual data entry, record by record; this was true of the Description, CostPerCase, Units Avail, and Reorder fields. However, for the other three fields, Eileen discovered simple ways to let Framework III fill in the data for her.

The Supplier field displays the supplier of each inventory item. The Sophisticated Palate regularly uses only six wholesale suppliers for its packaged retail goods:

> Scandinavian Fine Foods, Inc.
>
> Mediterranean Importers, Inc.
>
> Whole Earth Foods
>
> United Distributors
>
> Produits de France, Lté.
>
> Celestial Spice Co.

```
The Sophisticated Palate, Inc.        Packaged Goods Inventory                    May 17, 1989


  Stock No       Description      CostPerCase  Whsl Pr  Units Avail  Reorder        Supplier
  =======================================================================================================
      1001 Pate de foie gras          $14.50    $21.05      13        8 Produits de France, Lte.
      1002 Capers                     $19.83    $28.75      14       10 Produits de France, Lte.
      1003 Spanish saffron            $16.20    $23.49       5        8 Mediterranean Importers, Inc.
      1004 Cold pressed olive oil     $65.32    $94.75      10        5 Mediterranean Importers, Inc.
      1005 Tortellini (dried)         $13.20    $19.15       9       12 United Distributors
      1006 Norwegian Crispbread, lt.   $8.12    $11.79      36       20 Scandinavian Fine Foods, Inc.
      1007 Norwegian Crispbread, dk.   $8.12    $11.79      18       20 Scandinavian Fine Foods, Inc.
      1008 Norwegian Crispbread, heavy $8.12    $11.79      32       20 Scandinavian Fine Foods, Inc.
      1009 Artichoke hearts, marinated $72.00  $104.45      40       35 United Distributors
      1010 Dijon mustard              $21.00    $30.45      15       12 Produits de France, Lte.
      1011 Creole mustard             $19.60    $28.45       6       12 Whole Earth Foods
      1012 Hungarian Paprika           $8.62    $12.55       2        8 Celestial Spice Co.
      1013 Coriander seeds             $6.78     $9.85      12        8 Celestial Spice Co.
      1014 Anchovy paste               $9.22    $13.39      15       12 United Distributors
      1015 Turmeric                    $8.62    $12.55      12        8 Celestial Spice Co.
      1016 Lingonberry jam            $14.53    $21.09       8        5 Scandinavian Fine Foods, Inc.
      1017 Sardines in olive oil      $17.22    $24.99      40       20 Mediterranean Importers, Inc.
      1018 Escargots                  $43.12    $62.55      23       10 Produits de France, Lte.
      1019 Caviar, red                $56.40    $81.79       7        8 United Distributors
      1020 Caviar, black              $76.40   $110.79      12        8 United Distributors
      1021 Lemon curd                 $23.53    $34.15       9        5 Whole Earth Foods
      1022 Scots Shortbread           $19.76    $28.65      27       12 United Distributors
      1023 Miso                        $7.33    $10.65      15        5 Whole Earth Foods
      1024 Spaghetti, fresh           $12.60    $18.29      11        7 Whole Earth Foods
      1025 Spaghetti, spinach, fresh  $12.60    $18.29      12        5 Whole Earth Foods
      1026 Herring, in wine sauce     $13.54    $19.65      14        8 Scandinavian Fine Foods, Inc.
      1027 Herring, in sour cream     $13.54    $19.65      11       12 Scandinavian Fine Foods, Inc.
      1028 Herring, in tomato sauce   $13.54    $19.65      16        8 Scandinavian Fine Foods, Inc.
      1029 Herring, in mustard sauce  $13.54    $19.65      20        8 Scandinavian Fine Foods, Inc.
      1030 Minestrone                  $4.22     $6.15      27       12 Mediterranean Importers, Inc.
      1031 Beef Consomme               $4.77     $6.95       6       10 Produits de France, Lte.
      1032 Sage leaves, whole          $6.17     $8.95      13        8 Celestial Spice Co.
      1033 Couscous                    $9.45    $13.75       2        5 Mediterranean Importers, Inc.
      1034 Falafel mix                $13.21    $19.15      17        8 Mediterranean Importers, Inc.
      1035 Hoummous                    $8.52    $12.35       6        5 Mediterranean Importers, Inc.
      1036 Tomatoes, dried/olive oil   $9.12    $13.25      14        8 Mediterranean Importers, Inc.
      1037 Tuna/olive oil             $13.46    $19.55      11       12 Mediterranean Importers, Inc.
      1038 Whole rice flower           $6.85     $9.95      10        6 Whole Earth Foods
      1039 Filo                        $8.10    $11.75       8        6 Mediterranean Importers, Inc.
      1040 Major Grey's Chutney       $14.88    $21.59      12        8 Whole Earth Foods
      1041 Darjeeling Tea             $11.80    $17.15       9       10 Celestial Spice Co.
      1042 Oolong tea                 $11.80    $17.15      16       10 Celestial Spice Co.
      1043 Keemun tea                 $11.80    $17.15      17       10 Celestial Spice Co.
      1044 Bean thread noodles         $4.22     $6.15      11       20 Whole Earth Foods
      1045 Japanese horseradish        $8.48    $12.35       8        3 Whole Earth Foods
      1046 Dried seaweed               $3.17     $4.65       6        5 Whole Earth Foods
      1047 Bombay curry powder        $28.60    $41.49      13        7 United Distributors
      1048 Pineapple marmalade        $23.57    $34.19      12        8 United Distributors
      1049 Macadamia nuts             $57.60    $83.55      20       20 Whole Earth Foods
      1050 Cream of Coconut           $14.41    $20.89               12 United Distributors
```

Figure 5.17: The Sophisticated Palate's Inventory database

Rather than typing these six long names many times, Eileen simply entered the single-character abbreviations S, M, W, U, P, or C in the Supplier field. Then she used the Locate menu's Replace option to replace each of the abbreviations with the supplier's full name. Here is how she entered the name *Scandinavian Fine Foods, Inc.* into the database:

Ctrl-L	(to open the Locate menu)
R	(to select the Replace option)
S	(the target text)
Return	(to enter the target text into the menu)
Scandinavian Fine Foods, Inc.	(the replacement text)
Return	(to enter the replacement text into the menu)
End	(to replace all occurrences)

Eileen decided to assign stock numbers starting from 1001 to the packaged retail goods. (If she later decides to include other inventories in the database—such as a list of perishable goods—she can code them with another starting point, such as 2001.) To enter the consecutive stock numbers into the database, Eileen used a FRED function named @FILL.

This is exactly the kind of task that @FILL is designed for: entering a column of consecutive, or evenly incremented, numbers into a database or spreadsheet. The format of the @FILL function is:

@fill(*range, start, increment*)

where *range* is a database or spreadsheet range that will receive the numbers, *start* is the starting point of the numbers, and *increment* is the amount by which each number is increased (or decreased).

The @FILL function is an odd sort of tool, for a couple of reasons. Once it has performed its initial task, it is of no further use to the database or spreadsheet in which it was entered. Eileen therefore realized that once @FILL had done its work, she would be deleting the formula from the database. Furthermore, although @FILL does fill a range with values, it is not a field calculation formula. To prevent the database from treating it as though it were a field calculation formula, Eileen did not enter it behind a field name. Instead, she entered the function into the first record position of the Description column, before she had begun filling that column with data. (This location was an arbitrary choice; Eileen simply wanted to avoid placing the function in any location that already had data in it.) Here is the formula she entered:

@fill(Inventory.Stock No, 1001, 1)

The formula instantly filled in the Stock No column with numbers from 1001 to 1050. Eileen remembered to delete the formula, by pressing the Delete key, before she began entering the item descriptions into the Description column.

CALCULATING THE RETAIL PRICES CATEGORY

Finally, Eileen wanted the retail prices for the inventory items to be calculated automatically, based on the wholesale price. Eileen knew she could simply enter the following formula into the area behind the Whsl Pr field name:

Whsl Pr : = 1.45 * CostPerCase

She tried this formula, and it worked just fine, computing each wholesale price as a 45 percent markup from cost. But Eileen was not satisfied; she wanted to find some way to incorporate her concept of "attractive pricing" into the formula for retail prices.

Looking at the Whsl Pr column in Figure 5.17, you can see that she found a solution to this problem. The last digit of each price is either 5 or 9, following Eileen's specifications. In order to achieve this, she had to write a small FRED program behind the Whsl Pr field name, rather than just a simple calculation formula. We will look at Eileen's program in Chapter 7; for now, simply keep in mind that the program has two purposes:

1. To compute the 45 percent markup.
2. To increase each retail price by a few cents, when necessary, to ensure a final digit of 5 or 9.

PRINTING
THE INVENTORY DATABASE

Once Eileen had completed the database, she wanted to print it out on paper. Because of the width of the columns, she realized that to fit all the information across a standard $8^1/_2$- × -11-inch page, she would have to print the database in a condensed mode. She used the Print menu options for the purpose. First, she opened the Format Options submenu, and entered the values shown in Figure 5.18. She selected

Condensed Print   on

Then she set the margins. A page offset of 2 and a line length of 128 ensured that the entire line would be printed in condensed mode. A top margin of 8 and a bottom margin of 5 allowed plenty of room for a header.

Next, Eileen inserted the header text. She wanted three headers: one left, one centered, and one right. The left header would read

The Sophisticated Palate, Inc.

The center header would contain the text

Packaged Goods Inventory

The right header would display the date.

There was only one problem: Eileen wanted the company name to be in boldface type. Now, as we've seen, you can get boldface type into a header by using one of the FRED printing functions or, in Framework III, by selecting the style to add. If you use the printer code, the @HL function, which creates a header at the left margin, also destroys the spacing of the headers established in the menus, so they print continuously:

The Sophisticated Palate, Inc. Packaged Goods InventoryMay 17, 1989

She solved the problem by inserting a printer control code in the header text. For the left header, she entered

←HThe Sophisticated Palate, Inc←|

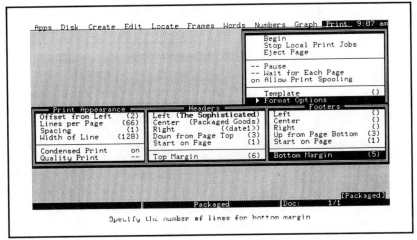

Figure 5.18: Print format options for the Inventory database

starting the text with the code her dot-matrix printer uses to begin boldfacing and ending it with the code to stop boldfacing (your printer may use different codes). As you can see from Figure 5.17, this worked perfectly.

FILTERING TO DETERMINE INVENTORY REORDER TIMES

Finally, Eileen is ready to deal with her most important inventory problem: determining which products she needs to reorder at any given point. She has entered numeric values into the Reorder column; these values represent what she considers the minimum acceptable stock level for each item. She has also entered the current stock levels into the Units Avail column, and she plans to update this field on a weekly basis. Here is the filtering formula she'll use each week to find the items that need to be reordered:

Units Avail < Reorder

Eileen moves the highlight to the Database frame's border and presses the Edit key (F2) so she can enter her filtering formula.

At that point, Eileen decides to add some more information to the header, so she revises the center header as follows:

Packaged Goods Inventory<return><return>Reorder List

As you may remember, inserting the symbol

<return>

into header text creates a multiple-line header. With this new center header, the text *Reorder List* will be centered two lines below the *Packaged Goods Inventory* portion of the header, as shown in Figure 5.19.

As Eileen examines the filtered database, she finds that it is time to reorder a dozen items. She sorts the filtered database into alphabetical order by supplier and then prints out the reorder list.

EXPLORING FURTHER

To complete our discussion of Database frames, we'll look at several more topics in this section:

• Working with databases in Forms view

```
The Sophisticated Palate, Inc.          Packaged Goods Inventory                    May 17, 1989

                                              Reorder List

Stock No        Description      CostPerCase  Whsl Pr  Units Avail Reorder          Supplier
==================================================================================================
     1012 Hungarian Paprika          $8.62     $12.55        2        8 Celestial Spice Co.
     1041 Darjeeling Tea            $11.80     $17.15        9       10 Celestial Spice Co.
     1003 Spanish saffron           $16.20     $23.49        5        8 Mediterranean Importers, Inc.
     1033 Couscous                   $9.45     $13.75        2        5 Mediterranean Importers, Inc.
     1037 Tuna/olive oil            $13.46     $19.55       11       12 Mediterranean Importers, Inc.
     1031 Beef Consomme              $4.77      $6.95        6       10 Produits de France, Lte.
     1007 Norwegian Crispbread, dk.  $8.12     $11.79       18       20 Scandinavian Fine Foods, Inc.
     1027 Herring, in sour cream    $13.54     $19.65       11       12 Scandinavian Fine Foods, Inc.
     1005 Tortellini (dried)        $13.20     $19.15        9       12 United Distributors
     1019 Caviar, red               $56.40     $81.79        7        8 United Distributors
     1011 Creole Mustard            $19.60     $28.45        6       12 Whole Earth Foods
     1044 Bean thread noodles        $4.22      $6.15       11       20 Whole Earth Foods
```

Figure 5.19: The reorder list filtered from the Inventory database

- Printing a mail-merge letter
- Printing mailing labels
- Using the dBASE view of databases
- Linking spreadsheets with databases

At the beginning of this chapter, we learned that there are three ways of looking at a Framework III database: the Table format, the Forms view, and the dBASE view. Up to now, we have seen databases only in the Table format. You may find yourself using the Forms and dBASE views less often than the Table format, but you should nonetheless know about the special features offered by these formats.

USING
THE FORMS VIEW OF A DATABASE

Let's return briefly to the Sales People database that we developed in the first part of this chapter. Bring back the database onto the desktop, and move the highlight inside the frame. Press the View key (F10) to switch into Forms view. Figure 5.20 shows approximately what your screen will look like.

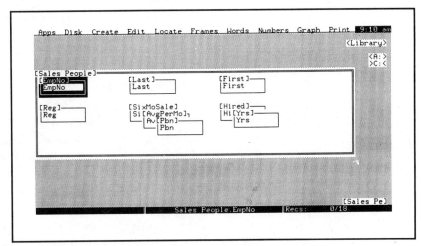

Figure 5.20: The Sales People database in Forms view

The Forms view of a database displays a single record at a time. Each field within the record becomes an individual frame inside the containing Database frame. You can use the arrow keys, located at the right side of your keyboard, to move the highlight from field to field or to display a new record:

    ←   (to move the highlight to the previous field)

    →   (to move the highlight to the next field)

    ↑   (to display the previous record)

    ↓   (to display the next record)

You can enter a new field value into a record simply by moving the highlight to the frame that represents the field and then typing the new value. Thus, the Forms view presents not only a different kind of display of the database, but also a new way to enter data into individual records.

The Forms view allows you to customize the organization of the screen for the display of a single record. You can use the Drag key (F3) to move the field frames to new locations on the screen, and the Size key (F4) to change the display dimensions of the field frames. (The modifications that you make on the Forms view arrangement will have no effect on the Table format.) By thus rearranging the fields on the screen, you can devise a record display that will be convenient both for viewing and for entering data.

Figure 5.21 shows a rearranged Forms view of the Sales People database. In this arrangement, the six input fields appear first, followed by the calculated fields. If you were using the Forms view to enter data, you might find this to be a more useful input screen than the original Forms view in Figure 5.20. Before you read on, try your hand at rearranging the Forms view screen on your own computer. Press the Zoom key (F9) to switch the Forms view into full-screen mode. Then experiment with the Size (F4) and Drag (F3) keys, and try to duplicate (approximately) the arrangement of Figure 5.21.

Forms view also allows you to expand the size of a text field so that you can enter multiple lines of information into the field. In this way, you can actually include a small word processed document in each record in your database. (Note that you can add multiple lines to any text field simply by bringing the field to the edit line and pressing the Zoom key, F9.) Figure 5.22 shows an example. A new field,

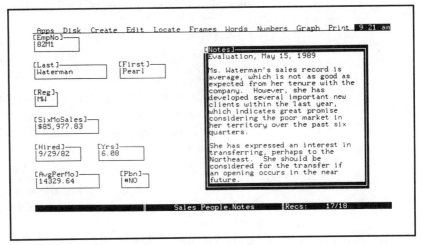

Figure 5.21: Rearranging the Forms view

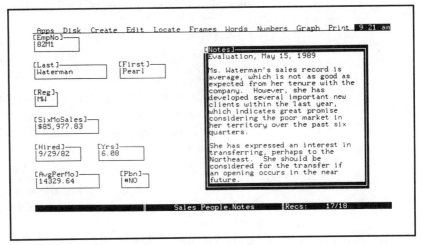

Figure 5.22: Adding a Notes field to the database

Notes, has been added to the database; the purpose of the field is to keep evaluative and personal notes about each salesperson. Let's examine the steps for creating and using this new field.

We should begin by adding a new field column to the Table format of the database. Press the View key (F10) twice to return to the Table format. Move the highlight to the last column of the database, Yrs, and press the following keys to add a new column:

Ctrl-C   (to open the Create menu)

C   (to add a column)

1   (to specify one column)

Return   (to complete the operation)

Move the highlight to the top of the new column, and enter the following field name:

Notes

Now press the View key (F10) to switch back to Forms view. You will find a new field frame devoted to the Notes field. Use the arrow keys to find the first record of the database, and move the highlight to the new Notes frame. Perform the following modifications:

- Press the Drag key (F3) to move the frame; use the → and ↑ keys to drag the frame to the empty upper-middle portion of the screen. Press the Return key to complete the Drag operation.

- Press the Size key (F4) to change the visual dimensions of the frame; use the ↓ key to enlarge the frame vertically and the → key to enlarge the frame horizontally. Try to match, approximately, the dimensions of the Notes frame shown in Figure 5.22. Press the Return key to complete the Size operation.

- Press the In key (+) to move the highlight into the frame. Using the Words menu, change the right margin of the text to 35.

Now start typing some notes; follow the example in Figure 5.22 if you like. You will find that the word processing features we discussed in Chapter 4 are in effect inside this frame. Wraparound will occur when you get near the end of each line. We have already seen that you can control the margins of the text from the Words menu. You can also change the alignment and the styling of the text. Be aware that the frame size controls only the *appearance* of the frame in Frames view; you can enter more text than will be visible in the frame. Press the Out key (–) to move the highlight back up to the frame's border.

As you move forward to subsequent records of the database, each new Forms screen will present you with a new empty Notes field. Using the Forms view, you can thus keep word processed notes about each member of your sales staff.

The Forms view can also be useful for printing your database. When you print a Database frame that is in Forms view, each record of the database is printed on a separate page. So, for example, if you were to print the new version of the Sales People database in Forms view, you would receive a one-page report, including all the information fields and the new Notes field, for each employee.

In summary, the Forms view of a database can be useful for four major activities:

- Viewing records, one at a time, in a customized screen format
- Entering data into a customized record input screen
- Incorporating a field of word processed text into each record of your database
- Printing each record of the database on a customized page format

MAIL-MERGE PRINTING

Framework III includes two powerful features for sending out form letters—mail-merge printing and label printing. Both are found in the Apps (Applications) menu, shown in Figure 5.23.

With mail-merge printing, you can create a form letter to be sent to several different people, and fill in the names, addresses, and any other relevant information, from a database. Figure 5.24 shows a new database, called Supervisors. This database, which we'll be returning to in Chapter 7, contains the names and addresses of the sales supervisors in each of your six national regions. The database has eight fields of information:

Reg
Last (name)
First (name)
Address
Suite

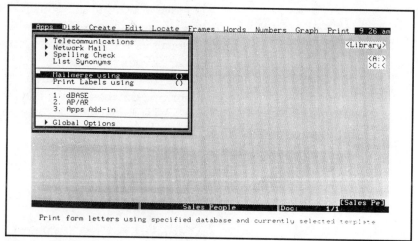

Figure 5.23: The Apps menu

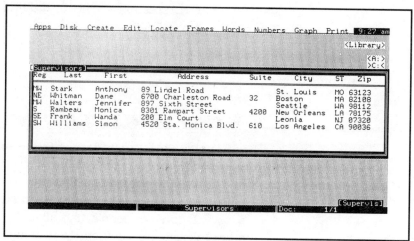

Figure 5.24: The Supervisors database

City
ST
Zip

You can see that the region abbreviations, in the first column of the database, correspond to the regions in the Sales People database.

We are going to send a form letter to each of the supervisors, but we will type this letter only once. The basic technique in creating a form letter for mail-merge printing is to substitute the names of the database fields that you want to appear in the letter for the actual text that those fields contain. As with keywords in the Print Format Options menu, these field names are enclosed in triangular brackets. Thus, the opening of the form letter might appear as in Figure 5.25.

Notice the marker

<Optional>

before the word *Suite*. This marker is used when the following field may be empty. It means, "If the following field contains data, print the text and the data, otherwise leave this line blank." Thus, you can use the same form letter for people whose addresses include a second line of information and for those who don't.

To print this letter, with the supervisors' names and addresses filled in appropriately, you must first have both the letter and the database on the desktop. Next, follow these keystrokes:

Ctrl-A   (to open the Apps menu)

M   (to select Mailmerge using)

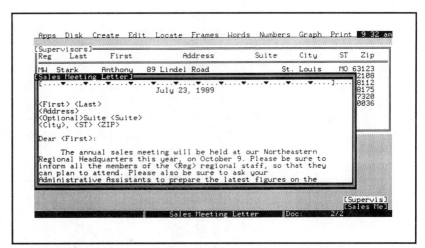

Figure 5.25: A form letter with mail-merge codes

supervisors (enter the name of the database to be used)

Return   (to record your selection)

Framework III will print one copy of the letter for each supervisor, with no further intervention from you.

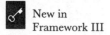
New in
Framework III

In Framework III, the mail-merge feature prints one letter for *each* record in the database, whether empty or not. Therefore, if you create a database that has room for 50 records, the program will print 50 letters, even if only 20 names have been entered. To avoid printing extra letters, first filter the database so that it contains only nonblank records (or the specific records you want to use), and then perform the mail merge.

PRINTING MAILING LABELS

Now that you have your form letter ready to go, you can have Framework III print your mailing labels, either from a roll of labels one label wide, or from sheets two or three labels wide. To print on a single-label roll, you will design a Word frame to match the label. Create a Word frame, and size it so that it is 5 lines deep and 40 characters wide. Set the right margin to 35. The text of your frame will read:

```
<First> <Last>
<Address>
<Optional>Suite <Suite>
<City>, <ST> <Zip>
```

Since the labels come on a continuous roll, you will print them as though each label were a "page." Thus, you should set the following options on the Print Format Options menu:

Offset from Left	{1}
Lines per Page	{6}
Spacing	{1}
Width of Line	{34}
Top Margin	{0}
Bottom Margin	{0}

Leave all the header and footer settings blank. Keep the Supervisors database on the desktop, and mount the labels in your printer. Select the frame that contains the label information. If necessary, filter the database. Finally, press

Ctrl-A	(to open the Apps menu)
P	(to select Print Labels using)
supervisors	(enter the name of the database to be used)
Return	(to record your selection)

Printing three-up labels is slightly more complicated. You must copy the single label into a containing frame, turn Allow Free Dragging on, and make three copies of the label frame. Line the frames up alongside each other so that they are laid out exactly the same as three labels across the page. It may take several attempts before your labels are printed correctly, so it might be a good idea to test with a small sample of records from your database (at least nine, so that you can see how several consecutive rows of labels will appear) before you print the entire list. Once you have a format that works, you might want to store it in the Library for future reference.

USING
THE DBASE VIEW OF A DATABASE

As you switched back and forth between the Table and Forms views of the Sales People database, you may have noticed a third view appearing. This is the dBASE view. This screen layout is identical to the data entry format used by the dBASE programs marketed by Ashton-Tate (as is Framework III). If you are accustomed to using any of the dBASE programs, you may find this view, which is illustrated in Figure 5.26, more congenial. The dBASE view has another distinct advantage: even though it shows you only one record at a time, it allows you to size the records so that all characters are displayed, no matter how wide the database is, or how narrow the columns in Table view are (except for multiple lines of text). It may even show you more information per record than Forms view.

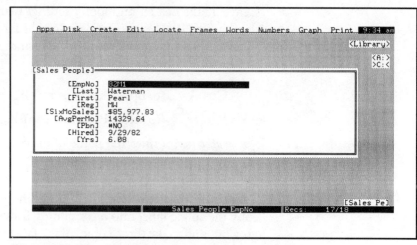

Figure 5.26: The dBASE view of a database

To display dBASE view, press the View key (F10) twice. As you can see in Figure 5.26, only one record is displayed. The field names appear on the left, in square brackets, and the contents of the field to the right of the field name. Only a few of Framework III's special keys function in the dBASE view of a database. These keys are summarized in Table 5.2.

LINKING SPREADSHEETS WITH DATABASE FRAMES

Another typical database management function involves calculating statistical values from database fields. For example, consider the following three values that you might want to calculate from the Sales People database:

- The total sales, of all the salespeople, during the six-month period covered by the database

- The average sales per employee

- The average number of years employees have worked for the firm

Table 5.2: Framework III Special Keys in dBASE View

KEYS	ACTION
↑, ←	Moves the highlight to the previous field.
↓, →	Moves the highlight to the next field.
Return	Moves the highlight to the next field.
Home, Ctrl-↑	Moves to the first field in the current record.
End, Ctrl-↓	Moves to the last field in the current record.
PgUp, Ctrl-Home	Moves to the first record in the database.
PgDn, Ctrl-End	Moves to the last record in the database.
Out (–)	Moves to the frame border.
In (+)	No effect.
Size (F4)	Changes the width of the field.

There is no convenient way to incorporate bottom-line statistics like these into a Database frame. Each row of a Database frame is supposed to represent a consistently formatted record of information; a bottom line of totals and statistics would go against the nature of a database.

Fortunately, you can easily draw database statistics into a Spreadsheet frame. We have already seen how different spreadsheets can contain interframe references for transferring information from one spreadsheet to another. A similar kind of linking is possible between spreadsheets and databases.

For an example, look at Figure 5.27. This figure shows two frames on the desktop: the Sales People Database frame, and a Spreadsheet frame called Sales Statistics. The spreadsheet contains three calculations from data drawn off the Database frame: the total nationwide sales for the six-month period, the average sales per person, and the average years of work for the firm.

To arrive at these calculations, we enter references to database fields into the appropriate cells of the Spreadsheet frame. From outside the Database frame, a reference to an entire field consists of the

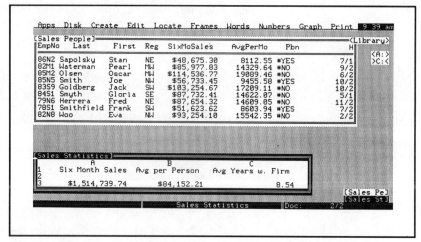

Figure 5.27: Linking a Spreadsheet frame with a Database frame

name of the frame and the name of the field. For example, here is the correct reference to the SixMoSales field:

Sales People.SixMoSales

Cell A3 in the Sales Statistics spreadsheet contains the following formula:

@sum(Sales People.SixMoSales)

This formula tells Framework III to find the sum of the entire Six-MoSales column.

The formula in cell B3 of the Sales Statistics spreadsheet contains the same reference but a different function:

@avg(Sales People.SixMoSales)

This formula finds the average of all the numbers in the SixMoSales column.

Finally, cell C3 of the spreadsheet contains the formula

@avg(Sales People.Yrs)

This formula yields the average of the numeric values in the Yrs column of the database.

In short, whenever you want to calculate values from entire columns in a database, you can simply create a Spreadsheet frame and write formulas that refer to the fields of the database.

SUMMARY

A Database frame is designed to store records of information in rows and columns. Each row holds one record, and each column represents a field category. The top row of the database is reserved for the field names. The adjustable width of each column determines the maximum number of characters that can be *displayed* in a given field of the database table. Once you have determined the data type of a field, you can use the Numbers menu to specify an appropriate display style for the column.

Framework III menus and function keys provide all the most important database management tools for a Database frame. The Locate menu allows you to sort the database, search for specific information in the database, and replace specified strings of text in the database. Using the Create menu, you can add new field columns or record rows to the database table.

The Edit key (F2) gives you access to the formula area behind the field names. Formulas that you enter in these areas can calculate values for entire columns of the database. There are two acceptable formats for such formulas: you can use the FRED @SET function to assign a calculation to a specific field, or you can use the assignment symbol, : = .

Formulas of another variety can be placed behind the Database frame itself. Specifically, you can write filtering formulas that express criteria for selecting specific groups of records from the database. A successful filtering formula will result in the display of a subset of the database. You can use the filtered database as you would the whole database; operations such as sorting, searching, deleting, and printing are all available for the filtered subset of records.

The Forms view of a database displays one record at a time on the screen. The Forms view is useful for producing customized data forms—for viewing, entering, or printing data. You can also expand the size of a field's frame in Forms view, to produce space for a word processed text to become part of each record.

You can link databases to Word frames to print form letters with the Mailmerge Using option of the Apps menu. You can also print mailing labels for all records in a database or for a filtered database with the Print Labels Using option of the same menu.

A third view of databases, the dBASE view, adds compatibility with the dBASE programs, and also affords you the opportunity to see complete records when the Table view is larger than the screen or has columns narrower than the data they contain.

Finally, you may sometimes want to link a spreadsheet to a database, to compute statistics from database fields. The tool that creates the link is simply a reference, in the spreadsheet, to a field name in the database.

Telecommunications

OVERVIEW

INTRODUCTION

IN ADDITION TO ITS MANY OTHER CAPABILITIES, Framework III can be used to communicate with other computers. Through its telecommunications component, you can send information to computers anywhere in the world, and you can capture and store information received from remote computers. You can receive information from services such as Dow Jones News/Retrieval, CompuServe, or The Source, or you can establish a direct connection with a computer on another desk.

Before you begin, you should be aware that telecommunications is the least standardized function in the nonstandardized world of computers. To use telecommunications you need patience, dogged persistence, and a willingness to experiment.

When you want two computers to talk to each other, a great many aspects of the process must be attended to. The computers must be matched carefully in several respects before any communication can take place. In addition, there are many different types of telecommunications equipment and many different brands of each type. Each of them has quirks that can disrupt the smooth flow of data communications if it has not been set up properly. The various computer programs that make telecommunications possible also have quirks, and Framework III is no exception.

In this chapter, we'll cover the basics of telecommunications, and then we'll practice using Framework III's telecommunications component. Later, we will walk through a communications session ourselves, and then watch as Eileen Wilcox of The Sophisticated Palate performs several communications tasks. Finally, we'll discuss some of the other telecommunications features available in Framework III.

We'll begin by introducing some of the background information you need to run a telecommunications program effectively. If you are already familiar with telecommunications, you may want to skip the following section.

TELECOMMUNICATIONS BASICS

Before any PC can communicate with another computer, both computers must have a *serial communications port,* either a *modem* or an *RS-232 interface,* and some form of *communications software.* Let's start with the hardware.

THE SERIAL PORT

The serial port is the physical connection through which a computer communicates with the outside world. A serial port is *not* standard equipment on the IBM PC, although most compatibles do have one. If you do not have one, you must purchase a *serial board.* IBM sells a serial board called the IBM Asynchronous Communications Adapter. However, most AT-class computers come with a serial port or serial adapter card already built in. Also, if you have a memory-expansion board installed in your computer, chances are excellent that it includes a serial board with a serial port. If you are not sure whether you have a serial port, look on the back of your computer. Older computers may have a 25-pin connector (in the shape of a trapezoid) that is *not* directly below the monitor interface. New computers will have a trapezoidal 9-pin *male* connector (not on the monitor interface).

The serial board is more than just a place to plug in a connection to another computer. To understand its importance, you must understand the way computers normally transmit information.

The smallest meaningful unit of information in a computer is a *bit*—represented in data communications as a voltage level. Each bit has one of two voltage levels, which are represented by 0 and 1, or off and on. It generally takes 8 of these bits, grouped together into a *byte,* to convey meaningful information. Each byte represents a single character.

Ordinarily, when information is transmitted among the various parts of a computer, or to peripheral devices such as monitors and printers, it is transmitted in *parallel* form. This means that the 8 bits that make up a byte are all transmitted at the same time, along eight parallel electrical paths.

In *serial* communication, however, the 8 bits in a byte are transmitted one after the other, in sequence. This is the mode of transmission normally used in telecommunications. (Some printers also use serial communication.) The reason for this is that most telecommunication involves transmitting signals along telephone wires, and telephone wires contain only two channels—one for receiving information and another for transmitting it. So the computer's 8-bit characters must be converted into a stream of consecutive bits before transmission. When these consecutive bits are received, they must be reconstructed into bytes. This rearranging of the data is the principal function of the serial board.

THE RS-232 INTERFACE

The serial board is connected to the outside world by means of either an *RS-232* or a *DB-9 interface*. The RS-232 is a more-or-less standard type of cable having a 25-pin trapezoidal connector, called a DB-25 connector, at each end. Although only two of the possible 25 pins are actually used in data communications, several other pins perform related functions, such as carrying commands from the computer to the modem. On newer machines, the smaller DB-9 connector is used on the computer end, though the DB-25 is usually still used to connect to the modem.

If you are communicating directly with another computer, you will need one type of serial cable. If you are using a modem, you will probably need a different type. In any case, successful communications depend on the pins of your serial board being connected correctly to those on the device at the other end of the cable. Check with your dealer to be sure that the cable you are using is suitable for your intended purpose.

THE MODEM

If you want to communicate with a computer that is more than a few feet away, you will also need a *modem*. A modem is a device that links a computer to a telephone line. The term is a contraction of *modulator-dem*odulator, terms that describe the modem's principal functions: translating the digital information that arrives at the serial port into sound frequencies that can be transmitted by telephone, and converting arriving sound frequencies back into the digital information that a computer can understand.

Modems vary greatly. Some, such as the Hayes Smartmodem 2400B, are boards that plug directly into slots in the computer. While they take less desk space, they also usurp some of the computer's expansion room. Free-standing modems come in two basic types: *acoustic couplers,* on which the telephone's handset is rested during transmission, and *direct-connect* modems, which are wired directly into the telephone lines. The latter generally transmit information more accurately than the former (which are virtually obsolete), because room noises cannot leak in and distort the signal.

Modems vary greatly in other ways. Some can communicate at high speeds (called *baud rates*), whereas others contain automatic error correction and data compression systems. They also vary in price, depending on speed and other features.

COMMUNICATIONS SOFTWARE

To communicate with another computer, you also need *communications software.* This is where Framework III's telecommunications component comes in. It allows you to control the modem and the serial board, and to configure the information being sent and received so that it matches the requirements of the computer with which you are communicating. It also takes care of such chores as storing incoming data, preparing frames on the desktop for sending, and setting up disk files to receive data directly.

You configure the information that passes through the serial port by setting a series of *communications parameters.* These parameters control the way the computers make sense of the electrical pulses arriving at their serial ports.

The communications parameters that must be set include the *baud rate,* the number of *data bits,* the *parity* setting, the *stop bits,* and the *source* and *direction* of communication. These terms will be explained shortly.

In addition to the parameters that determine the form of the data to be communicated and the rate at which it travels, there are several routines that check for errors when data is being sent or received. These routines are called *communications protocols.* All you really need to know about communications protocols is that the sending and receiving computers must both be using the same protocol. Framework III includes seven different protocols and some special settings, so that you can transfer files to and from computers using other communications programs:

 Version Note:

YMODEM, Kermit, and IBM Mainframe protocols are new in Framework III.

- *XMODEM.* This is one of the most popular communications protocols, used on virtually all CP/M-based remote bulletin boards and available in most microcomputer telecommunications packages.

- *Batch XMODEM.* This is a multiple-file, wildcard version of the XMODEM protocol.

You can also set CRC (cyclic reduncancy check) error correction on or off with both types of XMODEM transfers. In order to use it, both computers must have it available. You can also reset the *Timing Relaxation Factor*, which controls the amount of time allowed between sending and acknowledging the receipt of a packet. It is set in the Framework III Setup file, but should probably be left alone unless you are experiencing a lot of timeout errors during file transfers.

- *YMODEM.* This is a multiple-file protocol, a variant of XMODEM, but one that sends more information at a time, and is consequently faster in most situations. Additional options include *One File Only*; *Receive* to allow only one file at a time; and *No Acknowledgement* to turn off error correction from the software. This is used when the modem is already performing the error correction (such as one of the many MNP protocol modems or the Hayes V-series modems; MNP is a popular error-correction protocol developed by Microcom and widely adopted by other modem manufacturers).

- *Kermit.* This protocol is most often used when sending between a microcomputer and a mainframe or minicomputer. Several special setup options for Kermit transfers can be set in the Framework III Setup file.

- *IBM Mainframe.* This is a special setting for Kermit transfers between micros and IBM mainframe computers. It instructs Framework to wait for a ^Q after each line, which is necessary with IBM mainframe equipment.

- *CLINK/Crosstalk.* This protocol is designed for use with IBM PCs running the popular communications program Crosstalk.

- *HAYES.* This protocol is used by the Smartcom program supplied with the Hayes Smartmodem 1200B and 2400B.

BASIC TELECOMMUNICATIONS MODES

There are three fundamentally different ways to send and receive information through telecommunications.

- *Terminal mode.* In terminal mode, you converse directly with another computer.

- *Uploading and downloading.* These processes transfer text files informally (character-by-character, without error-checking) from one computer to another.

- *Protocol transfers.* Protocol transfers use error-checking routines that can be applied to all types of files.

Let's see how these operations work.

Before you can engage in any of these activities, your telecommunications software must be configured to match the software running on the computer you want to communicate with. When dealing with mainframes and online services, you must ensure that your computer conforms to the remote computer's communications parameters. In connecting to another PC, you and the user of the other PC must agree on the parameters you will use.

Once you have configured your telecommunications software properly, you can converse directly with other computer users or access the various online information services and electronic bulletin boards. In this mode, which is called *terminal mode,* you type the information you want to send at the keyboard, and it appears almost simultaneously on the remote computer's screen. Similarly, information generated by the remote computer will appear on your screen. A great deal of recreational telecommunications consists of this type of conversation.

If the conversation is not too long, it will all be saved in the Telecommunications frame. You can also open a file into which the text generated during the session will automatically be sent. In addition, you can use the Text Transfer options on the Telecommunications menu to receive a complete text file from another computer. These processes—saving information in a desktop frame, saving the session to a file automatically, and receiving files through a text transfer—are referred to as *downloading*.

In addition to downloading, you can also *upload* text files from the Framework III desktop, that is, transmit them to a remote computer through terminal mode. This process is also controlled by the Text Transfer submenu.

In the *protocol transfer* mode, controlled by the File Transfer options of the Telecommunications menu, you can send or receive any disk file, including programs. This mode of file transfer scrupulously checks the transmission for errors. It is especially appropriate for the following:

- Transmitting and receiving files in Framework III's format. Framework III files contain a great deal of formatting information along with the data you have entered into them. If you are sharing files with another Framework III user, you should use a protocol transfer method to ensure that the receiver can use the files within Framework III.

- Transmitting and receiving word processed text files created by other programs. The control codes used to format text in word processing programs may also be used to control terminal communications, and they may have undesirable effects when transmitted through the terminal as part of a file. (Other options of the Telecommunications menu allow you to control this process, too, however.) A protocol transfer prevents these undesirable effects from occurring.

- Transmitting and receiving program code. In a program, every character is significant, so you want to be sure that none are lost in the transfer process. Text files, in contrast, are relatively easy to reconstruct.

Figure 6.1 shows the main Telecommunications menu, which is displayed when you select Telecommunications from the Apps menu.

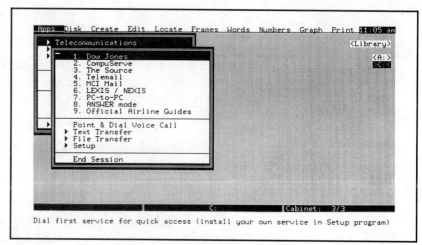

Figure 6.1: The Telecommunications menu

CREATING A TELECOMMUNICATIONS FRAME

Unlike all other types of frames, which are created from the Create menu, Telecommunications frames are created from the Apps menu. A Telecommunications frame is essentially a Word frame, but one that receives some of its contents from another computer. As your session proceeds, the frame will fill with text until it contains 32,000 characters, after which the first part of the session will be lost, as new text comes in and replaces it. You can, however, increase this figure from one of the Telecommunications submenus. When you have finished a telecommunications session, you can treat the contents of a Telecommunications frame as you would any other Word frame— edit the text, save the contents to a file, move or copy portions of the text to another frame.

To create a Telecommunications frame, press

    Ctrl-A (to open the Apps menu)

    T   (to select the Telecommunications submenu)

    S   (to select the Setup submenu)

    B   (to begin a telecommunications session)

If a Word frame is currently selected, Framework III will display the message

Use this frame for Telecommunications session? (y/n)

If you press Y, the session will begin after the last character in the frame.

Otherwise a new frame, occupying the full desktop except for the bottom line, will be created, with the label

Telecommunications.

In the third section of the status panel, the message

Tcom

will appear. Figure 6.2 shows a Telecommunications frame.

What happens when you choose to begin a session (which is what you did in order to create the frame) depends on whether you have a modem connected and turned on. If your computer is not connected to a modem, or if the modem is turned off, a peculiarity of the serial interface makes your computer respond as if a call is in progress. You will see, in quick succession, the messages

Dialing...   (Ctrl-Break to cancel)
Waiting for "trap" character from remote system...
(Ctrl-Break to cancel)
Telecomm is active

in the message area at the bottom of your screen. If your computer is connected to a modem and the modem is turned on (or if you have an internal modem), Framework III automatically attempts to dial a phone number and link with another computer. It will wait 45 seconds for the other computer's telephone to respond, displaying the message

Waiting for carrier detect...   (Ctrl-Break to cancel)

In any case, once you have selected the Begin/Resume session option, Framework III regards telecommunications as active. You can press the Out key (–) and leave the frame, and you can use most

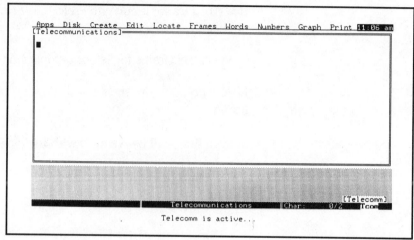

Figure 6.2: A Telecommunications frame

of Framework III's menu options, but you cannot delete the frame until telecommunications becomes inactive. If you do not have a modem active, you must return to the Telecommunications menu and formally end the session. Press

Ctrl-A   (to open the Apps menu)

T   (to open the Telecommunications submenu)

E   (to end the session)

If your modem is active, on the other hand, you can just press Ctrl-Break while the modem waits for a response, or wait 45 seconds, and telecommunications will become inactive.

As you can see, before you can actually use a Telecommunications frame for telecommunications, you must make certain preparations in advance. We'll now turn to the Telecommunications Setup Options menu, where you make these preparations.

PREPARING FRAMEWORK III FOR TELECOMMUNICATIONS

In a little while, we'll be logging onto Telenet, one of the major national networks through which you can log onto information services.

Before we do so, however, we'll have to configure telecommunications for the purpose. To do so, we'll have to set the communications parameters. These parameters are controlled by the Setup Options menu, which is shown in Figure 6.3. To display this menu, press

Ctrl-A	(to open the Apps menu)
T	(to select Telecommunications)
S	(to select the Setup submenu)
S	(to select the Setup Options submenu)

You will see that the Setup Options menu is divided into three sections. The left-hand section of the menu contains most of the communications parameters mentioned briefly at the beginning of this chapter. Two more parameters, the source and direction of communications, are in the right-hand section of the menu. We'll discuss the communications parameters at greater length here.

BAUD RATE

The *baud rate* is the rate at which bits are transmitted. Roughly, the baud rate divided by ten will yield the number of *characters* transmitted per second. Most modems allow baud rates of 110 to 1200. Others can handle baud rates of up to 2400, and some of the newer

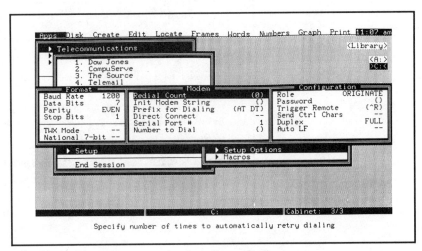

Figure 6.3: The Telecommunications Setup Options menu

models can transmit at baud rates as high as 9600 and above. It is essential that the baud rates of both systems be the same. If they are not, the information you receive or transmit will be meaningless. You will know that the two computers are not using the same baud rate if your screen resembles the one shown in Figure 6.4.

DATA BITS

The Data Bits parameter represents the number of bits used to transmit a single character. To transmit the characters from 0 to 127 in the ASCII code (see Appendix C), only 7 bits are required. These characters include the standard alphabet and the Ctrl-key combinations; the codes are almost completely standardized from computer to computer. The characters with ASCII codes greater than 127 vary greatly from one computer to another, however, and may even be modified by the software. Eight bits are required to transmit these characters.

The vast majority of intercomputer communication requires only 7 bits. The number of data bits, however, like so many aspects of data communications, varies from one system to another, and both systems must agree before successful communication can occur.

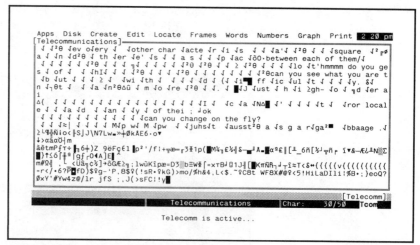

Figure 6.4: The result of telecommunicating with unmatched baud rates

PARITY

Parity is a primitive means of checking transmitted data for errors. If the system you are communicating with uses 7 data bits, the eighth bit is a *parity bit*. If the parity is set to *even*, the software will place 1 in the parity bit if the addition of the 7 data bits results in an odd number. If the result is already even, the software will place 0 in the parity bit. If the parity is set to *odd*, the reverse happens. Thus, when checking incoming data, the receiving computer will know that an error has occurred if the value of the 8 bits does not conform to the parity setting. If the system uses 8 data bits, no parity is used.

STOP BITS

If the receiving computer is to make sense of the stream of apparently random bits arriving at its serial port, the data has to be formatted in some way. Therefore, every 8-bit byte is preceded by a *start bit,* which is a binary 0. At the end of a byte are either 1 or 2 *stop bits,* which are binary 1s. This is the representation of the line signal's "resting" voltage. When stop bits are detected, the receiving computer waits until the next start bit is received. Different systems require different numbers of stop bits. Two stop bits are commonly used at low baud rates, and 1 stop bit is more prevalent at higher speeds.

CHANGING THE SETTINGS

The default settings shown in Figure 6.3 for the baud rate, data bits, parity, and stop bits are all correct for logging onto Telenet:

Baud Rate	1200
Data Bits	7
Parity	EVEN
Stop Bits	1

Version Note

Before Framework III, baud rate choices were 100, 300, 1200, 2400, 4800, and 9600 only.

Telenet can also function with 300-baud modems, however. If you have a 300-baud modem, select Baud Rate from the Setup Options submenu. The baud rate will cycle through the values 2400, 4800, 9600, 19200, 38400, 75, 110, and 300 (in fact, all the possible choices except 600, which follows 300), changing each time you press Return. Press Return two more times to return to 1200 baud.

You might want to try changing the other settings just for practice. Try selecting Data Bits and pressing Return. This setting will toggle between 7 and 8 each time you press Return. Similarly, the Stop Bits setting will toggle between 1 and 2. The Parity setting might be considered a "throggle"—it has three possible values instead of two. Press Return once and EVEN will be replaced by NONE. Press Return again, and NONE will change to ODD. Press Return a third time, and EVEN will reappear.

SOURCE OF COMMUNICATION

In the right section of the Setup Options menu are two more communications settings that must be established before you make a call (which is called *going online*). The first is called Role and refers to the *source* of communication.

When two computers communicate, one must be designated as the source, or originator, of the communication, and the other as the answering computer. It doesn't much matter which is which, so long as they are different. When dialing online services such as CompuServe, however, or logging onto electronic bulletin boards, the Role must be set to ORIGINATE (the default setting), because the remote service will always be set up to answer.

DIRECTION OF COMMUNICATION

Data communications also involve "directionality." The transmission of data can occur in one of three ways: in only one direction, in both directions at different times, or in both directions at the same time.

Transmission in only one direction is called the *simplex configuration*. It is rarely used with microcomputers. The other two configurations—*half duplex* (both directions at different times) and *full duplex* (both directions at the same time)—are much more common. Most communication between microcomputers takes place in full duplex mode, which is the default value for this option.

When you type characters at your keyboard for transmission, they do not automatically appear on your screen. Rather, they go directly to the serial port. What you see on your screen is an "echo" of the characters that are received at the remote computer. This may seem a roundabout way of getting characters on your screen, but it ensures that what you send is being received. This echoing process is possible only in full duplex mode. If you do not see characters when you type, try changing the Duplex setting to FULL (in case it has been switched away from the default) by selecting it and pressing Return. Sometimes, you'll get a double echo, so that when you type

> hello

you see

> hheelllloo

on your screen. In this case, try changing your Duplex setting to HALF.

The Role and Duplex default settings on the Setup Options menu are both correct for use with Telenet.

INTERACTING WITH YOUR MODEM

The center section of the Setup Options menu is where you set up telecommunications to make your call and interact properly with your autodial modem. (If you have a manual-dial modem, you do not need to enter anything in this section of the menu, unless your modem automatically goes online whether or not you are in communication with another computer. If it does, select Direct Connect and press Return. You must, however, set the ORG/ANS switch on the modem to ORG.) In this menu, you will see the following options and their current values:

Redial Count	{0}
Init Modem String	{}
Prefix for Dialing	{AT DT}
Serial Port #	{1}
Direct Connect	– –
Number to Dial	{}

The Redial Count specifies the number of times you want your autodial modem to redial a number after it reaches a busy signal. You can change this setting to any number up to 99.

Now check the manual that came with your modem to see if you need a *modem initialization string* and a *dial prefix*. If your modem requires an initialization string, select Init Modem String, press Return, and enter the characters that your manual indicates exactly as they appear. If any of them are control characters, enter them by pressing ^ (Shift-6), followed by the letter of the control character. Press Return a second time to record your selection. (If your modem does not require an initialization string, don't enter anything here.)

If your modem requires a dial prefix other than the one shown, select Prefix for Dialing and follow the same procedure, entering the dial prefix for your modem. If it requires none, select Prefix for Dialing, press Return, and type a space before pressing Return a second time.

Framework III will automatically attempt to dial a number whenever you begin a telecommunications session. To succeed, however, it must have a valid number to dial. It looks for this number in the Number to Dial option on the Setup Options menu. Since you have not yet installed one, you saw bizarre results when you created a Telecommunications frame. A bit later, when we log onto a network, we'll install a phone number in this space.

Let's summarize the setup procedure:

- The baud rate must be set to match *both* that of your modem and that of the remote computer (some modems offer the option of several different baud rates; some of the remote services can communicate at 300, 1200, or 2400 baud; and private bulletin board systems can communicate at up to 9600 baud).

- The number of data bits, the parity, the number of stop bits, and the telephone number (when using an autodial modem) must be set to match those of the remote computer. (By the way, most remote services and bulletin board systems use the settings 8 data bits, no parity, and 1 stop bit [8, N, 1]. You must be using 8 data bits to perform file transfers using protocols such as XMODEM, YMODEM, and Kermit. As you will see, there are exceptions to this rule.)

- The initialization string and dial prefix must be set to match your autodial modem.

LOGGING ONTO A NETWORK

Now that we have covered some of the basics of telecommunications, let's try using Framework III's telecommunications package. First, be sure that the following hardware requirements are met:

- Your modem is connected to your computer with the correct type of cable.

- The modem switches are set correctly (you can find all the correct settings in Table 10-1 of the *Using Framework III* manual).

- The telephone is attached to the modem (if you have an autodial modem)

- The modem is turned on.

Next, you will need somebody to communicate with. We will log onto Telenet, a *communications network* through which you can gain access to such remote services as CompuServe, The Source, and The Knowledge Index. Telenet has several services that can be used without charge, and we will begin with one of those, so you can practice using telecommunications without paying for the time.

To use the services Telenet offers, you need Telenet's local phone number. You can get it through Telenet's toll-free customer-service numbers:

(800) 336–0437

(800) 572–0408 (in Virginia)

First check whether your modem is 300, 1200, or 2400 baud. Then call the appropriate number and ask for the nearest phone number you can use with your baud rate.

When you have the phone number, press

Ctrl-A	(to open the Apps menu)
T	(to select Telecommunications)
S	(to select the Setup submenu)
S	(to select the Setup Options menu)
→ or ←	(to select the center section)

N	(to select Number to Dial)
Return	(to enter the number)
phone number	(the number to dial)
Return	(to record your entry)

MAKING THE CONNECTION

To actually start communications, make sure your modem is connected and turned on, then press the keys to begin the session.

| Out (–) | (to back up to the Telecommunications Setup menu) |
| B | (to begin the session) |

As before, a Telecommunications frame will be created, and if you have an autodial modem, it will immediately dial the number you just installed. (If you have a manual-dial modem, just dial the number. When you hear a high whining sound, either place the receiver on the acoustic coupler or unplug the modular cord from the receiver and plug it into the appropriate jack on the modem.)

Within the Telecommunications frame, the dial prefix and phone number you installed will appear, while the message

Dialing...   (Ctrl-Break to cancel)

appears in the message area. After the modem finishes dialing the number, the message

Waiting for carrier detect...   (Ctrl-Break to cancel)

will replace it. If you have a direct-connect modem with a speaker, you will then hear either a busy signal or a phone ringing, followed by a high-pitched tone. (If you dialed manually, these sounds will come from your telephone handset. Place the handset on the acoustic coupler, or unplug the handset and plug the wire into your modem, depending on which type of modem you have.) The message area will now read

Telecomm is active

You should now press Return twice, to alert the remote computer to your presence. The word

TELENET

will appear, followed on the next line by your local area code along with another code. When you see

TERMINAL =

type

d1

and press Return. This is your *terminal identifier code*. Telenet's system prompt is the @ sign. When you see it, type

mail

and press Return. This is the service you can have access to without charge. The next prompt asks for your user name:

User name?

For this service, type

phones

and press Return. When you see the prompt

Password?

type

phones

again and press Return. This time the word will not appear on your screen. This dialogue is illustrated in Figure 6.5.

Be careful when you type your responses to the prompts, because you may not be able to edit them. On some systems, the Delete key, while it appears to be deleting on your screen, instead sends a delete

```
 Apps  Disk  Create  Edit  Locate  Frames  Words  Numbers  Graph  Print  9 48 am
[Telecommunications]
 AT DT8364911

 TELENET
 415 15V

 TERMINAL=d1

 @mail

 User name?  phones
 Password?
```

Figure 6.5: Logging onto Telenet

character (ASCII 127), and the Backspace key sends a backspace character (ASCII 8, or Ctrl-H) in addition to the character you have deleted. If, for example, you typed *maio* instead of *mail,* and you tried to correct it before pressing Return,

   maio^HI

would be transmitted. (Your screen will look perfectly normal, but you can see graphic symbols representing the Backspace and Delete characters in a capture file, which you will learn how to establish shortly.) You will know you mistyped a response if you get a question mark followed by a repetition of the previous prompt. If that happens, do not be alarmed. Simply retype your response. Telenet is fairly forgiving at this level, and you can make quite a few mistakes before the network throws you off.

   In a short time, you will see several commercial messages. There will be prompts you can answer to get more information about Telenet local access numbers in various parts of the country. They will scroll across your screen, pausing periodically when the program sends a certain message. The pause is normal and is nothing to worry about. A sample section of Telenet's messages, with appropriate responses to Telenet's prompts, appears in Figure 6.6.

```
 Apps  Disk  Create  Edit  Locate  Frames  Words  Numbers  Graph  Print  6:02 pm
[Telecommunications]
o FOR INFORMATION BY STATE TYPE 'STATE'

o FOR INFORMATION BY AREA CODE TYPE 'AREA.CODE'

o FOR A COMPLETE LISTING TYPE 'ALL'

o TO EXIT THE PHONES LISTING TYPE 'QUIT'

state

DO YOU WANT INWATS OR A STATE BEGINNING WITH A-TO-L?   <YES OR NO>

y

PLEASE ENTER TWO-CHARACTER STATE IDENTIFIER.

ca
                                                              [Telecomm]
                          Telecommunications        |Char:      3/131  Tcom
                            Telecomm is active...
```

Figure 6.6: Messages, prompts, and responses from Telenet

You can continue as long as you like. When you are ready to stop, if you are at a Telenet prompt, type

> quit

To disconnect your own phone, or to quit when you are not at a prompt, press

> Ctrl-A   (to open the Apps menu)
>
> T   (to open the Telecommunications menu)
>
> E   (to end the session)

RECORDING A CONVERSATION

You have now completed your first online session. If it was short, the complete transcript of what you have seen will still be in the Telecommunications frame. But what if you want to record more extensive dialogues for future reference?

You can send the contents of the active Telecommunications frame to a disk file at any time by pressing Ctrl-PrtSc. The first time you press this combination of keys, you will be prompted to

> **Please enter a name for file to capture to**

After you enter the file name, the message

Capture file open

will appear. Thereafter, you can toggle capturing on and off by pressing Ctrl-PrtSc.

You can also create a file in advance into which the entire text of the dialogue will be written, at the same time as it appears in the Telecommunications frame. To do so, you will use the Text Transfer submenu, shown in Figure 6.7, which controls uploading and downloading of text. To set this option, press

Ctrl-A	(to open the Apps menu)
T	(to open the Telecommunications menu)
T	(to open the Text Transfer menu)
→	(to move to the Download portion of the menu)
Return	(to select Capture to File)

You will be prompted with

Please enter a name for file to capture to

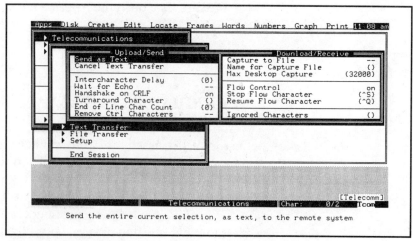

Figure 6.7: The Text Transfer submenu

Enter the file name and press Return. When you begin your next session, text will automatically be sent to the file you have named. If a file by that name exists, the new text will be appended to it.

If you are already involved in a session, you can begin to send text to a file at any point by using the Capture to File option. The text sent to the file, however, will include only what appears after you have named the file. You can also toggle the capturing process off and on at any point during a session by selecting this menu option and pressing Return. This is useful if, for example, you want to record a menu the first time it is displayed, for further perusal, but do not want to save all succeeding instances of the same menu.

Let's log onto Telenet again, but this time we'll save the conversation, to get some practice in downloading a file. Follow the steps just outlined, and type in the name under which you will save the dialogue, preceded by the drive designator of the disk on which you want the file to appear, and press Return. For example, you might type

    C:TELENET.TXT

You can open the disk directory by pressing the Shuttle key (Scroll Lock) at any time during or after the session, and you will see this file name in the directory. Once your session is over, you can load this file (which will be a Word frame) to the desktop and edit, print, or read it at leisure.

TRANSFERRING FILES

Strictly speaking, *all* computer files are binary files—that is, files of eight-place, binary-coded numbers whose values range from 0 to 255. Text files are simply a special case of binary files, in which these values are interpreted as ASCII character codes.

When files are transferred by means of telecommunications, text file transfer means that the information in the file is sent as a stream of characters, departing through the serial port one character at a time. Only files that are prepared as text files can be sent through text file transfer. If you want to send information from a Framework III frame to someone who does not use Framework III or who wants to use the information in another program, the frame *must* be prepared as a text file, so that the nontextual information that only Framework III uses is filtered out.

Text files can also be sent by means of a binary transfer, however, in which the information is sent and received in blocks of bytes rather than as a stream of characters. The advantage of sending a text file through a binary transfer is that special error-checking routines are used that ensure the integrity of each block of bytes. This is also a useful means of sending word processed files, which may contain control codes that would interrupt the smooth flow of communication if the file were sent character by character.

When you send a file that is on the desktop, it is always sent as a text file. Framework III automatically converts the frame to an ASCII text file, just as if you had selected the DOS File option from the Destination submenu of the Print menu (or if you had converted it to an ASCII text file yourself, as will be explained in Chapter 8). To send a file in this manner, first exit from the Telecommunications frame. Then select the file you want to send, and press

Ctrl-A   (to open the Apps menu)

T   (to open the Telecommunications menu)

T   (to select the Text Transfer submenu)

S   (to send the file as text)

You can, in fact, send any selected material from the desktop in this manner—parts of frames, whole frames, or several frames. Anything that would affect the printed appearance of the frame—such as title locking in a spreadsheet (except for special type styles, such as underlining)—will affect the appearance of the material that is sent. You can interrupt the transfer at any time by selecting Cancel Text Transfer from the same menu.

When you select Send as Text, Framework III creates a temporary file, just as it does when it prepares to print a file, and displays the message

PREPARING TO UPLOAD

As soon as the file is ready, the message area displays

> Waiting for "trap" character from remote system...
> (Ctrl-Break to cancel)

When the awaited character is received, a graphics character appears in the Telecommunications frame, and a message flashes briefly before the next segment of the file is sent. The "trap" character message then reappears. When the entire file has been sent, the message area displays

> Upload Completed

While this is going on, you can leave the Telecommunications frame and work elsewhere in Framework III. A beep will sound when the upload is completed, to remind you to return to communication. Be aware that telecommunications messages appear only while the Telecommunications frame is selected.

Once again, note that you need not use the Text Transfer option if your files are already on disk in the proper form. Any file that has been saved on disk through the DOS File Destination option from the Print submenu or the ASCII Text Export option (discussed in Chapter 8) on the Disk menu is a text file. These files can be sent either as text files from the desktop, or as binary files, using an error-checking protocol, from the File Transfer menu (which will be discussed shortly).

SETUP FILES

If you communicate on a regular basis with telecommunications services, such as Dow Jones News/Retrieval or CompuServe, or with electronic bulletin board services, you will find that each service uses a particular set of communications parameters, as well as a particular telephone number. Most of them will also require you to have an account number and a password.

For your convenience, you can save all the settings for a given remote computer or service in a *setup file*. As you can see from the Telecommunications menu in Figure 6.1, Framework III comes with eight preconfigured files: items 1 through 8. Included are files for connecting to Dow

Jones News/Retrieval, CompuServe, The Source, GTE's Telemail service, MCI Mail, the Lexis/Nexis information databases, connecting to another personal computer, and placing your computer into answer mode. These files, which are identified on disk by a .TCM extension, contain the communications parameters necessary to connect with these services. Before you can use them, however, you must insert the service's local phone number, your account number, and your password. After the necessary information has been inserted, selecting any of these options from the Telecommunications menu will automatically dial the phone number (assuming you have an autodial modem) and initiate the log-on sequence, leaving you ready to communicate. We'll learn how to perform these steps in the next section.

If the setup file you need is on the menu, you can load it simply by selecting it from the Telecommunications menu. (Doing so will automatically initiate a telecommunications session.) If not, you can load a setup file by pressing

Ctrl-A	(to open the Apps menu)
T	(to open the Telecommunications menu)
S	(to select the Setup submenu)
L	(to select the Load Setup File option)
Return	(to enter the name of the file)
filename	(enter the name of the file)
Return	(to record your selection)

The message area will then say

Your options have been set from setup file

Next time you begin a telecommunications session, the communications parameters, telephone number, and log-on sequence from this file will be used (until you reset the computer or load another setup file).

A setup file is really nothing more than a "snapshot" of the settings on all the Telecommunications submenus. You can create such a file at any time by selecting the Write Setup File option from the Setup submenu, and entering the file name. If you haven't changed the settings since your conversation with Telenet, you could write a setup file for Telenet just by selecting Write Setup File and entering the file name

telenet

To change the default settings that are automatically loaded when you start Framework III, establish the menu settings you want to use, then choose the Write Setup File option and enter the file name

telecomm

CONFIGURING SETUP FILES: TELECOMMUNICATIONS MACROS

There is, however, a bit more to organizing your setup files so that they will perform all their chores automatically. For this we need yet another submenu—the Macros submenu of the Setup submenu. To open this menu, which is shown in Figure 6.8, press

Ctrl-A   (to open the Apps menu)

T   (to open the Telecommunications menu)

S   (to select the Setup submenu)

M   (to open the Macros submenu)

Here you can add macros to your setup that will be sent by a combination of the Ctrl key and a function key. The right half of the menu gives you a place to add a comment explaining the purpose of the macro.

The macros on this menu can be used anywhere in Framework III, as well as in telecommunications. This means that you can load an additional ten macros by loading a setup file, even if you are not going to use telecommunications. (Macros established in the Library can be used in telecommunications as well.) Thus, you can send a

Figure 6.8: The Telecommunications Macros menu

series of characters to the remote computer by calling them from a macro, just as you can insert them anywhere else in a frame on the desktop. These macros differ from Library macros, however, in that they must be created on the edit line, rather than recorded from your keystrokes.

You can add macros that will smooth your communication with a particular remote computer. Ctrl-F10, in particular, is reserved for a macro that will be sent automatically as soon as connection is established with the remote computer. Thus, you can use it to perform your log-on sequence automatically. To accomplish this, however, you may need to use some special codes that act as telecommunications commands. These codes and their effects are listed in Table 6.1.

The WAIT code, @W, is useful if you use a long-distance service such as MCI. You can insert it between your local number (the number to dial) and your access code, so that the number to dial and the access code will not be sent until the appropriate moment.

To see how the other codes are used, let's create an automatic log-on macro for Telenet. Your first response upon connection to Telenet is two carriage returns, so your Ctrl-F10 macro will begin with

^M^M

Table 6.1: Special Codes for Telecommunications Macros

CHARACTER	FUNCTION
@W	WAIT code—waits for one second before sending the next character.
@S*string*@S	Waits for the *string* bracketed by @S codes. This command allows you to wait for strings longer than those allowed by @T.
@T*char*	Waits for the character *char* to be received.
@L*n*	Links to macro number *n*. Used if a single macro cannot hold enough keystrokes to complete your command. (Ctrl F10 is macro number 0.)
@@	Sends a Ctrl-@, an ASCII 0, or NULL.
^	Makes the following character a control character.

(As you can see from Table C.2, Ctrl-M is the equivalent of a carriage return.) You do not need to respond again until Telenet gives you the prompt

    TERMINAL =

so you want your macro to wait for this prompt. When the equal sign is received, you want to send your terminal identifier, so add

    @T = d1^M

to your macro. This tells the computer to wait for an equal sign, and then send

    d1

followed by a carriage return. The next prompt you need to respond to is an @ sign, to which you reply

    mail

so you will add

> @T@mail^M

The next prompt ends in a question mark and receives the response

> phones

so you can add another @T followed by a question mark, then the word *phones*:

> @T?phones

Your macro should now read:

> ^M^M@T = d1^M@Tmail^M@T?phones^M

Now, just to try something different, use the @S code to wait for the string *Password?* and then send the password string *phones*. (You could use the @T code again here, but let's do it a different way this time. Using @S codes to wait for an entire string instead of just one character avoids ambiguity and ensures that the macro is waiting for exactly the string you intend.)

> @SPassword?@Sphones

Now the completed macro reads

> ^M^M@T = d1^M@Tmail^M@T?phones^M@SPassword?@Sphones^M

You might want to try adding this macro to your Telenet setup and beginning another session, to make sure that it works.

It's also helpful to include (probably in Ctrl-F1) your log-off sequence. Many services use

> OFF

or

> BYE

as their log-off command. However, you should find out what each system that you communicate with regularly uses, and install that command as the macro for Ctrl-F1. In addition, you will need to tell your modem to hang up the phone. As you will remember, you hang up the phone by pressing

Ctrl-A   (to open the Apps menu)

T   (to select Telecommunications)

E   (to select End Session)

to get to the End Session command. However, you do not want to transmit the Ctrl A T E characters to the remote system—you want to send them to Framework III. Therefore, you must record them in Framework III's format. The log-off macro, therefore, should be in the form

    BYE^M@W{ctrl-a}te

If you had used ^A instead of {ctrl-a}, telecommunications would have attempted to send the Ctrl-A character to the remote computer. The @W is included so that the modem will wait until the remote computer's response to your log-off command has been received before hanging up.

CONFIGURING EXISTING SETUP FILES

If you use any of the services for which a setup file is included, you will find that the log-on and log-off sequences are already installed in Ctrl-F10 and Ctrl-F1 on the Macros menu. All you have to do is add your local access number, your password, and your account number. Begin by loading the setup file by means of the Load Setup File option on the Setup submenu. Otherwise, Framework III will immediately try to dial the number (which you have not yet installed) and connect to the service. You will need to install the phone number in the appropriate location, as we did in our Telenet setup file. Then you should go to the Macros menu and install your personal information. For example, the macro assigned to Ctrl-F10 for the Dow Jones setup is

```
^M^M@T = d1^M@T@c
60942^M@T?@Wdjns^M@TE@Wacct#^M
```

To customize this macro, bring it to the edit line with Return, delete the characters

```
acct#
```

and insert your Dow Jones account number in their place. If there are particular subsections of a service that you use regularly, you can install the series of commands needed to reach them in other macros on this menu, and execute the commands whenever you like just by pressing the appropriate Ctrl-function key combination. When you are finished, press

Ctrl-A	(to open the Apps menu)
T	(to open the Telecommunications menu)
S	(to open the Setup submenu)
W	(to choose the Write Setup File option)
Return	(to write the file using the name of the same file that you originally loaded)

The changes you made will be written to the setup file, and the next time you want to use the service, you can just select it from the main Telecommunications menu. If the services on the Telecommunications menu are not the ones you use, you will learn in Appendix A how to delete the ones you don't need and add the ones that you use. You will create the setup files necessary for the process simply by entering the appropriate values in all the menus and then using the Write Setup File option.

Now that you are familiar with the basics of telecommunications and have experienced an online session, we'll look at some examples of telecommunications at work. At The Sophisticated Palate, Eileen Wilcox is in charge of telecommunications. We'll watch as she uses telecommunications to receive a spreadsheet file from the recently established branch store, to place an advertisement on an electronic bulletin board, and to log onto an online service. Finally, we'll watch her put telecommunications into answer mode and send some spreadsheet files to the firm's accountant. In Chapter 8, we'll learn how George Farley prepared the spreadsheet file for the accountant, and how he integrated the information from the branch store into his own spreadsheets.

EXAMPLES

It was after hours at The Sophisticated Palate. Frank Osawa had just finished posting the day's expenses to a spreadsheet and George was taking care of the bank deposit. As soon as Frank finished, Eileen would begin a telecommunications session. She prepared her work carefully in advance, because some of her calls would be long distance, and connect time on the online services could be expensive. She wanted to save time and money.

During the course of her session, Eileen had several tasks to accomplish:

- Scanning a local bulletin board service to find advertisements for used equipment that could be used in the new branch store

- Receiving a spreadsheet from the newly opened branch store, to be integrated with the main store's spreadsheet

- Logging onto a major online service

- Sending a spreadsheet to the firm's accountant

Eileen had to take quite a few steps to ensure efficient use of her telecommunications time. First, she put a blank data disk in drive A. Next, she used Framework III's word processor to prepare an Equipment Wanted notice she would post if there were no appropriate items listed. When it was finished, she pressed Ctrl-P D D to save the frame as a DOS text file. That way, it could be used again without further preparation if she received no response during the two weeks that notices were permitted to remain on the bulletin board. She also left the notice in a tray on the desktop, so she could transmit it as a text file.

Now Eileen was ready to go online. She opened her Telecommunications menu, shown in Figure 6.9. (Notice that she has tailored her Telecommunications menu for her own purposes.)

Her first online task would be to receive a spreadsheet from the branch store. She wanted to finish that first so that Joe Escovedo, the manager of the branch store, could leave for the evening.

RECEIVING A FILE THROUGH A PROTOCOL TRANSFER

The branch store, which did not need to keep as extensive records as the main store, had an Apple IIe computer. George and Eileen had chosen the VisiCalc spreadsheet program for that computer, because Framework III can convert VisiCalc spreadsheets to Framework III spreadsheets, as we'll learn in Chapter 8. For telecommunications, they had chosen a package called Easycom/Easygo, because it included the XMODEM error-checking routine for file transfer, as well as an adequate word processor. It was important to have an error-checking protocol, because the information in the spreadsheets was too important to risk sending through a simple text transfer.

Although VisiCalc spreadsheets themselves are not compatible with Framework III, VisiCalc can create a special type of file, called a DIF file, which is a simple sequential text file. Framework III's file-conversion options include converting DIF files to Framework III files.

First, to make sure that Joe was ready, Eileen called him on the telephone. Having assured herself that Joe was prepared, she hung up the phone, switched on her Hayes Smartmodem 2400, moved the cursor to the Telecommunications menu, and pressed Return to load the Branch Store setup and begin the session. At that point she was in terminal mode, and her parameter file for the branch store had been set up to make the call automatically. Her parameter file had set the baud rate to 300, to match that of the Apple modem at the other end.

To make sure the connection was good, she typed

Are you there, Joe? –o–

Figure 6.9: The Sophisticated Palate's Telecommunications menu

(The symbol –o– is used in telecommunications to indicate "over.")
Joe responded with

> **Everything looks good at this end. –o–**

Then she typed

> **OK, let's go. –oo–**

(The symbol –oo– is used to indicate "over and out.")
Next, she pressed these keys:

Ctrl-A (to open the Apps menu)

T (to open the Telecommunications menu)

F (to open the File Transfer submenu)

R (to select the Receive a File option)

This brought the cursor to the edit line, so she could enter the file
name

> **a:brnchsls.dif**

This would be the name under which the VisiCalc file would be stored on her disk. She chose the name to indicate that the file contained the branch store's sales for the fourth quarter. She did not need to select the XMODEM protocol, because XMODEM is Framework III's default protocol.

Telecommunications responded to her file name with

T
Attempting to Synchronize
Now Receiving A:BRNCHSLS.DIF

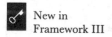 New in
Framework III

Now, in earlier versions of Framework, she would have seen some characters on the screen that represented information about the file transfer. However, in Framework III, a special display line appears at the bottom of the screen to show the progress of the protocol download (receiving a file) or upload (sending a file).

The file transfer line shows the most recent block number sent, the number of bytes transferred, the percentage complete (in some cases), and the number of errors that occurred during transmission. Below that line, another line shows the current mode (Receive a File, or Send a File) plus the file name. While Framework III was downloading the file, Eileen could watch the progress of the file on the line. Her screen looked like Figure 6.10.

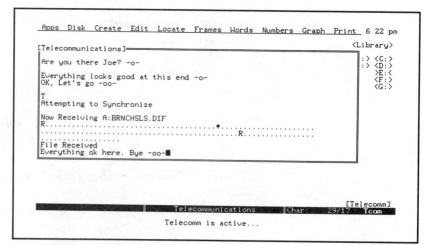

Figure 6.10: Receiving a protocol transfer

While a protocol transfer is being completed, the only action available to the user is to cancel the transfer by pressing Ctrl-Break. After about two minutes, the message

File Received

appeared. Eileen said goodbye to Joe and logged off. She hung up the phone by pressing Ctrl-F1, to activate the hang-up macro.

LOGGING ONTO A BULLETIN BOARD

Eileen's next task was to place an advertisement on the Merchandisers' Bulletin Board Service. She pressed

Ctrl-A   (to open the Apps menu)

T   (to open the Telecommunications menu)

6   (to select the Merchandisers' BBS setup file)

She had already set up her Ctrl-F10 macro to transmit her identification code and password automatically. When the log-on procedures were completed, her screen displayed the menu shown in Figure 6.11. Notice that it is only 40 columns wide, to accommodate those computers that

Figure 6.11: The Merchandisers' Bulletin Board Service menu

can display only 40 columns of text. This is quite common on electronic bulletin boards.

Eileen opened a download file from the Text Transfer menu, and chose the fourth option, Scan Mail. While any messages that might have been left for her were being written to disk, she took care of some paperwork. When she heard the computer beep, Eileen returned to it and closed the download file.

Next, she chose the third option, Read General Notices, selecting

Merchandise for Sale—Equipment

from a submenu, to see if anyone was advertising any of the equipment The Sophisticated Palate needed. She found an ad for a restaurant stove, and returned to the main menu to select the second option, Send Messages to Individuals. The remote computer prompted:

Enter name of new file, a / and your ID code:

Then she waited while the remote bulletin board responded with

Please wait. . .checking disk space.

When the remote computer had verified that there was enough disk space, it displayed the message

OK to begin sending.
Press Ctrl-C when done.

Eileen typed a response, right in the Telecommunications frame, to be posted as a message to the individual who had placed the ad. She finished by pressing Ctrl-C, and after a short time, the text

Message Received
Your Choice?

appeared on her screen. Eileen typed MENU and then pressed 1, to post her own advertisement. Finally, she typed MENU, and then chose the third option again, to assure herself that her notice had been posted. When she saw that it had, she pressed Ctrl-F1, to send the bulletin board's log-off message and hang up the phone. At her next telecommunications session, she would choose Scan Mail, to see if she had received any responses to her ad.

USING ANSWER MODE

Eileen's final task for the evening was to send a spreadsheet to the firm's accountant. Although the accountant used Lotus 1-2-3 rather than Framework III, this posed no problem, because Framework III can convert its files to the Lotus 1-2-3 format. She had previously broken George's Income and Expenses spreadsheets into two separate frames, because that was how the accountant wanted them, and converted them to 1-2-3 format using the procedures that we'll look at in Chapter 8. Using a method we'll look at shortly, she used Framework III to dial the accountant's number by way of the modem, and made sure he was ready.

She then turned to the Setup submenu, changed the Role setting from Originate to Answer, and opened the File Transfer submenu to select the Batch XMODEM protocol, which allows you to send several files at once. Then she set her modem to auto-answer, and waited for the accountant to call back. When the connection was made, the message

Welcome to Framework Telecommunications

appeared on both screens. This telecommunications session appears in Figure 6.12.

When the end of the file was reached, the messages

File Sent
Now Sending EXPENSES.WKS

appeared. After saying goodbye, Eileen used the Ctrl-F1 macro to hang up the phone, and proceeded to her final telecommunications activity for the evening.

LOGGING ONTO COMPUSERVE

Eileen liked to keep up-to-date with the latest developments in her areas of interest, one of which was, of course, Framework III.

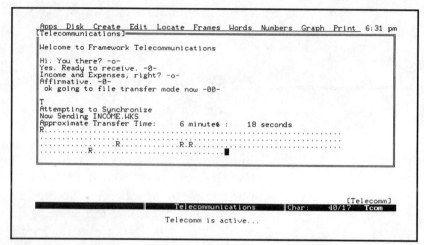

Figure 6.12: Beginning a telecommunications session

Ashton-Tate maintains a bulletin board on CompuServe for users of its products, and Eileen wanted to see if the library of technical notes had been updated. She opened a file on drive A to receive the contents of her session, selected CompuServe from the Telecommunications menu, and logged in automatically. At the top-level (main) menu, shown in Figure 6.13, she typed

GO ASHTON

and after a short pause was in the Ashton-Tate Support Library. The library is divided into sections by product, and the Framework III section includes two subcategories—Reference Notes, and Anomalies and Workarounds.

Eileen scanned Anomalies and Workarounds to see if there were any bugs that had been discovered or fixed. She scanned the screens quickly, knowing that she was paying for her time and that the information was secure in her download file, where she could peruse it at leisure. Having completed her scan, she typed

GO MAIL

to check her electronic mailbox. She found a request for a recipe from another CompuServe user, whom she had "met" earlier via one of the service's Citizens' Band Simulators. Not wanting to spend her

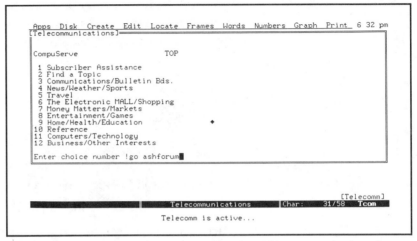

Figure 6.13: CompuServe's top-level menu in a Telecommunications frame

online time composing a response, Eileen made a mental note to check the download file for her correspondent's electric mailbox number, so she could prepare a response to send the next time she used CompuServe. By this time it was quite late, so Eileen bypassed the opportunity to chat on the Citizens' Band Simulator, and logged off instead.

Her work done for the evening, Eileen quit Framework III, shut down the computer, and closed up for the night.

EXPLORING FURTHER

Before we leave telecommunications, we should discuss several more telecommunications features of Framework III. First, we'll learn how you can create a Phone Book database in the Library and use it to have your modem dial your phone automatically. Then we'll take a brief look at Framework III's terminal emulation capabilities and at transferring files directly between computers without a modem.

AUTOMATIC PHONE DIALING

You can easily create a Phone Book frame in the Library. Since frames in the Library are always available on the desktop, you can call your Phone Book at any time. Later, in Chapter 7, you'll learn how to create a *macro* to do so. The Phone Book database is a four-column database, with the headings

Last Name
First Name
Home Phone
Work Phone

To create the Phone Book, press

Shuttle (Scroll Lock)	(to switch cabinets)
Home	(to move to the Library cabinet)
Return	(to open the Library cabinet)
In (+)	(to move inside the frame)
Ctrl-C	(to access the Create menu)
w4	(to set the width to 4; optionally, you could set a height value here)
d	(to create the new database)

Version Note

In Framework II, the Library included two preconfigured macros: Alt-F9 and Alt-F10. Pressing Alt-F9 displayed a Zoom view of the Phone Book, no matter where in Framework III you were currently working. Alt-F10 would dial a selected phone number. However, Framework III does not include these macros, but uses Alt-F9 and Alt-F10 for other purposes. You'll learn about the new Library macros as well as how to recreate the Framework II macros in Chapter 7.

Next, enter the four column headings for the fields in the database, and enter any names and phone numbers you want.

Having your telephone directory at hand on the desktop is, of course, a great convenience. Moreover, it need not be in the form described here—you can tailor it as you see fit. You might want to add addresses, notes, or other information.

To open the Phone Book from within any other frame, press:

Shuttle (Scroll Lock)	(to access the other cabinets)
Home	(to move up to the Library cabinet)
In (+)	(to move into the Library cabinet)
arrow keys, if necessary	(to move to the Phone Book frame)
Zoom (F9)	(to display the phone book on the screen)

To locate a number, follow these keystrokes after opening the Phone Book frame:

Home	(to move to the first column)
Ctrl-L	(to open the Locate menu)
S	(to select the Search option)
name	(enter the name to find)
Return	(to record your selection)
Tab, as many times as necessary	(to move the highlight to the phone number)

If you have a modem, Framework III will dial any number in this directory (or anywhere on the desktop) automatically, by means of the menu choice Point and Dial Number found on the Apps menu. When you select this option, the message

DIALING

will appear in the message area, along with your selected phone number. You will hear your modem play the tones of the number as it dials. The message area will then display

Pick up phone, then when dialing complete, press Spacebar

That's all there is to it! If you keep all your frequently used phone numbers in the Library's Phone Book, this feature can be a real timesaver. In the next chapter, we'll show you how to create a macro to open the Phone Book, and we'll look at a couple of programs you can write that will use these features to maintain a log of the calls you make.

TERMINAL EMULATION

Terminal emulation is a feature included principally for people who need to log onto a corporate mainframe computer. Such computers generally expect those who use their files to be working from a "dumb terminal"—a workstation including a keyboard and screen, but no computing powers of its own. Generally, a terminal will allow you full-screen editing, which is not available in most telecommunications software, although you have a form of it in Framework III's telecommunications component. To use terminal emulation, press

Ctrl-A	(to open the Apps menu)
T	(to select the Telecommunications menu)
S	(to open the Setup submenu)
E	(to turn Emulation on)

You can begin terminal emulation at any time during a telecommunications session by following these keystrokes. However, you will then have to press B to select the Begin/Resume Session option.

You may choose from among these five types of terminals:

- DEC VT-100
- Televideo 920
- IBM 3101
- Admiral 3A
- Adds Viewpoint

To select a terminal, select the Terminal option from the Setup submenu and press Return. The selected terminal will cycle through these five types, changing each time you press Return.

If you subscribe to an online service such as Dow Jones, CompuServe, or The Source, you can try out terminal emulation on these services. The most common type of terminal is the VT-100. Choose the appropriate menu from the service to let it know you will be using terminal emulation, and turn emulation on in the Setup menu.

Framework III behaves somewhat differently when terminal emulation is on:

- The screen will change so that it now looks similar to the form shown in Figure 6.14.

- Even if you have a color screen, the terminal screen will be black and white.

```
/SCR xyz    Scramble on "xyz"
/SMC xyz    Scr & Monitor Clear on "xyz"
/XCL xyz    Xmt CLear & monitor scr
/UNS        Unscramble (xmt & rcv clear)
/SQU x      Squelch by handle
/SQU uid    Squelch by User ID
/NOECHO     Turn off input echoing
/ECHO       Restore input echoing
/EXIT       Exit
/BAND x     Switch to Band "x"
/MENU       Exit
/TOP        Go to your TOP page
/MAIN       Go to page CIS-1
/GO mm-n    Go to Page "mm-n"
/FIND xxx   Find topic xxx
/OFF        Log off CompuServe
/VERSION    Displays CB version number




   Telecomm is active...
```

Figure 6.14: The telecommunications screen during terminal emulation

- If you press Ctrl-PrtSc while using terminal emulation, a snapshot of the screen, rather than the entire contents of the Telecommunications frame, is sent to the capture file.

- Control characters typed at the keyboard or contained in macros are sent to the remote computer, even if they normally activate Framework III menu commands.

To leave emulation mode while engaged in a telecommunications session, press Ctrl-Break or Instruct (Ins). This will not interrupt communications, but it will return you to the desktop. You can then move the cursor into the active Telecommunications frame, but you will have to use the Begin/Resume Session option to return to the terminal screen and resume communications. Alternatively—if the remote computer will permit it—you can turn emulation off, and resume communications inside the active Telecommunications frame.

HARDWIRE TRANSFERS

If you need to send information to another computer that is nearby—perhaps to send a text file to a computer that cannot read disks formatted under MS-DOS—you might consider the "hardwire" method. This involves connecting your computer's serial port directly to that of the other computer by means of a special type of RS-232 interface. (The technical description is that it has "pins 2 and 3 crossed," which simply means that the wires are crossed so that your computer's output channel is connected directly to the other computer's input channel, and vice versa.) The only other change you need to make is to select the Direct Connect option by pressing D while in the Setup Options submenu.

Assuming that the other computer has telecommunications software that is compatible with Framework III, you can then proceed just as though you were dealing with another computer by means of a modem. The advantages are twofold:

- There is less chance of interference in the signal, because you won't be dealing with potentially noisy phone lines.

- You are not limited by the speed of your modem. PCs can comfortably handle baud rates up to 19,200. If the other computer can be set to a comparable baud rate, you can communicate at 19,200 baud instead of the more common 2400 or 1200 baud that most modems can handle. In any case, you can communicate at the other computer's highest baud rate. In some special circumstances, you may even be able to communicate at rates as high as 38,400 baud!

SUMMARY

Telecommunications is Framework III's final productivity component. With this component, you can perform all of the standard telecommunications tasks:

- Conversing in terminal mode
- Uploading text files
- Downloading text files

- Performing protocol transfers in either direction
- Emulating a dumb terminal

Framework III telecommunications can be used easily from the desktop. You have access to all of Framework III's features while using it, and you can even work elsewhere on the desktop while telecommunications is proceeding.

Framework III will save the communications parameters you use most frequently in setup files, which you can install on the main Telecommunications menu and recall with three keystrokes. It will also automatically capture the contents of your telecommunications dialogues to disk.

An Introduction to FRED Programming

OVERVIEW

INTRODUCTION

WHILE STUDYING SPREADSHEET, DATABASE, AND word frames, we have learned to write formulas and to use several categories of functions that begin with the @ character. Formulas and functions are the elements of Framework III's built-in programming language, called FRED.

We've seen two general uses for formulas: producing calculated values and performing certain "programmed" activities. In spreadsheets and databases, we've written formulas primarily to calculate values. We've learned that a single formula can result in many calculated values. In spreadsheets, formulas can be copied down or across a range of cells; in databases, a single formula, entered into the area behind a field name, results in calculated values for an entire field column.

But we've also used formulas to perform tasks that deal with entire frames rather than a single cell or range of cells. Specifically, we've written formulas behind Database frames to *filter* the database according to a specific criterion for selecting records. Once again, the primary result of such a formula, from our point of view as Framework III users, is a process, not a value. We've also written some printing formulas that affect entire frames.

In this chapter, we'll expand upon the subject of writing formulas and using functions. We'll now begin to think of these formulas and functions as *FRED programs*. However, this shift in our thinking is taking place at an arbitrary moment in our study of Framework III. In fact, every formula in Framework III, no matter how large or small, is a FRED program; furthermore, any spreadsheet cell, database field, or frame can store a FRED program. In this sense, we have been writing FRED programs all along.

But much more is possible with FRED programming than what we have been doing up to this point. As we begin to explore the versatility of FRED—and to see the range of processes that FRED can control—keep in mind that FRED's resources are available in any Framework III context. We'll examine a variety of programming examples in this chapter, but these examples will represent only a brief first glimpse at the full power of FRED. The purpose of this chapter is not so much to provide a text on how to program in FRED as it is to show you the capabilities available to you through FRED.

WHY WRITE PROGRAMS?

Given all the Framework III features we have discussed in previous chapters, you might well wonder why we need a programming language at all. What powers can the complexities of programming add to the considerable capabilities that are already built into Framework III?

The answer is not simple, primarily because you can exploit FRED at several levels—beyond what you have already learned about writing formulas and using functions. Your use of FRED will depend on your own programming requirements, as well as on the extent to which you are inclined to explore and master the sometimes intricate details of the programming language. Some personal computer users enjoy learning the logic of computer programming; others prefer to work within the simpler confines of a predefined software environment.

Thinking in general terms, we could propose three levels of FRED programming. From first to last, these levels offer progressively more power and assume a progressively more sophisticated understanding of FRED:

1. The first level involves writing ''convenience'' programs that save time and give you shortcuts to accomplishing essential Framework III activities. At this level, we'll be discussing a special kind of FRED program called a *macro*. Macros are accessible to anyone—even people who do not care to learn how to program. A macro can streamline your day-to-day use of Framework III, allowing you to perform the most common tasks with just a couple of keystrokes.

2. The second level involves writing programs that actually add new computational or procedural capabilities to Framework III. In this category, you might write formulas—long or short—that perform specific arithmetic tasks for which Framework III does not already have a built-in function. Or you might write programs that work with Framework III documents in new ways—combining data, producing

reports, controlling procedures, and automating complex activities. This kind of programming delves more deeply into FRED's resources, as we will see in examples later in this chapter.

3. The most advanced level of programming involves writing "turnkey" programs that take complete control over an entire session with Framework III. Writing turnkey programs (in FRED or in any other computer language) is one of the jobs of the professional programmer. Turnkey programs are generally designed for users who want to accomplish a specific computerized task without having to learn anything about a particular software environment. The main goal of such a program is "user friendliness"—hiding the intricacies of computer operations and making the computer seem like a machine devoted exclusively to a single task.

As you explore FRED and gain experience with Framework III's features, you will find your own place in this range of programming levels. One guiding rule is that when Framework III is accomplishing everything you bought it for, you have reached your own appropriate level of expertise. A second rule is that Framework III, along with FRED, can always be stretched further than your current level, to achieve additional versatility and usefulness.

FRED PROGRAMMING

The programming features of FRED are represented by special categories of functions. Like the other functions we have seen, each programming function has its own name, beginning with the @ symbol.

Through these functions, FRED offers all the capabilities of other, more traditional PC programming languages, such as BASIC and Pascal. If you have already programmed in one of these languages, you will recognize the vocabulary that programmers use to describe these capabilities. Otherwise, the following brief descriptions of the various categories of programming activities and structures will help to introduce you to some of the concepts involved in programming:

- *Control over input and output.* Input and output activities involve accepting values from the keyboard, displaying information on the screen, sending data to the printer, and creating inter-active *dialogues,* in which the computer reacts appropriately to values entered from the keyboard.

- *Variables and arrays.* These programming structures allow you to set aside specific places for values that are required during a program's performance. You can establish *global* variables, available throughout the program, or *local* variables, available in only a certain section of the program.

- *Decisions and flow of control.* Often a program will have to choose among alternative courses of action, depending on some current condition in the program. For this reason, programming languages provide ways of expressing logical conditions on which decisions can be made.

- *Structured loops.* A loop allows a program to repeat the performance of a certain sequence of activity a controllable number of times.

- *Subroutines.* Subroutines make it possible to organize a program into functional *modules,* each of which is responsible for accomplishing a distinct task. Subroutines can operate on *parameters,* information passed to them from other parts of the program.

Unlike other languages, FRED is designed to operate exclusively in the Framework III environment and to take advantage of all of Framework III's features. A FRED program can access and perform any of Framework III's menu and keyboard operations—including creating new frames, sorting and searching, formatting and styling, graphing and printing, moving and copying information, selecting frames, recalculating formulas, and even placing a new formula behind a frame. In short, FRED and Framework III rely on each other for the resources that build upon each other's power.

GETTING READY TO WRITE A FRED PROGRAM

The Edit key and the Zoom key are the tools that allow us to enter a formula into the area behind a frame. We have seen the process several times: you begin by moving the highlight to the border of the frame (or to the spreadsheet cell or database field) where you want to store a formula. Then you press

Edit (F2)   (to move the cursor to the edit line)

Zoom (F9)   (to expand the edit line into full-screen mode)

The full-screen edit mode allows you to create a formula—or a FRED program, as we are now saying—that consists of multiple lines of text. While you are writing a program, you can use Framework III's menus and keyboard functions to edit or style your program. For example, the Locate menu allows you to perform search and replace operations on a program. The Words menu permits styles such as boldfacing and underlining in programs.

You'll often want some way of *documenting,* in English, the activities that a program performs, especially when a program is long or complex. Like most programming languages, FRED allows you to incorporate ''comments'' into your program. Any line of your program can contain a comment or a part of a comment. The semicolon character (;) marks the beginning of a comment.

A line can be entirely devoted to a comment, in which case you'll place the semicolon at the beginning of the line:

```
; FRED will read this line as a comment.
```

Or you can place a comment at some point following, but on the same line as, a part of the program itself. FRED ignores any text that you enter to the right of the semicolon character:

```
; The following line contains a formula and a comment:
SixMoSales > 100000      ; filter the database
```

In either case, the purpose of commenting is to provide explanations of the logic and structure of your program. Liberal use of commenting will help other people understand the programs you write. Commenting will also remind you of the logic of your own program, several weeks or months after you have written it.

Later in this chapter, we'll be writing some fairly complex programs. You should get into the habit of writing comments while you are developing a program. Many programmers promise themselves that they'll go back and insert comments after the program is complete; this promise is frequently broken. As we proceed, you'll see many examples of fully commented programs.

When you have finished writing a program behind a frame, press the Zoom key (F9) to move back to the single edit line. The Return key enters the formula into the frame and calculates its result. To enter a formula without immediately calculating it, press the Escape key. You can calculate a frame's formula at any time by moving the highlight to the frame's border and pressing the Recalc key (F5).

Framework III's Print menu allows you to print a FRED program at any stage of the programming task. To do so, first move the highlight to the border of the frame that contains the formula. Open the Output Options submenu of the Print menu, and toggle the Formulas Only option to its *on* status:

    on Formulas Only

Finally, select the Begin option of the Print menu. Framework III will print the formula that resides behind the frame, rather than the contents of the frame.

We refer to a printed copy of the lines of a program as a *listing*. Obviously, producing a program listing is a good way for you to study your work, search for mistakes, and consider ways to improve the program's performance.

In the remaining sections of this chapter, we will move rather quickly through the elements of FRED programming. First we'll look at the Library's tools, learning what they can do and how they are organized. Then we'll survey some of the most important FRED programming functions, and we'll learn about Framework III's help facilities for programming.

During our visit to The Sophisticated Palate, we'll return to Eileen Wilcox's Packaged Goods Inventory database, to look at a short program we talked about briefly in Chapter 5.

Finally, in the Exploring Further section of this chapter, we'll examine a complete example of a significant FRED program and learn how to create a user-defined function. The example program controls the process of merging information from two databases and producing printed documents from the combined data. Mastering the details of this program will be difficult if you have no programming background; however, you should read through to the end of this chapter anyway. Even if you don't understand the workings of the program itself, you'll finish with a better sense of what FRED can do.

THE USES OF THE LIBRARY

Framework III gives you a powerful tool to aid you in your programming—the Library. Within the Library cabinet you will see, among other things, four major subheadings, as shown in Figure 7.1:

- Macros
- Abbreviations
- User-defined functions
- Assumptions

Each of these headings contains examples of different types of FRED formulas and programs, some of which you can use as they stand. Others you can modify to suit your needs.

In addition, you can create new programs of each of these types. In this section, we'll examine each of these types of programs, and experiment with at least one of each. We'll look into the macros that are supplied with the Library in some detail, as they are quite powerful and useful. Since any frame in the Library can be called directly by other frames, this is an excellent way to keep handy any special blocks of text, formulas, or even complex programs that you will want to use often.

CREATING LIBRARY MACROS

You have already heard about Framework III's ability to create *macros*—strings of characters that can be invoked with a single keystroke combination. The command to create a macro is

Ctrl-C   (to open the Create menu)

M   (to create a macro or abbreviation)

You will then see the message

Enter macro or abbreviation for recording—ESC cancels entry

```
Macros
  -  (Alt-F1)      ; Display Library Frame
  -  (Alt-F2)      ; Save Library Frame
  -  (Alt-F3)      ; Type Current Date
  -  (Alt-F4)      ; Type Current Time
  -  (Alt-F5)      ; Available Memory
     1   (Alt-F6) ; Memos and Letters
     -  1.1  Memorandum
     -  1.2  Company Letter
     -  1.3  Personal Letter
     -  1.4  Exit
  -  (ALT-F7)      ; Cut
  -  (ALT-F8)      ; Paste
  -  (ALT-F9)      ; Display Phone Book
  -  (ALT-F10)     ; Point and Dial Voice Call
  -  Return to Caller
  -  Cut Paste Buffer
Abbreviations   —  alt-backspace
  -  CA    ; California
  -  MA    ; Massachusetts
  -  fed   ; federal government
  -  fw    ; Framework III    alt - number /letter .
Assumptions
  -  Your Name           ; For letters, memos
  -  Your Company        ;Company name
  -  Company Address 1
  -  Company Address 2
  -  Inflation           ;Avg rate for past qtr
  -  Interest            ;Prime rate for past wk
Phone Book
```

Figure 7.1: The Framework III Library

Before you create the macro, you must decide which key will execute it. It must be a combination of the Alt key and another key. All of the following characters are available for representing FRED macros:

- The 26 letters of the alphabet
- The 10 digits
- The 10 function keys

When you have entered the key you want to use, a frame will be created in the Library, under the Macros subheading, with a label containing the name of your chosen key. The message area then displays

Recording library macro/abbreviation entry—press Ctrl-Break to finish

All the keystrokes you type, until you press Ctrl-Break, will be recorded in the contents area of this special frame. This is probably the easiest way to write FRED programs, since you can include any keystrokes you might use in any task, as well as text, and Framework III takes care of all the syntax and structure for you. The only catch is that the keystrokes must be valid. You can't create text on an empty desktop, for example; there must be a frame of some sort to contain it. Similarly, if you issue commands among your keystrokes, they must be valid in the environment in which you issue them. Let's try a few examples. Then we'll look into the frames, to see what has happened.

A SIMPLE MACRO EXAMPLE

First, we'll create a macro that enters your first and last names into a frame. It's quite simple. Press

Ctrl-C	(to open the Create menu)
E	(to create an Empty frame where your keystrokes can be recorded)
Ctrl-C	(to open the Create menu)
M	(to create a macro)
Alt-N	(to select the key to which the macro will be assigned)
Fred Masters	(your name, followed by a space)
Ctrl-Break	(to terminate recording)

Now that you've recorded your macro, press Alt-N to invoke it. The macro will play back the keys that you have specified, entering your name into the contents area of the frame:

Fred Masters

Try it several more times, pressing Alt-N repeatedly. Each time you press Alt-N, the macro will perform its keystrokes:

Fred Masters Fred Masters Fred Masters

You can, of course, use a macro along with other keystrokes that you enter into the frame yourself. Press the Return key to move to the next line of what has now become a Word frame. Enter the following text:

My name is

Be sure to enter a space after *is*. Now press Alt-N once again, and the frame will read:

My name is Fred Masters

The name macro, though perhaps a bit trivial, illustrates a typical use of macros: to store a sequence of frequently used keystrokes that can be recalled with a single keystroke combination. But the power of macros goes well beyond this. Let's elaborate the name macro a bit, and incorporate a few commands.

We'll create a macro that enters your name and address into a frame, centered so that you can use it as a letterhead. In the steps that follow, substitute your own name and address for those in the example. Here are the keystrokes:

Ctrl-C	(to open the Create menu)
E	(to create an Empty frame where your keystrokes can be recorded)
Ctrl-C	(to open the Create menu)
M	(to create the macro)
Alt-N	(to select the key to which the name macro will be assigned)

Since you have already used Alt-N, this message will appear:

Library entry exists; overwrite it?
(y to overwrite, n to append, ESC to cancel)

Framework III warns you if you have already used a key for a macro, and gives you a chance to replace it, edit it, or choose another key.

(Of course, you can also edit a macro by opening its frame in the Library and editing it as you would any other text.) Press

Y	(to create a new macro with the same name)
Ctrl-W	(to open the Words menu
C	(to center the text)
Fred Masters	(your name)
Return	(to start a new line)
123 Calc Street	(your address)
Return	(to start a new line)
Ashton, TX 54321	(the rest of the address)
Return	(to start a new line)
Ctrl-W	(to open the Words menu)
A	(to align the following text of the letter with the left margin)
Ctrl-Break	(to terminate recording)

Now let's take a look at what has happened. Follow these steps:

Shuttle (Scroll Lock)	(to shuttle to the cabinets)
↑ or ↓	(to select the Library cabinet)
Return	(to open the Library cabinet)
In (+)	(to enter the frame)
↓	(to select the frame labeled Alt-N)
Zoom (F9)	(to look at the contents area of the frame)

You should see the text

```
{CTRL-W}cFred Masters{RETURN}123 Calc Street
{RETURN}Ashton, TX54321{RETURN}{CTRL-W}a
```

Note that this is the exact series of keystrokes you used to enter the macro. Notice also that if you made any mistakes, and corrected them with the Backspace or Delete key, the incorrect keys will also appear, followed by

{BACKSPACE}

or

{LEFTARROW}{DEL}

FRED gives a name to each keystroke, placing the nonalphabetic keys in curly braces, and records exactly what you type. You can see a sampling of nonalphabetic keys in Table 7.1.

Library macros are different from other programs in several important respects. First, as you noticed, the keystrokes you entered were recorded in the *contents* area of the frame, rather than the formula area. In our previous encounters with FRED programming, we used the formula area behind the frame, which we reached by pressing the Edit Formula key (F2). Second, Library macros require no FRED language commands other than the names of the keys. Third, because the macros are in the Library, you can call them whenever you are using Framework III.

ABBREVIATIONS

As we also noted in Chapter 1, you can store complex series of keystrokes in an abbreviation in the Library, as well as in a macro. If your macro is primarily a text macro to be used in a Word frame, as are the ones we've tried out so far, it might be more advantageous to store the text as an abbreviation. Framework III does not limit the number of abbreviations you can use, but you are limited as to how many macros you can create. Moreover, it's much easier to create a mnemonic abbreviation than a mnemonic macro name. For example, you might want to make your Alt-N macro into an abbreviation called NAD, for name and

Table 7.1: A Sampling of FRED's Key Names

Cursor-Movement or Highlight-Movement Keys	
{uparrow}	↑
{dnarrow}	↓
{rightarrow}	→
{leftarrow}	←
{ctrl-uparrow}	Ctrl-↑
{ctrl-dnarrow}	Ctrl-↓
{ctrl-rightarrow}	Ctrl-→
{ctrl-leftarrow}	Ctrl-←
{home}	Home
{end}	End
{ctrl-home}	Ctrl-Home
{ctrl-end}	Ctrl-End
{uplevel} or {out}	Out
{dnlevel} or {in}	In
{ctrl-uplevel} or {ctrl-out}	Ctrl-Out
{ctrl-dnlevel} or {ctrl-in}	Ctrl-In
{pgup}	PgUp
{pgdn}	PgDn
{ctrl-pgup}	Ctrl-PgUp
{ctrl-pgdn}	Ctrl-PgDn
{tab}	Tab
{backtab}	Shift-Tab
Miscellaneous Keys	
{return}	Return
{backspace}	Backspace
{del}	Delete
{esc}	Escape

Table 7.1: A Sampling of FRED's Key Names (continued)

Function Keys	
{f1}	Help
{f2}	Edit Formula
{f3}	Drag
{f4}	Size
{f5}	Recalc
{f6}	Extend Select
{f7}	Move
{f8}	Copy
{f9}	Zoom
{f10}	View

address, or LH, for letterhead (as in all other aspects of FRED, it doesn't matter whether you use uppercase or lowercase names).

It's easy to change a macro into an abbreviation. Select the frame in the Library labeled {alt-n}, edit the label so that the label is the abbreviation you want, and use the Move key (F7) to move the frame from the Macros subheading into the Abbreviations subheading.

Let's try creating an abbreviation from scratch.

Suppose you were writing a letter to a friend describing the wonders of Framework III. Naturally, you would be using the words *Framework III* quite frequently, so they would be a natural candidate for an abbreviation. To set up an abbreviation, press the following keys:

Ctrl-C   (to select the Create submenu)

M   (to select Macros and Abbreviations)

You will then see the message

Enter macro key or abbreviation for recording—
ESC cancels entry

in the message area. You now type

> **fw**

and the message

> **Recording library macro/abbreviation entry—press Ctrl-Break to finish**

appears in the message area. Type

> **Framework III**

and press Ctrl-Break. Your abbreviation is now recorded in the Library. To use the abbreviation, press Alt-Backspace, and in place of the letters *fw*, *Framework III* will appear.

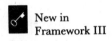 New in
Framework III

In Framework III, abbreviations can be expanded automatically when you type them. In the Word Options submenu of the Words menu, set Expand Abbreviations on. Then try typing the fw macro. As soon as you press the spacebar, or a punctuation key, the macro expands automatically. You can use this feature to speed up typing in word processing tasks as well as when entering FRED programs.

For instance, in the next section you'll learn about a common function called @PERFORMKEYS. You might create a macro called *pk* to expand to @PERFORMKEYS whenever you type *pk*. The @PERFORMKEYS function is always followed by a left parenthesis, which Framework III considers punctuation. Therefore, the abbreviation will expand. However, as you'll see, Framework III already offers a shorter version of @PERFORMKEYS.

THE @PERFORMKEYS FUNCTION AND SPECIAL KEY NAMES
There may be times when you want something that is similar to a macro—that is, a series of keystrokes to be entered automatically—but you don't want to create it "on the fly." The FRED function @PERFORMKEYS can accomplish the same thing as a macro in other contexts.

Significantly, FRED allows you to place *any* combination of keystrokes inside the @PERFORMKEYS string, including the cursor-movement keys, the Out (–) and In (+) keys, the Ctrl key, the function keys, and all the other keys that are essential to the Framework III environment.

@PERFORMKEYS recognizes special names for all these keys; Table 7.1 lists some of the most important of these names. Notice that all of these names must be enclosed in curly braces. They must also be included inside the quotation marks of the @PERFORMKEYS function's string parameter.

In Framework III, @PERFORMKEYS can be abbreviated @PK. You can use the two commands interchangeably.

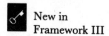

New in
Framework III

Here is a quick sequence of examples. Suppose you want to write a macro that creates an Empty frame. You could prepare the following function:

@performkeys("{ctrl-c}e")

The *{ctrl-c}* keyboard command opens the Create menu, and the *e* selects the Empty/Word Frame option. If you want to expand your macro to assign the label *Test* to this new frame, you would edit the formula to read like this:

@pk("{ctrl-c}eTest{return}")

After the Empty frame has been created, the keystrokes *Test* represent the label, and the *{return}* command enters the label into the frame's border. Finally, if you want the macro to move the highlight down into the contents area of the frame, you will add one more element:

@performkeys("{ctrl-c}eTest{return}{in}")

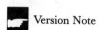

Version Note

Although In (+) and Out (–) are proper Framework III keys, earlier versions of Framework called them *Down Level* and *Up Level*, respectively. To keep FRED programs from one version to the next compatible, you can use {dnlevel} and {uplevel} interchangeably with {in} and {out}.

The *{in}* keystroke moves the highlight into the frame. Notice that a @PERFORMKEYS string can contain any combination of regular characters and special keys.

To implement this simple program, you create an Empty frame, and place the program in the programming area behind the frame by pressing the Edit key (F2), just as you did for spreadsheets and databases. When you select this frame and press Recalc (F5), the program will be executed, producing the Empty frame shown in Figure 7.2.

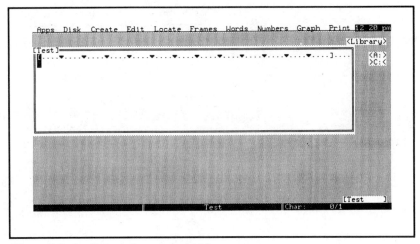

Figure 7.2: An Empty frame created by a macro

MACROS SUPPLIED WITH THE LIBRARY

Let's look now in greater depth at the macros that are supplied with the Library. Figure 7.1 shows you the names of these macros as they appear in the Library, and Table 7.2 briefly explains their functions. You are, of course, free to modify them as you see fit, or to assign completely different macros to the function keys. However, the ones supplied are quite useful.

There are two ways to view the Library. (Remember that you select the Library by pressing Shuttle [Scroll Lock] and the ↑ or ↓ key.) First, you can select the Library and press Return, which gives you a narrow frame. Second, you can get a full-screen (Zoom) view by selecting the Library and pressing Recalc (F5). This recalculates the formula that is behind the Library cabinet itself.

As you will see in the next section on Framework II macros, there is also a third way: by using a Library macro to give you a full-screen view of the Library cabinet from anywhere in Framework III.

The first Framework III Library macro is assigned to the Alt-F1 key combination. This relatively simple macro will automatically reset any margins to 0 and remove paragraph indents on a paragraph of text selection. You can use it to quickly change formatting. You might use this macro as a template for creating your own style macros.

Table 7.2: Functions of the Library Macros

Keyboard Name	Description
Alt-F1	Resets the left margin in text frame to 0 and removes paragraph indentation.
Alt-F2	Creates an empty frame at the top of the current outline section, highlighting the new frame.
Alt-F3	Types the date using the system clock.
Alt-F4	Shows the printed width of a spreadsheet or database (excluding offsets and margins).
Alt-F5	Displays the amount of unused memory still available in your system.
Alt-F6	Allows you to select any of several predefined formats for letters and memos from a menu.
Alt-F7	Creates a template for snaking columns. Prompts you for information about column length, characters per inch, number of columns, and whether you want Automatic Page Creation on or off.
Alt-F8	Sums the numbers in the spreadsheet column above the cursor.
Alt-F9	Removes hard carriage returns from the end of each line—especially helpful for telecommunicated files.
Alt-F10	Mini calculator for entering and evaluating a numeric expression on the fly.

The Alt-F2 macro creates an Empty frame at the top of the current section of an outline, leaving the highlight on that frame. You can use this macro to add to an outline quickly without having to worry about cursor position. Ordinarily, you would have to add a frame below the top position, then move it. This macro does it all in one step.

Alt-F3 types the current date (as read from the system clock). This date is a string value that can be inserted into any cell, field, or document that will accept a string value. For instance, typing Alt-F3 at the top of a document will insert

March 24, 1989

You cannot perform date arithmetic with the results, because they are string values, not date values. The formula used for this entry is

@pk(@date4(@today))

Alt-F4 will show you the actual printed width of a spreadsheet or database (not including offsets and margins). Use this macro to determine if a spreadsheet or database will fit onto your paper, or, if you are working with specific forms, if it will fit the form size.

Alt-F5 tells you how much memory is currently available in your computer. It uses a FRED function called @MEMAVAIL, which you can use behind any frame or cell for the same purpose. However, Alt-F5 will supply the information in the message area, in a form that is easily readable:

You have 488,992 more bytes of memory available.

Moreover, like other Library macros, it can be used at any point in Framework III, without disturbing your current working environment.

Alt-F6 is a menu of templates for letters and memos. Later in the chapter, you'll learn how to write a program that produces a menu like this one. You can, of course, add your own templates to the outline contained under the Alt-F6 subheading, or modify the existing ones.

Alt-F7 creates a template for snaked frames (a new feature of Framework III; see Chapter 2). This is the most complex of the ten function-key macros. It prompts you for information about the size and number of columns you want to create and other details, finally creating the appropriate frames for a multicolumn document. If you want to work with multiple snaking columns, you'll appreciate this macro. More advanced programmers may find it useful to examine this script.

Alt-F8 is an interesting macro that totals a column of values in a spreadsheet. Basically, it builds an @SUM statement that includes the rows above the cursor. The cursor should be placed in an empty cell at the bottom of the column to add. Only contiguous numeric cells will be totaled, so if there is a blank cell between two entries, only the cells after the blank will contribute to the total. However, Alt-F8 will ignore a label entry in the column, and it will include any cells containing formulas.

Alt-F9 is particularly useful if you use telecommunications to send and receive text files. It will remove the hard carriage returns from the ends of lines. The best way to use it is to be sure that two carriage returns separate paragraphs, then move to the frame border and press Alt-F9. All the paragraphs will be reformed. If paragraphs are not separated by two carriage returns, you can add them manually or use Extend Select (F6) to select those lines that belong in a single paragraph. Then press Alt-F9. Using this method, you can reform paragraphs one at a time.

Alt-F10 is a small calculator macro. It creates a frame called Calc and prompts you to enter a calculation. For instance, if you enter

    33*45/3*4

the value 1980 is entered in the frame. To calculate another formula, press Edit Formula (F2) and either edit the old calculation or enter a new one.

FRAMEWORK II LIBRARY MACROS   Although the macros that come with Framework III are useful, there were some built-in macros that worked well in Framework II. We thought you might like to see how they work, and maybe enter them into new Library macros if you like them.

The first Framework II macro opens the Library frame for you. This is the same as selecting the Library and recalculating it, but with two advantages. First, you need not leave your current location to select the Library before viewing it. Second, as the message area will indicate, you can return immediately to your previous working location by pressing the Escape key. This can save quite a few keystrokes. Here's the FRED program that runs the Library Open macro:

```
@echo(#OFF),@performkeys("{esc}{esc}{esc}{esc}{ctrl-L}
GLibrary{return}{f9}"),
```

```
@echo(#ON),@eraseprompt,("Press ESC to return to where you
were", 22),
@keyfilter({esc},Return to Caller)
```

To add a macro to your Library, you need to open an Empty frame and label it with an Alt-key combination. Press Edit Formula (F2), then press Zoom (F9). Now enter the formula. When you are finished entering the formula, press Zoom (F9) again, then press Return. Finally, use the Move key (F7) to place the frame into the Library under Macros. Label the frame with curly braces and an Alt-key combination. For instance, call this macro

```
{Alt-1}
```

The @KEYFILTER function assigns a key on the keyboard to a frame whose formula is then executed. The cryptically named Return to Caller frame mentioned in the last line of the program is the frame assigned to the Escape key. It resets the key filter, closes the Library frame, and returns you to your original position. You'll have to create this frame inside the Library. Then press Edit Formula (F2) and enter the following short script:

```
@keyfilter({esc})
@pk("{ctrl-out}{return}{ctrl-L}G{return}")
```

The macro assigned to Alt-F2 in Framework II was called Save Library Frame. It is also used to manage the Library. It will save the current version of the Library to disk anytime you invoke it. Again, you can accomplish the same thing by selecting the Library and pressing Ctrl-Return, but like the macro we just created, this one works no matter where you are located. If you have just created a new macro or abbreviation, you might want to use this key, for the same reason that you should always save your work frequently. Here is the script for the Alt-F2 macro:

```
@local(Start),Start : = @setselection("Library"),
@pk("{ctrl-return}"),@setselection(Start)
```

Warning: This macro will not work properly if you call it from a frame with no name. Be sure the frame you are on or in when you call this macro has a name.

Alt-F3 performs the same function in Framework II and Framework III.

In Framework II, Alt-F4 returned the current time as a string (much as Alt-F3 returns a date). We'll include a simplified form of the original Framework II Alt-F4 macro:

```
@pk(@time1(@today))
```

Notice that this formula and the one that returns a date (Alt-F3) do *not* include the quotation marks usually found in @PERFORMKEYS statements. If they did, the formula would be entered, rather than the result of the formula. You cannot perform time arithmetic with the results, because they are string values, not time values. Later, however, we'll modify the time for use in conjunction with a user-defined function so that we can use the string value to do time arithmetic. We'll also look at an application where this can be useful.

Alt-F5 and Alt-F6 perform the same functions in Framework II and Framework III.

In Framework II, Alt-F7 and Alt-F8 were used as cut-and-paste tools; however, the same tools are now available in Framework III as Shift-F7 and Shift-F8.

In Framework II, Alt-F9 was used to display a special Phone Book frame that was included in the Library. We showed you how to recreate the Phone Book in Chapter 6, and how to use it to first locate and then dial a number automatically. Here, we'll rewrite the Open Phone Book macro. In addition, we'll expand on that macro later in this chapter to show you how to create a Phone Log.

To create the macro that calls the phone book, first create an Empty frame inside the Library. The best way is to place the cursor over the last macro you created, {Alt-T}, and then press Ctrl-C E. Now label the new frame {*Alt-9*}. The macro you will enter is:

```
@echo(#OFF),@performkeys("{esc}{esc}{esc}{esc}{ctrl-L}
GLibrary.Phone Book{return}{f9}"),@echo(#ON),
@eraseprompt,("Press ESC to return to where you were", 22),
@keyfilter({esc},Return to Caller)
```

Notice that this is virtually the same macro we used to call the Library, but the frame Library.Phone Book has replaced the original call to the Library. Therefore, you can use the macro you already created. To do so, position the cursor on the {Alt-1} frame in the Library and press:

Edit (F2)	(to begin editing)
Zoom (F9)	(to zoom open)
Extend Select (F6)	(to begin selecting the macro)
PgDn	(to select the whole macro)
Cut (Shift-F7)	(to copy the macro to the buffer)
Escape	(to return to the frame)
↓, several times	(to highlight the {Alt-9} frame)
Formula Edit (F2)	(to begin formula edit)
Zoom (F9)	(to zoom the formula)
Paste (Shift-F8)	(to paste the formula)

Now you can edit the reference to the Library to read *Library.Phone Book*. Press Zoom (F9), then press Return to finish entering the macro.

You may want to enter several names and numbers to your phone book. Remember, the Phone Book database is always available. All you have to do is press Alt-9.

As you saw in the Chapter 6, you can select a phone number, then press Ctrl-A T P for the Point and Dial command. In Framework II, there was a macro that did the same (Alt-F10). You can easily create a macro of your own by pressing Ctrl-C M and then repeating the preceding keystrokes in the macro. Let's call this macro Alt-0. To create it, press:

Ctrl-C	(to open the Create menu)
M	(to begin macro recording)
Alt-0	(to name the macro)
Ctrl-A	(to open the Apps menu)
T	(to open the Telecommunications submenu)

P	(to Point and Dial)
Ctrl-Break	(to end the macro recording)

We'll use this macro in the next section.

WRITING A MACRO PROGRAM

Let's look at an example of some Library macros in use. First, we'll write the macro as a program, and then move it to the Library, just to get a better feel for programming and for the power of the Library macros. Suppose you need to log your phone calls for business purposes. You set up a database called Phone Log in the Library, with the following column heads:

Date
Time
Number
Party

Use the Entry Format for Data option on the Numbers menu to set the Date, Time, and Number fields to Character format.

Next, Framework III users will need to create a small macro that replaces the Alt-F4 macro used in earlier versions to provide the current time as a string value. Earlier in this chapter, we showed you how to recreate a version of the Framework II Alt-F4 macro. In case you didn't follow those steps, we'll recreate the Alt-T macro here.

Create an empty cell, name it {Alt-T}, and then press Edit Formula (F2). Enter the following line of FRED code:

```
@pk(@time1(@today))
```

Press Return to finish entering the formula, then move the {Alt-T} frame into the Library with the other macros.

We'll use several Library macros to fill in the column entries. Follow these steps:

Alt-9	(to open the Phone Book)
Home	(to move to the first column)
Ctrl-L	(to open the Locate menu)

S	(to select the Search option)
Name	(the name of the party you want to call)
Tab, several times	(to move to the phone number)
Alt-0	(to dial the number)
Cut (Shift-F7)	(to copy the number to the Cut Paste Buffer)
Zoom (F9)	(to close the Phone Book)

Next, you'll open the Phone Log, and move to the first empty cell in the Date column (later, you'll incorporate some FRED functions into a macro that will do this for you automatically). Continue with:

Alt-F3	(to record the date)
Tab	(to move to the Time column)
Spacebar	(to begin entering text)
Alt-T	(to enter the time, which begins with a number, as text)
Tab	(to move to the Number column)
Alt-F8	(to bring back the phone number from the Cut Paste Buffer)
Return	(to record the number)

Now we'll write the macro that accomplishes this task automatically. We'll create the macro as a frame on the desktop, to practice programming, and then use the Move key (F7) to move it to the Library.

A few considerations must be taken into account when setting up this Phone Log. Most obviously, why not simply enter the formula

`@date(@today)`

in the cells of the first column, and the formula

`@time1(@today)`

in those of the second? Principally because, if you used date and time formulas, they would all be recalculated automatically if you hit the Recalc key (F5) for any reason. If the dates and times were formulas rather than strings, every one of them would be reset to today's date and the current time whenever you used the log, which would result in no log at all. Thus, the string dates supplied by the Alt-F3 macro are much more useful for the purpose. We'll also use the Alt-T macro again.

Now let's create the Phone Log macro. Begin by creating an Empty frame. Label it

> {Alt-P}

and use the Edit Formula (F2) and Zoom (F9) keys to get to the full-screen programming mode. Figure 7.3 shows the formula that will be entered behind this frame.

Again, we'll assume that you have called the Phone Book by pressing Alt-9, and already dialed your call. When you press Alt-P, your call will be recorded automatically. The statement

> @performkeys("{shift-f7}{out}")

```
{Alt-P}        ; Log Phone calls:
    ; This macro must be used after a phone number is selected
    ; from the Phone Book. It will automatically log the date,
    ; time, and number called.

    ; First copy the phone number to the buffer with the Cut macro;
    ; then leave the Phone Book.

    @performkeys("{alt-f7}{uplevel}"),

    ; Next select the Phone Log

    @setselection("library.phone log"),

    ; Open the log and locate the first empty cell in the
    ; first column:

    @performkeys("{f9}{ctrl-home}{ctrl-dnarrow}{dnarrow}"),

    ; Enter the date, time, and phone number

    @performkeys("{alt-f3}{tab} {alt-f4}{tab} {alt-f8}{tab}"),

    ; Remind the user that the Library will disappear when you
    ; press the Escape key:

    @prompt("Press ESC when finished")
```

Figure 7.3: A macro to call the Phone Log

copies the phone number to the buffer, and gets you out of the Phone Book. Next, the @SETSELECTION function, which you will learn a bit more about in the following section, tells Framework III to look for the frame that is specified in its parameter. The next problem is finding the first empty cell in the Phone Log. The next @PERFORMKEYS statement opens the log with the Zoom key. Ctrl-Home makes sure that you start in the upper left corner of the database. Ctrl-↓ automatically moves the highlight to the last cell in the column that contains data. (Note that you must have something—perhaps a dotted line—in cell A2 of the Phone Log, or the Ctrl-↓ command will automatically jump to the last row of the spreadsheet. A second ↓ moves down to the next cell, which is the first cell in the first empty row.)

The third @PERFORMKEYS statement could be included as part of the previous one, but it is separated here for clarity. This statement pastes the three essential items of data into the proper cells in the spreadsheet: date, time, and phone number.

Each of the macro keys included in the last @PERFORMKEYS statement generates prompts in the message area that will replace the prompt

Press ESC to return to where you were

which appeared when the Phone Book was opened with Alt-F9. Therefore, a prompt reminds you to press the Escape key after you have finished entering the details of the conversation.

Now that the Alt-P macro is complete, you can open the Library and move the frame into it, under the Macros subheading, using the Extend Select key (F6) and the Move key (F7).

ASSUMPTIONS

Assumptions can be any values that you use repeatedly. The usual reason for storing Assumptions in the Library is to have them on hand for recalculating spreadsheets. Suppose, for example, you have made various cost-price-profit analyses for different purposes in different spreadsheets. Each of these spreadsheets includes some assumptions you have made about the current interest rate and the current rate of inflation. You can store these values in frames (in the contents area, not in the formula area) under the Assumptions subheading in the Library. To use them, just refer to them as if they were FRED functions. For example, if you want to use the inflation rate as part of a formula in a cell, you might write a formula like this:

@sum(B3:B17)*@inflation

If the inflation rate changes, replace the figure in the Library Assumptions frame labeled Inflation with the new value, and any spreadsheet that refers to that frame will automatically take on the new value when you recalculate it.

As you can see from a cursory glance through the Assumptions in the Library, these frames can also store text. If you place the name of your company in the frame labeled Your Company, then any cell behind which you enter the formula

@your company

will display the name of your company. This may not be so useful for text values such as a name (an abbreviation might be more appropriate). However, it is a distinct advantage when you want to treat numbers as text, as in addresses and zip codes.

USER-DEFINED FUNCTIONS

One of the joys of a programming language such as FRED is its extensibility—if you need a function that it doesn't include, you can write it.

Suppose, for example, that you use a computer at home. The Internal Revenue Service requires you to log the time you spend on your computer for business purposes. FRED does have functions that will perform date arithmetic—@SUMDATE and @DIFFDATE. However, its equivalent time functions are complex. After we have looked further at FRED programming functions, we'll write a simpler function that will find the time elapsed between two times—the @DIFFTIME function. We'll also look at how the log should be set up, and suggest some ways of making it work automatically.

The FRED macro functions, @PERFORMKEYS and @SETSELECTION, are only two of many available programming functions. The next section of this chapter presents a survey of several other programming categories.

FRED PROGRAMMING FUNCTIONS

In this section, we'll look briefly at the various categories of programming activities and structures we discussed earlier, and we'll mention some of the functions FRED provides in these categories. These are the programming categories we'll look at:

- Input and output
- Variables and arrays
- Decisions
- Loops
- Subroutines
- Control of frames

For more information about the functions we discuss here, consult Appendix B, which presents a complete glossary of all the FRED functions. Also, the sample program in the final section of this chapter shows examples of many of these functions in use.

INPUT AND OUTPUT

Programs are said to be *interactive* if they can accept information that is entered from the keyboard while the program is running. Such programs often present prompts on the screen to tell the user what kind of input information is expected at that point in the program. FRED includes a group of functions that allow you to plan and write interactive programs. These functions present messages on the display screen and accept input information from the keyboard.

The @PROMPT and @ERASEPROMPT functions allow you to make programmed use of the message area below the Framework III desktop. @PROMPT places a message on the screen; @ERASEPROMPT erases any information currently in the message area.

For receiving information from the keyboard, using the edit line as the input location, FRED offers the @INPUTLINE function. This function can display a prompt at the bottom of the screen, and if you wish you can make it imitate several of the usual edit line characteristics.

@INPUTLINE causes FRED to wait for a value to be entered from the keyboard. When the user presses the Return key (to complete the input process), the input value itself is returned as the value of the @INPUTLINE function. Within a program, this value can be assigned to a variable for storage; for example:

Company : = @inputline("What company do you work for?")

If a program needs to display more information than will fit in the message area at the bottom of the screen, the @DISPLAY function can be used for displaying an entire existing frame on the desktop.

FRED also offers the @MENU function for displaying programmer-prepared menus on the screen and waiting for the user to select an option from the menu. To set up a menu, you create an Outline frame, with subframes that represent the menu's options. The formula residing behind each subframe provides instructions that FRED will follow when the user selects the corresponding menu option. @MENU takes, as its single parameter, a reference to the Outline frame that represents a menu of options. We'll see an example of @MENU later.

VARIABLES AND ARRAYS

Programs often require temporary storage space for numeric and string data values that are generated during the course of a program's performance. Programming languages provide various means of defining *variables,* to which a program can refer by name, to store and later recall specific values when they are needed. FRED offers two kinds of structures that can act as variables: frames on the desktop and variables created through the @LOCAL function.

In FRED programs, any frame that is on the desktop during a program's performance, or in the Library, can act as a *global* variable in a program. Such space is available to any section of the program, even if the program is divided into many "subroutine" modules. In Chapter 5, we found two ways to assign values to a frame, spreadsheet cell, or database field: using the @SET function or the : = symbol.

You can also set up *local* variables, for the private use of a specific subroutine in a program. The @LOCAL function defines such variables simply by giving them names. Once you have defined local variables, you can use the @SET function or the : = symbol to assign values to those variables. However, when the work of a subroutine is complete and control passes to some other section of the program, any local variables defined by the previous subroutine are lost.

Sometimes it is convenient for a program to be able to work with lists or tables of variables; in programming languages such as BASIC and Pascal, such groups of variables are called *arrays*. In FRED, a programmer can simulate the structure of an array by providing a spreadsheet or a database of values for the program to work with.

Two special FRED functions, @GET and @PUT, allow the programmer to read from and write to a range of spreadsheet cells or database fields. These functions are used within a *loop* structure to process an entire range of cells or fields, one value at a time. This *range* processing, using @GET and @PUT, is similar to the way a BASIC program might process the information in an array, using a FOR loop. However, there is an important difference. Arrays in BASIC and Pascal are numerically *indexed*. If you want to access any particular value in an array of variables, you refer to the correct index value in the array.

The @GET and @PUT functions, on the other hand, set up a pointer in the range. As the range of values is processed, the @NEXT function is used to move the pointer forward in the range, value by value. Thus, the processing must occur sequentially, from the beginning of the range to the end. Direct access of a particular value in the range is not possible with @GET and @PUT, although the more complicated @HLOOKUP and @VLOOKUP functions can accomplish this.

FRED also has the @ITEM function, which is useful for passing up to 16 parameters of information from one subroutine to another. We'll examine this function when we discuss subroutines.

DECISIONS

The @IF function is a tool for introducing decision-making into a FRED program. We had some experience with @IF in Chapter 5. @IF takes three parameters—a logical expression and two values or formulas:

@if(*logical expression, formula1, formula2*)

If the *logical expression* has a value of #TRUE, the @IF function evaluates *formula1* and returns its value; otherwise, @IF evaluates and returns the value of *formula2*.

Sometimes the three-parameter structure of the @IF function is too confining. A programmer may want to choose between two *groups* of formulas, depending on the value of the logical expression. For times like this, FRED provides the @LIST function.

@LIST allows you to place a group of formulas in a location where structurally there is room for only one formula. In an @IF function, we might picture the use of @LIST as follows:

```
@if(logical expression,
    @list(formula1,
        formula2,
        formula3,
        formula4),   ; end of first list
    @list(formula5,
        formula6,
        formula7,
        formula8) ; end of second list
)       ; end of @if
```

In this example, a value of #TRUE for the logical expression will result in evaluation of the first list of formulas. A value of #FALSE sends control to the second list of formulas.

For building compound and complex logical expressions, FRED provides the three functions @AND, @OR, and @NOT. Both @AND and @OR take a series of parameters and result in a logical value, #TRUE or #FALSE.

For @AND to return a value of #TRUE, *all* its parameters must be #TRUE. @OR, however, returns a value of #TRUE if *any* of its parameters are true.

The @NOT function negates the value of its single parameter. If the parameter is #TRUE, @NOT returns a value of #FALSE. If the parameter is #FALSE, @NOT returns a value of #TRUE.

LOOPS

A programming loop provides a structure for repeated processing of a series of formulas. Different programming languages provide different kinds of looping structures. Loops in FRED are created by the @WHILE function.

@WHILE takes an unspecified number of parameters. Its first parameter is a logical expression; subsequent parameters are formulas to be processed:

> @while(*logical expression,*
>   *formula,*
>   *formula,*
>   *formula, ...*
>   ⌐ of @while

⌐rameters of the @WHILE function are processed ⌐uence from first to last, as long as the logical expres-⌐UE.

⌐e event within the repeated activity will ultimately ⌐ value to #FALSE. When this occurs, processing of ⌐s after the current iteration. (If the logical expres-⌐m the outset, the formulas will never be evaluated.)

⌐earlier the use of the @GET and @PUT functions to ⌐ of values within a loop. A special FRED constant ⌐s available for this kind of range processing. The ⌐eturns a value of #NULL! when it reaches the end of ⌐es it is processing.

⌐LE function that uses @GET to process a range of ⌐ will appear as part of the logical expression; for

> ⌐et(*range*) <> #NULL!,
>
> ⌐ ...
>
> ⌐ange)

⌐ocesses each value in the range, the @NEXT function ⌐e @WHILE loop) moves the range pointer forward by ⌐en the last range value has been processed and @NEXT ⌐e pointer forward again, the next evaluation of @GET ⌐lue of #NULL!, thus ending the @WHILE loop.

We'll see an example of this kind of range processing in the sample program at the end of the chapter.

SUBROUTINES

Framework III's outlining function makes it easy to write FRED programs that are well planned, modularized, and structured into logical levels of control. Frames at every level of the outline can contain subroutines, stored in the formula area behind the frame itself. The outer, containing frame might make a series of subroutine calls to the frames within the outline. Each subframe, in turn, might call upon the subroutines located in frames at lower levels.

Ideally, the frames located at the higher levels of the outline will control the broad structure of the program; they will be devoted primarily to subroutine calls to frames lower in the outline. The frames at the lowest levels will contain the FRED code for accomplishing specific details of the task at hand. This kind of organization leads to subroutines that are short, easy to identify, and easy to debug if necessary.

The structure of a subroutine call in FRED is identical to a function call. To perform a program contained in a given frame, simply place the @ symbol before a reference to the frame:

> *@frame name*

This call causes FRED to transfer control of the program to the frame you have referenced and to perform (or "recalculate") the formula residing behind the frame.

You can also send up to 16 parameter values to a subroutine, again in the same format that you would use for a FRED function:

> *@frame name(1st value, 2nd value, 3rd value, . . . , 16th value)*

To make use of the parameter values sent to it, the subroutine you are calling simply refers to the functions @ITEM1, @ITEM2, @ITEM3, . . . , @ITEM16. These functions return the values of the corresponding parameters that have been passed to the subroutine.

When the work of a subroutine is complete, control of the program returns to the program location from which the subroutine was originally called. The @RETURN or @RESULT function can be used to return a specific value from the subroutine.

CONTROLLING THE FRAMES ON THE DESKTOP

FRED also has a special set of functions that allow you to manipulate and work with frames from within a program. These functions are unique, with no real parallels in other programming languages. Through these functions, FRED and Framework III manage to work even more closely together than we have seen up to now.

These functions include @EXECUTE, for changing and then recalculating the formula behind a frame; @PRINT, for printing a frame from within a FRED program; @SETSELECTION, for moving the highlight to a specific frame on the desktop; and @PERFORMKEYS, for performing keyboard commands that affect frames (as we have already seen).

Together, these functions allow you to perform, from within a FRED program, any frame operation that is available in Framework III. In the program example at the end of the chapter, we'll see how efficiently all these functions can be used.

GETTING HELP

As you learn to program in FRED, several sources of help are available to you in Framework III. They include the online help system and the @TRACE function. Let's look briefly at these facilities.

ONLINE HELP

As with the rest of Framework III, online help is provided for programming in FRED via the Help key (F1). The help system includes an overview of the language, complete with descriptions of every constant, error code, and operator. There is also a brief tutorial on writing user menus. An additional portion of the help system is devoted to an index to FRED functions, containing brief descriptions of every FRED function and its syntax, and a quick review of the key names used in FRED.

THE @TRACE FUNCTION

When you have written a program that doesn't quite work as you intended, it is helpful to be able to follow the code, step by step, as it executes. For this purpose, the FRED language includes a function called @TRACE. To use this function, follow these steps:

1. Create two Empty frames.

2. Label one frame A and the other B (you can use other labels, but since the frames will probably be temporary, you might as well use something simple).

3. Select frame B, and press the Edit key (F2) to access the formula area.

4. Enter the formula

   @trace(a, #ON)

Once you have entered this formula, the name of every function that is executed will appear in frame A, followed on the next line by the result of that function's execution. For example, as soon as you enter the formula in frame B, frame A will display

TRACE Result: #ON

The results of formulas that make selections will appear underlined. Tracing will continue until you enter the formula

   @trace(a, #OFF)

or delete either frame A or frame B from the desktop.

Now it's time for a short visit to The Sophisticated Palate to follow up on a FRED program that we talked about in Chapter 5.

EXAMPLES

Look back at Eileen Wilcox's Packaged Goods Inventory database in Figure 5.15. Recall Eileen's dilemma as she prepared to write a formula to calculate the wholesale prices of her inventory items.

Eileen wanted this field, called Whsl Pr, to contain values showing a 45 percent markup on the price per case. She could have stored a simple calculation formula behind the Whsl Pr field name:

Whsl Pr : = CostPerCase * 1.45

But when Eileen tried this formula, she didn't like the wholesale prices that were calculated. Prices ended in odd numbers of cents; for example:

$2.31
$2.64
$1.82
$3.55
$2.97

She knew that her customers would be used to seeing wholesale prices assigned in a more consistent manner.

COMPUTING ''ATTRACTIVE'' PRICES

To achieve this effect, Eileen wrote the small FRED program shown in Figure 7.4. She entered this entire program behind the field name Whsl Pr at the top row of her database table. The program then calculated the final wholesale prices that you can see in Figure 5.15.

Let's examine this program. As you can see, the program contains rather extensive comments that describe what is happening on each line.

```
Packaged Goods Inventory.Whsl Pr:
  ;  Formula for "Attractiveness Pricing"

  @local(pr,         ; the calculated wholesale price
         temp,       ; the last digit aver the decimal point
         add         ; the amount, in cents, to add on
         ),
  pr := @round(CostPerCase * 1.45,2),          ; find the price
  temp := 10 * (pr * 10 - @int(pr * 10)),      ; isolate the last digit
  add := @if(temp>5, 9-temp, 5-temp),          ; find how much to add
  Whsl Pr := pr + add/100
```

Figure 7.4: Formula for computing ''attractive'' prices

The program begins by defining three local variables, using the @LOCAL function:

```
@local(pr,
   temp,
   add
   ),
```

These variables are used in the various steps of the calculation that the formula performs.

In the next line of the program, the variable PR receives the wholesale markup, calculated as a simple 45 percent increase over the cost per case:

```
pr : = @round(CostPerCase * 1.45, 2),
```

The @ROUND function rounds a value to a specified number of decimal places. @ROUND takes two parameters: the value to be rounded and the desired number of decimal places. As you can see, this formula rounds the calculated wholesale price, PR, to two decimal places.

The next line isolates the last digit in the value of PR and assigns it to the variable TEMP:

```
temp : = 10 * (pr * 10 − @int(pr * 10)),
```

This rather convoluted algorithm uses the @INT function to find the integral value of PR * 10. When this integral value is subtracted from the product of PR * 10, the last digit of PR is the result; this result needs to be multiplied by 10 again to yield a single-digit integer.

The value of the variable ADD, calculated in the next line, represents the number of cents that need to be added to the calculated wholesale price, PR, to yield a price ending in 5 or 9. The @IF function is instrumental in determining this value:

```
add : = @if(temp >5, 9 − temp, 5 − temp),
```

If the digit TEMP is greater than 5, Eileen will add enough pennies to yield a price ending in 9. Otherwise, if TEMP is less than or equal to 5, she will add enough pennies to yield a price ending in 5. Given

ADD, the number of pennies to add, the last line of the program actually calculates the field Whsl Pr:

Whsl Pr : = pr + add/100

Writing programs like this one can prove useful in many Spreadsheet and Database frames. Because you can use the full-screen edit mode to produce a formula for any spreadsheet cell or database field, you can easily write and experiment with customized, multistep arithmetic formulas like Eileen's.

EXPLORING FURTHER

THE LETTERS PROGRAM

In this section, we'll examine a complete and somewhat detailed FRED program. The program works with two databases we studied in Chapter 5: the Sales People database and the Supervisors database. (You can review these two databases by looking back at Figures 5.1 and 5.24.)

The Sales People database, you'll recall, contains the following fields of information about a group of 18 sales employees: employee number, last name, first name, work region, total sales for the last six months, average monthly sales, probation status (#YES or #NO), date hired, and years with the firm. The Supervisors database contains information about the six regions in which these salespeople work: the region name, the regional supervisor, the regional office address, the city, the state, and the zip code.

The program we're going to look at is called Letters. Its task is to write two sets of form letters to two different groups of salespeople. To create the letters, the program merges information from the Sales People and Supervisors databases.

The first group of salespeople consists of all the employees who are on probation. Each person in this group is to receive a warning letter like the example shown in Figure 7.5. Along with its actual message, the letter contains the salesperson's name and complete regional address; the average monthly sales that the person achieved; and the name of the person's supervisor, on the cc: line at the bottom of the letter.

```
                                    June 9, 1989

        Donny Brooke
        89 Lindel Road
        St. Louis, MO 63123

        Dear Donny:

               We are sorry to  note that your  sales record for
        the  last  six months  has not been  satisfactory. Your
        average monthly sales were  $9,739.89.  We hope you can
        do better than this in the future;  we'll be keeping an
        eye on your progress.

                                 Sincerely yours,




        cc: Anthony Stark
```

Figure 7.5: Warning letter to probationary salespeople

The second group of salespeople who are to receive letters consists of those who achieved sales of $100,000 or better during the six-month period. Figure 7.6 shows an example of the congratulatory letter written for these people. The letter contains the same individual information as the warning letter—name, address, average monthly sales, and supervisor.

The Letters program automatically prepares and prints these letters to all the salespeople in both groups. This exercise can be performed repeatedly. For example, suppose that you revise and update the Sales People database after six more months; the Letters program could once again generate two sets of letters to the salespeople who at that time fall into the two special groups.

In the process of preparing these letters to the sales force, the program works its way through a sequence of eight interesting programmed tasks:

1. It creates a new database, called Sales Addresses, with room for all the pertinent fields of the Sales People database, plus space to append the correct address to each record.

2. It copies the Sales People database into the containing frame, and moves the information from it into the Sales Addresses

```
                         June 9, 1989


      Anne Rizzo
      6700 Charleston Road
      Suite 32
      Boston, MA 02108

      Dear Anne:

           We are  delighted to note that your  sales record
      for the last six months has been  excellent. Your aver-
      age monthly sales were  $19,605.41.  Congratulations on
      your very high  achievement.  We hope you will continue
      to do as well in the future.

                         Sincerely yours,



      cc: Dane Whitman
```

Figure 7.6: Congratulatory letter to best salespeople

database, deleting the Sales People database when the task is completed.

3. It copies the Supervisors database into the containing frame, and merges data from this database (supervisor's last name and first name, address, suite, city, state, zip) into the Sales Addresses database, then deletes the Supervisors database.

4. It presents a menu on the screen, allowing you to select which group of letters you wish to produce. Figures 7.7 and 7.8 show two views of this menu. The menu has only two options, but the explanatory message displayed at the bottom of the screen changes according to the option that is highlighted.

5. Once you have chosen one of the two menu options, the program filters the Sales Addresses database according to the criterion that you have selected: all those who are on probation, or all those who achieved sales over $100,000.

6. The program uses the filtered database to perform a mail merge with one of two predesigned letter templates, representing the warning letter and the congratulatory letter. These templates contain the text of the two letters, with mail-merge fields included for the information from the database.

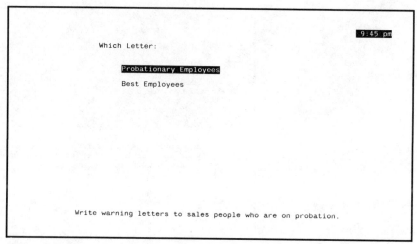

Figure 7.7: The Which Letter menu, with the highlight over the first option

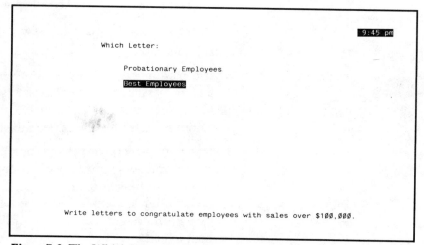

Figure 7.8: The Which Letter menu, with the highlight over the second option

7. The program then prints the filled-in form letters onto paper, generating one letter for each salesperson in the selected group.

8. Finally, before returning you to the desktop, the new Sales Addresses database is deleted.

Since this is a task that might be performed every six months, why not simply save the new database, with the information from both of the original databases, within the frame for later use? There are several reasons not to do this. First, there is no reason to store the same information (the address of every regional office, and the name of the local supervisor) twice. Second, by avoiding the redundancy of having two copies of the same information, you make it easier to keep the information current. If a new supervisor is hired, for example, only one database needs to be updated. Third, your information is more likely to be accurate. If a salesperson transfers to a different region, you need only change the Reg field in the Sales People database. There is no danger of your copying the address incorrectly, because it is safely stored in another database. For these reasons, it is much safer to create the database with the combined information only when you need it.

THE STRUCTURE OF THE LETTERS PROGRAM

The modules of the Letters program, along with the documents that the program works with, are stored in a single Outline frame called Letters. The frame is shown, in Outline view, in Figure 7.9. You can see that the first two subframes contained inside the outline are the form letters: Good and Bad. The print formatting for these

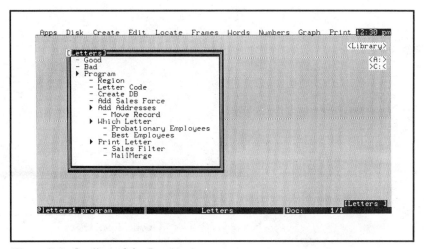

Figure 7.9: Outline of the Letters program

frames has been set up on the Print menu. The date, which does not appear in the form letter templates, is added by using the formula

<date4>

as a header, centered, on line 11. The top margin is set at 13 lines, to allow space for the company letterhead. Figure 7.10 shows the template for the "Good" letter.

The third subframe in the Letters frame is an outline within the outline. It is called Program, and its frames and subframes contain the FRED program modules that perform the letter-writing tasks.

The first two subframes under the Program heading represent the global-variable storage space that the program requires:

- Region is a frame that will contain the name of the region for which the addresses are being transferred to the merged database.

- Letter Code is a frame that is assigned one of two codes, depending on which kind of letter is currently being prepared—"P" for probation letter and "B" for best letter. This variable is used throughout the program, to determine

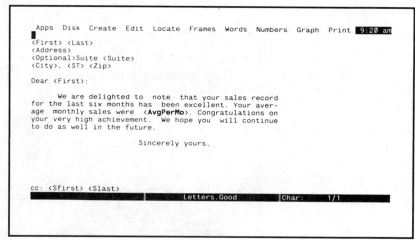

Figure 7.10: The "Good" form letter

which letter template should be used, to determine the formula that filters the Sales Addresses database, and to determine which letter template should receive the information from the Supervisors database.

The following three frames do most of the work of the program:

- Create DB uses a complex @PERFORMKEYS statement to create a database frame of appropriate dimensions for Sales Addresses and to fill in some of the column heads (the rest of the column heads will be transferred directly from the Sales People database).

- Add Sales Force brings the Sales People database into the frame from disk (it is assumed that this database is on the default drive and directory), and copies all but the last two columns of that database (Hired and Yrs, which are not needed for this task) into the Sales Addresses database.

- Add Addresses begins by bringing the Supervisors database into the frame from disk. It then repeatedly filters the Sales Addresses database so that the records for only one region are displayed. After the Sales Addresses database has been filtered, this frame calls a subroutine called Move Record, which performs the actual copying of information from the Supervisors database to the Sales Addresses database.

Continuing down the program outline, you'll see a frame called Which Letter. This frame is itself a short outline that the program uses for displaying the menu on the screen:

▶ Which Letter
– Probationary Employees
– Best Employees

We will see later how the @MENU function works with this outline, as well as the formulas that the outline contains.

Finally, the Print Letter outline contains two simple modules:

- Sales Filter filters the Sales Addresses database so that it includes only the records that are appropriate for the letter you want to print.

- MailMerge selects the correct form letter and performs the mail merge.

Let's look at the Letters program, module by module, and see what it can teach us about FRED programming.

INSIDE THE LETTERS PROGRAM

To run the program, first load the Letters Outline frame from disk. Make sure that the Supervisors and Sales People databases are in the default directory of the default drive. Then select the Letters frame, and press the Recalc key (F5). The first formula that is executed is behind the containing frame itself. As you may recall, you can cause the formula in a frame to be executed by referring to the frame with an @ symbol:

@Letters.Program

This formula simply directs FRED to execute the program in the frame called Program, which is shown in Figure 7.11.

The formulas behind the Letters.Program frame contain the master program. The first four formulas do nothing but call the subroutines that do the actual work:

@Letters.Program.Create DB,

```
Letters.Program:
    ; Call the subroutines to create the merged database.

    @Letters.Program.Create DB,
    @Letters.Program.Add Sales Force,
    @Letters.Program.Add Addresses,

    ; Call the menu to choose the letter to be printed.

    @menu(Letters.Program.Which Letter),

    ; When the program is finished, delete the new database.

    @setselection("Letters.Sales Addresses"),
    @performkeys("{del}"),

    ; If the program is interrupted, restore Outline view.

    @if(@isabend, @performkeys("{f10}{ctrl-out}"))
```

Figure 7.11: The formulas behind the Letters.Program outline

```
@Letters.Program.Add Sales Force,
@Letters.Program.Add Addresses,
@menu(Letters.Program.Which Letter),
```

The remainder of the frame contains some cleanup routines to be performed after the program is finished. First, the new database is selected and deleted:

```
@setselection("Letters.Sales Addresses"),
@performkeys("{del}"),
```

Finally, we have one of FRED's error-trapping functions. @ISABEND stands for "is abnormal end." It is contained in the formula

```
@if(@isabend, @performkeys("{f10}{ctrl-out}"))
```

Since most of the work of the program consists of entering data into the Sales Addresses database, the Letters frame must be switched from Outline view to Frames view before the work can begin, because you cannot go inside a frame in Outline view. If you interrupt the program by pressing Ctrl-Break before it has finished executing, this formula will notice the "abnormal end" to the program, and restore the containing frame to Outline view, placing the highlight on the outer frame.

CREATING THE SALES ADDRESSES DATABASE

The new database is created by three subroutines, one of which has a subroutine of its own:

```
– Create DB
– Add Sales Force
► Add Addresses
– Move Record
```

Each of these subroutines begins by displaying a message and then halting the screen display. The latter is accomplished by a call to the FRED function @ECHO, which controls whether the effects of FRED functions are displayed on the screen. @ECHO takes one of two constants, #ON or #OFF. @ECHO is set to its OFF status during the execution of these frames for two reasons. First, it spares the user from having to watch as the screen changes frantically. Second, the program executes much more quickly if it does not have to display every change on the screen as it proceeds.

The @PROMPT function displays a message as each subroutine begins, so you know that the program is still working while nothing changes on the screen. The second parameter in the @PROMPT statement, a number, determines how many spaces from the left margin the message will appear. Each subroutine ends by restoring the screen echo to #ON, so that the initial message of the next subroutine can be displayed.

Figure 7.12 shows the Create DB frame. It consists mostly of one long @PERFORMKEYS statement. Notice the use of the *string concatenation operator,* &. This symbol allows you to add a string to the end of the previous string. Although a FRED program statement can be as long as 255 characters, it is much easier to read if it is broken into small sections that will fit on the screen. You could, alternatively, create a whole series of short @PERFORMKEYS statements, but a single statement executes much more quickly than a series of statements, because Framework III has to look up the meaning of each FRED function before it executes it.

```
Letters.Program.Create DB:
  ; Create the empty Sales Addresses database.

  @prompt("Please wait . . . creating database.", 22),  ; Display message.

  @echo(#OFF),        ; Freeze screen activity during program performance.

  ; Use the Create menu to create a database of appropriate dimensions,
  ; inside the Letters frame.

  @performkeys("{f10}{in}{ctrl-c}w14{return}h18{return}d"

              ; Label the database frame.

            & "Sales Addresses{return}"

              ; Widen the SixMoSales column.

            & "{f9}{tab}{tab}{tab}{tab}{tab}{f4}"
            & "{rightarrow}{rightarrow}{rightarrow}{return}"

              ; Label the columns for the new data.

            & "{tab}{tab}Slast{tab}Sfirst{tab}Address"
            & "{tab}Suite{tab}City{tab}ST{tab}Zip{return}{out}"),

  @echo(#ON)         ; Restore screen activity so next message can be displayed.
```

Figure 7.12: The Create DB subroutine

Breaking up the statement into several lines also allows you to add comments, so that you will remember what each segment of the statement is supposed to do. In the first line, you will see

```
@performkeys("{f10}{in}{ctrl-c}w14{return}h18{return}d"
```

F10 first switches to Frames view, so that the frame can be entered. Next, the In key (+) ensures that the database will be created within the Letters frame, but not within the Program frame. The rest of this line issues the Create menu commands to create a Database frame with appropriate dimensions.

The following lines place a label in the new frame, move the high-light to the fifth column and widen it, and place labels in the columns that will hold the new data, so that the fields can be referred to by name in the mail-merge form letter. It is necessary to widen the fifth column, which contains the AvgPerMo field, because it is not wide enough to display the numbers, displaying asterisks instead. This is no problem when the formulas are recalculated, because the formula resides behind the frame. When a mail merge is performed, however, it is the text displayed in the cells that is copied into the form letter. If the AvgPerMo field were not widened, asterisks would appear in the form letters, instead of the correct sales figures. It is not necessary to widen the SixMoSales column because, although the column is used to determine the best employees, the figures themselves are not used in the letters.

Finally, column labels are placed in the right-hand columns of the database, to be used as field names in the form letter. This is not necessary for the left-hand columns because they will be copied from the Sales People database.

If you want to see exactly how this routine works, you can place a semicolon before the

```
@echo (#OFF)
```

statement, or type in all the keystrokes of the @PERFORMKEYS statement.

The Add Sales Force subroutine, shown in Figure 7.13, transfers the data from the Sales People database to the new Sales Addresses database. With one exception, this routine is also essentially one long @PERFORMKEYS statement.

First, the database is brought from disk into the Letters frame by the following menu command:

@performkeys("{ctrl-d}gSALESPE{return}"

Next, the Open All command from the Frames menu is issued, in case the database had been stored on disk in a filtered state, and the cursor is placed in the upper left corner:

& "{ctrl-f}o{in}{ctrl-home}"

The highlight is extended over the entire contents of the frame, and then moved back two columns by the keystokes

{leftarrow}{leftarrow}

This is the quickest way to select the portion of the database that we want to use.

```
Letters.Program.Add Sales Force:
    ; Transfer the data from the Sales People database to the Sales
    ; Addresses database.

    @prompt("Adding Sales People to database", 25),      ; Display message.
    @echo(#OFF),      ; Freeze screen activity during program performance.

    ; Load the Sales People database from disk.

    @performkeys("{ctrl-d}gSALES_PE{return}"

    ; Initialize the database by opening all frames and placing
    ; the cursor in the upper left corner.

                & "{ctrl-f}o{in}{ctrl-home}"

    ; Select the columns to be copied.

                & "{f6}{ctrl-end}{leftarrow}{leftarrow}{f7}{out}"),

    ; Copy the data to the Sales Addresses database.

    @setselection("Letters.Sales Addresses"),
    @performkeys("{in}{ctrl-home}{return}{out}"),

    ; Delete the Sales People database.

    @setselection("Letters.Sales People"),
    @performkeys("{del}"),

    @echo(#ON)        ; Restore screen activity so next message can be displayed.
```

Figure 7.13: The Add Sales Force subroutine

When issuing keystrokes by means of a program, it is difficult to know exactly where a frame will be located, especially if it has been created or put in place by the program itself. Therefore, instead of using

{uparrow}

or

{dnarrow}

to move to another frame, the @SETSELECTION statement is used. It makes the frame named in its argument the currently selected frame. In this instance, it selects the destination where we want to move the data:

@setselection("Letters.Sales Addresses")

In a FRED program like this one, the @SETSELECTION statement can function as though it were part of the @PERFORMKEYS statement. The move, which was started in the previous @PERFORMKEYS statement, is still waiting for the Return key to establish its destination while the @SETSELECTION statement is executed. The move is finally completed by the statement

@performkeys("{in}{ctrl-home}{return}{out}"),

after which the Sales People database is deleted.

The third subroutine, Add Addresses, is the most complex part of the program. It appears in Figure 7.14. The complexity arises from the use of two *region-walking* functions, @GET and @NEXT. Because of its complexity, it deserves a thorough explanation.

Like the Add Sales Force subroutine, the Add Addresses subroutine begins by displaying a message, bringing the appropriate database from disk into the Letters frame, and initializing it. This frame, however, requires two types of initialization. Because the region-walking is quite separate from any cursor movement, the @PERFORMKEYS statement places the cursor in the upper left cell to prepare for copying, while the statement

@reset(Letters.Supervisors.Reg),

places the range pointer at the beginning of the range.

```
Letters.Program.Add Addresses:
    ; Copy addresses from Supervisors database to the proper records
    ; in the Sales Addresses database.

    @prompt("Transferring addresses to database", 23),      ; Display message.
    @echo(#OFF),        ; Freeze screen activity during program performance.

    ; Load the Supervisors database from disk.

    @performkeys("{ctrl-d}gSUPERVIS{return}"),

    ; Initialize the database for both copying and region walking.

    @performkeys("{in}{ctrl-home}{out}"),
    @reset(Letters.Supervisors.Reg),

    ; Process the first record.

    Letters.Program.Region := @get(Letters.Supervisors.Reg),
    @execute(Letters.Sales Addresses, Reg = Letters.Program.Region),
    @Add Addresses.Move Record,

    ; Process the first record.

    Letters.Program.Region := @get(Letters.Supervisors.Reg),
    @execute(Letters.Sales Addresses, Reg = Letters.Program.Region),
    @Add Addresses.Move Record,

    ; Process the remaining records.

    @while(@next(Letters.Supervisors.Reg) <> #NULL!,
        @setselection("Letters.Sales Addresses"),
        @performkeys("{ctrl-f}o"),       ; Reopen the database after filtering.
        Letters.Program.Region := @get(Letters.Supervisors.Reg),
        @execute(Letters.Sales Addresses, Reg = Letters.Program.Region),
        @Add Addresses.Move Record,
    ),                                   ; End of the @WHILE loop.

    ; Delete the Supervisors database.

    @setselection("Letters.Supervisors"),
    @performkeys("{del}"),

    @echo(#ON)          ; Restore screen activity so next message can be displayed.
```

Figure 7.14: The Add Addresses subroutine

The bulk of the subroutine is an extensive @WHILE loop, but because of some peculiarities of the region-walking functions in FRED, the first record must be processed before the loop begins. The first step in processing each record is to use the @GET statement to read the name of the next region in the Reg column. However, the @NEXT statement, which determines when the loop should end, moves the pointer to the next record. If the first record were not processed before the loop began, it would be skipped.

The @WHILE loop steps through the Supervisors database, repeatedly filtering the Sales Addresses database for each region, and copying the supervisor's name and regional office address to the appropriate records. The Reg field controls iterations of the loop itself:

@while(@next(Letters.Supervisors.Reg) < > #NULL!,

@NEXT, like @GET, takes a *range* parameter. In the case of a Database frame, the field name itself represents a range—that is, an entire column in the database.

If the @GET statement were used to control the loop instead of the @NEXT statement, the column would be read until the condition indicated by #NULL! (the end of the database column) were reached. However, since the copying occurs *after* the @WHILE statement, the last record would be read twice. Since the @GET statement is used to filter the database, the final pass through the loop would copy the last record to a database filtered on a null value. That is, the database would appear to have no records in it; as a result, the last record would be copied into the column heads, replacing the field names, with disastrous results. The peculiar construction of this subroutine avoids the problem.

The statement

Letters.Program.Region : = @get(Letters.Supervisors.Reg),

reads the first record in the Reg column, and assigns it to the global variable contained in the frame Region. This is necessary if the result of the reading process is to be available to the Sales Addresses database, because otherwise the results of region-walking functions are known only in the frame in which they occur.

The next statement filters the Sales Addresses database so that it contains only the salespeople for the region whose name is stored in the Region frame. The main tool for doing this is the @EXECUTE function. @EXECUTE, you may recall, places a new formula behind a specified frame and then recalculates the formula. One of its most useful applications is filtering databases during a program's performance. The format of @EXECUTE is

@execute(*frame name, formula*)

After the database is filtered, the Move Record subroutine, which we will look at shortly, performs the actual copying of the data. You will note that these three statements—the statement containing @GET, the @EXECUTE statement, and the call to the Move Record subroutine—also appear inside the @WHILE loop.

The only other statements in the @WHILE loop are in charge of reopening the database before it is filtered again. The database is selected, and the Frames menu is used to restore it:

```
@setselection("Letters.Sales Addresses"),
@performkeys("{ctrl-f}o"),
```

Because these statements are at the end of the loop, the database will be fully open after all the addresses have been added, so that it can be filtered to select the employees to whom letters will be written.

At the end of the subroutine, the Supervisors database is deleted, in the same manner as the Sales People database was deleted.

The Move Record subroutine, which is called after the first record in the Supervisors database is selected, and then again during each pass through the loop, simply selects the appropriate records of the field to be transferred, and copies them to all the records in the filtered database. It is illustrated in Figure 7.15. Since, if the program executes properly, you will never see the Sales Addresses database in its final form, part of it is illustrated in Figure 7.16.

THE MENU

Now that we have created a database that contains all the information we need, we are ready to begin creating the letters. The @MENU statement in the Program frame begins this portion of the program by displaying the menu on the screen (see Figures 7.7 and 7.8).

```
Letters.Program.Add Addresses.Move Record:
   @setselection("Letters.Supervisors.Last"),
   @performkeys("{dnarrow}{f6}{end}{f8}{out}"),
   @setselection("Letters.Sales Addresses.Slast"),
   @performkeys("{dnarrow}{f6}{ctrl-dnarrow}{return}{return}")
```

Figure 7.15: The Move Record subroutine

```
        Apps  Disk  Create  Edit  Locate  Frames  Words  Numbers  Graph  Print  6:21 am
         Last      First    Reg  SixMoSale  AvgPerMo    Pbn   Slast      Sfirst    Addre

        SmithfielFrank     SW   ********   $8,603.94  #YES   Williams   Simon    4520
        Goldberg  Jack     SW   ********  $17,209.11  #NO    Williams   Simon    4520
        Smith     Ashleigh SW   ********  $11,188.74  #NO    Williams   Simon    4520
        Petrakis  Bill     SE   ********  $18,718.72  #NO    Frank      Wanda    200 E
        SchroederArt       SE   ********  $15,707.20  #NO    Frank      Wanda    200 E
        Smyth     Gloria   SE   ********  $14,622.07  #NO    Frank      Wanda    200 E
        Smith     Joe      NW   ********   $9,455.58  #YES   Walters    Jennifer 897 S
        TakahashiBruce     NW   ********  $17,110.80  #NO    Walters    Jennifer 897 S
        Woo       Eva      NW   ********  $15,542.35  #NO    Walters    Jennifer 897 S
        Sapolsky  Stan     NE   ********   $8,112.55  #YES   Whitman    Dane     6700
        Rizzo     Anne     NE   ********  $19,605.41  #NO    Whitman    Dane     6700
        Herrera   Fred     NE   ********  $14,609.05  #NO    Whitman    Dane     6700
        Brooke    Donny    MW   ********   $9,739.89  #YES   Stark      Anthony  89 Li
        Olsen     Oscar    MW   ********  $19,089.46  #NO    Stark      Anthony  89 Li
        Waterman  Pearl    MW   ********  $14,329.64  #NO    Stark      Anthony  89 Li
        Curtis    Amy      S    ********   $7,876.12  #YES   Rambeau    Monica   8301
        WashingtoEd        S    ********  $17,062.52  #NO    Rambeau    Monica   8301
        HernandezEsther    S    ********  $13,873.53  #NO    Rambeau    Monica   8301

                                Sales Addresses.Reg      Recs:    18/18
```

Figure 7.16: The Sales Addresses database

The @MENU statement calls the Outline frame Which Letter, and causes it to act like a menu:

@menu (Letters.Program.Which Letter)

To display and work with a menu, the @MENU function makes use of every part of this outline—the frame labels, the frame contents, and the formulas residing behind the frames. This is how @MENU operates:

- The frame labels—in this case, the labels *Probationary Employees* and *Best Employees*—become the actual menu options.

- Any contents of the option frames are displayed as explanatory messages at the bottom of the screen. The two messages seen in Figures 7.7 and 7.8 are stored in the contents areas of the Probationary Employees frame and the Best Employees frame, respectively.

- When the user selects an option from the menu, control of the program passes to the formula residing behind the frame that represents the selected option.

From the user's point of view, a menu created by the @MENU function has the same operational features as a regular Framework menu. You can use the ↑ and ↓ keys to move the highlight over a menu selection. Pressing the Return key selects the current selection. Alternatively, you can simply press the first letter of the option you want to select—in this case, P or B. If you want to exit from the menu without selecting an option, press the Escape key.

As we have seen, selecting a menu option results in execution of the formula that resides behind the corresponding Outline frame. Figure 7.17 shows a listing of the formulas behind the two frames Probationary Employees and Best Employees.

Both routines are simple. They begin by assigning a single-character code to the variable frame Letter Code. If the user has selected the Probationary Employees option from the Letter menu, a ''P'' is placed in Letter Code:

> Letters.Program.Letter Code : = ''P'',

If the user selected the Best Employees option, the frame receives a ''B'':

> Letters.Program.Letter Code : = ''B'',

The value stored in this frame, Letter Code, will be used to determine which of the two letters is being processed, the warning letter or the congratulatory letter.

```
Letters.Program.Which Letter.Probationary Employees:
   ; Prepare to write letters to the
   ; employees who are on probation.

   ; Begin by placing a "P" in Letter Code:

   Letters.Program.Letter Code := "P",

   ; Now call the Print Letter Program:

   @Letters.Program.Print Letter


Letters.Program.Which Letter.Best Employees:
   ; Prepare to write letters to the
   ; employees whose sales levels are above $100,000.

   ; Begin by placing a "B" (for "Best") in Letter Code:

   Letters.Program.Letter Code := "B",

   ; Now call the Print Letter Program:

   @Letters.Program.Print Letter
```

Figure 7.17: The formulas behind the Which Letter menu outline

Finally, both of the menu option formulas end by sending control of the program to the Print Letter frame. Notice the form of the subroutine call:

@Letters.Program.Print Letter

As we have discussed, a subroutine call consists simply of a reference to the frame that contains the subroutine. The reference must be preceded by the @ symbol.

PRINTING THE LETTERS

The Print Letter program module appears in Figure 7.18. It consists primarily of subroutine calls to the two lower-level subroutines that do the real work of the module:

@Letters.Program.Print Letter.Sales Filter
@Letters.Program.Print Letter.MailMerge

As we will see, Sales Filter selects the appropriate group of salespeople, and MailMerge selects the appropriate letter template and prints the letters.

The Print Letter subroutine contains a call to another FRED function, @QUITMENU. This function exits the menu and returns the user to the desktop.

```
Letters.Program.Print Letter:
    ; Write letters to selected sales people

    @echo(#OFF), ; Freeze screen activity during program performance

    ; Filter the Sales People database and process each
    ; person in the filtered group:

    @Letters.Program.Print Letter.Sales Filter,
    @Letters.Program.Print Letter.MailMerge,

    ; End the program:

    @echo(#ON),
    @quitmenu,
    @performkeys("{ctrl-out}{f10}")
```

Figure 7.18: The Print Letter subroutine

The Sales Filter subroutine, shown in Figure 7.19, is in charge of filtering the Sales Addresses database according to the appropriate criterion for the selected group. Once again, the filtering is performed by the @EXECUTE function. The task of this subroutine is to choose one of two different filter formulas. You may recall the two filters we used in Chapter 5 to examine different groups of employees. If we want to print warning letters to probationary employees, the formula will be simply

    Pbn

If we print congratulatory letters to the most successful salespeople, the filter formula will be

    SixMoSales > 100000

To choose between these two formulas, Sales Filter examines the value currently stored in the variable frame Letter Code. If the frame contains a "P", we are writing to probationary employees; otherwise, we are dealing with the best employees. Sales Filter uses the @IF function to decide between two possible @EXECUTE commands:

    @if(Letters.Program.Letter Code = "P",
      @execute(Letters.Sales Addresses, Pbn),
      @execute(Letters.Sales Addresses, SixMoSales > 100000)
)

Once the Sales Addresses database has been correctly filtered, the MailMerge subroutine can print the letters. A listing of MailMerge is shown in Figure 7.20.

```
Letters.Program.Print Letter.Sales Filter:
    ; Filter the Sales Addresses database so that
    ; only the selected employees (Probationary or Best)
    ; will be displayed.

    @if(Letters.Program.Letter Code = "P",
        @execute(Letters.Sales Addresses, Pbn),
        @execute(Letters.Sales Addresses, SixMoSales > 100000)
        )
```

Figure 7.19: The Sales Filter subroutine

```
Letters.Program.Print Letter.MailMerge:
    ; Select the correct letter.

@if(Letters.Program.Letter Code = "P",
    @setselection("Letters.Bad"),
    @setselection("Letters.Good")
    ),

; Call the Mailmerge using function from the Apps menu.

@performkeys("{ctrl-a}mLetters.Sales Addresses{return}")
```

Figure 7.20: The MailMerge subroutine

The MailMerge subroutine uses the value stored in Letter Code to identify the correct letter template to use:

```
@if(Letters.Program.Letter Code = "P",
    @setselection("Letters.Bad"),
    @setselection("Letters.Good")
    ),
```

Finally, the @PERFORMKEYS statement calls the *Mailmerge using* option from the Apps menu, and tells it to use the Sales Addresses database for the mail merge.

As you can see, the Letters program is a complex example of what you can do using FRED and Framework III's outlining capability to organize a program. This example is provided not to confuse you, but rather to show you how many of the functions and capabilities you learned about in Framework's other components—databases, mail merge, and so on—can be used to provide power and flexibility in the context of FRED programming.

CREATING A USER-DEFINED FUNCTION

Now that we have some experience with programming in FRED, let's try writing the @DIFFTIME function. This function should calculate the time elapsed between two times, just as the @DIFFDATE function calculates the time elapsed between two dates.

In earlier versions of Framework, there was no function that would find the difference between two times. However, in Framework III, the

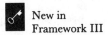
New in
Framework III

@DIFFDATE function can do so. To see how this works, see @DIFFDATE in Appendix B.

We've included this example anyway, for two reasons. First, it is a good example of a user-defined function. Second, it is easier to use in your calculations because it requires a simpler syntax and will work with string values (which the @DIFFDATE function will not do).

We could conceivably write a version of the function that would work with the time displayed in *any* form. However, to simplify our work, the function we'll write will assume that the time is given as a string value, as hours and minutes on a *24-hour* clock, the same form as given by the function

    @time2(@time)

We've chosen not to use a 12-hour clock because 1PM would be later than 11AM, for example, and we'd have to find a way of converting the PM times so that we could easily perform arithmetic. There *are* ways to convert a date-type function into numbers. However, there are also ways to convert strings into numbers, and any date-type function will also include extraneous information, such as seconds. In addition, after we've created the function, an application will be suggested where you'll want to use strings to prevent recalculation, just as you did with the Phone Log example. Also remember that you can use Copy (F8) with the pound sign (#) to place the *result* of a formula into a field or cell as a string.

The basic form of the function, when used in (or as) a formula, is

    @difftime(*early, late*)

where *early* and *late* are two times, the second one being later than the first. Since we will ultimately generate the times on which we work by using the @TIME2 function, which presents times in the form

    HH:MM

the strategy will be to:

1. Select the first two characters from the string: HH.

2. Convert the characters to numbers to find the number of hours.

3. Multiply the number of hours by 60 to find out how many minutes they represent.

4. Select the last two characters, MM, and convert them to numbers.

5. Add these minutes to the number of minutes represented by the hours.

We'll do this for both the early time and the later time, and then subtract the early time from the later time. Since the operation for determining both times is identical, we'll use a subroutine so we don't have to write the code twice. This subroutine, called Calculate, is shown in Figure 7.21. The two times that serve as the function's parameters are treated within the program as @ITEM1 and @ITEM2. However, since each of the times is sent to the subroutine separately, each one is treated by the subroutine as @ITEM1.

The Calculate routine does three things. First, it uses the @MID function (which behaves virtually the same as BASIC's MID$ function), to count two characters from the beginning of the string, and assign them to the local variable HOURS. Second, it starts with the fourth character (the third is the colon), and assigns the following two characters to the local variable MINUTES. Finally, these strings are converted to numbers by the @VALUE function, which returns the value of a string consisting of numbers, and the arithmetic is performed. The result is returned to the main program at the same time. The following formula accomplishes the last three tasks:

```
@return((@value(hours)*60) + @value(minutes))
```

The main program is shown in Figure 7.22. Again, local variables called HOURS and MINUTES are defined. They are not the same as those used in the Calculate subroutine, because they are defined as local. One statement passes both times to the subroutine, receives the result from the subroutine, and divides the result by 60, to find out how many hours have elapsed:

```
hours : = (@difftime.calculate(@item2)
 - @difftime.calculate(@item1))/60,
```

```
Library.User-defined functions.difftime.Calculate:
  @local(hours, minutes),


                                ; First find the colon in the time string
                                ; colon is third character
  hours := @mid(@item1,1,2),    ; hours are characters to left of colon
  minutes := @mid(@item1,4,2),  ; minutes are characters to right of colon
                                ; convert strings to numbers
                                ; calculate total number of minutes,
                                ; return to main program

  @return((@value(hours)*60) + @value(minutes))
```

Figure 7.21: The Calculate subroutine of the @DIFFTIME function

```
Library.User-defined functions.difftime:
  ; @difftime(early, late)
  ; Calculates the number of minutes and hours between two specified times.
  ; Times should be recorded as strings generated by @time2, that is
  ;   hours and minutes on a 24-hour clock.

  ; The Calculate subroutine breaks apart the string into minutes and hours,
  ;   and performs the arithmetic to convert each time string into a number of
  ;   of minutes, on which arithmetic can be performed.

  @local(minutes, hours),

  ; @item1 is the early time, @item2 the later time.
  ; The following formula sends both values to the Calculate subroutine,
  ; and subtracts the later from the earlier, then divides by 60 to
  ; get the number of hours elapsed.

  hours := (@difftime.calculate(@item2) - @difftime.calculate(@item1))/60,

  ; Minutes is the remainder after subtracting whole hours. This decimal
  ; fraction must be multiplied by 60 to convert to minutes.

  minutes := (hours - @int(hours))*60,

  ; The result is converted to a string by the @integer function.

  minutes := @integer(minutes),

  ; If the string is one character long, a zero is placed before it,
  ;   to conform to conventional time formats.

  @if(@len(minutes) = 1, minutes := "0" & minutes),
     ; Hours is converted to a string value.
     hours := @integer(@int(hours)
     ),

  ; A string of the form "HH:MM" is returned.

  @return(hours & ":" & minutes)
```

Figure 7.22: The Difftime program

The rest of the routine is designed to convert the fraction left over after dividing by 60 into a number of minutes, and put together a string representing hours and minutes elapsed in conventional format. First, the formula

minutes : = (hours − @int(hours))*60

finds the fraction left over after dividing HOURS by 60. Subtracting the integer part of the number leaves the fraction. This is multiplied by 60 to convert the fraction into minutes, which is then converted back into a string by the @INTEGER function. This is the inverse of the @VALUE function, and it can be used to convert both date and numeric data into strings.

Finally, for a touch of elegance, the length of the MINUTES string is checked. If the number of minutes is less than ten, the resulting string might appear in the form

7:3

Therefore, the @LEN function is used to see if the MINUTES string is only one character long. If so, the concatenation operator, &, is used to add a zero before the number of minutes. Finally, HOURS is converted to a string by the @INTEGER function, and a string of the proper form is created:

hours : = @integer(@int(hours)),
@return(hours & ":" & minutes)

If the elapsed time were seven hours and three minutes, the display would now be

7:03

AN APPLICATION
FOR THE @DIFFTIME FUNCTION

You may wonder what the @DIFFTIME function is good for. Consider the fact that, if you use a computer at home for business purposes, the Internal Revenue Service requires you to keep a log of the percentage of time you use it for such purposes. This function is handy in maintaining such a record.

The programming details will not be presented, so you can work them out as an exercise, but here are the outlines of the problem. To start, create a spreadsheet with five columns, labeled

Date
Start Time
Project
End Time
Time Elapsed

You can use Alt-F3 to enter the date. Create a modified version of the Alt-F4 macro that places a string of the proper form in the second column. You'll have to fill in the name of the project by hand. Use your new macro to log the ending time when you have finished your work. Finally, place the formula

@difftime(B2,B4)

in cell E2, and copy it downward into every cell in column E.

If you want to get elaborate, you can create a program that will do most of the work automatically. The outline for the program is shown in Figure 7.23. Create an Empty frame. Move your spreadsheet into it, and copy it twice with the Copy key (F8). Label the frames

Business
Personal
Financial

Now you can create a menu, following the principles you learned in the Letters program. But this menu will have submenus. The menu is the frame called

Which function

and each of its options displays a second menu with the options

Begin session
End session

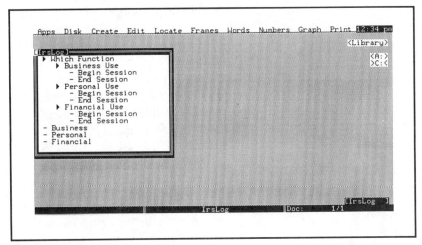

Figure 7.23: Outline frame for the IRS Log program

With what you have learned from the Phone Log example, you should be able to construct a program that will let you choose the appropriate spreadsheet and enter the starting or ending time into the appropriate cell. Later, you can create an @SUMTIME function, to add up the total hours for each function. You might even want to create a Library macro that automatically calls the program from disk and begins execution, and stores the frame on disk again as soon as the new data has been entered.

SUMMARY

FRED programming is attractive for a range of Framework III applications, from simple to complex. Your own programming level will depend partly on your inclination to learn about and work with the details of the FRED language. Your motivation for writing a program might include any of the following:

- A desire to streamline your work with Framework III, using keyboard macros

- The need to add new calculating or processing power to Framework III applications

- The ambition to produce turnkey applications for professional programming projects

One feature of Framework III that is helpful to both novices and experienced programmers is the desktop Library. Items in the Library can be called by FRED formulas anywhere on the desktop. It also provides a home for programs that you write automatically, as macros or abbreviations. In it you can store:

- Macros, which capture a series of frequently used keystrokes, ready to be performed whenever you enter an Alt-key command from the keyboard.

- Abbreviations, which allow you to type a simple mnemonic, and recall a block of text by pressing Alt-Backspace.

- Assumptions, which you can reference from a spreadsheet cell or database field, which will automatically take on the values stored in them upon recalculation.

- User-defined functions, which allow you to extend the scope of the FRED language, and which can be called from any point in Framework III.

FRED is also a complete programming language, with facilities for all the usual processes and structures that such a language must offer. In particular, FRED includes functions for handling all of the following:

- Keyboard input and screen output
- Local and global variables
- Decisions and flow of control
- Structured loops
- Subroutines

In addition, FRED has several unique functions that allow you to perform any Framework III operation from within a program. In short, the individual resources of Framework III and FRED are designed to work together to accomplish more than either could do alone.

Working with Other Programs

483

OVERVIEW

INTRODUCTION

ONE OF FRAMEWORK III'S ADVANTAGES IS THAT AS an integrated software package it allows you to perform all the important productivity functions—word processing, spreadsheet analysis, database management, creating business graphs, telecommunications, outlining, and printing documents and reports—in the same environment. The same commands, which you enter with the same keystrokes, are used in all activities. Framework III thus spares you from having to learn a different set of commands—and keystrokes to activate them—for different purposes. If you had separate programs for each function, each one would undoubtedly require you to learn different commands. In addition, Framework III's outline-based structure, and its move, copy, and cut-and-paste functions, allow you to move data between different types of frames with ease.

However, not everyone uses Framework III. Sometimes even people who do use Framework III have to use other programs to accomplish tasks for which they normally use Framework III. And sometimes you may have a need for a specialized program that performs some function more efficiently than Framework III's generalized components.

You may, for example, have an accounts receivable program that efficiently handles all your accounts receivable transactions, and needs no design or programming on your part. You might not want to invest the time needed to create a database that would perform all the functions of this program equally well. Or, you might want to use some sort of paint or graphics program to enhance Framework III's graphs for presentation—changing the colors or smoothing out the edges of the labels, for instance.

You might also want to use files created by your accounts receivable program within a Framework III spreadsheet or in conjunction with other data, or use data created by a dedicated database management program in a Framework III database. In addition, you may need to share your data with people who use other programs to accomplish the tasks you perform with Framework III.

Framework III is designed for maximum flexibility in these areas. In this chapter, we'll explore:

- *Importing files into Framework III:* What kinds of files Framework III can read, how to load them into a Framework III frame, and what you can do to make other types of files readable

- *Exporting files from Framework III:* What kinds of files Framework III can write

- *Ways to run other programs:* By using a DOS Access frame, by running a FRED program on the desktop, or by adding programs to the Apps menu

You'll learn how to write a program that allows you to run another program right from the desktop, and we'll take our first look at the Setup program (explored more fully in Appendix A), which we'll use to add the program to the Apps menu. In our visit to The Sophisticated Palate, we'll see how George Farley integrates the VisiCalc DIF file, which Eileen downloaded in the previous chapter, into his Activity Comparisons spreadsheet. Finally, we'll look at ways of importing types of files that are not on the menus, and ways of approaching the process of transferring files between applications to minimize potential problems and difficulties.

CONVERTING FILES

If you open the Disk menu, you will notice that it includes two options we have not yet explored: Import and Export. Each of these options opens a submenu. The Import submenu is shown in Figure 8.1, and the Export submenu in Figure 8.2. The items on these menus call up special FRED programs (which are on the Apps disk if you are using a floppy disk system) that convert files from one format to another.

IMPORTING FILES INTO FRAMEWORK III

Framework III includes options to import ten types of files. If a file on a disk is (or appears to be) in any one of these formats, you can load it to

Version Note

Framework II supported only seven of these formats: dBASE III, IBM DCA, WordStar, Multi-Mate, ASCII text, Lotus 1-2-3, and VisiCalc DIF. If you are using Framework II, you will notice some differences.

the desktop simply by selecting the file name in a disk drive cabinet. (If you prefer, however, you can choose any of these file formats from the Import submenu, entering the name of the file to be converted.) Framework III can import files specific to six programs, and four more general formats. The four specific formats are as follows:

- Files from earlier versions of *Framework*. Simply load them in, and Framework III will convert them automatically.

Figure 8.1: The Import submenu

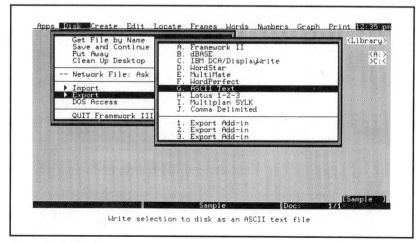

Figure 8.2: The Export submenu

- Database files from the programs *dBASE II, III, and III PLUS*. These programs are products of Ashton-Tate, as is Framework III, and are fully compatible with Framework III. These files normally have the extension .DBF. They will appear on the desktop as Database frames.

- *Lotus 1-2-3 worksheet files*. If you select a Lotus file with the .WKS or .WK1 extension from a disk drive cabinet, it will be brought to the desktop as a Framework III Spreadsheet frame. Although earlier versions of Framework imported only the contents of the cells, Framework III will read numbers, formulas, formats, and column widths, but not macros or graph information. However, Lotus 1-2-3 files grow larger when imported into Framework III, so it may be a good idea to divide them into smaller units when first importing them.

- *WordStar* word processing files. These files need not have any special extension. All versions of WordStar *except* WordStar 2000 can be imported directly.

- *MultiMate* word processing files. These files generally have the extension .DOC.

- *WordPerfect 4.1* and later files can be imported, though not using the direct-to-frame import method explained later in this chapter.

If you select a file of any of these types (except WordPerfect), Framework III will perform the conversion automatically. (If you have a floppy disk system, you will be prompted to insert the Apps disk in drive A.) Framework III will load a conversion program and check to see that there is no frame on the desktop with the same name. If there is, it will prompt you

> Name conflict: rename desktop frame and try again—
> Press SPACE to continue

Otherwise, it will create the appropriate type of frame on the desktop and convert the data, displaying various messages in the message area and in a special frame called *Messages*. You can cancel the conversion by pressing Ctrl-Break. Figure 8.3 shows an example of the Messages frame.

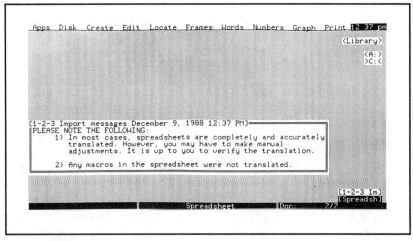

Figure 8.3: A Messages frame created by importing a Lotus 1-2-3 worksheet

In addition, Framework III includes programs to convert four more general types of files to its own format:

- *DCA.* A DCA (*Document Content Architecture Revisable-Form Text*) file is a special type of file format owned by IBM, which is used by both the DisplayWrite word processing programs and by many programs that run on IBM mainframe and minicomputer programs. If you download text files from an IBM mainframe, the chances are good that they will be in this format. These files have the extension .DCA. They are completely unreadable without some means of converting them to text.

- *ASCII text files.* These files contain nothing but the standard ASCII characters, and are similar to the files created by selecting the DOS File option from the Print Output Destination submenu, except that, as a rule, they do not contain printer escape sequences or the results of selecting printing formats. (DOS files created by way of the Print menu are loaded as ASCII text files, however.) ASCII text files may have almost any extension. If you select an ASCII text file in a disk drive cabinet, it will be loaded directly, without the intervention of a conversion program.

- *Multiplan SYLK files.* A SYLK (*SYmbolic LinK*) file is a special type of ASCII text file that contains the data from the spreadsheet (but not the formulas), plus enough additional information to reconstruct the spreadsheet.

- *DIF files.* A DIF (*data interchange format*) file is a special type of ASCII text file that contains the data from a spreadsheet (but not the formulas), plus enough additional information to reconstruct the spreadsheet. DIF files have the extension .DIF.

These types of files can be created by many different programs. If you need to import a file from a program other than the six named earlier (Framework, dBASE, Lotus 1-2-3, WordStar, MultiMate, or WordPerfect), the chances are fairly good that that program can create a file in one of these formats (DCA, ASCII, SYLK, or DIF). We'll look at some details of these formats shortly.

If you select a file that is neither in Framework III format nor in any of the formats that Framework III includes conversion programs for, Framework III will load it to the desktop without attempting to perform any type of conversion. If the file is a text file of any type, there is some chance that you will be able to read it, although you may have to reformat it extensively before you can do anything else with it. One new feature in Framework III is the Alt-F9 macro, which removes hard carriage returns from such a file. If it is a program file, most of the contents will probably be lost. Later in this chapter, we'll look at ways to read files of other types.

WRITING FILES FOR OTHER PROGRAMS

Also on the Disk menu is an Export submenu of file formats that Framework III can create on request. They include formats specific to most of the programs that Framework III can import files from:

- Framework II
- dBASE
- WordStar
- MultiMate

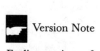 Version Note

Earlier versions of Framework supported fewer export types. Specifically, they supported WordStar, MultiMate, and Lotus 1-2-3 as well as ASCII Text, DCA, and comma-delimited (which was called dBASE Delimited in Framework II).

Also note that the new Framework III export option, dBASE, will export to dBASE III or IV. To export a file for dBASE II, you must use the Comma Delimited option. Finally, for Framework II users, the menus are constructed differently, so some of the specific keys to press will be different in the examples that follow.

- WordPerfect
- Lotus 1-2-3

(This is how Eileen Wilcox created a Lotus 1-2-3 file for the accountant.) Framework III can also write ASCII text files, DCA files, and SYLK files. Although it cannot write DIF files, Framework III can write a third general file format, the *comma-delimited* file, which appears on the menu as

J. Comma Delimited

This is one of several formats used by the dBASE programs, and some others as well, for exchanging data with other programs. Most programs that can write comma-delimited files can also read them. A comma delimited file is like a DIF file for database programs—it contains the data plus enough information to reconstruct the table.

You cannot create the file types on the Export submenu automatically. You must first bring the frame you want to convert to the desktop. Next, you must select it. Finally, you must select the export format from the menu. For example, to export a frame called LETTER to WordStar, you must select the frame, then press

Ctrl-D	(to open the Disk menu)
E	(to open the Export submenu)
D	(to export to WordStar)

If you are using a floppy disk system, Framework III will prompt you to place the Apps disk in drive A. Framework III will then load the appropriate conversion program and perform the conversion, writing the result to disk. You can interrupt the process at any time by pressing Ctrl-Break, but you may end up with an empty file on the disk anyway.

WordStar files are written with the extension .WSD so you can identify them, although WordStar does not require an extension. ASCII text and comma-delimited files are written with the extension .TXT, although comma-delimited files created by dBASE programs have the extension .SDF.

The export format must be appropriate to the frame you want to convert. You cannot export a Database or a Spreadsheet frame directly to a word processing format, for example. You can, however, export such frames to ASCII text files.

SOME CHARACTERISTICS OF THE ASCII FILE FORMATS

An ASCII text file contains nothing but the displayable characters of the ASCII code. These are the characters from 32 through 127 in Table C.1. They include all the characters that you can type at the keyboard, and none of the control characters. Since most word processing programs can produce ASCII text files, you can probably arrange to read files from almost any word processing program if you plan your work carefully. Virtually all word processing programs can also read ASCII text files, so you can use the ASCII format to create files for word processors that are not on the Export menu, and for many spreadsheet and database programs as well. However, you will lose any print styling that was in the original frame. DIF and comma-delimited files are special types of ASCII text files, so they have some of the same advantages.

ROW-ORDER DIF FILES   Although the VisiCalc spreadsheet program was the first to produce DIF files, many spreadsheet programs (and, indeed, quite a few other programs) can produce DIF files. These files can be set up so that the information is recorded row-by-row or column-by-column. However, Framework III can read only DIF files that are in *row order*. Such files will be converted into a normal Framework III spreadsheet frame. If the DIF file is in *column order*, however, the information in the resulting spreadsheet will appear sideways, with the row labels in row 1, the column labels in column A, and the data correspondingly rearranged. This may not be a problem with a small spreadsheet, but if you are importing a spreadsheet that is a few columns wide and many rows long, you may have trouble reading the result. Later in this chapter, we'll look at the DIF file that Eileen Wilcox downloaded from the branch store.

If you find yourself dealing extensively with DIF files, you may find the book *Mastering VisiCalc,* by Douglas Hergert (SYBEX, 1983), extremely useful. It contains an extensive description of the characteristics of DIF files, including BASIC programs to write and read them. If you must interact with a program that can create DIF files only in column order, you may be able to adapt some of these programs to convert the files to row order. Indeed, if you become adept at FRED programming, you may be able to write the program in FRED.

COMMA-DELIMITED FILES Comma-delimited files convert the data from a database or spreadsheet one row at a time. Each field (or cell) in a row is separated from the next by a comma. Non-numeric data is also surrounded by quotation marks. There are three potential hazards in exporting comma-delimited files:

- Since quotation marks delimit text fields, a text field that contains quotation marks will be broken into several fields. To prevent this, replace double quotation marks with single quotation marks before you perform the conversion.

- Since numeric fields are delimited only by commas, attempting to import a spreadsheet or database in which the numeric format includes commas will result in the numeric information being broken into several fields. Convert numeric fields to general or integer format before performing the conversion.

- If the columns are not wide enough to display their entire contents on the screen, some characters will be lost. The conversion program converts only those characters that would be displayed in the tabular form of the original frame.

Figure 8.4 shows a comma-delimited file created from the Sales People database we worked with in Chapter 5. If you want to try this for yourself, bring the file to the desktop and press

Ctrl-D	(to open the Disk menu)
E	(to open the Export submenu)
J	(to export a comma-delimited file)
Sales People	(enter the name of the file to export)
Return	(to record your selection)

(If you're using floppy disks, you need to insert the Apps disk first.) When you see the message

Export file written

select the file SALESPE.TXT from your default disk drive cabinet, and press Return. The file will be brought to the desktop as an ASCII text file, exactly as it appears in Figure 8.4. Later in this chapter, we'll look at some specialized techniques for dealing with comma-delimited files.

You might also try the following experiments:

1. Create a spreadsheet, convert it to 1-2-3 format, and then read it back.

2. Create a Word frame, convert it to WordStar, DCA, or MultiMate format, and then read it back. To see the other program's format, use the Import submenu to import the file into Framework III as an ASCII text file.

You will find that 1-2-3, MultiMate, and DCA files are completely unreadable when imported as ASCII text files. When you attempt to

```
"EmpNo","Last","First","Reg","SixMoSales","AvgPerMo","Pbn","Hired","Yrs"
"82M1","Waterman","Pearl","MW",85977.83,14329.64,"#NO","Sep 29, 1982",4.6
"84M3","Brooke","Donny","MW",58439.33,9739.89,"#YES","Dec 1, 1984",2.5
"85M2","Olsen","Oscar","MW",114536.77,19089.46,"#NO","Jun 20, 1985",1.9
"66N3","Rizzo","Anne","NE",117632.48,19605.41,"#NO","May 21, 1966",21.0
"79N6","Herrera","Fred","NE",87654.32,14609.05,"#NO","Nov 20, 1979",7.5
"86N2","Sapolsky","Stan","NE",48675.30,8112.55,"#YES","Jul 13, 1986",.8
"74N4","Takahashi","Bruce","NW",102664.78,17110.80,"#NO","Mar 23, 1974",13.2
"82N8","Woo","Eva","NW",93254.10,15542.35,"#NO","Feb 25, 1982",5.2
"85N5","Smith","Joe","NW",56733.45,9455.58,"#YES","Oct 23, 1985",1.6
"69S3","Washington","Ed","S",102375.10,17062.52,"#NO","Aug 29, 1969",17.7
"78S4","Curtis","Amy","S",47256.70,7876.12,"#YES","Apr 12, 1978",9.1
"82S9","Hernandez","Esther","S",83241.20,13873.53,"#NO","May 5, 1982",5.0
"72S6","Schroeder","Art","SE",94243.22,15707.20,"#NO","Jan 24, 1972",15.3
"81S5","Petrakis","Bill","SE",112312.34,18718.72,"#NO","Aug 24, 1981",5.7
"84S1","Smyth","Gloria","SE",87732.41,14622.07,"#NO","May 17, 1984",3.0
"78S1","Smithfield","Frank","SW",51623.62,8603.94,"#YES","Jul 22, 1978",8.8
"83S9","Goldberg","Jack","SW",103254.67,17209.11,"#NO","Oct 29, 1983",3.6
"86S2","Smith","Ashleigh","SW",67132.45,11188.74,"#NO","Mar 4, 1986",1.2
```

Figure 8.4: A comma-delimited version of the Sales People database import files using an importing standard that appears to be incorrect for the type of file, you will see a message of the form

> **File appears to be (1) MultiMate, not (2) ASCII**
> **Load as (1), (2), or Cancel (ESC)?**

To force Framework III to load the file in the format you want to see, press 2 to choose the ASCII format.

 You now have a sense of the ways in which Framework III can talk to other programs—how it can read files they have created and write files they can read. Let's look now at ways of running other programs while using Framework III.

MORE ABOUT DOS ACCESS FRAMES

 The easiest way to run another program while using Framework III is to create a DOS Access frame, and enter the command that invokes the program when the DOS prompt appears in the frame. If you wanted to run WordStar, for example, you would simply type

> **WS**

DOS commands will actually be executed in the DOS frames. Many other programs, however, will take over the whole screen. When you exit from a program like WordStar, your screen will look as though Framework III has disappeared. In fact, it has not. To return to Framework III from DOS or any other program, you simply enter the DOS command

> **exit**

If the desktop seems to have disappeared, no text will be captured in the DOS Access frame after its disappearance. You can keep the DOS Access frame from capturing characters by issuing the CLS (clear screen) command at the DOS prompt. You can also increase the amount of text Framework III will store in a DOS Access frame by means of the Setup program, which we will look at in Appendix A. If you use the ANSI.SYS device driver, it will be impossible to capture any text in a DOS Access frame, as the desktop will disappear as soon as the DOS prompt appears.

What if you want to capture the information displayed on the screen while you are working in DOS, or in another program, and the desktop has disappeared? If you are working in another program, you may be able to write a file in a format that Framework III can read, and import it when you return to the desktop.

If you are working in DOS, you may be able to use "output redirection" to create a file. For example, suppose you wanted to keep copies of the directories of several different diskettes on the desktop for easy reference. If your DOS Access frame does not disappear, this is no problem—simply type the command

```
dir
```

at the DOS prompt, and keep the frame after you return to the desktop. If the desktop does disappear, however, you can have DOS send the directory to a file instead of to the screen, and then read the file as an ASCII text file when you return to the desktop. For example, you might type

```
dir > disk1.dir
```

to have the directory sent to a file called DISK1.DIR. The > symbol tells DOS to send the output to whatever is specified after it.

Alternatively, if you use a RAM-resident "background" program such as SideKick or SuperKey that has a cut-and-paste feature, you can capture anything on the screen with it. When you return to Framework III with the EXIT command, create an Empty frame, and use the background program's paste feature to send the text from the screen into the frame.

A FEW WORDS OF CAUTION

Some kinds of programs must be run *before* you start Framework III, rather than from within it. DOS programs that include a portion that remains in memory, such as MODE.COM and GRAPHICS.COM, will place an upper limit on the memory available to Framework III. If you load such a program from a DOS frame, it will be located at the upper limit of the memory currently in use, and you will no longer have access to any of the computer's memory that is located above the point at which the resident program now ends. The same thing will happen if you load a RAM-resident "background" utility program.

If any of the programs you plan to run from the desktop requires a special device driver, it, too, must be loaded before Framework III, to prevent the same kind of limitation.

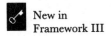 New in
Framework III

In Framework III, if you are using a mouse, you should load the mouse driver program before loading Framework III.

ADDING APPLICATIONS TO THE APPS MENU

In addition to using DOS Access frames, you can run other applications directly from the desktop. Figure 8.5 shows the Apps menu. As you can see, the third section of the menu includes three numbered items: dBASE III, and space for two application "add-ins." Thus, you can run dBASE III directly from the desktop (if you have it) by pressing

Ctrl-A   (to open the Apps menu)

1   (to run dBASE)

If you press these keys, the desktop will clear, and a frame will appear displaying the text shown in Figure 8.6. (Although this figure implies you must run dBASE III from a diskette, it will prompt you for a drive and directory.) If you have dBASE III, then the program will create an output frame for it, and display messages and prompts to guide you in running dBASE III from the desktop. Of course, if you don't have dBASE III, after a bit of disk whirring and opening and closing of menus, you will be returned to the desktop.

The key to this process is a FRED program called RUNDBASE.FW3, which is on the Help disk. Careful study of the program will show you how to deal with running a complex program such as dBASE III. However, most programs are much simpler to run than dBASE III. Let's

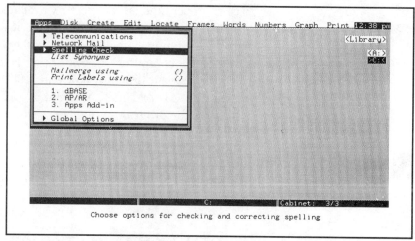

Figure 8.5: The Apps menu

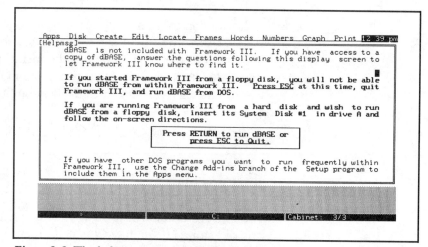

Figure 8.6: The help message from RUNDBASE.FW3

imagine that you have an accounting program called AP-AR.EXE, which handles your accounts payable and receivable quite effectively, and you would like to run it from the desktop. We will write a relatively simple program to accomplish this. We'll assume that the program is in a separate directory on your hard disk, called \ACCOUNTS. We'll start with a simple version of the program, and then add a few niceties.

Let's call the program Accounts. Create an Empty frame and label it *Accounts*. Next, press In (+) to enter the frame, and create another

Empty frame inside the first. Label this frame *Output*. (FRED programs always need a destination for their output.)

Now select the frame labeled Accounts. Press the Edit key (F2) to get to the programming area, and then press the Zoom key (F9) to get a full screen on which to write your program. The program will have to direct your computer to find the proper directory and select it, and then run the program, finally returning you to your Framework III directory when it is finished.

The key function for running another program is the @RUN function. For example, to run the program AP-AR.EXE, you would need a statement of the form

```
@run(accounts.output, "c:ap-ar.exe"),
```

This tells Framework III to run the program, using the Output frame within the Accounts frame for its output. But you also need to tell your computer where to find the program to be run. The following program is really all you need:

```
@setdirectory("c:\accounts"),
@setdrive("c:"),
@run(accounts.output, "c:ap-ar.exe"),
@setdirectory("c:\framewk"),
```

The @SETDIRECTORY function is FRED's equivalent of the DOS CHDIR (change directory) command. The @SETDRIVE function has the same effect as selecting a different drive at a DOS prompt. This short program will select the \ACCOUNTS directory, make sure you are logged onto drive C, run the accounting program, and return you to the \FRAMEWK directory before returning you to the desktop. To run the program, select it and press the Recalc key (F5).

A MORE ELABORATE PROGRAM

Let's try a somewhat more advanced version of the same program. Use the Alt-F2 macro to create another Empty frame inside the Accounts frame, above the Output frame. (Remember to use Alt-F2 in Outline mode. Otherwise, you'll have to create the frame, then—using F7—move the Output frame below it.) Label the new frame HELPMESSAGE.

If you need to give a user some special instructions, such as "Insert a disk in drive A", you can enter the text in the HELPMESSAGE screen. We'll assume that you do not need to add instructions. Use the Size key (F4) to make the frame relatively small. Then press

Ctrl-F   (to open the Frames menu)

S   (to select Size All)

This will make all the inner frames small enough to be fully displayed in the containing frame. Press In (+) twice to enter the HELP-MESSAGE frame, press Return to get to the second line, and perform the following keystrokes:

Ctrl-W   (to open the Words menu)

R   (to set the right margin)

36   (to select a right margin of 36, the size of the frame)

Return   (to record your selection)

Instruct (Ins)   (to reopen the Words menu)

C   (to center the text)

Enter the text

Press Return to run AP/AR

using the Words menu to boldface the program name. Now press

Out (–)   (to move the highlight to the frame's border)

Ctrl-F   (to open the Frames menu)

D   (to turn Display Labels off)

Ctrl-W   (to open the Words menu)

W   (to open Word options)

D   (to hide ruler line)

Your frame should look like Figure 8.7.

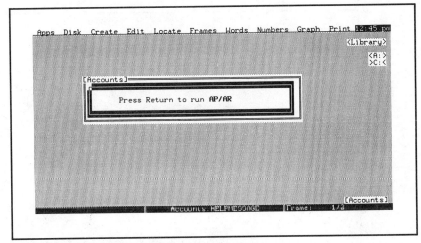

Figure 8.7: The Accounts frame on the desktop

Next, select the outer frame and enter the programming area. Modify the program so that it matches the one shown in Figure 8.8.

Again, to run the program, select it and press Recalc (F5). This version of the program begins by cleaning up the desktop, which conserves memory, and then using the @DISPLAY function to display the HELPMESSAGE frame in the upper left corner of the desktop. When you press Return, it checks to see if there is enough memory available in your computer to run the AP/AR program, which we'll assume requires 128K, or somewhat over 131,000 bytes. If there's not enough memory, your computer will beep and tell you so:

```
@if(@memavail < 132000,
   @list(
      @eraseprompt,
      @prompt("Not enough memory to run AP/AR—Press a key
to continue"),
      @beep,
      @nextkey,
      @eraseprompt,
      @return(#FALSE)
   )
)
```

```
@performkeys("[ctrl-d]c"),
@display(accounts.helpmessage),
@eraseprompt,
@local(ch),ch := @nextkey,
@echo(#on),
@if(@memavail < 132000,
        @list(
                @eraseprompt,
                @prompt("Not enough memory to run AP/AR -- Press a key to continue"),
                @beep,
                @nextkey,
                @eraseprompt,
                @return(#FALSE)
                )
        ),
@if(ch = [return],
    @list(
                @setdirectory("c:\accounts"),
                @setdrive("c:"),
                @eraseprompt,
                @prompt("Loading AP/AR . . . Please Wait"),
                @echo(#OFF),
                @performkeys("[ctrl-d]c"),
                @run(accounts.output, "c:ap-ar.exe"),
                @setdirectory("c:\framewk"),
                @echo(#ON),
                )
    )
```

Figure 8.8: The Accounts program

The statement

@return(#FALSE)

ends the program immediately at that point.

If there is enough memory, however, the program proceeds to the second @IF statement. This statement waits for the Return key to be pressed, and then executes substantially the same program that we wrote the first time. The only differences are that it displays a prompt while loading the accounting program, and that screen echoing is turned off, so you don't have to watch menus opening and closing.

You can use variations on this program to run almost any program that will fit in your available memory from the desktop. If you plan to run the program from a different disk drive, change the @SETDRIVE and @SETDIRECTORY statements accordingly. (If you are using a floppy disk system, you will probably want the application program you will run to be in drive B, because ultimately the FRED program will reside on the Help disk in drive A.)

You can also execute almost any DOS commands within your FRED program. For example, if you want your FRED program to copy data files to a RAM disk before running the application, you can use a series of statements such as

```
@prompt("Insert data disk in drive B and press a key"),
@nextkey,
@eraseprompt,
@run(accounts.output, "\command.com /c copy b:*.dat d:"),
@prompt("Insert AP/AR Program Disk in drive B and press a
key"),
@nextkey,
@eraseprompt,
```

before the @RUN statement that actually runs the application program.

Notice the form of the @RUN statement in this segment of the program. The syntax

```
\command.com /c
```

must be used when you want to use any of the DOS commands. The other statements in this segment simply display a prompt, wait for a key to be pressed, and then erase the prompt.

If you include statements like these, you will probably also want to prompt the user to place the data disk in drive B and use an @RUN statement to copy the modified files back onto it:

```
@run("\command.com /c copy d:*.dat b:")
```

ADDING YOUR PROGRAM TO THE APPS MENU

Up to now, you've been using a frame on the desktop to run other application programs. Presently we're going to install the accounting program on the Apps menu, so you can select it without having to load the FRED program first. To do this, we'll have to leave Framework III. Use the Move key (F7) to save your program on the Help disk if you are using floppy disks, or simply save the program to the Framework III directory on your hard disk before you exit from Framework III.

To install the program on the menu, we need the SETUPFW program. (Floppy disk users will find it on the Setup disk; see Appendix
A.) For now, just follow the steps outlined below. When your screen
displays the appropriate drive prompt, type

setupfw

Once the program is loaded, the screen should look like Figure A.1 in
Appendix A. Press

2   (to select All Other Uses of the Setup Program)

If you have a hard disk, you will probably then press 2 again, if the
Setup program is in your Framework III directory. If you have a
floppy disk system, insert the Help disk in drive A and press 1. Next,
press

5   (to select Add-ins)

1   (to select Applications Add-ins)

You will see the screen shown in Figure 8.9. We'll assume for now
that you want to keep dBASE on the menu. Press

4   (to enter the Add-in 2 menu name)

AP/AR   (enter the name of the application to appear on the
             menu)

Return   (to record your entry)

as shown in Figure 8.10. Next, press

5   to enter the Add-in 2 file name)

accounts.fw3   (enter the name of the FRED program to run
                    the application)

Return   (to record your entry)

6   (to enter the Add-in 2 user message)

Run Accounting   (enter the message to be displayed in the
from the Desktop   message area)

Return   (to record your entry)

At this point, your screen will look like Figure 8.10. Now press

M   (to return to the main menu)

7   (to record the changes you have made)

You will be prompted if you need to change disks. Figure 8.11 shows the completed entry.

```
APPLICATIONS ADD-INS                    CURRENT SETTING      NEW SETTING
(1) Add-in 1 menu name                      dBASE               same
(2) Add-in 1 file name                   RUNDBASE.FW3           same
(3) Add-in 1 user message           Run dBASE within Fra       same
(4) Add-in 2 menu name                   Apps Add-in            same
(5) Add-in 2 file name                                          same
(6) Add-in 2 user message           Use Setup to add you        same
(7) Add-in 3 menu name                   Apps Add-in            same
(8) Add-in 3 file name                                          same
(9) Add-in 3 user message           Use Setup to add you        same




              PRESS A NUMBER to indicate which option you want to change.
  Or press       [F1] for Help      [Esc] to back up one screen     M for Main menu.
```

Figure 8.9: The Applications Add-ins Setup menu

```
APPLICATIONS ADD-INS                    CURRENT SETTING      NEW SETTING
    Add-in 1 menu name                      dBASE               same
    Add-in 1 file name                   RUNDBASE.FW3           same
    Add-in 1 user message           Run dBASE within Fra       same
--> Add-in 2 menu name                   Apps Add-in            same
    Add-in 2 file name                                          same
    Add-in 2 user message           Use Setup to add you        same
    Add-in 3 menu name                   Apps Add-in            same
    Add-in 3 file name                                          same
    Add-in 3 user message           Use Setup to add you        same
                              ENTER NEW MENU NAME


SETTINGS
Current: Apps Add-in
    New: same
                                    (entry cannot exceed 21      characters)
  Newest: AP/AR
                                    (enter "none" to clear the setting)

                 Enter name or symbol and then press [RETURN].
                    Or press [Esc] to back up one screen.
```

Figure 8.10: Entering an application add-in

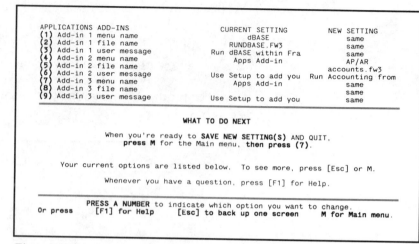

Figure 8.11: A completed application add-in

If you would rather replace dBASE, select 1, 2, and 3 in place of 4, 5, and 6, respectively, on the Applications Add-ins menu screen. Figure 8.12 shows the Apps menu with three applications added and one selected. Next time you want to run the AP/AR program, open the Apps menu and press the appropriate number key. The HELP-MESSAGE frame will appear on the desktop as shown in Figure 8.13, waiting for you to press Return.

EXAMPLES

When we last looked in on The Sophisticated Palate, Eileen Wilcox had completed a telecommunications session in which she downloaded a spreadsheet from Joe Escovedo, manager of the new branch store. It was in the form of a VisiCalc DIF file. The next morning, George wanted to integrate those figures into the spreadsheet he developed in Chapter 3.

INTEGRATING THE VISICALC DIF FILE

Before he could do anything with Joe's spreadsheet, George first had to convert the VisiCalc DIF file into a form that Framework III

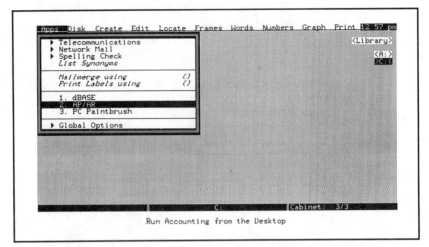

Figure 8.12: The Apps menu with three add-in applications installed

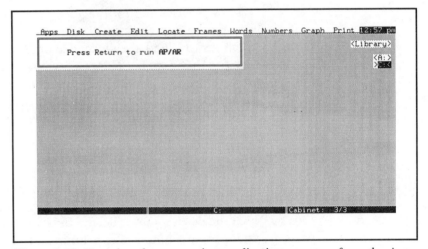

Figure 8.13: Running the accounting application program from the Apps menu

could read. Since DIF is one of the formats that Framework III recognizes, it converted the spreadsheet automatically. Next, George watched as Framework III created a spreadsheet and transferred all the figures from the file to the spreadsheet. When the process was finished, the spreadsheet shown in Figure 8.14 appeared on his screen. For comparison, the text of the original BRNCHSLS.DIF file is shown in Figure 8.15.

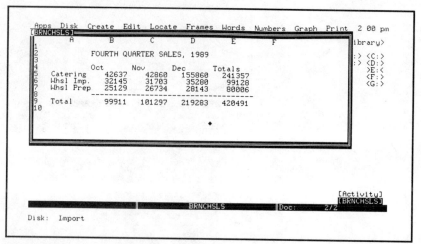

Figure 8.14: A Framework III spreadsheet from a DIF file

Now George had to integrate the information into his Activity Comparisons spreadsheet, so he could see the totals for both stores combined. He had already loaded the Activity Comparisons Outline frame to the desktop. (This frame contains the spreadsheet and graph we first saw in Chapter 3, Figures 3.18 and 3.19. The spreadsheet and graph have been updated and now reflect the sales figures for the second half of the year.) Next he renamed his new spreadsheet (which was still called BRNCHSLS) *Activity Comparisons: Branch Store* and moved it inside the Outline frame. He also renamed his original spreadsheet *Activity Comparisons: Main Store.*

To make comparing and combining the spreadsheets easier, he had to change the format of Joe's spreadsheet to match his own. First, he deleted Joe's title and the blank line beneath it. Second, he added three columns after column A, so the last three months of the quarter were at the right side of the spreadsheet. Third, he centered the month headings of Oct, Nov, and Dec. Then he moved the highlight to the border of the Branch Store spreadsheet, set the Decimal Places option in the Numbers submenu to 0, and chose the Currency format, to make the display of numbers match his spreadsheet. Finally, he locked the titles.

Now his spreadsheets were laid out identically. He copied the Main Store spreadsheet to a new frame within the Sales Activity outline. He

```
TABLE
0,1
""
VECTORS
0,6
""
TUPLES
0,9
""
DATA
0,0
""
-1,0
BOT
1,0
""
1,0
"FOURTH QUARTER SALES, 1989"
1,0
""
1,0
""
1,0
""
-1,0
BOT
1,0
""
1,0
""
1,0
""
1,0
""
1,0
""
-1,0
BOT
1,0
""
1,0
"Oct"
1,0
"Nov"
1,0
"Dec"
1,0
"Totals"
1,0
""
-1,0
BOT
1,0
"Catering"
0,4.263700000000000E+04
V
0,4.286000000000000E+04
V
0,1.558600000000000E+05
V
0,2.413570000000000E+05
V
1,0
""
```

Figure 8.15: The BRNCHSLS.DIF text file (one long column on disk)

```
-1,0
BOT
1,0
"Whsl Imp."
0,32145
V
0,31703
V
0,3.528000000000000E+04
V
0,9.912800000000000E+04
V
1,0
""
-1,0
BOT
1,0
"Whsl Prep"
0,25129
V
0,26734
V
0,28143
V
0,8.000600000000000E+04
V
1,0
""
-1,0
BOT
1,0
""
1,0
"---------"
1,0
"---------"
1,0
"---------"
1,0
""
-1,0
BOT
1,0
"Total"
0,9.991100000000000E+04
V
0,1.012970000000000E+05
V
0,2.192830000000000E+05
V
0,4.204910000000000E+05
V
1,0
""
-1,0
EOD
```

Figure 8.15: The BRNCHSLS.DIF text file (one long column on disk) (continued)

labeled it *Activity Comparisons: Both Stores*. Behind the cell for July Wholesale Prepared Food sales, he created a formula to add the values from the equivalent cells of the spreadsheets for each store. He used Framework III's pointing mode to create the formula, which read

@sum([Activity Comparisons: Main Store].B2,
[Activity Comparisons: Branch Store].B2)

He copied this formula to all the cells in the spreadsheet except the titles and the cells containing dotted lines, and then waited as Framework III recalculated all the values. When the process was complete, he printed out the Outline frame so he could compare the spreadsheets easily. His printout of the spreadsheets is shown in Figure 8.16. Next July, when George would prepare another activity comparisons summary, he could just copy the formulas into a new *Activity Comparisons: Both Stores* spreadsheet.

EXPLORING FURTHER

Before we leave our discussion of working with other programs, let's look at ways to import and export file formats that are not

```
Activity Comparisons: Main Store

            Jul       Aug       Sep       Oct       Nov       Dec       Totals
Catering  $83,639   $79,243   $75,621   $77,821   $84,260   $87,402    $487,986
Whsl Imp. $60,218   $61,732   $61,482   $59,709   $64,821   $65,201    $373,163
Whsl Prep $45,521   $45,443   $42,879   $43,826   $47,365   $47,888    $272,922
          -------------------------------------------------------------------
Total    $189,378  $186,418  $179,982  $181,356  $196,446  $200,491  $1,134,071


Activity Comparisons: Branch Store

            Jul       Aug       Sep       Oct       Nov       Dec       Totals
Catering                               $39,325   $42,637   $42,860    $124,822
Whsl Imp.                              $31,703   $35,280   $35,343    $102,326
Whsl Prep                              $25,129   $26,734   $28,143     $80,006
          -------------------------------------------------------------------
Total                                  $96,157  $104,651  $106,346    $307,154


3  Activity Comparisons: Both Stores (S)

            Jul       Aug       Sep       Oct       Nov       Dec       Totals
Catering  $83,639   $79,243   $75,621  $117,146  $126,897  $130,262    $612,808
Whsl Imp. $60,218   $61,732   $61,482   $91,412  $100,101  $100,544    $475,489
Whsl Prep $45,521   $45,443   $42,879   $68,955   $74,099   $76,031    $352,928
          -------------------------------------------------------------------
Total    $189,378  $186,418  $179,982  $277,513  $301,097  $306,837  $1,441,225
```

Figure 8.16: Integrating a DIF file into a Framework III spreadsheet included on Framework III's Import and Export menus. We'll explore ways to integrate columnar data from an ASCII text file into a spreadsheet or database, import a comma-delimited file, and export a spreadsheet or database to a word processing program.

INTEGRATING A COLUMNAR ASCII FILE INTO A SPREADSHEET OR DATABASE

As you may have discovered, you can transfer data among different types of frames. You can copy the contents of a Database or Spreadsheet frame into a Word frame, and sometimes you can copy the text from a Word frame into a Database or Spreadsheet frame. How successfully you can do so depends on the format of the data in the original frame.

When moving columnar text from a Word frame to a Spreadsheet or Database frame, the important point to remember is that commas between text items, and single-character spaces between numeric fields, behave as delimiters between fields. Also, if you have some tabular data in which some items are blank, the data will not fall into the proper columns when you move it to a columnar frame.

Suppose, for example, that you were beginning a project schedule, or importing one from another program, and the data appeared in the following form:

Date	Task	Person
6 July89	Make initial contacts	George
	Send Purchase orders	Francine
	Write ad copy	Sue
12July89	Pick up Merchandise	Marie
14July89	Place ads	Sue
	Follow up on purchase orders	George
	Call Deliveries, Inc.	Harold

This seems like a natural format for a database frame. However, there are some hazards you must watch out for:

- Spaces between numbers act as field separators

- A single space between text items does *not* act as a field separator

- A comma within a text field acts as a field separator

If you copy this text to a database frame, the result will appear as in Figure 8.17. The space between *6* and *July* will result in the 6 being treated as numeric data and placed in a separate field. Similarly, the comma in *Deliveries, Inc.* will result in this text field being spread across two columns. As a result, the third field in these rows will be placed in a fourth column. Finally, the fact that

Follow up on purchase orders

is separated by only a single space from the responsible person's name will result in the name being included in the Task field, and the Person field will be blank.

Moreover, sometimes the leading spaces in some rows will be ignored, so that the tasks in column 2 of this text will end up in column 1. Clearly, some editing of the text form of the data—such as replacing `` July'' with ``July'', adding more space between columns 2 and 3, and replacing commas with nothing, will improve the results.

SPECIAL TECHNIQUES FOR COMMA-DELIMITED FILES

Comma-delimited files can be imported with relatively little difficulty. Again, the technique is to bring the file to the desktop as an

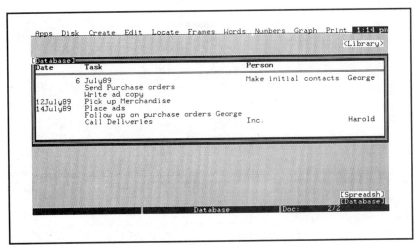

Figure 8.17: A database from columnar data in a Word frame

ASCII text file in a Word frame, and then copy the contents to a Database frame. The same things can go wrong as in a transfer in the opposite direction, however. That is, you must be sure that the imported file has no quotation marks embedded within text fields, and no commas within numeric fields. Again, a bit of editing of the data while it's in the Word frame can help to ensure a smooth transfer with the results you desire. To see the results of such an import, you might take the comma-delimited version of the Sales People database, bring it to the desktop, and copy it to a Database frame of appropriate size. The result should be a reasonable duplication of the original database, as shown in Figure 8.18, provided that you converted all the numeric cells from currency to general format before you created the comma-delimited file.

EXPORTING COLUMNAR DATA TO A WORD PROCESSING PROGRAM

As mentioned earlier, you will get an error message if you try to export a Spreadsheet or Database frame to WordStar or MultiMate. One way around this is to export the frame to an ASCII text file, and then read the text file into the word processing program. However, when you export a frame to an ASCII text file, you will lose any styling and formatting information the frame may contain. If you want to

Apps	Disk	Create	Edit	Locate	Frames	Words	Numbers	Graph	Print	1:55 pm

EmpNo	Last	First	Reg	SixMoSale	AvgPerMo	Pbn	Hired
82M1	Waterman	Pearl	MW	85977.83	14329.64	#NO	Sep 29, 1
84M3	Brooke	Donny	MW	58439.33	9739.89	#YES	Dec 1, 19
85M2	Olsen	Oscar	MW	1.15E+5	19089.46	#NO	Jun 20, 1
66N3	Rizzo	Anne	NE	1.18E+5	19605.41	#NO	May 21, 1
79N6	Herrera	Fred	NE	87654.32	14609.05	#NO	Nov 20, 1
86N2	Sapolsky	Stan	NE	48675.30	8112.55	#YES	Jul 13, 1
74N4	Takahashi	Bruce	NW	1.03E+5	17110.80	#NO	Mar 23, 1
82N8	Woo	Eva	NW	93254.10	15542.35	#NO	Feb 25, 1
85N5	Smith	Joe	NW	56733.45	9455.58	#YES	Oct 23, 1
69S3	Washingto	Ed	S	1.02E+5	17062.52	#NO	Aug 29, 1
78S4	Curtis	Amy	S	47256.70	7876.12	#YES	Apr 12, 1
82S9	Hernandez	Esther	S	83241.20	13873.53	#NO	May 5, 19
72S6	Schroeder	Art	SE	94243.22	15707.20	#NO	Jan 24, 1
81S5	Petrakis	Bill	SE	1.12E+5	18718.72	#NO	Aug 24, 1
84S1	Smyth	Gloria	SE	87732.41	14622.07	#NO	May 17, 1
78S1	Smithfiel	Frank	SW	51623.62	8603.94	#YES	Jul 22, 1
83S9	Goldberg	Jack	SW	1.03E+5	17209.11	#NO	Oct 29, 1
86S2	Smith	Ashleigh	SW	67132.45	11188.74	#NO	Mar 4, 19

| Comma-Delimited File].EmpNo | Recs: | 25/25 |

Figure 8.18: A database from a comma-delimited file

preserve such information, first copy the Spreadsheet or Database frame into a Word frame, and then export the Word frame directly to the word processing program's format. Since formulas residing behind cells or column heads are not converted in any of the import or export formats, you will lose nothing by taking this extra step.

SPECIAL CONSIDERATIONS IN EXPORTING TO WORD PROCESSORS

The export programs for word processing programs are not as clean as they might be. Not everything is translated entirely accurately. There are three aspects of frames that you need to be particularly careful about:

- Tabs
- Page breaks
- Frame labels and frames that are not Word frames

No matter what size tabs and paragraph indentations you use in your Word frames, the translation programs automatically convert all tabs to eight spaces. This is because the conversion is done by means of the Tab character (ASCII 9). Although you can set a typewriter's tabulator at any point you want, in the world of computers the tab character has traditionally been converted to eight spaces when a file is converted to text.

SUMMARY

Framework III includes several different types of tools to help you work with other programs. It can convert Framework III frames into ten different types of files:

- Framework II files
- dBASE III or III PLUS files
- ASCII text files

- Lotus 1-2-3 worksheet files
- DCA files
- WordStar word processing files
- MultiMate word processing files
- WordPerfect
- Multiplan SYLK files
- Comma-delimited files (dBASE III)

It can also convert ten other types of files into Framework III frames:

- Earlier Framework files
- ASCII text files
- dBASE .DBF files
- Lotus 1-2-3 worksheet files
- DCA files
- WordStar word processing files
- MultiMate word processing files
- WordPerfect
- Multiplan SYLK files
- VisiCalc DIF files

In addition to its file-translating capabilities, Framework III allows you to run other programs without actually unloading Framework III from memory. You can run other programs using three different methods:

- In a DOS Access frame
- By means of a FRED program on the desktop
- By installing a FRED program on the Apps menu

These capabilities make Framework III a flexible tool for working in a variety of environments. They allow you to customize Framework

III so that you can use other types of software conveniently, and to share files with other programs that you may use. They also simplify considerably the task of sharing data with people who use software other than Framework III to accomplish similar tasks.

Installing
and Customizing
Framework III

IN THIS APPENDIX, WE WILL EXAMINE THE SETUP program and some of the most important options it provides for making Framework III conform to your hardware and your work habits.

The Setup program is easy to use. You make all your choices by selecting items from menus, using the number keys at the top of the keyboard. You are prompted whenever you need to enter any text. If the instructions are not clear enough, context-sensitive help is available at any point via the Help key (F1). Since the program is so easy to use, we will not direct you keystroke by keystroke. Rather, we will point out some of the most useful options, or the most useful settings for the options that are available to you.

You must run the Setup program at a DOS prompt, not from the Framework III desktop. It is also best not to have any RAM-resident programs active while you are using Setup. When you are finished using the program, you have the choice of either saving the settings you have changed, or leaving the program without saving the settings. Therefore, you can feel free to experiment, knowing that you can cancel any changes you have made. You can use the Setup program to change Framework III's default settings as often as you like.

INSTALLING FRAMEWORK III FOR THE FIRST TIME

If you have never used Framework III before, you must run the Setup program to accomplish two tasks: First, you must *personalize* your copy, and second, you must configure the program for your hardware.

To run the Setup program, place the Setup in disk drive A, and at an A prompt, type

    setupfw

Then press Return. When the ID screen appears, you will be prompted to enter your name, the name of your company (which is optional), and the serial number of your disk, which you can read either from the label or from the warranty card. Once you have completed these steps, you can make working copies of all the program disks, or install Framework III to a hard disk.

In a short time, you will see the screen shown in Figure A.1. Press 1, and follow the directions that appear on the screen for floppy or hard disk systems, as appropriate. You will need to tell Framework III the kind of video resolution you want and the model of your printer. Choose the appropriate models from the lists provided. If you have more than one printer—a text printer and a graphics printer, for instance—you can run the Setup program again to define a second printer.

TEXT VERSUS GRAPHICS MODE

Originally, when there were two display modes—monochrome and color—there were two ways to install Framework. Today, however, there are many different video display modes, and so you have more options when installing Framework III for your screen.

Whether you have a color or a monochrome display, you may choose to install in text mode or in graphics mode. Table A.1 shows how each mode will display text attributes (such as bold, underlined, and italics), and how it will display graphics.

As you can see, you can choose a graphics or a text mode whether you have a monochrome or a color display. You might expect to always choose graphics with color systems, but in some cases, you

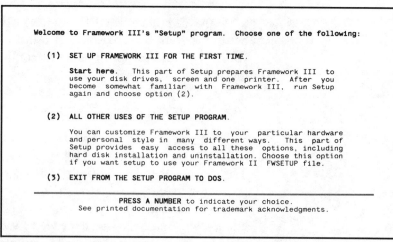

```
Welcome to Framework III's "Setup" program.  Choose one of the following:

(1)  SET UP FRAMEWORK III FOR THE FIRST TIME.

     Start here.   This part of Setup prepares Framework III  to
     use your disk drives,  screen and one  printer.  After  you
     become  somewhat  familiar  with  Framework III,  run Setup
     again and choose option (2).

(2)  ALL OTHER USES OF THE SETUP PROGRAM.

     You can customize Framework III to  your  particular hardware
     and personal  style in  many  different ways.   This  part of
     Setup provides  easy  access to all these  options, including
     hard disk installation and uninstallation.  Choose this option
     if you want setup to use your Framework II  FWSETUP file.

(3)  EXIT FROM THE SETUP PROGRAM TO DOS.

                   PRESS A NUMBER to indicate your choice.
           See printed documentation for trademark acknowledgments.
```

Figure A.1: The introductory screen for the Setup program

Table A.1: Display of Text Attributes and Graphics

MODE	TEXT ATTRIBUTES	GRAPHICS
Color Graphics	Text attributes and special effects appear as they will print	True color graphics
Color Text	Text attributes appear in different colors	Graphics in windows appear as character graphics; zoomed graphics (using F9) appear as true color graphics
Monochrome Graphics	Text attributes show up as they will print	True monochrome graphics (on cards that support true graphics)
Monochrome Text	Text attributes are not differentiated	Graphics display as character-based graphics

may prefer the text mode. For instance, on CGA color systems, you can display more colors if you choose text mode.

The Setup program allows you to do a great deal more to tailor Framework III to your hardware and your working habits. Let's look now at some of the options it provides.

TAILORING FRAMEWORK III TO YOUR HARDWARE

If you have already installed Framework III and want to go further with the options provided by the Setup program, load the program as though you were going to install Framework III, but press 2 (All Other Uses...) when the screen shown in Figure A.1 appears. Next, you will have an opportunity to choose which setup file to use—whether to create a new one or use the existing file. In most cases, you will want to press 2 to use your current setup file. Finally, you will be greeted by the Setup program's main menu, shown in Figure A.2. Press 1 (Configuration), and the screen shown in Figure A.3 will be displayed. To customize Framework III for your hardware, you will use options primarily from the Configuration Options menu. Let's look at some of the options it provides.

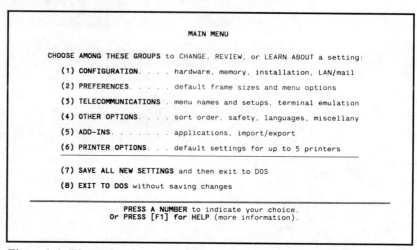

Figure A.2: The main menu of the Setup program

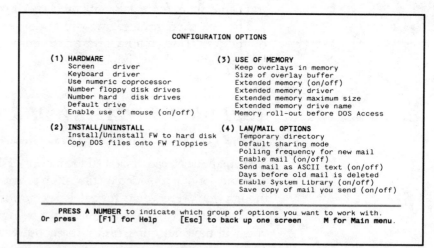

Figure A.3: The Configuration Options menu

INSTALLING DISK DRIVES

 Version Note

Earlier versions of Framework worked differently with disk drives and directories. For details, see the manual for the version you are using.

Framework III is "well-behaved" with respect to disk drives and directories—it can navigate through subdirectories with ease. However, you should make sure that the program can access all the drives in your system, or all the drives that you want it to have access to.

Ordinarily, Framework III can sense your computer's environment when you run the program—including such factors as dip switch settings, parameters in RAM, and the presence or absence of a network. However, in some cases, you will need to tell it what drives you are using. For instance, if you have a typical system with one floppy drive and one hard disk, Framework III will sense their presence automatically. If you use a RAM disk or other nonstandard disk, you may have to use the Setup program to tell Framework III what you are using.

When you press 1 from the Configuration Options menu, you will see the list of hardware setup options. Ordinarily, the settings for floppy drives and hard drives will read *0*. This is the setting for automatic sensing.

If you run Framework III, and each of your drives is represented by a separate cabinet, leave the drive settings to 0. However, if any drives are not recognized, run the Setup program and change the appropriate setting.

INSTALLING MULTIPLE
PRINTER CONFIGURATIONS

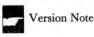 Version Note

In earlier versions, Framework supported only two printers.

As you can see from Figure A.2, you can install up to five printers and/or plotters. Press 6 (Printer Options) from the Setup main menu to access the main printer options. If your printer or plotter has two different modes of operation, one of which emulates another device, you may want to install the driver for the emulated device as a second printer/plotter. However, even if you have only one printer, you may still find it useful to install two or more printer configurations. To make the most of this possibility, you will need to use the Printer Options submenu for the printer you wish to redefine. For instance, to redefine Printer 3, you would select 3 from the Printer Options submenu to display the screen in Figure A.4.

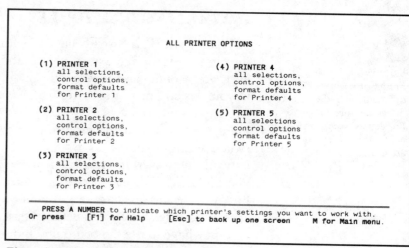

Figure A.4: The Printer Options submenu

Notice that the Printer Options submenu allows you to determine the default number of lines per inch and characters per inch separately for two printers. You could, for example, have two default configurations for a single printer, one for 6 lines per inch and 12 characters per inch, and the other for 8 lines per inch and 10 characters per inch. Simply enter the appropriate values in the Printer Options submenu.

MANAGING MEMORY

Let's turn our attention now to the Use of Memory submenu on the Configuration Options menu. It includes at least one seductive option that generally does not have the desired effect.

Framework III is a large program. Ordinarily, it reads sections of code from an *overlay file* when you switch from one function to another, and only a small portion of the actual program code is in memory at any given time. You can increase the size of the overlay buffer, which theoretically should speed up performance by reducing the number of times code has to be read from disk. In fact, increasing the size of the overlay buffer will severely reduce the amount of memory available for your files, which may hamper your operations, and even slow the program down. We recommend *not* increasing the size of the overlay buffer.

You can use extended memory (above 640K) or expanded (EMS) memory with Framework III if it is available in your system. To do so, you must make two entries in the Use of Memory submenu. First, you must install the name of the program that initializes your extended or expanded memory. Second, you must specify the maximum amount of extended or expanded memory that you want Framework III to use. You should be aware, however, that the largest file on the desktop is always kept in conventional memory, and conventional memory is also used to store *pointers* to the location of any files that are located in extended memory. Therefore, if you do not have enough conventional memory to store the pointers, you will not be able to use extended memory. You will need at least 640K to use extended memory.

The Use of Memory submenu includes an option to use a disk drive as though it were extended memory. If you have a hard disk, this option may be tempting. However, since reading from and writing to disk is the slowest aspect of computer operations, using your hard disk as extended memory will probably slow down Framework III's performance markedly. Unless you need to work with immense databases, we strongly recommend that you do not use a hard disk as extended memory.

You can also set the DOS roll-out feature on or off. If you set this feature on, a frozen picture of Framework will be saved in memory or on disk while you access DOS. This frees some space in conventional memory. However, you should be aware that this will affect the operation of the DOS frame. In particular, DOS roll-out will prevent any text from being captured in a DOS frame.

CUSTOMIZING THE DESKTOP

Let's turn now to the Preference Options menu, which is shown in Figure A.5. To display this menu, press 2 (Preferences) at the Setup main menu. As you can see, this menu allows you to determine several default settings for the options that appear on Framework III's menus. You can choose the size of various types of frames, the default dimensions of databases and spreadsheets on the Create menu, and some of the default settings for the Words and Print menus. If you

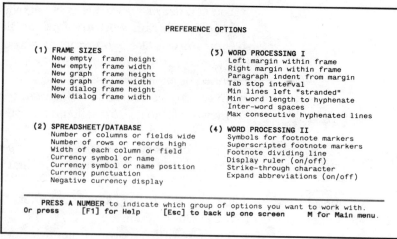

Figure A.5: The Preference Options menu

would prefer larger disk drive cabinets, for example, or if you characteristically work with small spreadsheets, this is the easiest way to tailor these features to your style of working.

When you select one of the items on the Preference Options menu to modify, its minimum, maximum, and default settings are shown, along with its current setting. This makes it easy to determine what is available, and reminds you of the settings you are currently using.

Our only specific recommendation is that you leave the Paragraph Indent setting at 0. If you do not, the line after any carriage return in a Word frame will automatically be indented. This can be inconvenient if you want to place the inside address of a letter at the left margin.

INSTALLING TELECOMMUNICATIONS SETUPS

In Chapter 6, we noted that you can streamline your telecommunications work by saving the settings you need for remote computers that you frequently communicate with in setup files. You can further streamline your work by installing your most frequently used setup files on the desktop Telecommunications menu.

To do so, press 3 (Telecommunications) at the Setup main menu. As you will see, you can install up to nine setups. They appear in groups of three, with each group of three on a separate menu. For each setup, you will need to enter both the name to appear on the menu and the file name of the setup. The procedure for making these installations is the same as the one described in Chapter 8 for installing applications add-ins.

MISCELLANEOUS FEATURES

You should be aware of three options on the Other Options menu, reached by pressing 4 at the Setup main menu. When you use either of the Sort options on the Locate menu, Framework III normally arranges the items to be sorted in Dictionary order. This will cause Framework III to place words in alphabetical order regardless of capitalization.

If you prefer, you can use this menu to change the sorting order to *ASCII* order. That is, the order is determined by the ASCII code of the characters in the field to be sorted. As you can see in Table C.1, the entire range of uppercase letters appears before any of the lowercase letters in the ASCII code.

If your system allows you to capture text in a DOS Access frame, you can use this menu to change the number of characters that will be retained. Normally, after 2,000 characters have appeared in a DOS Access frame, any subsequent characters will replace characters at the beginning of the frame. You can increase or decrease the number of characters retained. (Remember, this is different from the Capture setting on the Telecommunications menu, which can capture incoming characters when you are connected to a remote computer by modem. The default for capturing to a frame is 32,000 characters.)

You can also set the new Framework III Safety feature on or off as well as determine how big to make tabs in exported files.

You may have noticed that the Disk menu includes room for three import add-ins and three export add-ins. In theory, choosing 5 (Add-ins) from the Setup main menu allows you to add options to these sections of the Disk menu the same way you added the applications add-ins to the Apps menu. However, the format-translation files are complex, involving many direct calls to machine language (the computer's native language), and they are difficult to modify. Ashton-Tate was expected to make such translation files available for other file formats; however, as of this writing, none have been created.

USING RAM-RESIDENT SOFTWARE WITH FRAMEWORK III

Framework III is such a comprehensively designed software package that you should have little need for RAM-resident "background" programs such as macro processors, online dictionaries, and DOS access tools. However, if you are accustomed to using programs of this nature, you can still use them with Framework III. Most of them are quite compatible with it. The principal limitation is the amount of memory available in your computer. Remember that Framework III requires a full 640K, so you'll do best with background programs that put most of their code in EMS memory.

The only type of background software that does not generally work with Framework III is path-extension software. These programs allow you to use software that requires overlay or driver files without first logging onto the package's directory. When such a program is loaded, Framework III will look in drive A for many of its files, even if you are logged onto Framework III's directory on a hard disk. Even so, you can use this type of software successfully if neither your DOS search path nor your extended path includes the Framework III directory.

FRED Functions

INTRODUCTION

This appendix presents a listing and brief explanation of all the FRED programming functions, with their syntax formats. The functions are listed alphabetically. By way of introduction, the following comments describe the major categories of FRED functions.

NUMERIC FUNCTIONS

The numeric functions all perform some operation on a numeric expression and return a numeric value. The parameters to these functions usually consist of a number, a numeric expression, or a reference to a number. This category includes rounding functions (@ROUND, @FLOOR, @CEILING); logarithmic and exponential functions (@LN, @EXP, @LOG); a random-number generator (@RAND); and trigonometric functions, among others. The parameters to the trigonometric functions @COS, @SIN, and @TAN must be angles expressed in radians.

STATISTICAL FUNCTIONS

FRED's statistical functions all return statistical information about a series of parameters. The parameters to these functions must be in the form of a range or list of numbers or numeric expressions. This category includes functions for finding sums, averages, minimum and maximum values, and the variance and standard deviation, as well as for counting the number of values in a range of values.

FINANCIAL FUNCTIONS

FRED's financial functions include the present and future value functions (@PV and @FV), the net present value function (@NPV), a function for calculating loan and mortgage payments (@PMT), and functions for finding the internal rate of return of a business investment (@IRR and @MIRR).

DATE AND TIME FUNCTIONS

FRED's date and time functions fall into two groups: those that return a date and time—and display the date; and those that convert the date-type value returned by the first group into a text string and format that string in various ways. The distinction is important: the first group returns date-type values, which can subsequently be sorted, used in the date arithmetic functions, or formatted. The results of the second group of functions can be used only as text strings—they cannot be sorted chronologically, used in the date arithmetic functions, or formatted in any other way. These are the functions that return date-type values:

    @date
    @datetime
    @diffdate
    @sumdate
    @time
    @today

All other date and time functions take one of these functions as a parameter and return text strings.

Of the functions that return date-type values, @DATE, @DATETIME, @TIME, and @TODAY all return both a date and a time and display the *date*. The times that @DATE (without parameters) and @TODAY return are always the current time on the system clock. When @DATE is used with parameters, the time it returns is Framework III's default time—12:00 AM. The dates that @TIME (without parameters) and @TODAY return are always the current date on the system clock. When @TIME is used with parameters, the date it returns is in the same format that the @DATE function displays. To get any of these functions to display the time, you must convert their results into a text string using one of the time-formatting functions.

STRING FUNCTIONS

The string functions fall into two classes: those that perform some type of operation on a string, and those that convert numeric values to text values. The former include @LEN, @MID, @INT, and @VALUE. The rest of the string functions, with the exception of @TEXTSELECTION, convert numeric values to text values in various formats.

NUMERIC DISPLAY (OR "TAILORING") FUNCTIONS

In this category are several functions that control the display of currency and other numeric values. The fundamental currency-formatting function is @NATIONALIZE. The functions that @NATIONALIZE takes as parameters are @DOLLAR, @POUND, and @YEN, to display currency values with their appropriate symbols and formatting. For other currencies, use @UNIT. Finally, the @THOUSANDS and @MILLI functions will control the display of decimal points and commas.

PRINTING FUNCTIONS

The printing functions determine the way printed output from a frame will appear on the page. The horizontal positioning of text on the page is determined by the two functions @PO (page offset) and @LL (line length). The functions that place headers and footers on the page determine left, right, and center relative to the printed line established by @PO and @LL, not the physical page edges. For example, if you set up your printed line so that it starts in column 15 and runs 50 characters, flush left will be at column 15 and flush right at column 65.

In those functions where the parameter appears in quotes, the parameter must be a text-type value. All other parameters represent numeric values.

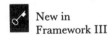
New in
Framework III

In Framework III, the print functions are mostly replaced by the Format Options and Control Options submenus of the Print menu.

MACRO-BUILDING FUNCTIONS

Macro-building functions are used to process the responses of a user to the macros you have created. They check the keyboard for responses, execute preprogrammed keystrokes in series, retrieve selected blocks of text, and select a particular frame or cell.

PROGRAMMING FUNCTIONS

FRED's programming functions handle all the standard programming operations. They fall into several classes:

- Control functions
- Logical functions
- Input and output functions
- Region-walking functions

The control functions include a loop controller (@WHILE), an assignment function (@SET), functions that pass values (@ITEM, @RESULT, and @RETURN), and a case structure (@SELECT). The logical functions include @IF, @AND, @OR, and @NOT, error-testing functions, and tests for alphabetic and numeric values. The input/output functions include @INPUTLINE, which prompts for user input; @PROMPT, which displays a prompt below the desktop; and @MENU, which processes a user-defined menu. FRED also includes the disk functions @WRITETEXTFILE and @WRITEFRAMEFILE, plus several other disk-related and directory-related functions.

The *region-walking* functions are a special class. They include the following functions:

```
@choose
@hlookup
@vlookup
@fill
@get
@next
@put
@reset
```

The first three functions are used for looking up items in tables. The rest are used to move a pointer within a specified range of frames or cells, and either retrieve values from or place values into them.

In addition, Framework III has functions that fetch formulas from specified locations and place formulas in other locations and execute them, so FRED programs can modify themselves.

MISCELLANEOUS FUNCTIONS

In addition to all its other function categories, FRED includes graph-generating functions, sound and graphics sublanguages (which are only touched upon briefly in this appendix), and a function for reading records from a dBASE file into Framework III.

THE FUNCTIONS

@ABS (numeric expression)
@ABS calculates the absolute value of its parameter.

@ACOS (numeric expression)
@ACOS returns the arccosine of its parameter, expressed in radians.

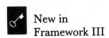
New in
Framework III

@ALARM (date-time value, frame ref)
@ALARM (# of minutes, frame ref)
@ALARM is used to activate a frame when a specified time or date is reached, or when a specific number of minutes has passed. The frame might contain a program (for instance, to activate a telecommunications session), or it might simply place a reminder message on the screen at the specified time. For instance, to begin a preprogrammed telecommunications session at 11:30 PM, you would place the FRED program to run the session in a frame (call it TELECOM) and then write the following formula in the program area of a Word frame:

```
@alarm(@datetime(@today, @time(23,30,00)),TELECOM)
```

@AND (expression1, expression2, . . .)
@AND is a logical function that returns #TRUE if *all* the logical statements among its parameters are true. Otherwise, it returns #FALSE. At least one of its parameters must be a logical statement—that is, a statement that can be evaluated as true or false. The @AND function is often used as part of the first parameter of the @IF function.

@ASIN (numeric expression)
@ASIN returns the arcsine of its parameter, expressed in radians.

@ATAN *(numeric expression)*

@ATAN returns the arctangent of its parameter, expressed in radians.

@ATAN2 *(expression1, expression2)*

@ATAN2 returns the arctangent of the angle, expressed in radians, whose opposite and adjacent sides are represented by *expression1* and *expression2*, respectively. @ATAN2 allows you to calculate the arctangents of all four quadrants of an x-y axis system.

@AVG *(expression1, expression2, . . .)*
@AVG *(range)*

@AVG returns the average of all the numbers in its parameter list.

@BEEP
@BEEP *(pitch, hundredths)*

When used without parameters, @BEEP causes the computer to emit a standard beep. However, you can cause the computer's sound generator to produce any tone it can produce by specifying a particular pitch in cycles per second and the duration of the sound in hundredths of a second.

If you want to use @BEEP to play music, first set up a series of local variables assigning the various pitch frequencies to their letter names. Then you can use the letter names as parameters in a series of @BEEP expressions.

@BM *(lines)*

@BM sets the bottom margin for a page of printed output. Its parameter is the number of *lines* that will be left blank between the last line of text (not including the footer) and the bottom of the physical page. The default value is 6.

@BOP
@BOP *(indentation, format, left margin, right margin)*

@BOP starts a new paragraph of text by inserting a hidden beginning-of-paragraph character. When used without parameters, it takes the default values of no indentation, flush right, a left margin of 0, and a right margin of 65. Choose a *format* by selecting its number from the following table:

0   Flush right

1   Align left

2   Justify

3   Center

The formula

"This is the end." & @bop(5,1,0,65) & "This is the beginning."

displays the text

This is the end.
This is the beginning.

@*BUSINESS* (*numeric expression*)
@*BUSINESS* (*numeric expression, decimal places*)
@*BUSINESS* (*date*)

@BUSINESS rounds the numeric value in its parameter to two decimal places, formats the result with a comma between every three digits, and converts the result into a text value. If a positive number of decimal places is specified as the second parameter, @BUSINESS rounds its first parameter to the specified number of places. If the second parameter is a zero, @BUSINESS rounds its first parameter to an integer before converting it into a text value. If the second parameter is negative, the first parameter will be rounded to the nearest 10, 100, 1000, and so on. For example, the expressions

@business(2654.7, – 1)
@business(2654.7, – 2)
@business(2654.7, – 3)

will return the text strings 2,650, 2,700, and 3,000, respectively.

If the parameter to @BUSINESS is a date-type value, it will convert that value to a text string and display the result in the format

Month dd, yyyy

This result is identical to that returned by the @DATE4 function. For example, the function

@business(@date(1989, 8, 30))

will produce the text string

August 30, 1989

@CEILING *(numeric expression)*

@CEILING computes the smallest integer that is not less than its parameter. In other words, it rounds its parameter upward. (Negative numbers are also rounded upward—that is, toward zero.)

@CHOOSE *(index, references)*

@CHOOSE retrieves a value from a specified position in a list or range of values. The first parameter, *index*, represents the position in the specified list or range where the desired value will be found. The subsequent parameter or parameters represent the list or range of values to be searched.

@CHR *(ASCII)*
@CHR *(ASCII, type style)*

@CHR is used to convert an ASCII code number into the character it represents. You can use it to display the graphics characters from the extended ASCII code—that is, characters with codes from 128 to 255. You can also use it to supply special printing control characters to the @ST function.

You can specify a second parameter to assign a *type style* to the character returned by the first parameter. Choose a style by selecting its number from the following table:

1   Boldface

2   Italic

4   Underline

The effects are additive. For example, a value of 6 in the second parameter would indicate that the character returned by the first parameter should be italicized and underlined.

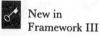
New in
Framework III

@COL

@COL returns the current column or field location of the cursor as a number. For instance, if you are in column E of a spreadsheet,

@COL will return 5. The function @ROW is the counterpart to @COL.

@COS *(numeric expression)*

@COS returns the cosine of the angle in its parameter, expressed in radians.

@COUNT *(expression1, expression2, . . .)*

@COUNT returns the number of numeric values in its list of parameters.

@CURRENCY *(numeric expression)*

The action of the @CURRENCY function is identical to that of the @BUSINESS function, except that @CURRENCY also includes a currency symbol in the resulting text value. Framework III's default currency symbol is $, which you can change using the @NATIONAL-IZE function.

@CURRENCY is used to embed figures derived from other frames or cells in text. For example:

"The tax on your order will be " &@currency(tax)

@DATE
@DATE *(yyyy, mm, dd)*

@DATE is usually used with three parameters, representing the year, month, and day, expressed as numbers. The result is a date-type value that can subsequently be sorted or used in the date arithmetic functions, @DIFFDATE and @SUMDATE. For example, the function

@date(1989, 10, 12)

will return a date-type value that will be displayed as

Oct 12, 1989

When used without parameters, @DATE returns the current date and time on the system clock and displays the date. The result of the @DATE function without parameters is identical to the result of the @TODAY function.

@DATE1 *(date)*

@DATE1 converts the date-type value in its parameter into a text string. Date arithmetic and chronological sorting cannot be performed on the result of @DATE1, because this result is a text value.

The parameter to this function must be another date function that produces a date-type value. For example:

> @date1(@date(1989, 8, 30))

will produce the text value

> Aug 30, 1989

Note that this resulting string is identical to the display format produced by @DATE and @TODAY. However, keep in mind the important difference: @DATE and @TODAY return date-type values, whereas @DATE1 (like @DATE2, @DATE3, and @DATE4) returns a string value.

@DATE2 *(date)*

@DATE2 converts the date-type value in its parameter to a text string and displays the result in the format

> Mmm yyyy

For example, the function

> @date2(@date(1989, 8, 30))

will produce the text value

> Aug 1989

The parameter to this function must be another date function that produces a date-type value.

@DATE3 *(date)*

@DATE3 converts the date-type value in its parameter to a text string and displays the result in the format

> Mmm dd

For example, the function

@date3(@date(1989, 8, 30))

will produce the text string

Aug 30

The parameter to this function must be another date function that produces a date-type value.

@DATE4 (date)

@DATE4 converts the date-type value in its parameter to a text string and displays the result in the format

Month dd, yyyy

For example, the function

@date4(@date(1989, 8, 30))

will produce the text string

August 30, 1989

The parameter to this function must be another function that produces a date-type value.

@DATETIME (date, time)

@DATETIME takes two parameters, *date* and *time*. The @DATE, @TIME, or @TODAY function can be used for either parameter. The @SUMDATE function can also be used for the *date* parameter. @DATETIME returns the date and time specified in its parameters and displays the date. For example, the function

@datetime(@date(1989, 4, 18), (@time 14, 53, 10))

will display the date

Apr 18, 1989

If the parameters are entered without their own parameters, this function—like @DATE, @TIME, and @TODAY—returns the current date and time from the system clock and displays the current date. To force the @DATETIME function to display the time, use @DATETIME with the *date* and *time* parameters as the parameter of @TIME1, @TIME2, @TIME3 or @TIME4.

@DBASEFILTER (*"drive:filename.dbf"*, *criteria*)
@DBASEFILTER (*"drive:filename.dbf"*, *criteria, starting record, ending record*)

@DBASEFILTER is used to load selected records from a dBASE II, dBASE III, or dBASE IV file into Framework III. It has two required and two optional parameters. The first parameter gives the drive on which the file will be found and the name of the database file. The second specifies a criterion or criteria for selecting records from the database file. It may be a complex expression, choosing records on the basis of multiple criteria through the @AND, @OR, and @NOT functions.

The optional parameters tell Framework III at which record to begin searching for the selected criteria, and at which record to stop.

If you load a dBASE file onto the desktop from one of the disk drive cabinets, Framework III will automatically create a Database frame with a @DBASEFILTER formula behind it. Pressing the Recalc key (F5) and then the Return key causes Framework III to read as many of the records from the dBASE file as will fit in the memory of your computer. Alternatively, you can edit the @DBASEFILTER formula, expressing your own selection criteria, before Framework III begins reading records into the frame.

New in
Framework III

@DBLOOKUP (*search, "searchfield", "retrievefield"*)

Use @DBLOOKUP to find specific information within a database and enter it at a specific place. The first parameter, *search,* is the value or string to be found. The second parameter is the field to look in, and the third parameter is the information to retrieve. For instance, to find out what Anne Rizzo's monthly average sales were (from the Sales People database used earlier in this book), you could write the expression

```
@dblookup(Rizzo, "sales_pe.Last", "sales_pe.AvgPerMo")
```

@DECIMAL *(numeric expression)*
@DECIMAL *(numeric expression, decimal places)*

@DECIMAL rounds its parameter to two decimal places and then converts the result into a text value. If a positive number of decimal places is specified as the second parameter, @DECIMAL will round to the number of places specified. If the second parameter is negative, @DECIMAL rounds the first parameter to the nearest 10, 100, 1000, and so on, before converting it into a text value.

@DELETE *("framename")*
@DELETE *("region")*

New in
Framework III

You can use @DELETE to delete a frame or to specify a region in a spreadsheet or database. If you use @DELETE with no parameters, it will delete the current selection. The information that is deleted using @DELETE is not placed in the Undo buffer, so use this command with caution. When the deletion is successful, the function returns #TRUE. Otherwise, it returns #FALSE.

@DIFFDATE *(date1, date2)*
@DIFFDATE *(date1, date2, type)*

@DIFFDATE calculates the number of days between *date1* and *date2*. If *date1* is earlier than *date2*, the result will be positive; if *date2* is earlier, the result will be negative. The parameters for @DIFFDATE must be any of the following functions:

@date
@time
@sumdate
@today
@datetime

New in
Framework III

In Framework III, @DIFFDATE can also accept an optional parameter to determine the *type* of value to return. The valid types are:

0	Days (default)
1	Complete months
2	Complete years
3	Hours
4	Minutes
5	Seconds
6	Hundredths of a second

New in
Framework III

@DISPLAY *(frame name)*
@DISPLAY *(frame name, col, row)*

You can use @DISPLAY within a program to display the contents of any frame that currently resides on the desktop or even on the "hidden" desktop. You can use this function to display specially prepared frames of information during a program's performance.

In Framework III, you can use the optional parameters, *col* and *row,* to position the frame on the desktop. *Col* determines the column of the upper left corner of the frame, and *row* determines the row of the upper left corner. The default value for *col, row* is 0,0.

@DOLLAR

You can use @DOLLAR as a parameter to the @NATIONALIZE function. See the @NATIONALIZE entry for details of usage.

@DRAW

The @DRAW function puts at your disposal a complete graphics language for use in Framework III. Shapes can be drawn, lines plotted, and text placed anywhere within a frame. Areas can be filled with any of several patterns. Each of these commands is expressed as a number, followed by numbers representing various points within the frame as x and y coordinates. See your Framework III manual for details.

@DRAWGRAPH *(source, #orientation, #type)*
@DRAWGRAPH *(source, #orientation, #type, "title", "x-axis title", "y-axis title", low value for x-axis, high value for x-axis, increment for x-axis values)*

The @DRAWGRAPH function draws graphs following the specific instructions selected from the Graph menu. Framework III places a @DRAWGRAPH function behind every Graph frame that you create.

Selecting options from the Graph menu is by far the easiest way to draw graphs in Framework III. You can, however, change the graphs by editing the formula behind the resulting Graph frame. The easiest way to master the @DRAWGRAPH function is to create graphs from the menu and then study the formulas from which they are drawn.

@DRAWGRAPH has three required parameters:

- *source* is the section of a Database or Spreadsheet frame that will provide the data to be graphed. It may be referred to by row and column numbers or by their English-language labels.

- *orientation* is the axis of the source frame indicating the source of x-axis titles for the graph. Either of two values is permissible:

  #row
  #column

- *#type* refers to the type of graph to be drawn. The following are the permissible values for this parameter:

  #bar
  #stackedbar
  #line
  #markedpoints
  #xy
  #pie

All types of graphs can have the following parameters included, in the following order:

''*title*''	Graph title, in quotes
''*X-axis title*''	Title for horizontal axis, in quotes
''*Y-axis title*''	Title for vertical axis, in quotes

In addition, all types of graphs except pie graphs can have any of the following parameters included, after those mentioned above:

low value for x-axis

high value for x-axis

increment for x-axis values

In place of these parameters, pie graphs can have a parameter that tells which slice of the pie should be separated from the others. (Note that pie graphs can only be drawn from one row or one column of figures.)

If you wish to use some, but not all, of the optional parameters, enter a comma in place of the skipped parameter. For example, to skip the titles but specify the numbers for the x-axis, your expression might read

> @drawgraph(Income.A2:C5, #row, #bar, ,,, 200, 900, 50)

This expression would draw a bar graph from cells A2 through C5 of the Income spreadsheet, taking its x-axis orientation from the spreadsheet's rows. No titles would be included, but the x-axis would be numbered from 200 to 900 in increments of 50.

@ECHO(#OFF)
@ECHO(#ON)
@ECHO(#ON, n)

@ECHO determines whether the effects of the keystrokes in a macro will be displayed. The expression

> @echo(#OFF)

will execute the keystrokes specified in the macro without displaying any effects on the screen.

Be careful in using @ECHO(#OFF). If you use this function in a program and fail to turn the echo on again, no further keystrokes will be displayed. For an example of this function in use, see Chapter 7.

The expression

> @echo(#ON)

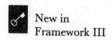

New in
Framework III

turns the display of keystroke activity back on again. In Framework III, a new option *(n)* has been added to allow programmers to determine how the ECHO(#ON) function will work. The value of *n* can be

- 0　Everything is redisplayed and repainted (default)
- 1　Screen is repainted only when an action changes the display
- 2　Current frame is repainted

@ERASEPROMPT

@ERASEPROMPT erases a prompt displayed in the message area below the desktop.

@EXACT *("string1", "string2")*

@EXACT returns #TRUE if *string1* and *string2* are identical, #FALSE if they are not. Unlike comparisons of strings with the = operator, @EXACT compares every character in both strings. The result is #FALSE if one string is longer than the other, or if any character in one string is of a different case from the equivalent character in the other string. Wildcard characters cannot be used.

@EXECUTE *(frame reference, formula)*

@EXECUTE places a new formula behind a specified frame and then performs the formula. Any formula that previously resided behind the frame is replaced.

@EXP *(exponent)*

@EXP returns a power of e, where e is 2.7182818. Therefore, the expression

   @exp(x)

is the same as e^x.

@FC *("footer text")*

@FC defines a string of text for the footer and specifies that the footer be centered below the last line of text.

@FILL *(range, startvalue)*
@FILL *(range, startvalue, increment)*

@FILL is used to fill a range in a database or spreadsheet with incrementing or decrementing values. It has three parameters. *Range* specifies the range that is to receive the values. *Startvalue* is the beginning value, and *increment* is the amount by which each subsequent value is to be increased. If the optional third parameter is not included, @FILL places the same value in every cell in the specified range. If the third value is negative, the values are decremented. The second parameter can also be a string parameter for filling columns or rows with text. Normally, @FILL should be deleted from the spreadsheet or database once the function has performed its task.

@FL *("footer text")*

@FL defines a string of text for the footer and specifies that the footer be printed flush left below the last line of text.

@FLOOR *(numeric expression)*

@FLOOR returns the largest integer that is not greater than its parameter. In other words, it rounds its parameter downward. (Negative numbers are also rounded downward—that is, away from zero.)

@FP *(line)*

@FP (footer position) determines the number of lines that will be left blank between the footer and the bottom of the paper. Its value must be less than that of the bottom margin, @BM. The default value for the footer position is 3.

@FR *("footer text")*

@FR defines a string of text for the footer and specifies that the footer be printed flush right below the last line of text.

@FRAMETYPE
@FRAMETYPE *("frame reference")*

@FRAMETYPE returns the type of frame currently selected or, if the cursor is not within a frame, the location of the cursor, as a number from the following table:

11	Cabinet
12	Library
13	Menu
14	Help screen
15	Outline frame
16	Spreadsheet frame
17	Database frame
18	Empty frame
19	Word frame
10	Graph frame
11	Cell
12	Field
13	Telecommunications frame
14	Inside a Word frame

15   Inside the formula area

16   On the edit line

17   Inside a Telecommunications frame

18   In a local variable

If a *frame reference* is given, @FRAMETYPE returns the frame type of the specified frame.

@FRAMEVIEW
@FRAMEVIEW (''frame reference'')

@FRAMEVIEW returns the type of frame currently selected as a number from the following table:

1   Database in Table view

2   Database in Forms view

3   Database in dBASE view

4   File cabinet showing file names only

5   File cabinet showing dates and times

6   Frames view of other types of frames

7   Outline view of other types of frames

If a *frame reference* is given, @FRAMEVIEW returns the frame type of the specified frame. You can use this function to test before issuing commands. For example, if you want to leave a frame called OUT-LINE on the desktop in Outline view after executing a program it contains, you might use the formula

```
@if(@frametype("outline") = 6, @performkeys("{f10}"))
```

@FV (*payment, rate, periods*)

@FV returns the compounded future value of a series of payments, given the following:

- A value representing an amount of money that is repeatedly added to the investment at regular intervals *(payment)*

- A value representing the periodic interest *rate*

• A value representing the number of payments *(periods)*

Be aware that the interest rate given must be the interest rate *per period*. Therefore, you must divide the annual interest rate by the number of periods per year.

@GET *(range)*

@GET is a region-walking function that returns the value of the current position in a specified range. The @NEXT function is used along with @GET to select a subsequent value after the current value has been processed.

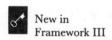
New in
Framework III

In Framework III, @GET *(range)* can take several forms; for example:

1. For region-walking in spreadsheets and databases, you can specify the boundaries of the range with *frame.cell* or *frame.field*:

        @get(Quarterly Income.B5:Quarterly Income.E5)
        @get(Sales People.SixMoSales:Sales People.AvgPerMo)

2. For working with a spreadsheet, you can use the spreadsheet name only:

        @get(Quarterly Income)

3. For *record-walking* in databases, you can specify the *range* as *(frame, field)* or *(frame, field number)*:

        @get(Sales People, SixMoSales)
        @get(Sales People, 5)

   The second example uses the number of a field instead of its name.

Both @GET and @NEXT normally appear within a @WHILE loop. See Chapter 7 for more examples.

@GETENV *("variable")*

@GETENV retrieves a DOS environment variable. For more details, see the DOS manual.

@GETFORMULA *(frame reference)*

@GETFORMULA retrieves a copy of the formula from behind the specified frame. A program might subsequently place the retrieved formula behind another frame, using either the @SETFORMULA or @EXECUTE function.

@HC ("header text")

@HC defines a string of text for the header and specifies that the header be centered above the first line of text.

@HF (pages)

@HF determines the number of pages after the current one at which headers and footers will begin to appear. If you are on page 1, for example, and you use the function

@hf(9)

headers and footers will commence on page 10. You can use this form of the function to allow for a title page, table of contents, and so on.

@HIDE (frame reference)

The @HIDE function hides the frame named in its parameter. In other words, @HIDE moves the frame from the normal desktop to a special "hidden" desktop, where the frame will still be available in memory but not visible on the screen. The @UNHIDE function makes the frame visible again.

@HL ("header text")

@HL defines a string of text for the header and specifies that the header be printed flush left above the first line of text.

@HLOOKUP (n, range, offset)

@HLOOKUP retrieves a value from a horizontally oriented lookup table. The function has three parameters: a lookup value (n), the *range* that contains the lookup table, and an *offset* row location from which to retrieve the target value.

@HLOOKUP searches the first row of the lookup table for the value n of its first parameter. When it finds n, or the last value in the lookup row that is not larger than n, @HLOOKUP moves down the specified number of offset rows and returns the value stored in that location.

@HP (lines)

@HP (header position) determines the number of lines that will be left blank between the top of the page and the header. Its value must be less than that of the top margin, @TM. The default value for the header position is 3.

@HR ("header text")

@HR defines a string of text for the header and specifies that the header be printed flush right above the first line of text.

@IF (logical statement, expression1, expression2)
@IF (logical statement, expression)

The @IF function evaluates the logical statement in its first parameter to either true or false. If the statement is true, the expression specified by the second parameter is evaluated. If the statement is false, the expression in the third parameter is evaluated. For example:

```
@if(a>b, a: = b, a: = 0)
```

In English, this would read, "If *a* is greater than *b*, set *a* equal to *b*; otherwise set *a* equal to 0."

The third parameter is optional. Without a third parameter, @IF performs no action when the logical statement is false.

@INPUTLINE ("prompt", "starting text", cursor-pointing, auto-delete, firstchar)
@INPUTLINE

@INPUTLINE allows a FRED program to make use of the edit line located below the desktop. The function takes five parameters, all of them optional. If you don't use any parameters, the cursor appears on the input line without a prompt. To use one to four parameters, be sure to leave commas in the command in place of the parameters you are not using. The parameters and their effects are

"*prompt*"	A word or phrase, in quotes, that will appear in the message area to tell the user what to do.
"*text*"	A word or phrase, in quotes, that will appear as the default value on the edit line. Pressing Return will enter this text as a response to the prompt.
cursor-pointing	This parameter determines whether pointing will be allowed as a technique for

entering a value onto the edit line. If this parameter is #TRUE or #YES, pointing is allowed; if it is #FALSE or #NO (the default), pointing is not allowed.

auto-delete   If this parameter is set to #TRUE or #YES, pressing a character key will automatically delete the default text on the edit line. However, the text can be edited if a navigation key is pressed before a character key. If this parameter is set to #FALSE or #NO (the default), the starting text will not be deleted automatically.

firstchar   If this parameter is set to #TRUE or #YES, the highlight will appear on the first letter of the starting phrase. If it is set to #FALSE or #NO, the selection will remain where it was before the @INPUTLINE command was issued.

@INT *(numeric expression)*
@INT *("string")*

When the parameter of @INT is a numeric expression, @INT returns the integer part of its parameter; that is, it strips off any fractional parts of its parameter.

When the parameter of @INT is a string value, @INT returns the ASCII value of the first character in the string, expressed as a decimal number.

@INTEGER *(numeric expression)*
@INTEGER *(numeric expression, decimal places)*
@INTEGER *(date)*

@INTEGER converts the numeric value in its parameter to an integer and then turns the result into a text value.

If the value of the second parameter is negative, @INTEGER rounds the first parameter to the nearest 10, 100, 1000, and so on, before converting it to a text value. If the value of the second parameter is greater than or equal to zero, the second parameter has no effect.

If the parameter to @INTEGER is a date-type value, it will convert that value to a text string displayed as numerals not separated by any markings, in the form

yyyymmdd

For example, if today were January 1, 2000, @INTEGER(@TODAY) would return the string

20000101

@IRR *(estimate, cash flow1, cash flow2, . . .)*

@IRR computes the internal rate of return on an investment. An investment's internal rate of return is the discount rate at which the present value of the negative cash flows equals the present value of positive cash flows. The parameters to this function are an *estimate* of the rate of return, and a series of positive and negative *cash flows* reflecting net periodic revenues or outlays. The *estimate* must be between 0 and 1.

@ISABEND
@ISABEND *(expression)*

@ISABEND detects whether a program ended abnormally. It returns #TRUE if it did, #FALSE if it did not. If a parameter is given, the parameter receives the value returned by the function.

@ISALPHA *(expression)*

@ISALPHA returns #TRUE if the value of its parameter is a string or text value, #FALSE if it is not.

@ISBOP *(string)*
@ISBOP *(string, number of characters)*

@ISBOP returns #TRUE if the first character of the specified *string* is a (hidden) beginning-of-paragraph character; otherwise, it returns #FALSE. If a *number of characters* is specified, @ISBOP returns #TRUE if the character at the specified location is a beginning-of-paragraph character.

@ISCAPSLOCK

@ISCAPSLOCK returns #TRUE if the Caps Lock key is on; otherwise, it returns #FALSE.

@ISDOCUMENT
@ISDOCUMENT ("frame reference")

@ISDOCUMENT returns #FALSE if the currently selected frame is contained within another frame; otherwise, it returns #TRUE. If a frame reference is given, it returns #FALSE if the specified frame is contained within another frame.

@ISERR (expression)

@ISERR is used to detect error conditions. If the value of its parameter is one of FRED's error constants, @ISERR returns #TRUE; otherwise, it returns #FALSE. This function can be used to filter values from databases and to prevent erroneous values from being copied to numerous spreadsheet cells by internal formulas. It is often used in @IF expressions; for example:

@if(@not(@iserr(Column1)), @set(Column1, Column1 * .12))

This formula will multiply the values in *Column1* by .12, skipping those that contain error constants.

@ISNA (expression)

@ISNA is used to detect the constant #NA!, which means that the value is not available. If the value of its parameter is #NA!, @ISNA returns #TRUE; otherwise, it returns #FALSE.

@ISNUMERIC (expression)

@ISNUMERIC returns #TRUE if the value of its parameter is a numeric value, #FALSE if it is not.

@ISNUMLOCK

@ISNUMLOCK returns #TRUE if the Num Lock key is on; otherwise, it returns #FALSE.

@ITEM (index)

@ITEM is used in the construction of user-defined functions, to receive the parameters passed to the function. In the called function, the parameters that are to be received are represented by @ITEM1, @ITEM2, @ITEM3, ... , @ITEM16. The actual values to be used by the function are passed to the @ITEM functions.

You can also reference a series of @ITEM values by using a variable index, in the form

@item *(i)*

In this case, the value of the variable *i* selects one of the series of parameter values.

The number of values passed to a subroutine need not match the number of parameters set up to receive them. You can use the @ITEM-COUNT function to determine how many values have actually been passed.

@ITEMCOUNT

@ITEMCOUNT returns the number of values passed to a user-defined function. It is used in the called function. It is especially useful when the calling formula may pass a variable number of parameters to the called function. For example, to index through the correct number of passed parameters, you could use a statement like this:

@while(INDEX < = @itemcount, . . .)

This @WHILE loop would contain references to @ITEM(INDEX). After each parameter was processed, the loop would increment the value of INDEX in a statement like this:

INDEX : = INDEX + 1

@KEY

@KEY is used in macros to record the last key that has been pressed. It reads keys, not character values, so any expressions involving @KEY should refer to keys by name, in curly braces. For example:

@if(@key = {esc}. . .)
@if(@or(@key = {X}, @key = {x}). . .)
@if(@key = {scroll-lock}. . .)

Note that the @KEY function considers uppercase and lowercase letters as separate keys.

@KEYFILTER *({keyname})*
@KEYFILTER *({keyname}, frame reference)*

The @KEYFILTER function is used to control user input into a program by reinterpreting various keys, groups of keys, or the entire keyboard. You can reinterpret the following groups of keys by using these parameters:

{char}	All the white keys in the center of the keyboard
{ctrl-a}	All the Ctrl-letter key combinations
{ctrl-1}	All the Ctrl-number key combinations
{alt-a}	All macro commands
{all}	The entire keyboard

The remaining keys—the function keys, Framework III's cursor-movement keys, and the rest of the gray keys—are filtered individually. Note that with the Ctrl- and Alt-key combinations, you must specify an additional key, but it doesn't matter which one. Ctrl-A or Ctrl-X will filter all combinations of the Ctrl key and letter keys, but Ctrl by itself is illegal.

It takes two frames to set up a key filter, just as it does with a macro. The first frame must contain a formula that defines the key or group of keys that will invoke the formula behind the second frame. For example,

   @keyfilter({End}, Frame2)

will execute the formula behind *Frame2* anytime the End key is pressed. If you want to control input by restricting a user to parts of the keyboard, you should begin by turning off the entire keyboard with the expression

   @keyfilter({all})

and then activate the keys you want to have usable with succeeding @KEYFILTER expressions that invoke formulas to be executed by those keys.

To cancel an established filter, enter the @KEYFILTER function a second time, omitting the frame reference.

@KEYNAME (key)

@KEYNAME returns the name of a *key,* expressed as a text string. Its parameter can be any key name enclosed in curly braces, or either of the functions @KEY or @NEXTKEY. One of this function's primary uses is in building macros. It receives the name of a key and returns a text string that can then be used as a parameter to the @PERFORMKEYS function.

@KP

@KP is a printing function that establishes a conditional page break. That is, if the current frame has the formula @KP behind it, the frame will begin a new page if the text in the frame cannot all fit on the current page.

@LEN ("string expression")

The @LEN function returns the number of characters in the string represented by the expression in its parameter.

@LIST (expression1, expression2, . . .)

@LIST is used to group several functions or expressions together where only one is normally used. For example, use @LIST when you want several actions to be performed as the result of an @IF function:

```
@if(test = #TRUE,
  @list(
    expression1,
    expression2
  ),
  @list(
    expression3,
    expression4
  )
)
```

In the performance of this statement, expressions 1 and 2 will be evaluated if TEST is #TRUE; otherwise, expressions 3 and 4 will be performed.

@LL (characters)

@LL (line length) is a printing function that determines the maximum number of characters that can be printed on any line of text in a document. The parameters of @LL and @PO should not add up to more than the number of characters your printer can print on a line. You must coordinate this setting with the margin settings on the Words menu.

@LN *(numeric expression)*

@LN returns the natural logarithm of the *numeric expression* that is its parameter. The base of the natural logarithm is *e*, where *e* = 2.7182818. (The parameter must be positive.)

@LOCAL *(variable1, variable2, . . .)*

@LOCAL defines variables that are created for use only within a given subroutine. Local variables can be used for the temporary storage of values within the subroutine in which they are defined.

@LOG *(numeric expression)*

@LOG returns the base-10 logarithm of the numeric expression that is its parameter. (The parameter must be positive.)

@MAX *(expression1, expression2, . . .)*
@MAX *(range)*

@MAX returns the largest numeric value in its parameter list.

@MEMAVAIL

@MEMAVAIL has two effects: it clears the undo buffer, thus increasing the amount of available memory, and it returns as a numeric value the amount of memory available in the computer. It takes no parameter.

@MENU *(frame reference)*

@MENU turns the Outline frame named in its parameter into a user-defined menu. The frames within the frame named in the parameter become the items on the menu. If one of these frames contains additional frames, selecting that frame will cause the titles of the frames contained in it to be displayed as a submenu.

If the frame is set up with number labels turned off, the menu will be a full-screen menu. If the number labels are turned on, the menu options will be listed horizontally on the edit line. Text contained inside the frames that are part of a menu will be displayed in the message area when the menu option is highlighted. Each frame within the menu frame should contain a formula behind it, to be executed when the option is selected.

You can choose an item on a user menu by using the cursor keys and pressing Return when the selected item is highlighted, or by selecting the first letter of the menu option—just as with Framework III's own menus. The user can always return to the next highest level from a menu frame by pressing the Escape key; however, the programmer can also set up one item on the menu as an exit option. To do so, use the @QUITMENU function.

@MID *("string expression", startpoint, characters)*

The @MID function extracts a group of characters from a string. Given three parameters—*string expression,* the point in the string at which to begin counting *(startpoint)*, and the number of characters to extract *(characters)*—this function will return a substring.

@MILLI

@MILLI is used as a parameter for the @NATIONALIZE function to control the form in which numbers are displayed. If @MILLI is used, numbers are formatted with periods between each group of three digits, and whole numbers are separated from decimal fractions by a comma, in the Continental style. The alternative format function is @THOUSANDS. (See @NATIONALIZE.)

@MIN *(expression1, expression2, . . .)*
@MIN *(range)*

@MIN returns the smallest numeric value in its parameter list.

@MIRR *(risky rate, safe rate, cash flow1, cash flow2, . . .)*

@MIRR calculates the internal rate of return on an investment, using a modified method of calculation. It takes the following parameters:

- The interest rate on the money you borrow to make the investment (the *risky rate*)

- The interest rate at which you could invest the money you make (the *safe rate*)

- Positive and negative *cash flows,* representing revenues from the investment and outlays toward the investment

@MOD *(dividend, divisor)*

Given two parameters, the *dividend* and the *divisor,* the @MOD function calculates the modulus, or the remainder resulting from the division. The divisor cannot have the value of zero.

@NATIONALIZE *(currency, format)*

The @NATIONALIZE function is used to control the way numbers are displayed. @NATIONALIZE takes either one or two parameters, allowing you to control the type of *currency* symbol used and the *format* in which numbers are displayed (Continental or Anglo-American style). @NATIONALIZE can take any of the following parameters for the *currency* parameter:

@dollar
@pound
@unit
@yen

You can use either @MILLI or @THOUSANDS as the *format* parameter. Framework III's default display parameters are @DOLLAR and @THOUSANDS.

@NEXT *(region)*

@NEXT moves the selection from the current cell or frame of the *region* specified by its parameter to the following frame or cell, and it retrieves the value stored there. @NEXT is typically used in a @WHILE loop, along with the @GET and @PUT functions to walk through a range of values.

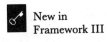
New in
Framework III

In Framework III, @NEXT can work with whole spreadsheets (starting with cell A1 and moving left to right, top to bottom) or with specified database fields, moving record by record. For example, the command to specify a whole spreadsheet would be

@next(Quarterly Income)

where Quarterly Income is the frame name. For record-walking in a database, the command would read

@next(Sales People, SixMoSales)

where Sales People is the frame name and SixMoSales is the field name. For more examples, see Chapter 7.

@NEXTKEY
@NEXTKEY *(seconds)*

@NEXTKEY waits for a key to be pressed and then returns the value of the key. Its optional parameter tells how many seconds to wait before executing the next expression. If there is no parameter, @NEXTKEY waits indefinitely. The function can be used to create a delay, as in the following program segment:

```
@prompt("Press any key to continue"),
@nextkey,
```

@NOT *(expression)*

@NOT returns #TRUE if its parameter is false and #FALSE if its parameter is true. You can use @NOT as a parameter of the @AND, @IF, and @OR functions. For example:

```
@if(@and(A>B, @not(B = 0)) . . .)
```

In English, this would read, "If *A* is greater than *B,* and *B* is not equal to 0, then . . .".

@NP
@NP *(page number)*

@NP is a printing function that tells Framework III to begin printing the current frame on a new page. Its optional parameter tells Framework III to begin printing the current frame on a new page whose page number is determined by the parameter.

@NPV *(discount rate, cash flow1, cash flow2, . . .)*

@NPV computes the net present value of a series of *cash flows* (positive and negative) at a given *discount rate.*

@OR *(expression1, expression2, . . .)*

@OR is a logical function that returns #TRUE if at least one of the logical statements among its parameters is true. Otherwise, it returns #FALSE. At least one of its parameters must be a logical statement—that is, a statement that can be evaluated as true or false. The @OR function is often used as part of the first parameter of the @IF function.

@PANEL1
@PANEL1 (''frame reference'')

@PANEL1 returns the left-hand number in the third status panel. If a parameter is given, it returns this number for the frame specifed as its parameter.

@PANEL2
@PANEL2 (''frame reference'')

@PANEL2 returns the right-hand number in the third status panel. If a parameter is given, it returns this number for the frame specified as its parameter.

@PERFORMKEYS (''keystrokes'')
@PK (''keystrokes'')

The @PERFORMKEYS function executes the *keystrokes* that comprise its parameter. Special key names should be placed in curly braces. The entire sequence must be enclosed in double quotes.

New in
Framework III

Framework III has added the short form @PK, which is equivalent to @PERFORMKEYS.

The expression

        @performkeys("Hi. How are you? {Return}")

will enter the text

        Hi. How are you?

followed by a carriage return. The expression

        @performkeys("{ctrl-c}eTest{Return}{in}")

will create an Empty frame, label it *Test*, and place the cursor within it. The same expression could be written:

        @pk("{ctrl-c}eTest{Return}{in}")

For more examples, see Chapter 7.

@PI

@PI returns the value of pi calculated to 14 decimal places. For those trigonometric functions that require parameters expressed in radians, use the following formula to convert degrees to radians:

```
radians = angle*@pi/180
```

@PL *(lines)*

@PL (page length) is a printing function that specifies the length, in lines, of your physical page. All text, headings, and top and bottom margins must be planned within this line limit. The default value is 66, which is the normal number of lines on an 11-inch page.

Use this function if you are using longer or shorter paper, changing the vertical spacing on your printer to increments other than lines, or finding that your text isn't fitting properly on a page.

@PMT *(principal, rate, periods)*

@PMT computes the payment required to pay off a loan, assuming a constant periodic payment. To calculate this result, it must be given the following parameters:

- A value representing the *principal* of the loan
- A value representing the periodic interest *rate*
- A value representing the number of payments *(periods)*

The interest rate given must be the interest rate *per period.* Therefore, you must divide the annual interest rate by the number of periods per year.

@PN

@PN (page number) is used within header or footer functions to specify that the current page number should be printed as part of the header or footer. It can be used in conjunction with other text; for example:

```
@fc("Page "& @pn)
```

@PO *(spaces)*

@PO (page offset) is a printing function that determines the size, in spaces, of the left margin of your printed document. The default value is 10. Printing on a line will begin in the column after the number of spaces specified in the parameter of @PO. However, the text's actual left margin is determined by adding the @PO setting to the frame's Left Margin setting, specified in the Words menu. The parameters of @PO and @LL should not add up to more than the number of characters your printer can print on a line.

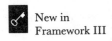
New in
Framework III

@POSITION *("framename", top left x, top left y, width, height)*

@POSITION allows you to place any frame on the desktop as well as size it with one command. The placement parameters *top left x* and *top left y* determine the position of the upper left corner of the frame relative to the top line of the desktop. *Width* and *height* determine the size of the frame. For example, the command

@position("Test Frame",10,3,40,12)

would place the frame called Test Frame 10 spaces from the left edge of the desktop and 3 lines down from the top. The frame would be 40 characters wide and 12 lines high.

@POUND

You can use @POUND as a parameter to the @NATIONALIZE function. See the @NATIONALIZE entry for details of use.

@PR *(@printfunction1, @printfunction2, . . . , @printreturn)*

@PR is used to group printing functions within a FRED program, to prevent the subsequent formulas from being recalculated during printing. It should appear before any other functions in the program. Its parameters consist of printing functions followed by the @PRINTRETURN function. (In Framework III only, turn on *Recalc Formula during Printing* from the Print Control Options menu.)

You can set the following specific print functions in the Format Options and the Control Options submenus. For more information, see the specific entries:

@bm	@hp	@pr
@fc	@hr	@printreturn
@fl	@kp	@sk
@fp	@ll	@sp
@fr	@np	@st
@hc	@p	@tm
@hf	@pn	
@hl	@po	

These commands are retained largely for compatibility with earlier versions of Framework.

@PRINT (*document or region reference*)

The @PRINT function issues the command to begin printing the document, frame, or region referred to in its parameter. When the @PRINT function is encountered, the frame referred to will be printed automatically.

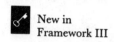
New in
Framework III

The *region* option of the @PRINT command is new in Framework III.

@PRINTRETURN

You should use @PRINTRETURN to close a list of printing functions that are parameters of the @PR function. For further details, see @PR. You can also use @PRINTRETURN by itself to separate a series of printing functions from subsequent formulas and thereby prevent the recalculation of the other formulas.

@PROMPT (*"message"*)
@PROMPT (*"message"*, *position*)

@PROMPT places the *message* specified in its first parameter on the message line. The second parameter, which is optional, specifies the *position* as a number of spaces from the left edge of the screen to the beginning of the message. To be sure that your message does not remain on the screen longer than you want it to, use the @ERASE-PROMPT function to remove it after appropriate action has been taken.

@PUT (*range, expression*)

@PUT places the value of the *expression* that is its second parameter in the current cell or frame of the region specified by its first parameter. @PUT is used along with @NEXT, typically in an @WHILE loop, to place a set of values in a range.

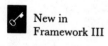
New in
Framework III

@PUT can take several forms. The following examples put the value 10 in the appropriate locations:

1. For region-walking in spreadsheets and databases, specify the range with *frame.cell* or *frame.field*:

        @put(Quarterly Income.B5:Quarterly Income.E5, 10)
        @put(Sales People.SixMoSales:
          Sales People.AvgPerMo, 10)

2. For working with a spreadsheet, use the spreadsheet name only:

   @put(Quarterly Income, 10)

3. For *record-walking* in databases, specify the *range* as *(frame, field)* or *(frame, field number)*:

   @put(Sales People, SixMoSales, 10)
   @put(Sales People, 5, 10)

@*PV* *(payment, rate, periods)*

@PV returns the present value of a constant stream of payments, given the following:

- A value representing an amount of money that is repeatedly withdrawn or paid at regular intervals *(payment)*

- A value representing the periodic interest *rate*

- A value representing the number of payments *(periods)*

This stream of payments can represent an investment from which regular withdrawals are made or a loan on which regular payments are made.

@*QUITMENU*

@QUITMENU should be placed in the formula area of a quit or exit option on a user menu. Pressing Return when the highlight is on a frame with the @QUITMENU function behind it causes exit from the menu to the next highest level of organization.

@*RAND*

@RAND is FRED's random number generator. It generates a random number from 0 to 1, inclusive, to 15 decimal places. It does not take a parameter.

@*REPT* *("string", count)*

The @REPT function produces a string value consisting of a repeated character or group of characters. The first parameter is the character or characters to be repeated, and the second specifies the number of repetitions.

To display a row of 60 asterisks, for example, you would use the formula

@rept("*", 60)

@RESET *(range)*

@RESET selects the first cell, field, or frame in the range specified by its parameter and returns the value of that element. @RESET is used in conjunction with the @GET, @PUT, and @NEXT functions.

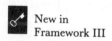
New in
Framework III

In Framework III, you can use @RESET to select the first cell or field in a spreadsheet or database, or to select a specific cell or field. @RESET uses the same parameters as @GET, @NEXT, and @PUT.

@RESULT *(expression)*

@RESULT causes a formula to stop executing; the function returns the value of its parameter when execution stops. It is usually used as part of an @IF or @WHILE expression.

@RESUME

New in
Framework III

@RESUME will resume a program that has been paused by the @SUSPEND function. When a formula reaches an @RESUME function, it begins execution of the formula following the most recent @SUSPEND function. If no @SUSPEND function has been encountered, the program ignores the @RESUME function.

A common way to use the @RESUME function is to assign it to a key filter, then use @SUSPEND to pause execution of the formula. After performing appropriate manual operations, press the key assigned to the @RESUME routine, and execution of the formula will continue from the point after the @SUSPEND.

@RETURN *(expression)*

@RETURN causes a formula to stop executing and returns the constant #FUNCTION as a value. It is usually used within an @IF or @WHILE expression.

@ROUND *(numeric expression)*
@ROUND *(numeric expression, decimal places)*

@ROUND can have one or two parameters. If it has one, it rounds the *numeric expression* to the nearest integer. If it has two, it rounds to the number of *decimal places* given in the second parameter.

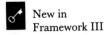

New in
Framework III

@ROW

@ROW returns the number of the current spreadsheet row or data-base record. This command is similar to the @COL command. Use @ROW and @COL within a spreadsheet or database to identify the *current* location.

@RUN(frame reference, "drive:progname.ext")
@RUN(frame reference, "drive:progname.ext", #TRUE/#FALSE)
@RUN(frame reference, "command line")
@RUN(frame reference, "command line", #TRUE/#FALSE)

You can use the @RUN function to run any .COM or .EXE program that resides on a disk in one of your drives, provided there is enough free memory to run the program. The first parameter names a frame in which whatever is written to the screen by the program will be cap-tured. Any error messages will also be returned in this frame. The second parameter must contain the drive designation (and the path name, where appropriate), the name of the program, and its exten-sion. The frame referred to in the first parameter can also be the frame behind which the formula itself resides. For example, placing the formula

@run(WordStar, "c:ws.com")

behind a frame called WordStar will cause Framework III to look for the WordStar word processing program on drive C and run it, taking over the whole screen. Any error messages will appear in the frame called WordStar.

If you want to use this technique to run "internal" DOS com-mands or batch files, you must include the DOS COMMAND.COM file as one of the command line arguments. In addition, you must include the /c option to issue instructions to the command processor as though they were typed at the DOS prompt. For example:

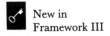

New in
Framework III

@run(DosFrame, "command.com /c copy a:*.fw2b:")

The optional #TRUE or #FALSE parameter of the @RUN command tells Framework III whether to implement the new *memory roll-out* fea-ture. If the option is #TRUE, Framework III will attempt to take itself out of memory to give DOS more room to run the program. How-ever, the memory roll-out requires either a hard disk or extended memory. If you have a hard disk without extended memory, Framework III creates a virtual file in the root directory. Upon completion of the @RUN command application, this file is used to recreate the Framework III desktop.

Roll-out has no effect on the status of files that were locked for use on a network before roll-out; they remain locked. However, the number of files an application can have open is reduced by the number of locked files.

If you are working with dBASE IV in the dBASE Apps Add-In option, Framework III automatically tries to use memory roll-out. You can also change the SETUPFW program to have Framework III automatically use memory roll-out before DOS access.

@SCAN(*"target string"*, *"containing string"*)
@SCAN(*"target string"*, *"containing string"*, *start location*)

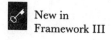
New in
Framework III

@SCAN returns the number of the character in the *containing string* at which the *target string* is matched. The match must be exact. For example, if a local variable CONTAINING were assigned the value

> "apes & grapes have similar shapes"

the function

> @scan("apes", CONTAINING)

would return the value 1. If the variable CONTAINING were assigned the value

> "Apes & grapes have similar shapes"

the value 10 would be returned, because the string "Apes", beginning with an uppercase A, would not match the target string.

You can specify the point in the containing string at which to start searching. If the formula read

> @scan("apes", CONTAINING, 12)

then the value 30, the location of the a in "shapes", would be returned.

@SCIENTIFIC *(numeric expression)*
@SCIENTIFIC *(numeric expression, decimal places)*
@SCIENTIFIC *(date)*

@SCIENTIFIC rounds the numeric value in its parameter to two decimal places, converts its format to scientific notation, and then turns the result into a text value. If the number of *decimal places* is specified as the second parameter, @SCIENTIFIC rounds its first parameter to the specified number of places.

If the parameter to @SCIENTIFIC is a date-type value, it will convert that value to a text string and display the result in the format

mm/dd/yyyy

For example, the function

@scientific(@date(1989, 8, 30))

will produce the text string

08/30/1989

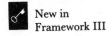
New in
Framework III

@SCREENINFO *(integer)*

@SCREENINFO returns the following information about screen values when you enter these values for *integer*:

0   #TRUE for text display; #FALSE for graphics display

1   Full height of screen

2   Full width of screen

3   Top left x (absolute coordinate of desktop); normally 0

4   Top left y (absolute coordinate of desktop); normally 1

5   Bottom right x (absolute coordinate of desktop); normally 79

6   Bottom right y (absolute coordinate of desktop); normally 21

These values will vary with different types of screen resolution.

@SELECT *(index, expression1, expression2, . . .)*

@SELECT chooses and evaluates one expression from a list of expressions included among its parameters. The first parameter, *index,* must be a numeric value. If *index* is 1, *expression1* will be evaluated; if *index* is 2, *expression2* will be selected; and so on. If the value of *index* is greater than the number of expressions in the parameter list, an error message will be generated.

@SENSE *(menu toggle)*
@SENSE *(menu toggle, ''frame reference'')*

@SENSE returns #TRUE if a menu option that is a toggle is set to ON. If a *frame reference* is given, @SENSE returns #TRUE if the specified option is toggled to ON in the specifed frame. Otherwise, @SENSE returns #FALSE.

If the menu item is not a toggle, @SENSE will return the value it is currently set to.

The menu toggles are given by the series of keystrokes necessary to access them, with the first character being the pound sign (#), and the Ctrl-character combination that accesses the menu specified only by its letter. In Framework III, the correct syntax is @SENSE(MENU#ET). Using MENU# with English initials will ensure compatibility with different versions of Framework. Thus,

> @sense(MENU#ET)

would return #TRUE if the current frame were in Typeover mode on the Edit menu. Similarly,

> @sense(MENU#PFW)

would return the current setting for the width of line in the Print menu's Format Options submenu.

@SET *(reference, value)*

@SET is FRED's assignment function. It takes two parameters—the name of a reference or local variable, and the value to be assigned to that reference or variable. The value may be either a literal value, a variable, or an expression. @SET behaves exactly the same as FRED's assignment operator (: =). For example, the following two

New in
Framework III

Version Note

In earlier versions of Framework, the syntax @SENSE(MENU#ET) was appropriate. Also, some menu commands have changed between versions, so be aware of new locations and commands. For instance, the Insert Soft Hyphens command that now reads @SENSE(MENU#EHI) would read @SENSE(#EI) in Framework II.

expressions perform identical operations:

```
@set(TESTVALUE, – 1)
TESTVALUE : = – 1
```

@SETDIRECTORY
@SETDIRECTORY (*"path name"*)

@SETDIRECTORY, when used without a parameter, returns the name of the current default directory. For example, if the default directory on drive C is FRAMEWK, the following expression will assign the string "c:\framewk" to the variable DEFAULT:

```
DEFAULT : = @setdirectory
```

When used with a parameter, @SETDIRECTORY sets the default directory to the directory specified in its parameter. The parameter must be a string representing a legitimate path name; for example:

```
@setdirectory("c:\framewk\workfile")
```

You can use @SETDIRECTORY to change the current subdirectory of a directory simply by giving it the desired subdirectory name as a parameter. If the current directory is C:\FRAMEWK\WORKFILE, you can set the current directory to C:\FRAMEWK\DBASES with the following expression:

```
@setdirectory("dbases")
```

@SETDRIVE
@SETDRIVE (*drive*)

@SETDRIVE, when used without a parameter, returns the name of the current default drive. When used with a parameter, @SETDRIVE sets the default drive to the drive specified in its parameter. The parameter must be a drive name in quotes; for example:

```
@setdrive("a:")
```

@SETFORMULA (*frame reference, formula*)

@SETFORMULA places the specified formula behind the specified cell or frame. The second parameter may be the formula itself or the value returned by an @GETFORMULA expression. For example:

```
@local(FORMULA),
FORMULA : = @getformula(oldframe),
@setformula(newframe, FORMULA)
```

@SETFORMULA does not immediately execute the new formula.

@SETMACRO ({alt-key}, frame reference)

The @SETMACRO function is used to establish the command for a macro. It has two required parameters: the name of the Alt-key combination that invokes the macro, and the name of the frame behind which the macro resides. To cancel a macro you have set up, enter the @SETMACRO function again, omitting the frame reference.

@SETSELECTION ("frame name")
@SETSELECTION

The @SETSELECTION function moves the highlight to the frame named in its parameter. It is a more efficient means of navigation than an @PERFORMKEYS expression using a series of cursor-movement key names. See the Letters program in Chapter 7 for an example of @SETSELECTION in a program.

When used without a parameter, @SETSELECTION returns the name of the currently selected frame.

@SIGN (numeric expression)

@SIGN returns a value of – 1, 0, or + 1, depending on whether its parameter evaluates to a negative value, zero, or a positive value, respectively.

@SIN (numeric expression)

@SIN returns the sine of the angle in its parameter, expressed in radians.

@SK (lines)

@SK is a printing function that tells Framework III to skip the number of *lines* specified in its parameter before printing the current frame.

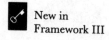

New in
Framework III

@SORT (range, order)

@SORT sorts a range of adjacent spreadsheet cells or database fields. The *order* option is either #ASCEND for ascending sorts, or

#DESCEND for descending sorts. You can also create multilevel sorts by entering multiple sets of ranges and orders, placing the primary sort last in the list, the secondary sort second to last, and so on. For instance, to sort a database called Addresses in descending order by Zip, with the Last Name field sorted in ascending order within zip codes, you would enter:

> @SORT(Addresses.Last Name, #ASCEND, Addresses.Zip, #DESCEND)

@SP *(lines)*

@SP is a printing function that determines the line spacing of a printed document. @SP(1) will result in a single-spaced document, @SP(2) a double-spaced document, @SP(3) a triple-spaced document, and so on.

@SQRT *(numeric expression)*

@SQRT returns the square root of its parameter. Its parameter cannot be negative.

@ST *("printer codes")*

The @ST function is used to send printer codes to your printer. If the codes are sent as keys, they must be enclosed in quotation marks. You can use key names if they are also enclosed in braces. To cause an Epson printer to print in "enhanced" mode, for example, the code is Escape E. To send this code to the printer, use the formula

> @st("{esc}e")

Alternatively, the printer codes can be sent by using the @CHR function as a parameter to the @ST function.

@STD *(expression1, expression2, . . .)*
@STD *(range)*

@STD returns the standard deviation of the numbers in its parameter list.

@SUM *(expression1, expression2, . . .)*
@SUM *(range)*

@SUM returns the sum of all the numbers in its parameter list.

@SUMDATE *(date, days)*

@SUMDATE adds the specified number of *days* to *date* and yields the resulting date. The date specified in the first parameter must be a date-type value produced by one of the following functions:

@date
@time
@sumdate
@today

The second parameter specifies the number of days from the first parameter for which the date is to be calculated. If today were February 25, 1993, the expression

@sumdate(@today, 10)

would return a date-type value displayed in the format

Mar 7, 1993

If the second parameter is negative, the number of days specified will be subtracted from the first parameter.

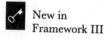
New in
Framework III

@SUSPEND

The @SUSPEND function pauses execution of a program for an unlimited time. During that time, a user can perform any ordinary Framework tasks. Only the @RESUME function can reactivate the suspended program again, beginning just after the last @SUSPEND. For more information, see @RESUME.

@TAN *(numeric expression)*

@TAN returns the tangent of the angle in its parameter, expressed in radians.

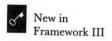
New in
Framework III

@TCHR *(n)*

@TCHR waits the specified number of seconds *(n)* for the next character received from a remote system during a telecommunications session. Entering @TCHR(0) will cause the computer to wait indefinitely. Pressing Ctrl-Break will interrupt the function.

Be careful if you are in full duplex mode. In full duplex, each character you send is repeated (echoed) on your own system, and it will be interpreted by the @TCHR function. This is true if you are at the originating computer. If you are at the answering computer, it will not be a problem.

@TEXTSELECTION

@TEXTSELECTION makes available the currently highlighted text of a Word frame for internal use in a program.

@THOUSANDS

@THOUSANDS is used as a parameter for the @NATIONALIZE function, to control the form in which numbers are displayed. If @THOUSANDS is used, numbers are formatted with commas between each group of three digits, and whole numbers are separated from fractions by a period, in the Anglo-American style. The alternative format function is @MILLI.

@TIME
@TIME *(hr, min, sec)*
@TIME *(hr, min, sec, hundredths)*

When used without parameters, @TIME displays the current date on the system clock. The result is a date-type value that can subsequently be sorted or used in the date arithmetic functions, @DIFFDATE and @SUMDATE. The result of the @TIME function is identical to that of the @DATE function when neither function takes a parameter.

@TIME can also be used with three or four parameters (hundredths of a second are optional). No matter what values you enter as parameters, @TIME will still display the date rather than the time, in the same format that the @DATE function displays the date. To display a time, you must use @TIME as the parameter of one of the time-formatting functions. If you use @TIME as the parameter of one of these functions without any parameters of its own, it will display the time on the system clock. If used in this manner with parameters, the resulting display will be the time represented by its parameters.

@TIME1 *(time)*

@TIME1 converts the date-type value in its parameter to a text string and displays the result in the time format

    hh:mm XM

For example, the function

> @time1(@time(15, 33, 57))

will return the text string

> 3:33 PM

@ *TIME2* (*time*)

@TIME2 converts the date-type value in its parameter to a text string and displays the result in the time format

> hh:mm

For example, the function

> @time2(@time(15, 33, 57))

will return the text string

> 15:33

@ *TIME3* (*time*)

@TIME3 converts the date-type value in its parameter to a text string and displays the result in the time format

> hh:mm:ss.hh

For example, if the system clock's time happens to be 15:33:57.12, the function

> @time3(@time)

will return the text string

> 15:33:57.12

@ *TIME4* (*time*)

@TIME4 converts the date-type value in its parameter to a text string and displays the result in the time format

> hh:mm:ss

Thus, if the time is 15:33:57, the function

@time4(@time)

will return the text string

15:33:57

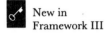 New in
Framework III

@TLIMIT(#ON/#OFF)

You can use @TLIMIT(#ON) to limit the processing of telecommunications activities to explicit @PERFORMKEYS, @TCHR, @TLINE, and @TWAIT statements. Use this function to control the sending and receipt of characters during a telecommunications session.

@TLIMIT must be turned off before the end of execution of your FRED program. However, if you press Ctrl-Break to interrupt the execution of the program, @TLIMIT(#OFF) is automatically executed.

 New in
Framework III

@TLINE(n)

@TLINE waits the specified number of seconds (n) for the next entire line sent by the remote system during a telecommunications session. It can capture up to 253 characters; the end of the line is signaled by ASCII code 13. Line feeds (ASCII code 10) are discarded. Setting @TLINE to 0 causes the computer to wait indefinitely for the next line.

Be careful if you are in full duplex mode. In full duplex, each character is repeated (echoed) on your own system, and it will be interpreted by @TLINE. If you are at the originating computer, your output may be echoed to the screen. The @TLINE function will not distinguish between those characters and the characters coming from the remote system.

@TM(lines)

@TM (top margin) is a printing function that determines the number of lines that will be left blank between the top of the paper and the first line of text, not including the header. The default value is 6.

@TODAY

@TODAY returns the current date and time on the system clock and displays the date. The result is a date-type value. The result of the @TODAY function is identical to that of the @DATE function used without parameters.

@TRACE *(frame reference, #ON)*
@TRACE *(#OFF)*

@TRACE turns the tracing function off and on. When used with a frame reference and #ON, it will trace each step in the execution of a program, and it will store the record of the performance in the specified frame. @TRACE(#OFF) turns the tracing function off again.

@TWAIT *(n)*
@TWAIT *(n, list)*

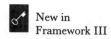

New in
Framework III

The @TWAIT function is used in telecommunications to wait a specified number of seconds *(n)* to receive a specific string response from the other computer. The *list* option allows you to specify up to 15 strings to match against the incoming response. Setting the wait time to 0 causes your system to wait indefinitely, as with @TCHR and @TLINE.

When no string is entered, as in @TWAIT(5), the computer waits the specified amount of time (in this case, 5 seconds) and then continues, *if no response is received in that time.*

If you specify one or more strings, @TWAIT returns the index of the string that was received (1 for the first, 2 for the second, and so forth). Case is not considered, so "HERE I AM" and "here I am" are equivalent.

When defining strings that contain other strings (for instance, "abc" and "abcd"), be sure to define the longer one first, or @TWAIT will stop checking after finding the shorter string. For instance:

> @TWAIT(5,"abcd","abc")

would find both "abc" and "abcd".

@UNHIDE *(frame reference)*

@UNHIDE is used to make visible a frame that has been hidden via the @HIDE function.

@UNIT *("symbol", #position)*

@UNIT is used as a parameter for the @NATIONALIZE function to format numbers using currency symbols other than those for pounds, dollars, and yen. It takes two parameters. The first is the characters representing the currency *symbol* to be used, enclosed in quotes. The second is a constant, either #BEFORE or #AFTER, which indicates the position of the symbol relative to the number to be formatted. For example, the formula

@nationalize(@unit("DM", #BEFORE), @milli), 13846.44

would result in the display

DM   13.846,44

The same expression without the ensuing number or numeric expression would result in all subsequent numbers being displayed as deutsche marks in the illustrated form.

@ *VALUE* ("*string expression*")
@ *VALUE* ("*string expression*", *expr*)

The @VALUE function converts the *string expression* that is its parameter to a numeric value, provided there are numbers in the expression. This function will work with numbers enclosed in quotes, with numbers expressed as text, or with numbers that have been converted to a text format by the @CURRENCY, @DECIMAL, @INTEGER, or @SCIENTIFIC function.

There are a few tricks to using this function without generating errors:

- A numeric expression in quotes must not include parentheses.
- A numeric expression in quotes cannot include letters.
- A numeric expression containing commas will generate an error unless the expression also includes a dollar sign.

Negative numbers, decimal points, and dollar signs cause no problems. The optional parameter, *expr*, allows you to set the format for the expression. The options are:

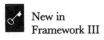
New in
Framework III

0	General (the default)
6	Numeric
7	Logical
8	Time
9	Date, in the form M D Y

10   Date, in the form D M Y

11   Date, in the form M Y

12   Date, in the form Y M D

13   Date, in the form D M

14   Date, in the form M D

15   Date, in the form M

The number in *expr* can be entered directly or as the result of any expression or formula that results in the appropriate value. This allows you to determine the type of data to return. For instance, in the expression

Time : = @value(@inputline("enter the time "), 8)

the value entered would be in a format suitable for time comparisons and calculations.

@*VAR* (*expression1, expression2, . . .*)
@*VAR* (*range*)

@VAR returns the statistical variance of the numbers in its parameter list.

@*VLOOKUP* (*n, range, offset*)

@VLOOKUP retrieves a value from a vertically oriented lookup table. The table can be a spreadsheet or a database. The function has three parameters: a lookup value (*n*) to be located, the *range* that contains the lookup table, and an *offset* column location from which to retrieve the target value.

@VLOOKUP searches the first column of the lookup table for the value *n*. When it finds *n*, or the last value in the lookup column that is not larger than *n*, @VLOOKUP moves to the right by the specified number of offset columns and returns the value stored in that location.

@*WHILE* (*condition, expression1, expression2, . . .*)

The @WHILE function is used to construct loops in FRED. The expressions that are its second through last parameters will be executed repeatedly until the first parameter becomes false. For example:

```
@local(count, total),
count : = 1,
total : = 1,
@while(count < = 10,
    total : = total * count,
    count : = count + 1
    ),
ResultFrame : = total
```

This program will find the value of 10! (1 * 2 * 3 * 4 * . . . * 10) and store the value in the frame called ResultFrame.

An @WHILE loop will normally execute 2048 times unless interrupted by a normal terminating condition or by an @RETURN or @RESULT expression. You can change this through the Setup program.

@WORDCOUNT
@WORDCOUNT ("frame reference")

@WORDCOUNT returns the number of words in the currently selected frame or cell. If a frame or cell reference is given, it returns the number of words in the specified frame or cell.

@WRITEFRAMEFILE (file name, frame reference)

@WRITEFRAMEFILE writes the specified frame to disk as a standard Framework III file with the specified file name. The file name can include a drive identifier, a DOS path name, and an extension. The effect of this function is identical to choosing *Save and Continue* from the Disk menu.

@WRITETEXTFILE (file name, frame reference)

@WRITETEXTFILE writes the specified frame to disk as a DOS text file with the specified file name. The file name can include a drive identifier, a DOS path name, and an extension. The effect of this function is identical to choosing *Write DOS Text File* from the Disk menu.

@YEN

@YEN can be used as a parameter to the @NATIONALIZE function. See the @NATIONALIZE entry for details of its use.

■

Tables of
ASCII Characters

THE FOLLOWING TABLES LIST THE CHARACTERS OF the ASCII code for computers using the MS-DOS operating system. The codes are listed in decimal and hexadecimal notation.

Table C.1 shows the complete set of displayable characters available in Framework III. Table C.2 displays the standard ASCII control codes and their keyboard equivalents. These codes are used primarily in communication with other devices (including the screen), to control the flow and appearance of data. Most are not directly available in Framework III, which uses the key combinations for menu commands. You will, however, need to use some of the codes with the telecommunications component, as explained in Chapter 6.

Every ASCII code except 0 and 255 has a corresponding displayable character; however, the characters corresponding to ASCII codes 9 (Ctrl-I) and 13 (Ctrl-M) cannot be displayed in Framework III. Instead, these codes generate a Tab character and a carriage return, respectively. The characters that cannot be found on the keyboard can be displayed in a Framework III frame by holding down the Alt and Shift keys and pressing the keys corresponding to the decimal value of the code (reading from left to right) on the numeric keypad, letting up the Alt key after all the digits have been entered. Alternatively, you can display them by means of the FRED function @CHR(n), where n is the decimal value of the ASCII code. Whether the characters can be printed on paper depends on the capabilities of your printer.

The "standard" portion of the ASCII code consists of the 32 control codes shown in Table C.2 plus the printable characters numbered 32 through 127, and the Backspace character, ASCII 128. The additional displayable characters are part of the MS-DOS extended character set, and can be used to create various types of borders, or to display symbols and characters of non-English alphabets.

Table C.1: MS-DOS ASCII Displayable Characters

ASCII	PRINTS	HEX		ASCII	PRINTS	HEX
0 *		0		32 **		20
1	▣	1		33	!	21
2	◙	2		34	"	22
3	♥	3		35	#	23
4	♦	4		36	$	24
5	♣	5		37	%	25
6	♠	6		38	&	26
7	•	7		39	'	27
8	◘	8		40	(	28
9		9		41	)	29
10	◙	A		42	*	2A
11	♂	B		43	+	2B
12	♀	C		44	,	2C
13		D		45	–	2D
14	♬	E		46	.	2E
15	☼	F		47	/	2F
16	►	10		48	0	30
17	◄	11		49	1	31
18	↕	12		50	2	32
19	‼	13		51	3	33
20	¶	14		52	4	34
21	§	15		53	5	35
22	▬	16		54	6	36
23	↨	17		55	7	37
24	↑	18		56	8	38
25	↓	19		57	9	39
26	→	1A		58	:	3A
27	←	1B		59	;	3B
28	∟	1C		60	<	3C
29	↔	1D		61	=	3D
30	▲	1E		62	>	3E
31	▼	1F		63	?	3F

* non-printable character   ** space

Table C.1: MS-DOS ASCII Displayable Characters (continued)

ASCII	PRINTS	HEX		ASCII	PRINTS	HEX
64	@	40		96	`	60
65	A	41		97	a	61
66	B	42		98	b	62
67	C	43		99	c	63
68	D	44		100	d	64
69	E	45		101	e	65
70	F	46		102	f	66
71	G	47		103	g	67
72	H	48		104	h	68
73	I	49		105	i	69
74	J	4A		106	j	6A
75	K	4B		107	k	6B
76	L	4C		108	l	6C
77	M	4D		109	m	6D
78	N	4E		110	n	6E
79	O	4F		111	o	6F
80	P	50		112	p	70
81	Q	51		113	q	71
82	R	52		114	r	72
83	S	53		115	s	73
84	T	54		116	t	74
85	U	55		117	u	75
86	V	56		118	v	76
87	W	57		119	w	77
88	X	58		120	x	78
89	Y	59		121	y	79
90	Z	5A		122	z	7A
91	[	5B		123	{	7B
92	\	5C		124	¦	7C
93	]	5D		125	}	7D
94	^	5E		126	~	7E
95	_	5F		127	△	7F

Table C.1: MS-DOS ASCII Displayable Characters (continued)

ASCII	PRINTS	HEX	ASCII	PRINTS	HEX
128	Ç	80	160	á	A0
129	ü	81	161	í	A1
130	é	82	162	ó	A2
131	â	83	163	ú	A3
132	ä	84	164	ñ	A4
133	à	85	165	Ñ	A5
134	å	86	166	ª	A6
135	ç	87	167	º	A7
136	ê	88	168	¿	A8
137	ë	89	169	⌐	A9
138	è	8A	170	¬	AA
139	ï	8B	171	½	AB
140	î	8C	172	¼	AC
141	ì	8D	173	¡	AD
142	Ä	8E	174	«	AE
143	Å	8F	175	»	AF
144	É	90	176	░	B0
145	æ	91	177	▒	B1
146	Æ	92	178	▓	B2
147	ô	93	179	│	B3
148	ö	94	180	┤	B4
149	ò	95	181	╡	B5
150	û	96	182	╢	B6
151	ù	97	183	╖	B7
152	ÿ	98	184	╕	B8
153	Ö	99	185	╣	B9
154	Ü	9A	186	║	BA
155	¢	9B	187	╗	BB
156	£	9C	188	╝	BC
157	¥	9D	189	╜	BD
158	₧	9E	190	╛	BE
159	ƒ	9F	191	┐	BF

Table C.1: MS-DOS ASCII Displayable Characters (continued)

ASCII	PRINTS	HEX
192	L	C0
193	⊥	C1
194	⊤	C2
195	⊢	C3
196	—	C4
197	+	C5
198	⊦	C6
199	‖	C7
200	⸀	C8
201	⌐	C9
202	⸤	CA
203	⊤	CB
204	⊩	CC
205	=	CD
206	⧺	CE
207	⸲	CF
208	⊔	D0
209	⊤	D1
210	⊓	D2
211	⊔	D3
212	⊦	D4
213	F	D5
214	⊓	D6
215	╫	D7
216	╪	D8
217	⌐	D9
218	⌐	DA
219	■	DB
220	▬	DC
221	▌	DD
222	▐	DE
223	▀	DF

ASCII	PRINTS	HEX
224	α	E0
225	β	E1
226	Γ	E2
227	π	E3
228	Σ	E4
229	σ	E5
230	μ	E6
231	τ	E7
232	Φ	E8
233	Θ	E9
234	Ω	EA
235	δ	EB
236	∞	EC
237	φ	ED
238	∈	EE
239	∩	EF
240	≡	F0
241	±	F1
242	≥	F2
243	≤	F3
244	⌠	F4
245	⌡	F5
246	÷	F6
247	≈	F7
248	°	F8
249	·	F9
250	·	FA
251	√	FB
252	ⁿ	FC
253	²	FD
254	∎	FE
255 *		FF

* non-printable character

Table C.2: MS-DOS ASCII Control Codes and Their Effects

ASCII VALUE	CONTROL CHARACTER	HEX VALUE	KEYBOARD EQUIVALENT	DEVICE CONTROL EFFECT
00	NUL	00	Ctrl-@	Null
01	SOH	01	Ctrl-A	
02	STX	02	Ctrl-B	
03	ETX	03	Ctrl-C	
04	EOT	04	Ctrl-D	
05	ENQ	05	Ctrl-E	
06	ACK	06	Ctrl-F	
07	BEL	07	Ctrl-G	Beep
08	BS	08	Ctrl-H	Backspace
09	HT	09	Ctrl-I	Tab
10	LF	0A	Ctrl-J	Linefeed
11	VT	0B	Ctrl-K	Cursor home
12	FF	0C	Ctrl-L	Form feed
13	CR	0D	Ctrl-M	Carriage return
14	SO	0E	Ctrl-N	
15	SI	0F	Ctrl-O	
16	DLE	10	Ctrl-P	
17	DC1	11	Ctrl-Q	
18	DC2	12	Ctrl-R	
19	DC3	13	Ctrl-S	
20	DC4	14	Ctrl-T	
21	NAK	15	Ctrl-U	
22	SYN	16	Ctrl-V	
23	ETB	17	Ctrl-W	
24	CAN	18	Ctrl-X	
25	EM	19	Ctrl-Y	
26	SUB	1A	Ctrl-Z	

Table C.2: MS-DOS ASCII Control Codes and Their Effects (continued)

ASCII VALUE	CONTROL CHARACTER	HEX VALUE	KEYBOARD EQUIVALENT	DEVICE CONTROL EFFECT
27	ESC	1B	Ctrl-[or Esc	Escape
28	FS	1C	Ctrl-\	Cursor right
29	GS	1D	Ctrl-]	Cursor left
30	RS	1E	Ctrl-^	Cursor up
31	US	1F	Ctrl-_	Cursor down

INDEX

FUNCTION INDEX

GENERAL INDEX

SYMBOLS

A

loading setup files for, 390
logging onto bulletin boards during, 401–403
protocol transfers during, 398–401
receiving files for, 398–401
recording conversations during, 370, 385–387
transferring text files in, 387–397
using answer mode in, 403
Telecommunications menu, 371–372
telecommunications networks. *See also* telecommunications
  file cabinets, 14
  logging onto, 381–382
  making connections, 382–385
  recording conversations, 385–387
telecommunications parameters, 368, 389–390
telecommunications protocols, 368
Telecommunications Setup menu, 371–372, 374–375, 390
telecommunications software, 368–370
Telenet, 374
  ? error message, 384
  @ prompt for, 383
  automatic log-on macro for, 392–394
  baud rates in, 377
  disconnecting from, 385
  making connections to, 382–385
  telephone numbers for, 381
templates
  for keyboard functions, 22
  in Library macros, 433
  for outlining, 37–38
  for printer settings, 64
  in snaked frames, 433
  storing, in the Library, 284–285
terminal emulation, 407–409
terminal identifier code, 383
terminal mode, 370
text blocks
  copying, 249–250
  deleting, 246–247
  mixing styles in, 273
  moving, 249–250
  selecting, 230–232
text fields, " designation, 491
text mode, installing Framework III, 520–521
text styling. *See* styling of text

Text Transfer option, 388–389
thesaurus files, 262
Thesaurus key (Shift-F6), 263
time functions. *See* date and time functions
Timing Relaxation Factor, 369
toggle keys, 22
trays, 12, 23
triangular brackets, in date formatting, 268
true/false evaluations, 328–331, 336. *See also* #TRUE/#FALSE values
#TRUE/#FALSE values, 328–331, 336–339, 446–447
turnkey programs, 417. *See also* FRED programming language
TXT file extension, 489
typeover mode, 245–246

U

underlining text, 47, 178, 248
underscore character (_), as illegal DOS character, 52
undoing deletions, 54–55
  in outline headings, 87–88
Undo option, 54
Up level key, 430. *See also* Out key
uploading files, 51, 370–371, 400
user-defined functions, 64, 442

V

values, = designation, 325, 327, 444–445
variables in FRED programs, 418, 444–445
VGA resolution displays, 193
View key (F10), 25
  in databases, 349, 351–352, 358
  in outlines, 105, 108–110
  for printing frames, 55
  for shifting between Outline and Frames view, 39–40, 99
View Pagination option, 101
VisiCalc, 490
  integrating DIF files into, 504–509
  receiving through telecommunications, 398–401

W

wildcard characters, 319

TO JOIN THE SYBEX MAILING LIST OR ORDER BOOKS
PLEASE COMPLETE THIS FORM

NAME _____ COMPANY _____

STREET _____ CITY _____

STATE _____ ZIP _____

☐ PLEASE MAIL ME MORE INFORMATION ABOUT **SYBEX** TITLES

ORDER FORM (There is no obligation to order)

PLEASE SEND ME THE FOLLOWING:

TITLE	QTY	PRICE
_____	___	___
_____	___	___
_____	___	___
_____	___	___

TOTAL BOOK ORDER _____ $_____

CUSTOMER SIGNATURE _____

SHIPPING AND HANDLING PLEASE ADD $2.00 PER BOOK VIA UPS _____

FOR OVERSEAS SURFACE ADD $5.25 PER BOOK PLUS $4.40 REGISTRATION FEE _____

FOR OVERSEAS AIRMAIL ADD $18.25 PER BOOK PLUS $4.40 REGISTRATION FEE _____

CALIFORNIA RESIDENTS PLEASE ADD APPLICABLE SALES TAX _____

TOTAL AMOUNT PAYABLE _____

☐ CHECK ENCLOSED ☐ VISA
☐ MASTERCARD ☐ AMERICAN EXPRESS

ACCOUNT NUMBER _____

EXPIR. DATE _____ DAYTIME PHONE _____

CHECK AREA OF COMPUTER INTEREST:

☐ BUSINESS SOFTWARE

☐ TECHNICAL PROGRAMMING

☐ OTHER: _____

THE FACTOR THAT WAS MOST IMPORTANT IN YOUR SELECTION:

☐ THE SYBEX NAME

☐ QUALITY

☐ PRICE

☐ EXTRA FEATURES

☐ COMPREHENSIVENESS

☐ CLEAR WRITING

☐ OTHER _____

OTHER COMPUTER TITLES YOU WOULD LIKE TO SEE IN PRINT:

_____

_____

OCCUPATION

☐ PROGRAMMER ☐ TEACHER

☐ SENIOR EXECUTIVE ☐ HOMEMAKER

☐ COMPUTER CONSULTANT ☐ RETIRED

☐ SUPERVISOR ☐ STUDENT

☐ MIDDLE MANAGEMENT ☐ OTHER:

☐ ENGINEER/TECHNICAL _____

☐ CLERICAL/SERVICE

☐ BUSINESS OWNER/SELF EMPLOYED

CHECK YOUR LEVEL OF COMPUTER USE

☐ NEW TO COMPUTERS

☐ INFREQUENT COMPUTER USER

☐ FREQUENT USER OF ONE SOFTWARE

PACKAGE:

NAME _____

☐ FREQUENT USER OF MANY SOFTWARE

PACKAGES

☐ PROFESSIONAL PROGRAMMER

OTHER COMMENTS:

_____

_____

_____

_____

_____

_____

_____

_____

PLEASE FOLD, SEAL, AND MAIL TO SYBEX

SYBEX, INC.
2021 CHALLENGER DR. #100
ALAMEDA, CALIFORNIA USA
94501

SEAL

SYBEX Computer Books are different.

Here is why . . .

At SYBEX, each book is designed with you in mind. Every manuscript is carefully selected and supervised by our editors, who are themselves computer experts. We publish the best authors, whose technical expertise is matched by an ability to write clearly and to communicate effectively. Programs are thoroughly tested for accuracy by our technical staff. Our computerized production department goes to great lengths to make sure that each book is well-designed.

In the pursuit of timeliness, SYBEX has achieved many publishing firsts. SYBEX was among the first to integrate personal computers used by authors and staff into the publishing process. SYBEX was the first to publish books on the CP/M operating system, microprocessor interfacing techniques, word processing, and many more topics.

Expertise in computers and dedication to the highest quality product have made SYBEX a world leader in computer book publishing. Translated into fourteen languages, SYBEX books have helped millions of people around the world to get the most from their computers. We hope we have helped you, too.

For a complete catalog of our publications:

SYBEX, Inc. 2021 Challenger Drive, #100, Alameda, CA 94501
Tel: (415) 523-8233/(800) 227-2346   Telex: 336311
Fax: (415) 523-2373

Mouse Techniques

ACTION	KEY EQUIVALENT	MOUSE TECHNIQUE
Open/close frame	Return	Double-click LB on frame cabinet or frame, or anywhere on open frame border
Zoom frame	Zoom (F9)	Double-click LB inside frame
Toggle drive cabinet/frame	Shuttle (Scroll Lock)	Click RB on closed frame or drive cabinet
Open menu	Instruct (Ins)	Click button on desired menu
Select from menu	First letter or arrow keys	Move mouse to desired menu item and click LB
Move up menu level	Out (−)	Click RB
Close all menus	Escape	Click LB and RB together
Scroll text	PgUp/PgDn	Press RB inside frame and drag mouse in direction you wish to scroll
Select frames	Extend Select (F6)	Press LB and drag mouse over frames to select, then release
Select outline elements	Extend Select (F6)	Press LB and drag mouse over outline elements to select, then release
Select text	Extend Select (F6)	Press LB and drag mouse over text to select, then release
Select cell range (SS)	Extend Select (F6)	Press LB and drag mouse over cells to select, then release
Select records (DB)	Extend Select (F6)	Press LB and drag mouse over fields or records to select, then release
Drag frame	Drag (F3)	Position mouse cursor on upper left corner of frame, press LB and drag mouse to reposition frame
Resize frame	Size (F4)	Position mouse cursor on lower right corner of frame, press LB and drag mouse to size frame
Edit formula	Formula Edit (F2)	Click mouse in formula display area of cell

Mouse Terms and Abbreviations

Click	Press button quickly and release	LB	Left button
Double-click	Press button twice quickly	RB	Right button
Press	Press and hold button	SS	Spreadsheet
Drag	Move mouse with button depressed	DB	Database